P9-DTE-007

# The Privacy Engineer's Manifesto

## Getting from Policy to Code to QA to Value

*Welcome to the Data Revolution!*

Michelle Finneran Dennedy

Jonathan Fox

Thomas R. Finneran

Selected For Intel's Recommended Reading List

(intel)

Apress
**open**

## The Privacy Engineer's Manifesto

Michelle Finneran Dennedy, Jonathan Fox, and Thomas R. Finneran

Copyright © 2014 by Apress Media, LLC, all rights reserved

**ApressOpen Rights**: You have the right to copy, use, and distribute this Work in its entirety, electronically without modification, for non-commercial purposes only. However, you have the additional right to use or alter any source code in this Work for any commercial or non-commercial purpose which must be accompanied by the licenses in (2) and (3) below to distribute the source code for instances of greater than 5 lines of code. Licenses (1), (2), and (3) below and the intervening text must be provided in any use of the text of the Work and fully describes the license granted herein to the Work.

(1) **License for Distribution of the Work**: This Work is copyrighted by Apress Media, LLC, all rights reserved. Use of this Work other than as provided for in this license is prohibited. By exercising any of the rights herein, you are accepting the terms of this license. You have the non-exclusive right to copy, use, and distribute this English language Work in its entirety, electronically without modification except for those modifications necessary for formatting on specific devices, for all non-commercial purposes, in all media and formats known now or hereafter. While the advice and information in this Work are believed to be true and accurate at the date of publication, neither the authors nor the editors nor the publisher can accept any legal responsibility for any errors or omissions that may be made. The publisher makes no warranty, express or implied, with respect to the material contained herein.

If your distribution is solely Apress source code or uses Apress source code intact, the following licenses (2) and (3) must accompany the source code. If your use is an adaptation of the source code provided by Apress in this Work, then you must use only license (3).

(2) **License for Direct Reproduction of Apress Source Code**: This source code, from *TouchDevelop: Programming on the Go, ISBN 978-1-4302-6136-0* is copyrighted by Apress Media, LLC, all rights reserved. Any direct reproduction of this Apress source code is permitted but must contain this license. The following license must be provided for any use of the source code from this product of greater than 5 lines wherein the code is adapted or altered from its original Apress form. This Apress code is presented AS IS and Apress makes no claims to, representations, or warrantees as to the function, usability, accuracy, or usefulness of this code.

(3) **License for Distribution of Adaptation of Apress Source Code**: Portions of the source code provided are used or adapted from *TouchDevelop: Programming on the Go, ISBN 978-1-4302-6136-0* copyright Apress Media LLC. Any use or reuse of this Apress source code must contain this License. This Apress code is made available at Apress.com/978143026136-0 as is and Apress makes no claims to, representations or warrantees as to the function, usability, accuracy or usefulness of this code.

ISBN-13 (pbk): 978-1-4302-6355-5

ISBN-13 (electronic): 978-1-4302-6356-2

Trademarked names, logos, and images may appear in this book. Rather than use a trademark symbol with every occurrence of a trademarked name, logo, or image we use the names, logos, and images only in an editorial fashion and to the benefit of the trademark owner, with no intention of infringement of the trademark.

The use in this publication of trade names, trademarks, service marks, and similar terms, even if they are not identified as such, is not to be taken as an expression of opinion as to whether or not they are subject to proprietary rights.

While the advice and information in this book are believed to be true and accurate at the date of publication, neither the authors nor the editors nor the publisher can accept any legal responsibility for any errors or omissions that may be made. The publisher makes no warranty, express or implied, with respect to the material contained herein.

President and Publisher: Paul Manning
Lead Editor: Steve Weiss
Technical Reviewers: Richard Schaefer and Stuart Tyler
Coordinating Editor: Jill Balzano
Copy Editor: Mary Bearden
Cover Designer: Anna Ishchenko

Distributed to the book trade worldwide by Springer Science+Business Media New York, 233 Spring Street, 6th Floor, New York, NY 10013. Phone 1-800-SPRINGER, fax (201) 348-4505, e-mail orders-ny@springer-sbm.com, or visit www.springeronline.com.

For information on translations, please e-mail rights@apress.com, or visit www.apress.com.

# About ApressOpen

## What Is ApressOpen?

- ApressOpen is an open access book program that publishes high-quality technical and business information.

- ApressOpen eBooks are available for global, free, noncommercial use.

- ApressOpen eBooks are available in PDF, ePub, and Mobi formats.

- The user friendly ApressOpen free eBook license is presented on the copyright page of this book.

- Interested in sponsoring a book on the ApressOpen platform? Please contact us at apressopen@apress.com.

*To our children, our families, and privacy engineers everywhere*
*—past, present, and future.*

# Contents at a Glance

# Contents

# About the Authors

**Michelle Finneran Dennedy**
VP, Chief Privacy Officer, McAfee

Michelle currently serves as McAfee's Chief Privacy Officer where she is responsible for the development and implementation of McAfee's data privacy policies and practices, working across business groups to drive data privacy excellence across the security continuum. Before coming to McAfee, Michelle founded The iDennedy Project, a public service organization to address privacy needs in sensitive populations, such as children and the elderly, and emerging technology paradigms. Michelle is also a founder and editor in chief of a new media site—theIdentityProject.com—that was started as an advocacy and education site, currently focused on the growing crime of Child ID theft.

Michelle was the Vice President for Security & Privacy Solutions for the Oracle Corporation. Before the Oracle acquisition of Sun, Michelle was Chief Data Governance Officer within the Cloud Computing division at Sun Microsystems, Inc. Michelle also served as Sun's Chief Privacy Officer.

Michelle has a JD from Fordham University School of Law and a BS degree with university honors from The Ohio State University. In 2009, she was awarded the Goodwin Procter-IAPP Vanguard award for lifetime achievement and the EWF – CSO Magazine Woman of Influence award for work in the privacy and security fields. In 2012, she was recognized by the National Diversity Council as one of California's Most Powerful & Influential Women.

**Jonathan Fox** is the Global Director of Data Privacy at McAfee. Previous to McAfee, he was the Worldwide Director of Privacy at eBay Inc., and before that, Deputy Chief Privacy Officer at Sun Microsystems, Inc. Jonathan's principal areas of focus are product development, behavioral advertising, training, mobile applications, data licensing, government relations, social shopping, quality assurance, and mergers and acquisitions. He has worked closely with marketing, information security, engineering, internal audit, professional services, technical support, and cloud teams to establish policies and operate programs to ensure the protection of customer and employee personal information. He is a Certified Information Privacy Professional (CIPP/US), a Certified Information Privacy Manager (CIPM), and was a Certified Information Security Manager (CISM). He is on the International Association of Privacy Professional's Certification Advisory Board. His prior roles have included Editor-in-Chief of sun.com, business development manager for a new media startup, senior manager of electronic and intellectual property licensing for Random House, and Program Delivery Manager for the Oracle Developer's Programme. He is a graduate of Columbia University. He regularly speaks at industry events on privacy issues.

His writing credits include:

THE CIO AND THE CPO — A VISION FOR TEAMWORK AND SUCCESS, Sun Microsystems, 2006

ESTABLISHING A PRIVACY OFFICE, Sun Microsystems, 2007

PRIVACY IN THE PARTICIPATION AGE, Sun Microsystems, Inc., 2008

**Thomas R. Finneran** is a principal consultant for the IDennedy Project. He has proposed an approach to use the Organization for the Advancement of Structured Information Standards (OASIS) UML Standard for privacy analysis. He was a consultant for over 25 years for CIBER, Inc. He has acquired over 25 years of experience in the field of information technology. His strengths include enterprise (including data, information, knowledge, business, and application) architecture, business and data analysis, UML object analysis and design, logical data modeling, database systems design and analysis, information resource management methodologies, CASE and metadata repository tools, project management, and computer law. He is experienced in almost all application system areas, including real-time data collection systems, inventory control, sales and order processing, personnel, all types of financial systems, the use of expert systems, and project management systems. He has developed and taught training courses in the areas of use cases, relational concepts, strategic data planning, logical data modeling, and the utilization of CASE tools, among others. He is also an experienced intellectual property patent lawyer. For various companies, he has held such titles as director, MIS; manager, corporate data strategy; manager, data administration; managing consultant; manager, standards and education; and systems designer. These companies include the Standard Oil Company, Corning Glass Works, ITT, ADR, and the U.S. Navy. In addition, he was vice president and general counsel of TOMARK, Inc., the developer of the highly successful ABEND-AID software package. He has a bachelor of arts (Ohio State University), a master's of business administration (Roosevelt University), and a juris doctor's degree (Cleveland State). He is a member of the bar of the U.S. Supreme Court and a member of the bar of Ohio, New Jersey, Connecticut and a member of the Patent Bar. His published papers include:

> Enterprise Architecture: What and Why
> (www.tdan.com/i007ht03.htm);
>
> Enterprise Architecture: The What's and How's
> (www.tdan.com/i018ht02.htm);
>
> A Component-Based Knowledge Management System
> (www.tdan.com/i009hy04.htm);
>
> A Best Practices Assessment (www.tdan.com/i012ht04.htm);
> E-Biz Metrics (www.tdan.com/i014hy03.htm);
>
> Doing .Net Right: Looking at the Critical Success Factors
> (www.tdan.come /i020hy04.htm);
>
> "Data Deliverables", Database Management
> (Auerbach Press) (1990);
>
> "Business Analysis for Database Design"
> (Datamation, Nov. 1977)

# About the Technical Reviewers

**Richard Schaefer** is the director of technical alliances at Good Technology. He is responsible for all aspects of ISV integration with Good's secure mobility platform including security compliance. His longtime career focus is market adoption of evolutionary technologies primarily via partner ecosystems. His roles have spanned engineering, marketing, and business development in the application of nascent computing platforms and processes to a broad range of industries. His achievements have earned him awards and executive recognition at Sun Microsystems and Good. He has edited and contributed to books on the Solaris operating system, multithreading, and Java. Michelle Finneran Dennedy frequently introduces him as the one who taught her about garbage collection.

**Stuart Tyler** is a senior privacy analyst at Intel Corporation with more than 13 years of hands-on privacy experience gained in Europe and the United States, covering every conceivable aspect of privacy including operational compliance, product and service development, and external public policy.

# Acknowledgments

From all of us:

Our spouses and family were key members of our team, who gave us support and sacrificed much.

To the wonderful team at Apress Media, particularly Steve Weiss, Jill Balzano, Nyomi Anderson, and Mary Bearden, the Manifesto would likely still be in draft form were it not for your firm but encouraging hands. To Javiar Leija, Patrick Hauke, and the rest of the Intel Press team, thank you for encouraging us to convert our ideas and speeches into this book. Your guidance, experience, and generosity to a pack of newbie authors will never be forgotten. Steve, if coaching and cajoling authors ever loses its charm, you have a promising career in stand-up or e-mail comedy.

To the marketing and promotions teams at Intel & McAfee, thank you for all of your support for this rather rogue project. To the wonderful Dr. Eric Bonabeau, visionary, big data, analytics, and human decision-making expert to the stars, we thank you for trusting us enough to read the manuscript and provide the Foreword that is indeed a tie to the massive data challenges that lie ahead. Your insight highlights their proximity to other, solvable, big data challenges that you and your team are tackling today. To the many contributors who selflessly heeded our calls and graciously put fingers to the keyboard and provided articles based on their real-world experiences, thank you. Your contributions not only break up the monotony of our collective voice, they also give our book deeper texture and richer content than we had ever hoped for. Our thanks to Richard Purcell and John Dutra, whose early reviews of an amorphous manuscript helped us recognize the book we were writing was a manifesto, a call to action, and not just a book on engineering. Last but most certainly not least, to our technical reviewers, Stuart Tyler and Richard Schaefer, it is impossible to thank you enough for your time, your patience, and your creativity and insights. We knew you would both be critical in shaping this book into the tool for change that we hope it will become. We were right; you were. We have loved having you all on our team.

From Michelle Finneran Dennedy:

This short section is the hardest of all to write. I am not a pithy author so I have an expansive and grateful heart. There are countless contributors, family, and friends, who remain nameless in this book but are all known and honored by me. To the many creative and talented people who have inspired, taught, challenged, scoffed at, picked up, loved, and bought me many drinks to lament the state of privacy over the years, I thank you. To my coauthors, thank you for writing this book, keeping me on task, and putting up with my impossible dreams and making them happen. One of you taught me to walk, the other brought privacy into my life, and both have made pigs fly. To my dear husband, Tom Dennedy, your constancy and excellence as a father to our girls have kept us all going during the many months when "The Manifesto" became our sole waking activity, and

I will always love you for that and for so much more. To my bright, talented, effervescent, and limitless daughters, Reilly Finn and Quincy Esther Dennedy, your future was at stake in every creative thought I have ever had in the fight for privacy. This book was written with my unfettered hope that your generation will do a better job at loving and respecting one another and the stories and information about one another that we will leave behind. You ladies are my Magnus Opus.

From Jonathan Fox:

Books, too, take a village and there are many to thank. Unfortunately, there are too many to include in one place.

There are a few, however, to whom I would like to give special recognition. First, my coauthors. Tom, I have learned much from you. Michelle, the adventure continues. Thanks to you both. Next, my wife, Nicki, you are my foundation and ballast; and my children, Sophie and Adam, your cheer and interest in life continues to inspire.

Finally, there are those who helped put me on the path to this book: my parents, who introduced me to the world and encouraged me to be curious; Nancy Novogrod and Arnold Ehrlich, who introduced me to publishing; Michael Mellin, who introduced me to technology; Franz Aman, who put privacy under my watch when I was editor-in-chief of sun.com, and Kate Rundle, who had the good sense to assign a newly hired attorney named Michelle Dennedy to support the privacy program when we were at Sun Microsystems.

To those not mentioned, your help, support, and insights are appreciated, valued, and remembered. This book, like so many other things, stands on the shoulders of you and others.

From Thomas R. Finneran:

Writing and producing a book is a struggle that impacts both family and friends. Norma, my wife, has supported me throughout the process, picking up the many balls that I dropped along the way. She facilitated the project with both actions and prayers. This has turned out to be a family project. We thank all the kids and their kids for their support.

Jonathan and Michelle had, for a number of years, been fighting the privacy wars. Michelle called me and told me that she felt that privacy engineering was a necessity. I said that I knew how to do that. The three of us developed an outline and we were off to the races.

# Foreword, with the Zeal of a Convert

It's a call I get every 6 to 12 months. My credit card has been "compromised" and needs to be replaced with a new one. Once a major annoyance, this has become a well-oiled, mildly inconvenient ritual for updating useful accounts and dropping the ones I no longer need or want—an effective method for canceling sticky subscriptions. It is a tribute to the resilience of human beings that we can adapt so easily to a bad state of affairs. And so it is for me, and many others I suspect, the way that I am reminded about privacy and its protection, by accident, every 6 to 12 months, for just a few days. It's not that I don't like privacy; it's just that I really didn't care all that much.

The book you are holding at this instant is what made me care, deeply. It didn't happen for ideological reasons, nor because I favor anonymity, although I do like it, at times of my choosing. No, I care because the "privacy engineering" framework, methods, and processes the authors have put together are critical enablers to unlock value from data. However strange that may sound (after all, isn't privacy all about preventing companies from gaining access to customer data?), it makes sense when you consider the complexity of dealing in practice with the absurd amounts of data individuals, companies, and governments are producing and accumulating at an accelerating pace. The keyword here is complexity. Having spent the past two decades studying and modeling complex systems, I am not the most unbiased of observers, but, given that we all have our biases, I hope you will find mine useful.[1] I tend to view the most interesting problems through the lens of complex systems, and data, particularly in large quantity, strike me as a complex system of sorts.

## Data as a Complex, Evolving, Self-Organizing System

Let's consider, for the purpose of this Foreword, data about individuals—their attributes and behaviors as they have been captured digitally, with or without consent from the individuals, often redundantly and with errors. All those data about one single individual constitute a mini-ecosystem, a mini-PIE (personal information ecosystem). The mini-PIE is populated with many interacting species: when a ZIP code interacts with a list

---

[1] A mutation of the great mathematician George E. P. Box's statement that "essentially, all models are wrong, but some are useful." G. E. P. Box, and N. R. Draper, *Empirical Model Building and Response Surfaces* (New York: Wiley, 1987).

of recently visited web pages, an (allegedly relevant) advertisement may be created, the response to which will be added to the mini-PIE. When a misspelled version of a name interacts with a web site account, it results in a rejection; but when the same misspelled version of a name interacts with a Department of Homeland Security database, it may wreak havoc in the individual's life.

Each time there is an interaction, it adds richness and complexity to the mini-PIE. Your very own mini-PIE, which is in fact your digital identity, exhibits many coexisting dynamical patterns of behavior: you pay your bills on time, you travel domestically about three times per month and overseas twice a year, you visit 57 news sources on average in a given week, you purchase a lot of items on Amazon around December 18, and, to play on the infamous Target-knows-everything example, your daughter's buying patterns suggest she is pregnant even though you don't know (yet). The truth is, there are millions, even billions of possible patterns in your mini-PIE: yes, your PIE can be sliced in that many ways.

Now consider bringing together the mini-PIEs of thousands or even millions of individuals, a typical number for, say, a midsize retailer. All these interacting species can now interact between individuals, not just within one individual's mini-PIE. Some of these interactions are implicit: "my ZIP code is the same as your ZIP code," while others are explicit: "my (pregnant?) daughter is Facebook friends with your (suspicious?) son." The interacting species from all the mini-PIEs form a big PIE covering many individuals, with each species a building block that can be combined in many different ways to address many different questions. The trouble is, the number of possible combinations is, well, combinatorial, which means that it increases faster than exponentially with the number of building blocks and therefore the number of individuals in the PIE, a concept we will encounter again soon. I hope to have convinced you, however imperfectly, that personal information is a complex system. Now is a good time to examine the consequences.

# Complexity

The problem with increasing the number of interacting building blocks in a PIE is that finding the right combinations becomes a quixotic task. If you are looking for correlations in the data, which seems to be the new scientific method, the number of spurious correlations increases much faster than their more meaningful counterparts. In *Antifragile*, economist and author Nassim Taleb sums it up: "in large data sets, large deviations are vastly more attributable to noise (or variance) than to information (or signal)."[2] He adds, "falsity grows faster than information." In other words, we can expect many correlations that are statistically significant but ultimately meaningless. It follows that in order to exploit the complexity inherent in very large datasets, you need a way to weed out most of the meaningless correlations that inevitably show up all over the place.

---

[2] N. N. Taleb, *Antifragile. Things that Gain from Disorder* (New York: Random House, 2012).

# Emergence

In addition to the combinatorial complexity of putting together the right building blocks, there is the delicious problem of emergence: the whole is more (or less) than the sum of its parts (building blocks), meaning that you cannot know ahead of time what a combination of building blocks will produce. Put two or three innocuous building blocks together and the result might be equally innocuous—or spectacularly interesting. To use a national security example, let's assume that the three building blocks are as follows: (1) Suspicious individuals are learning to fly aircraft without learning how to land. (2) Web site chatter indicates that a terrorist event will take place on 9/11. (3) A suspected terrorist told his friends in a chat room that there will soon be an attack against the World Trade Center in New York. I wouldn't call any of these building blocks innocuous, so they are not, individually, actionable. However, if you know to put them together, you get a very actionable piece of intelligence. Of course, I am assuming here that you know to put these three particular building blocks together, but the main point is that the value of the combination is much, much greater than the sum of the individual building block's value. This type of emergence is ubiquitous in PIEs. Just as the combination of unclassified individual parts can produce classified information, the combination of perfectly legal parts can be illegal. Another kind of emergent phenomenon happens when building blocks are plunged into a new environment, revealing previously concealed properties: for example, a combination of building blocks that is legal to store in one country could become illegal the minute you cross a border, reflecting a change in the legal environment. That makes the calculus of privacy tricky.

# Self-Organization

Some of the more interesting emergent patterns that can be observed in PIEs are patterns of self-organization. It is an interesting property of ecosystems that species interact with one another, thereby modifying their environment, which in turn changes the way they interact with other species. To see how the concept applies here, let's consider the very, very big Amazon PIE. Amazon customers leave data trails similar to the pheromone trails of ants: the more pheromone on a trail, the more ants are attracted to the trail, further reinforcing the trail's pheromone concentration, a well-known example of self-organization in biological systems. The net result for Amazon customers is well-groomed trails to the most popular products as these products attract more reviews, which makes other customers more comfortable and gives Amazon an incentive to promote them since these products sell more easily.

Recommender systems seem largely stuck in the collaborative filtering model, an inherently self-reinforcing method corralling the masses toward self-defining blockbusters and away from the "long tail," those products that sell just a few pieces every year. Collaborative filtering does not rely on your personal characteristics but rather on a generic set of PIE building blocks: the overlap between what you have purchased and what other people have purchased. Beyond recommender systems, you will find a similar kind of self-reinforcing dynamics in every situation where a certain type of building block from your PIE will be used to increase its own importance. For example, if you are a frequent traveler on an airline, you can very easily become a "known traveler" and peruse the keep-your-shoes-on-and-your-laptop-in-the-bag security line at the airport, a perk that increases the likelihood that you will continue to pile up the miles with that airline. What is missing in this picture is creativity and innovation. Even ants sometimes wander off their columns and get lost when finding new food sources, and so must data-mining algorithms, or we will be stuck on boring, self-reinforcing highways for a long time, ignoring other opportunities. One example of a company that should give us hope uses evolution as its creativity engine. Its name? Pandora.

# Evolution

Pandora has identified the building blocks of music and musical tastes. A team of experienced musicologists have painstakingly analyzed tens of thousands of songs spanning all musical genres using a set of 450 well-defined attributes that characterize the music and listeners' musical preferences. Pandora calls this treasure trove of precise taxonomic information the Music Genome Project (MGP), a key asset that has made the company a beloved personalized radio station: discovery is not based on what others like but on what you like. Pandora asks a listener to rate multiple songs and uses its MGP to evolve and mutate the genomes of the preferred songs to discover songs that might be of interest to that particular listener. A common experience with Pandora is to discover an artist or song that you love but had no idea even existed: you wouldn't have been able to search for it, but you know it is a great match in the first seconds of hearing it. In other words, Pandora provides an example of evolutionary dynamics in a mini-PIE. But for this to work, "the MGP's database is built using a methodology that includes the use of precisely defined terminology, a consistent frame of reference, redundant analysis, and ongoing quality control to ensure that data integrity remains reliably high."[3] Similarly, if we are to discover not just songs but more general patterns in data, the underlying data need to have the same characteristics as the Pandora MGP data.

As dean of a College of Computational Sciences, focused on critical analysis and creative thinking, I have established "Know thy data" as one of the core learning objectives of our curriculum. Well, it's expressed in less memorable terms: "Consider the nature, scope, quality, sampling, origin and context of the data, including the existence of a control group." In other words, the integrity and traceability of data are crucial to what you can do with it, a core theme of privacy engineering. Modelers have a well-known expression: garbage in, garbage out. Problem is, you don't know for sure that it's garbage if you haven't prepared your data properly.

Once the underlying data structure is in place and all methods and processes are properly implemented, amazing things become possible if you view data as the genetic code of value propositions. In the case of the Pandora value proposition, it is literally true. But it is generally true that data building blocks are combined, mutated, and recombined to create new value propositions. Innovation comes from combining and reconfiguring existing building blocks differently. Consider Capital One, the credit card company that invented balance transfer and is famous for experimenting at scale by creating and

---

[3]www.pandora.com/about/mgp

sending out tailored offers to potential customers, waiting for results to come in, and then modifying its offers in response to the profitability of a particular combination of offer and segment. The continuous feedback, although it was taking place on a longer timescale than Pandora's, is of the same nature, with the data building blocks defining [offer] × [segment] being mutated and recombined in response to customer behavior. The same principle is widely applicable, from the mundane A/B testing used by savvy Internet companies to the design of entire business strategies. But before anything can be done, you need a privacy engineering strategy.

# Foreword's Epilogue

"My company has been collecting a megaton of data over the years and we have used it for reporting but we think there is value in it that we're not exploiting. But we don't know where and how to look. Help us discover the value in it." In just one year, this kind of statement has become commonplace in my conversations with executives all over the world. Privacy is rarely mentioned, and even then, only as a hindrance. Let me note in passing that privacy, as a field, should probably be renamed. There is no sense of urgency or value in the word privacy, a problem that has plagued the field and will one day be addressed by shrewd marketers. Therein lies the beauty of privacy engineering: not only do data that have been "privacy engineered" comply with rules and regulations, they are also ready for exploitation, thereby transforming a legal burden into an opportunity for value creation.

Just as a prelude, consider what privacy engineering can do to clinical trials in the drug development process. The future of clinical trials is the quasi-disappearance of clinical trials: they are slow, large, expensive, indiscriminate, and produce flawed results—they need to go in their current incarnation. The most promising alternative approach is based on "real-world outcomes," that is, observational studies that do not rely on the randomized controlled trial (RCT) concept. Powerful statistical techniques can to a large extent "replicate" RCTs and establish causation. With this approach, the same data building blocks (age, race, gender, genotypic attributes, lifestyle attributes, drugs used, etc.) can be used, reused, and recombined multiple times depending on the question being studied, lowering drastically the cost and duration of studies and boosting innovation. But for that approach to be possible, well, the building blocks need to be legal, and dependable and their integrity ensured. In other words, the data have to be privacy engineered.

As for that credit card call, if the appropriate data building blocks had been kept separate, I wouldn't have received it. But it's become my best strategy to get out of sticky subscriptions.

—Dr. Eric Bonabeau, PhD

# Introduction

The world is certainly flat. Everyone said so. The government said so. The church said so. Your wise old aunt and the richest guy in town said so. Everyone.

Except, a few explorers, dreamers, scientists, artists, and plain-spoken folks who looked out at a sky that looked more like a bowl and noticed that the ground and sky always met for a brief kiss before the observer wandered ever closer and the meeting became elusive. And shadows, tides, and other indications seemed to suggest that there might be something more than dragons beyond the edge of the world. And so, as it turned out, the world was not, in fact flat. There was a seemingly endless set of new possibilities to discover.

Privacy is *certainly* dead. Everyone said so. Rich people with big boats who sold stuff to the CIA in the 1970s said so. Founders of important hardware companies said so. Someone who blogs said so. The government cannot make up its mind which person should say so or if the polling numbers look right, but it might say so. Someone tweeted. Even really old technologists who helped invent the whole thing said so. *Everyone.*

Except, a few explorers and inventors and philosophers and children and parents and even government regulators who looked out at a seemingly endless sea of data and could still see how a person can be distinguished from a pile of metadata. This is true for people who wish to decide for themselves the story they wish to tell about themselves and see a different horizon. The privacy engineer sees this horizon where privacy and security combine to create value as a similarly challenging and exciting time for exploration, innovation, and creation; not defeat.

The purpose of this book is to provide, for data and privacy practitioners (and their management and support personnel), a systematic engineering approach to develop privacy policies based on enterprise goals and appropriate government regulations. Privacy procedures, standards, guidelines, best practices, privacy rules, and privacy mechanisms can then be designed and implemented according to a system's engineering set of methodologies, models, and patterns that are well known and well regarded but are also presented in a creative way. A proposed quality assurance checklist methodology and possible value models are described. But why bother?

The debate about data privacy, ownership, and reputation poses an irresistible and largely intractable set of questions. Since the beginning of recorded history, people have sought connection, culture, and commerce resulting from sharing aspects about themselves with others. New means of communication, travel, business, and every other social combination continue to evolve to drive greater and greater opportunities for the solo self to be expressed and to express oneself in person and remotely. It is all terribly exciting. Yet, every individual desires a sense of individuality and space from his or her fellow man; a right to be left alone without undue interference and to lead his or her individual life.

Governments have played a stark role in the development of data privacy. Laws are created to protect, but there are also abuses and challenges to individual rights and freedoms in the context of multiple governments in a world where people have become free to travel with relative ease and comfort—sans peanuts—around the globe and back again. National and international security norms have been challenged in both heroic and embarrassing fits and starts. The role of total information vs. insight and actionable information is debated again and again. "Insiders" and fame seekers have exposed massive data collection programs.

In the information technology sector, data privacy remains a matter for heated debate. At times the debate seems as if technologists somehow wished (or believed) they could escape the norms of general social, cultural, and legal discourse simply by designing ever more complex systems and protocols that "need" increasing levels of sensitive information to work. The lawyers come trooping in and write similarly complex terms and conditions and hope to paper over the problem or find a cozy loophole in unholy legislative agendas. Investors search in vain for beans to count. Everyone else finds privacy *boring* until their own self-interests are compromised.

At the same time, just as automotive technology eventually became a ubiquitous and necessary part of many more lives, so too has information technology, from phones to clouds, become such an essential part of industrialized nation-states. Personal data fuel and preserve the value of this new information boom. Thus, the technical elite no longer can dismiss the debate or pretend that data privacy doesn't matter, nor can they fail to build new creations that defy basic privacy precepts, which we will discuss herein, if they wish to see this new world unfold and grow.

If an executive at a global company publicly were to state that he doesn't believe in taxes and therefore will not pay them to any government, he would likely be removed or at least considered to be a great humorist. Not so for data privacy in the past. In the past decades, executives and other makers and consumers of information technologies regarded data privacy as some sort of religion that they could believe in or not at will and without earthly consequence. They certainly did not regard privacy as a *requirement* to measure, to debate in the boardroom, or to build at the workbench. We see these uninformed days of privacy as religion as nearly over. The age of data privacy as a set of design objects, requirements for engineering and quality measures, is dawning, and we hope to help the sun come shining in.

In fact, plain old-fashioned greed and an instinct for value creation will *hasten* the age of privacy engineering and quality. We know that the concept of privacy regarding one's person, reputation, and, ultimately, what can be known about the person has been the inspiration of law and policy on one hand, but we also know that innovation and the recognition that privacy—informational or physical—has value.

Andrew Grove, cofounder and former CEO of Intel Corporation, offered his thoughts on Internet privacy in an interview in 2000:

> *Privacy is one of the biggest problems in this new electronic age. At the heart of the Internet culture is a force that wants to find out everything about you. And once it has found out everything about you and two hundred million others, that's a very valuable asset, and people will be tempted to trade and do commerce with that asset. This wasn't the information that people were thinking of when they called this the information age.[4]*

Thus, people living in the Information Age are faced with a dichotomy. They wish to be connected on a series of global, interconnected networks but they also wish to protect their privacy and to be left alone—sometimes. Both business and governmental enterprises, striving to provide a broad base of services to their user community, must ensure that personal information and confidential data related to it are protected. Those who create those systems with elegance, efficiency, and measurable components will profit and proliferate. History is on our side.

We call the book and our approach "privacy engineering" in recognition that the techniques used to design and build other types of purposefully architected systems can and should be deployed to build or repair systems that manage data related to human beings.

We could have similarly called the book "design principles for privacy" as the techniques and inspirations embraced by the design communities in informatics, critical design, and, of course, systems design are also a part of the basic premise where one can review an existing successful framework or standard and find inspiration and structure for building and innovation. The very nomenclature known as privacy engineering is left open to the possibility of further design.

The models shown are abstractions. Models are never the reality, but models and patterns help designers, stakeholders, and developers to better communicate and understand required reality.

Confidence in privacy protection will encourage trust that information collected from system users will be used correctly. This confidence will encourage investment in the enterprise and, in the case of charity enterprises, will encourage people to donate.

There are many books and papers on privacy. Some focus on privacy law, others on general privacy concepts. Some explain organizational or management techniques. This book is intended to be additive. This book crosses the boundaries of law, hardware design, software, architecture, and design (critical, aesthetic, and functional). This book challenges and teases philosophical debates but does not purport to solve or dissolve any of them. It discusses how to develop good functionalized privacy policies and shows recognized methodologies and modeling approaches adapted to solve privacy problems. We introduce creative privacy models and design approaches that are not technology specific nor jurisdiction specific. Our approach is adaptable to various technologies in various jurisdictions.

---

[4]"What I've Learned: Andy Grove," *Esquire*, May 1, 2000.

Simply put, this is a book of TinkerToy-like components[5] for those who would tinker, design, innovate, and create systems and functional interfaces that enhance data privacy with a sustainability that invites transparency and further innovation. We wish to demystify privacy laws and regulations and nuanced privacy concepts into concrete things that can be configured with flexible, engineered solutions.

The *Privacy Engineer's Manifesto: Getting from Policy to Code to QA to Value* is a unique book. We introduce privacy engineering as a discrete discipline or field of inquiry, and innovation may be defined as using engineering principles and processes to build controls and measures into processes, systems, components, and products that enable the authorized processing of personal information. We take you through developing privacy policy to system design and implementation to QA testing and privacy impact assessment and, finally, throughout the book, discussions on value.

- Chapter 1 discusses the evolution of information technology and the network and its impact on privacy.

- Chapter 2 discusses a series of definitions: policy, privacy engineering, personal information (PI), and the Fair Information Processing Principles (FIPPS).

- Chapter 3 covers data and privacy governance, including data governance, Generally Accepted Privacy Principles (GAPP), Privacy by Design (PbD), and other governance frameworks.

- Chapter 4 introduces a privacy engineering development structure, beginning with the enterprise goals and objectives, including privacy *objectives*, that are used to development privacy policy.

- Chapter 5 discusses privacy engineering requirements. We then introduce use cases and use-case metadata.

- Chapter 6 introduces enterprise architecture and the various views of it. We dig into the privacy engineering system engineering lifecycle methodology. We show the Unified Modeling Language (UML) usage flow from the context diagram, using the UML use-case diagram, to the use of business activity diagrams, including showing key data attributes, then on to data and class modeling using the UML class modeling diagram, and then to user interface design. We use the system activity diagram to show where FIPPS/GAPP requirements are satisfied within the privacy component design (scenario 1) and then we move to dynamic modeling where we define service components and supporting metadata, including the inclusion of privacy enabling technologies (PETs). We then discuss the completion of development, the development of test cases, and the system rollout.

---

[5] See www.retrothing.com/2006/12/the_tinkertoy_c.html for a random, cool TinkerToy creation by MIT students.

- Chapter 7 discusses the privacy component app, which will be used to maintain the Privacy Notice. The privacy team, along with the data stewards, will enter and maintain the privacy rules. When an embedding program requires personal information, the privacy component will ensure that the personal information is collected according to privacy policies.

- Chapter 8 presents, as an example, a small mobile app, using a simplified version of the privacy component to support a high school cross-country runners app.

- Chapter 9 covers an example vacation planner app that utilizes a privacy component that has already been developed, tested, and implemented by a large hospitality company that requires a system to help its customer community plan a vacation at one of their hospitality sites.

- Chapter 10 covers quality assurance throughout the development lifecycle, data quality, and privacy impact assessments (PIA).

- Chapter 11 discusses privacy awareness assessments and operational readiness planning.

- Chapter 12 covers the organizational aspects of privacy engineering and aligning a privacy function to IT, to data governance or data stewardship, and to the security management function.

- Chapter 13 discusses how data and data privacy may be valued.

- Chapter 14 covers our musings about the future of privacy and privacy engineering along with our Privacy Manifesto.

# Why Anyone Should Care About Privacy, Privacy Engineering or Data at All

It's time to serve humanity.

Humanity is people.
Humanity is empowered stewardship of our surroundings—
Our universe, planet, and future.

Humanity is described by data;
Data about humans;
Data about all things human.

Data is not humanity;
Data tells a story;

Data is leverage;
Data is not power.

Humanity can capture data.
Data cannot capture humanity.

It's time to serve humanity.
There is no one else.
We are already past due.

This is the paradox in which the privacy engineer discovers, inspires, and innovates. *Let's begin.*

# PART 1

# Getting Your Head Around Privacy

# CHAPTER 1

■ ■ ■

# Technology Evolution, People, and Privacy

*It isn't all over; everything has not been invented; the human adventure is just beginning.*

—Gene Roddenberry

This chapter takes a look at the history of information, technology, beneficiaries of that technology, and their relationship to data governance development over time. Innovation in business models, technology capabilities, and the changing relationships in the ownership and accessibility to data has resulted in a fundamental shift in size and complexity of data governance systems. Additionally, the increasing trend where collective numbers of individual consumers actually drive information technology, also known as consumerization of information technology (IT), adds yet more complexity to business relationships, fiduciary duties toward data about people, and underlying system requirements.[1] In short, this chapter introduces the context of informational privacy evolution and its relationship to new, shiny, and complex things.

Complexity—in requirements, systems, and data uses—has led to increasingly sophisticated personal data management and ethical issues, the dawning of the personal information service economy, and privacy engineering as a business-critical and customer satisfaction imperative and necessity. This book will unpacked that complexity and then examine how technology and people have interacted and how this interaction has led to data privacy concerns and requirements.

---

[1]One of the first-known uses of the term consumerization to describe the trend of consumer to business technological advancement is in the early 2000s. See David Moschella, Doug Neal, John Taylor, and Piet Opperman, *Consumerization of Information Technology*. Leading Edge Forum, 2004. http://lef.csc.com/projects/70

# The Relationship Between Information Technology Innovation and Privacy

Throughout history, one can correlate innovation and the use of information technologies to pivotal moments in the history of privacy. In fact, there are many examples where technology either directly or indirectly impacts the sharing of personal details.

Take, as an example, the Gutenberg press and the invention of movable type. The development of the printing press and movable type not only directly led to the emergence of inexpensive and easily transportable books but also contributed to the development of the notion of personal space, privacy, and individual rights, as noted in Karmaks "History of Print": "[Print] encouraged the pursuit of personal privacy. Less expensive and more portable books lent themselves to solitary and silent reading. This orientation to privacy was part of an emphasis on individual rights and freedoms that print helped to develop."[2]

Then in the19th century, technology took privacy in another direction. The book *The Devil in the White City*[3] describes another time where movement and communication, facilitated by rail travel, inexpensive paper and writing implements, and increasing literacy, also added to the mass documentation and sharing of everyday life—from grocery lists to documented invention notebooks to planning for grand world fairs. This documentation of personal life created additional rights and obligations to share that information in culturally acceptable ways. So much temporal information also helped to piece together the lives of those living in that period of explosive innovation and growth in a manner never before available to historians or anthropologists. One wonders, will we feel the same about our old MySpace postings throughout time?

Another example (also in the late 1800s) of innovation of information technology that resulted in a pivotal privacy moment was the invention of the camera—or more precisely, rolled film. In 1888, George Eastman invented film that could be put on a spool, preloaded in easy-to-handle cameras, and sold much like today's disposable cameras.[4] The technical innovation of this new film and packaging allowed for cameras to become more portable (or mobile) and thus allowed more people access to becoming "Kodakers" or photographers. These technical advances widened the range of subject matter available to the photographers to include people who did not necessarily desire their behavior to be captured on film.[5]

Two years later, prominently citing the example of photography as technology capable of intrusion upon individual space and publicity, Warren and Brandies wrote an article that first articulated the right to privacy as a matter of US jurisprudence.[6] Note, the Warren and Brandies article, "The Right to Privacy," was not the first articulation of privacy rights; in fact, one can go back to biblical times to find discussions of substantive privacy.

---

[2]"Printing: History and Development." http://karmak.org/archive/2002/08/history_of_print.html. Copyright © 1994-99 Jones International and Jones Digital Century. All rights reserved.
[3]Erik Larson, *The Devil in the White City*. New York: Vintage Books, 2003.
[4]http://inventors.about.com/od/estartinventors/ss/George_Eastman.htm
[5]As discussed in later chapters, placing value on data, reputation, and brand creates incentive for privacy preservation and assigns appropriate weight and value on technology that would escalate or diminish that value.
[6]Samuel Warren and Louis Brandeis, "The Right To Privacy," *Harvard Law Review*, 4, no. 193 (1890). www.english.illinois.edu/-people-/faculty/debaron/582/582%20readings/right%20to%20privacy.pdf

# SACRED REFERENCES TO PRIVACY

By Jay Cline, President of privacy consulting firm MPC

The inventions of the camera, database, and Internet browser gave rise to modern Western ideas about privacy. But the seeds of privacy were planted in world cultures and religions long before these technological innovations.

Perhaps the first privacy-enhancing technology was the fig leaves of Adam and Eve, the first couple of the Jewish, Christian, and Islamic faiths. In Genesis 3:7, the pair implemented a bodily privacy control: "Then the eyes of both were opened, and they knew that they were naked. And they sewed fig leaves together and made themselves apron."

In Genesis 9:23, after several generations had passed, the value of bodily privacy had become a broader social objective people helped one another accomplish. This was apparent when Noah's sons discovered him drunk and unclothed in his tent: "Then Shem and Japheth took a garment, laid it on both their shoulders, and walked backward and covered the nakedness of their father. Their faces were turned backward, and they did not see their father's nakedness."[7]

This respect for bodily privacy expanded within Jewish culture to encompass all private activity, even in the public space. You could harm someone if you viewed their private affairs without their awareness. According to Rabbi David Golinkin, author of *The Right to Privacy in Judaism*,[8] the Talmud contains two teachings on this topic:

> The Mishnah in *Bava Batra* 3:7 states: "In a common courtyard, a person should not open a door opposite a door and a window opposite a window."

> The *Rema* adds in the *Shulhan Arukh* (*Hoshen Mishpat* 154:7) that it is forbidden to stand at your window and look into your neighbor's courtyard, "lest he harm him by looking."

The Book of Proverbs, a collection of wisdom of right living prevalent in the ancient Jewish culture, contains three verses praising the value of confidentiality:

> "Whoever goes about slandering reveals secrets, but he who is trustworthy in spirit keeps a thing covered." (11:13)

> "Whoever covers an offense seeks love, but he who repeats a matter separates close friends." (17:9)

---

[7] www.biblehub.com/genesis/9-23.htm

[8] "The Right to Privacy in Judaism," David Golinkin, Schechter Institute of Jewish Studies, http://www.myjewishlearning.com/practices/Ethics/Business_Ethics/Contemporary_Issues/Privacy/A_Responsum.shtml.

"Argue your case with your neighbor himself, and do not reveal another's secret." (25:9)

The Christian scriptures didn't highlight the concept of privacy. But Mohammed, living 600 years after the time of Jesus, continued the Jewish respect for private affairs. Abdul Raman Saad, author of "Information Privacy and Data Protection: A Proposed Model for the Kingdom of Saudi Arabia," identified the following privacy-friendly verses in the Quran:

> "O ye who believe! enter not houses other than your own, until ye have asked permission and saluted those in them: that is best for you, in order that ye may heed (what is seemly). If ye find no one in the house, enter not until permission is given to you: if ye are asked to go back, go back: that makes for greater purity for yourselves: and God knows well all that ye do." (An-Nur: 27–28) (24:27–28)[9]

> "O ye who believe! Avoid suspicion as much (as possible): for suspicion in some cases is a sin: And spy not on each other behind their backs. Would any of you like to eat the flesh of his dead brother? Nay, ye would abhor it. . . . But fear God: For God is Oft-Returning, Most Merciful." (Al-Hujurat: 12) (49:12)[10]

As Christianity matured, its high regard for confidentiality—as an expression of obeying the biblical commandment to not bear false witness against a neighbor— became more evident. Chapter 2477 of the *Catechism of the Catholic Church*[11] states:

> *"Respect for the reputation* of persons forbids every attitude and word likely to cause them unjust injury. He becomes guilty:
>
> —of *rash judgment* who, even tacitly, assumes as true, without sufficient foundation, the moral fault of a neighbor;
>
> —of *detraction* who, without objectively valid reason, discloses another's faults and failings to persons who did not know them;
>
> —of *calumny* who, by remarks contrary to the truth, harms the reputation of others and gives occasion for false judgments concerning them."

---

[9]Information Privacy and Data Protection A Proposed Model for the Kingdom Of Saudi Arabia, Abdul Raman Saad, *Abdul Raman Saad & Associates, Malaysia,* 1981, page 3.

[10]"Information Privacy and Data Protection A Proposed Model for the Kingdom Of Saudi Arabia," Abdul Raman Saad, Abdul Raman Saad & Associates, Malaysia, 1981, page 29.

[11]*Catechism of the Catholic Church*, Libreria Editrice Vaticana, Citta del Vaticano, http://www.vatican.va/archive/ENG0015/_INDEX.HTM, 1993.

It could well be that it was these ancient cultural foundations, and not primarily the rise of technology, that led delegates to the United Nations in 1947 to embed a right to information privacy in section 12 of the Universal Declaration of Human Rights: "No one shall be subjected to arbitrary interference with his privacy, family, home or correspondence, nor to attacks upon his honour and reputation. Everyone has the right to the protection of the law against such interference or attacks."[12]

Interestingly, these seeds of privacy found in the monotheistic faiths did not grow in the same way in the East. The Mandarin word for privacy—*yin si*—generally translates as "shameful secret." According to Lu Yao-Huai, a professor at Central South University in Changa City, a person asserting a need to withhold personal information could easily be seen as selfish or antisocial. "Generally speaking, privacy perhaps remains a largely foreign concept for many Chinese people," she wrote in "Privacy and Data Privacy Issues in Contemporary China."[13]

Similarly, in their article "Privacy Protection in Japan: Cultural Influence on the Universal Value," Yohko Orito and Kiyoshi Murata, professors at Ehime and Meiji universities, respectively, explain that Japanese citizens may not share the European view that privacy is an intrinsic right. "[I]nsistence on the right to privacy as the 'right to be let alone' indicates a lack of cooperativeness as well as an inability to communicate with others," they wrote.[14]

In related research, Masahiko Mizutani, professor at Kyoto University, and Dartmouth professors James Dorsey and James Moor stated, "[T]here is no word for privacy in the traditional Japanese language; modern Japanese speakers have adopted the English word, which they pronounce *puraibashi*."[15]

In the late 1960s, there were many concerns that governments had access to massive stores of personal information in easily accessible formats. The US government's use of databases in what was then the Department of Health, Education, and Welfare, in particular, led to the first articulation of the Fair Information Practice Principles (FIPPs). The FIPPs, which will be discussed in more detail in later chapters, are widely considered the foundation of most data privacy laws and regulations.

We are at another pivotal privacy moment given the ongoing and ever accelerating pace of information technology innovation and consumerization. This acceleration is being driven by market demand—individuals who want new and different functionality

---

[12]www.ohchr.org/EN/UDHR/Documents/UDHR_Translations/eng.pdf

[13]Privacy and Data Privacy Issues in Contemporary China, Lü Yao-Huai, Kluwer Academic Publishers, 2005.

[14]Privacy Protection in Japan: Cultural Influence on the Universal Value, Yohko Orito and Kiyoshi Murata, http://bibliotecavirtual.clacso.org.ar/ar/libros/raec/ethicomp5/docs/htm_papers/52Orito,%20Yohko.htm

[15]The internet and Japanese conception of privacy, Masahiko Mizutani, James Dorsey, James H. Moore, Journal Ethics and Information Technology, Kluwer Academic Publishers, Volume 6, Issue 2, 2004, pages 121-128.

from technology and uses of information—and market creation—enterprises and governments attempting to capitalize on new and expanded business models. The time for privacy engineering has arrived as a necessary component to constructing systems, products, processes, and applications that involve personal information. In today's world, systems' products, processes, and applications that involve personal information must be thought of as personal information or privacy "ecosystems" and like any ecosystems must be treated in a certain way to not only exist, but also to grown, thrive, and flourish.

To better understand this moment and the precipice we stand on, it is worth taking a few steps back and reviewing the history of information technology through a history of the network.

# The Information Age

Technological support for the Information Age can be described as starting with the invention of the Gutenberg press and moveable type, where documentation, movement, and sharing of information left the realm of the elite few and entered into the popular culture. Suddenly, the possibilities for data transfer and influence expanded far beyond the social circle of the "author."

The introduction of the telegraph and telephone or the ENIAC (for Electronic Numerical Integrator and Computer, which went online in 1947 and which many IT historians call the "first electronic general-purpose computer") was a similarly remarkable leap in the ability to process and data.

For the sake of simplicity, this book will focus on the recent past to discuss various stages where information technology, norms, practices, and rules combined to allow for data gathering and sharing within an enterprise and with individuals. Framing and noting the various risks and opportunities within various stages in the Information Age creates a context for the ensuing discussion surrounding the mission and purpose of the privacy engineer and the call to action for the privacy engineer's manifesto, as presented later in this book.

Within the Information Age, this discussion will focus on five separate evolutionary stages, as shown in Figure 1-1.

## Five Stages of the Information Age

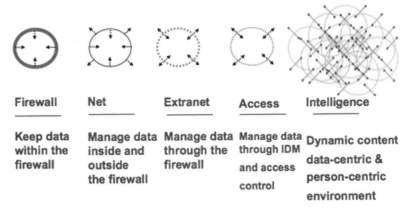

| Firewall | Net | Extranet | Access | Intelligence |
|---|---|---|---|---|
| Keep data within the firewall | Manage data inside and outside the firewall | Manage data through the firewall | Manage data through IDM and access control | Dynamic content data-centric & person-centric environment |

*Figure 1-1.* *Five stages of the age of information*

Each of these stages has evolved from one to the next in a cumulative fashion, not only because information technology became more consumer friendly and more easily accessed and implemented, but also because user, creator, and builder-driven innovation forced its evolution. Also this evolution was enabled in no uncertain terms by the realities of such things as Moore's law,[16] which correctly predicted that base technologies would become inexpensive, ubiquitous, and available for experimentation and growth.

## The Firewall Stage

In the firewall stage, technology was limited[17] to discrete islands of compute capabilities (Figure 1-2). Where systems were connected to external systems, a fairly simple firewall was sufficient to maintain system integrity and exclude unauthorized users. This is that period of time before the Internet was leveraged widely as a commercial tool. Online activity, for example, was limited to networks such as Prodigy, CompuServe, and AOL. Bulletin board systems (BBS) and the Internet were the province of academics and researchers.

---

[16]Gordon Moore, one of the founders of Intel, observed in 1965 that the number of integrated transistors doubles approximately every 2 years with concomitant falling costs and rising efficiencies associated with production.

[17]In all of these discussions, technology limitations and capabilities are those that are widely deployed and accessible by enterprises or individuals. The first working mobile phone, for example, existed in the 1940s but did not have the innovative impact until decades later.

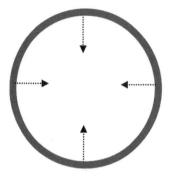

***Figure 1-2.*** *Firewall stage*

## MY LIFE WITHIN THE FIREWALL

By Michelle Finneran Dennedy

In the late 1980s I was, in fact but not title, one of the early chief information security officers for a conglomerate, multinational oil and gas company. My title, in reality, was temporary summer receptionist.

My retrospective title is based on one of the many duties required of me at the company. In addition to fetching coffee, screening visitors, and locking up packages when the addressee was unavailable, I was also in possession of "the Key." The Key opened the all-important broom closet that housed, in addition to brooms, the Wang computer that I unlocked to allow the monthly reconciliation work to happen within the accounting department, under the direction of a very distinguished white-haired gentleman named Mr. Gerold.[18]

I was never hacked. The spread sheeting capabilities were never compromised. The data was never leaked or misaddressed to the wrong party. I had a rare perfect security track record for confidentiality, integrity, and availability.

Now, the Wang computer was not linked electronically to other systems; nor did it do very much more than help the basic computations of a limited number of authorized people during the 9-to-5 workday. Limited functionality helps security and prevents privacy and confidentiality intrusion but it is also, well, not very functional or exciting.

That said, I dare any current CISO to claim that they have a perfect security track record.

---

[18]Not his real name, but he was truly a lovely man.

The network was still a highly controlled and governed environment where connectivity was limited by the features of the operating systems, hardware, compatibility with telephone networks, and by the expectations and practices of information technology users. An enterprise would often operate using a local area network (LAN) set of networking protocols, but its functionality and capacity were limited. Typically, data from outside sources were brought into the enterprise by means of batches or created internally and converted from analog to digital. In a like fashion, data would be moved from the enterprise in batches. People still communicated using letters created on a once ubiquitous, now museum quality, IBM Selectric typewriter. During the firewall stage, enterprise data was maintained within the protection of a digital firewall[19] as well as a physical firewall: brick, mortar, and locked filing cabinet.

Because data was contained inside physical organizational boundaries, security and privacy issues were limited and were essentially defined by the perimeters of the secure environment.

It was during the firewall stage when forward-thinking policymakers documented the FIPPs and they were adopted by the Organisation for Economic Co-operation and Development (OECD).[20] These principles became an internationally accepted set of guidelines for processing personal information. And, although the FIPPs clearly indicate the firewall stage was not without privacy concerns or the potential for greater harms, the primary focus at the time was the fear for government misuse of private information rather than commercial enterprise abuse. In addition, policymakers recognized the increasing pressure to establish a standard for handling data across jurisdictions.

Although the cost of memory, bandwidth, throughput, and compute and processing power were all still at a premium compared to today's capabilities, the increasing mobility of people and the pressure to create new, global communities foretold of an innovation bubble

Market dynamics and innovation brought compute power and network capabilities within reach of individuals and not solely the province of business and government with the availability of the affordable personal computer and Mosaic, the first Internet "browser" for the World Wide Web.

## The Net Stage

The combination of the Mosaic browser, HTML (HyperText Markup Language), and customer-ready hardware and software (i.e., hardware and software that did not require an advanced engineering degree) may have been the mixture of combustibles that ignited and accelerated market dynamics and led to the consumerization of information technology that we take for granted today because it allowed nontechnical users to access and share information in a convenient fashion. It also accelerated and set in motion the dynamics that have led to the widespread consumerization of data (including personal

---

[19]A firewall is a system designed to prevent unauthorized access to or from a private network.
[20]Organisation for Economic Cooperation and Development (OECD), "OECD Guidelines on the Protection of Privacy and Transborder Flows of Personal Data" (September 23, 1980). www.oecd.org/internet/ieconomy/oecdguidelinesontheprotectionofprivacyand transborderflowsofpersonaldata.htm

information) and the need for privacy engineering to reap this opportunity because individuals became the focus of observation, processing, and preference mining, which became one of the most powerful business models in modernity.

The net stage was a golden time for perceived anonymity (Figure 1-3). The belief was that with the net, no one knew who you were unless you announced yourself. The *New Yorker* ran a now famous cartoon showing a dog at the keyboard of a PC with the caption of "On the Internet, nobody knows you're a dog."[21] No one thought of him- or herself in a public space online unless they announced themselves (i.e., published content or by participating in an online forum).

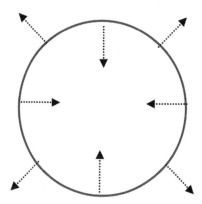

***Figure 1-3.*** *Net stage*

The two primary privacy conversations during this time were e-marketing (i.e., spam) and identity theft. Data was increasingly transported and shared through the net, but this sharing was somewhat unidirectional. The Internet pushed data out to the public; the intranet pushed data into the enterprise. Targeted advertising and profiling were in their infancy. The net was a means of publishing and marketing. PDAs (personal digital assistants) were not connected devices for the most part. E-mail and job listings were the killer apps of the Web.

---

[21]http://en.wikipedia.org/wiki/File:Internet_dog.jpg

# The Extranet Stage

With the introduction of the extranet,[22] the network moved into another major phase. The extranet stage[23] can be described as the age of the portal (Figure 1-4). If during the net stage the network was largely a push medium primarily used for publishing (business and governments) and reading information (consumers and citizens), extranets signaled the net as an interactive medium—an environment where one was invited behind the velvet rope into the enterprise but still not necessarily included as a fiduciary, contractor, or employee. Extranets were controlled spaces where authorized users could access information and tools and take care of limited things themselves. So-called self-service services were available to customers and other interested parties for everything from tech support to banking to benefits administration and more. Extranets allowed systems and functionality that used to exist only behind the firewall to be surfaced and exposed to "authorized" individuals.

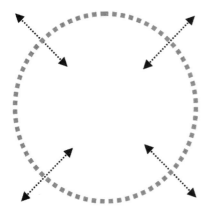

***Figure 1-4.*** *Extranet stage*

These developments meant two things. First, an enterprise was no longer monolithic with a distinct "inside" and "outside" the firewall. The firewall became more porous as more and more ports had to be opened to allow users, functionality, and external applications in. Second, though the notion of user IDs and passwords existed before the extranet stage, the rapid growth of extranets as an enterprise facilitating and expediting medium resulted in the rapid growth of identity management solutions. The use of the extranet is significant for more reasons than the thinning of the firewall.

---

[22]An extranet is a private network that uses Internet technology and the public telecommunication system to securely share part of a business's information or operations with suppliers, vendors, partners, customers, or other businesses. It will typically have an inner firewall that protects crucial enterprise databases. There is usually an outer firewall that screens incoming data so that only invited source data is allowed in. Between the two firewalls, there may be databases that share data between external enterprises and the enterprise itself.

[23]During this stage, data were managed through a sophisticated firewall environment, but the corporate network was essentially extended to enable remote access by trusted parties.

Functionality, which heretofore was only possible in proprietary online environments, was now within reach of the many (not quite the masses yet). Users began to use the net in a fundamentally different way. It became a "private" space of interaction between designated teams, circles, and groups. Whereas before, the Web had been a publishing medium, it was now a sharing and collaboration medium.

Without a doubt, the ability to join groups changed the nature and kind of information that was now traveling the information highway. This also meant a change in "business intelligence." Whether it was the data shared, the interactions, or just the metadata[24] (data about the data and data about the interactions), business intelligence had a new resource to draw from.

## Access Stage

As technology has continued to advance, more open and ubiquitous access tools and functionality information began to change the ways that people used technology, how they communicated, and, most important, what they shared. Participants were not just acquiring information, but they were also contributing, refining, sharing, and broadcasting it—sometimes to closed, selected groups and sometimes to all (i.e., the public). The key difference between the extranet stage and the access stage was the magnitude of sharing and the ease of access to enabling technology (identity management [IDM], social networks, blogs, and smartphones) (Figure 1-5). More and more, people used technology to connect with one another, to participate, and to share their lives—work and personal. Just as people had once used meetings, the water cooler, or parties as places to meet and chat and access one another, now they used the net.

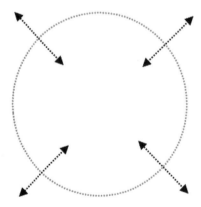

*Figure 1-5. Access stage*

---

[24]We will discuss metadata in detail throughout Part 2 of this book.

As the nature and ability to share grew during the access stage, so too did privacy concerns. Some of these concerns relate to the type and nature of information that individuals were willing to share in public and quasi-public settings as well as questions surrounding the general public's understanding of the power and potentially lasting impact of tools and technologies. This is a fundamental awareness or behavioral cognizance asymmetry that we still suffer from today.

Additional concerns were raised by the growing desire for governments and other enterprises to use and exploit larger and larger datasets about individual and aggregate users of technologies in the name of providing "service" or "creating community" or just plain "marketing."

Struggling legislators have grappled with these consumer and governmental interference issues by attempting to add increasing legal penalties to the miscollection and use of data. California's now watershed SB1386[25] data breach notification law is one such example, where collectors and keepers of information about people were forced to reveal data loss or theft to individual data subjects[26] in the hope of helping individuals to prepare against identity theft or other misuse.

Although this law did not come into effect until 2003—far after other comprehensive data protection laws and frameworks—this California State statute was arguably one of the first laws to create rapid, expensive, and inevitable change in corporate and governmental planning and prevention. Breach notification requirements continue to be adopted across the globe as more territories seek to protect their citizens and create requirements for tangible and measurable data protection protocols, tools, organizations and education.[27]

## The Intelligence Stage

The intelligence stage is the new, now and future frontier (Figure 1-6). This stage in computing and communicating and creating is about people, devices, and systems seamlessly making handshakes, connecting, processing information, and providing services that are designed to improve the quality of life and are tailored to our needs. It is driven by increased bandwidth, throughput, processing power, analytic skills, data-reading abilities, and the desire to provide value. Here, at last, consumerization— where individuals alone or collectively—is able to drive the changes of the feature sets of computing as much as the former stages of technology forced conformity to the technology.

---

[25]www.leginfo.ca.gov/pub/01-02/bill/sen/sb_1351-1400/sb_1386_bill_20020926_chaptered.pdf

[26]A data subject is simply the individual who is described by data elements either alone or in combination with other data elements.

[27]The advent (or development) of the chief privacy officer (CPO) role, in particular, as well as the need for the professionalization of privacy as a distinct profession, in general, were other key developments during this stage of the Information Age.

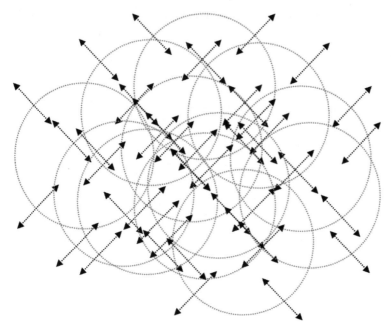

**Figure 1-6.** *Intelligence stage*

Some early examples of the computing in the intelligence stage are:

- Smart grid technologies recording and optimizing energy use on homes within communities

- Mapping apps that provide real-time traffic updates and suggest course corrections

- Connected appliances such as mini-bar refrigerators that automatically inventory themselves

- Augmented reality and gaming as a tool as well as recreation

- Localized shopping applications that give real-time pricing comparisons

These apps take in user-provided information, observed information or behavior, and output results that can be life improving, labor saving, and time efficient.

Whereas the hallmark of the access stage was the sharing of information, the intelligence stage may be considered as far more person and data centric rather than tool centric. In this stage, the use of information provided or collected and behavior and information observed can drive technology, social, cultural, and ethical change.

One of the implications of the dawning intelligence stage is the implication that power may be derived from being a creative, flexible thinker who can effectively gather, distill, and communicate information from a variety of sources.

# THE INTERNET OF THINGS AND PRIVACY

By Tyson Macaulay, Vice President, Global Telecommunications Strategy, McAfee

Pity the fool who insists on a definition of the Internet of Things (IoT). There are literally dozens (50+ at last count by the IOS Special Working on the IoT in March 2013), originating from august and well-regarded institutions. So let's put one out there for the purposes of this discussion and leave it as a stake in the ground and reference point.

Here we go: the IoT includes devices that are manipulated by people (smartphones, desktops, tablets), devices that support very limited interfaces with people or animals (point of sale devices, medical devices), and devices that observe or manage the physical world (remote sensors, location trackers, meters, industrial controls, smart anything) in automated or semiautomated manners. And it all sits on a common network technology like Internet protocol (IP) or behind a gateway sitting on an IP network. One way or another, most of these networks are connected.

## When Is Personally Identifiable Information in the IoT Actually Personally Identifiable Information?

Pity the fool who looks for consensus related to what equals personally identifiable information (PII) in the IoT.

The massive amount of data present in the IoT means there is no question that the IoT, en masse, is personal. It simply is. If you can access, correlate, and associate identity and activity in the IoT, you will pretty much be able to write a biography that will shock mothers and end marriages. Every time.

For instance, *if* you could capture the data flows from a given device (say a power meter), and *if* you could sift out the extraneous signaling and network handshakes from the service payloads, and *if* you could get the mapping of the device IP address to a subscriber ID held in a usage database, and *if* you could map the ID to a subscriber's real name held in a customer management database, *then*, maybe you might have personal information for a bachelor in a bachelor apartment and have breeched a law. Maybe.

That is a lot of *ifs*. But more important, it assumes that all this information—already segregated for business reasons unrelated to privacy—can be brought together without obstacle.

## A Proposed PII Code of Conduct

What would be useful for risk mangers in the IoT are some basic rules or a code of conduct for dealing with privacy in the IoT.[28] For instance, start with a truth we can agree on, hopefully:

---

IoT Privacy Maxim: Information is personal if identity can be correlated with activity.

---

If information is about activity or events that are not about people, then it is not intrinsically personal. For instance, information about the temperature of the nickel smelter is probably not personal even in the wildest dreams of the most partisan privacy advocate.

However, if the identity of a person getting on a bus is recorded in their transit pass, and the time, date, and GPS coordinates of the bus are also logged somewhere, then PII could certainly, but not necessarily, have been generated. It is about correlation between identity and activity.

If IoT data flows contained information that could be correlated for later use or disclosure about a identifiable person, it might be PII. But not so fast!

Move to rule number 1:

---

IoT Privacy Rule #1: PII exists if correlation of identity to activity is viable and probable.

---

A frequently cited tenant of the audit profession is "would a well-informed and reasonable person agree?" When it comes to privacy and the IoT, the same tenant should apply. Is the assertion of both viability and probably of correlation rendered by reasonable and well-informed people? Is it reasonably possible to affect the correlation? Are the sources accessible such that a reasonable and well-informed person believes that it would come to pass given the time, skills, resources, and motivations of putative threat agents? Without the security jargon: is this a serious risk?

The IoT is personal to the extent that data containing both identity and activity can be correlated. Correlating an identity to the data generated by everything else a person comes into contact with physically and logically and you have the whole picture. But getting access to that identity is all too often assumed to be simple or even viable, when in fact it is not. This is where the delta between technically competent and incompetent advocates will become apparent and a danger that

---

[28]We do recognize this as a fraught proposition of addressing complex questions with simple answers, as Isaac Asimov so famously illustrated over 50 years ago.

swallows IT project whole, like Charybdis from Homer's *Odyssey*, sucking in ships and crew.

To people who contend an IP address is PII, we say "show us." Show us how to (legally or illegally—you choose) get logs from the devices that issue the temporary IP addresses (carrier DHCP) to gateway devices (home modems or business routers), then get account IDs assigned by different systems (RADIUS), and then the logs from the account ID system that relate the (yet again) separate billing systems, which ultimately identifies people. Then show us how you get event logs from the gateway devices (which rarely do any logging at all) and match those to the temporarily assigned internal IP addresses (home/business DHCP) within the home or business. And then make sure the person using the internal device is the same as the person paying the bills. Seriously.

This could bring us to a second rule, about viability and probability if the nature of the information is still uncertain:

---

IoT Privacy Rule #2: PII exists if identity and activity information exists in the same repository.

---

So what might "viable and probable" look like as far as identity correlation in the IoT is concerned? Identity data stored in the same repository (information source managed and accessible by the same applications, users, and administrators) as the activity artifacts associated with that identity (logs, transactions, media recordings, etc.) would viably be PII. Even if the identity data were obscured in some manner, it would still be possible through this single repository to correlate activity and an obscured identity. Meaningless but unique identifiers, over time, will usually yield identity if they can be readily compared to IoT activity.

As a counterbalance to Rule 2 is Rule 3:

---

IoT Privacy Guideline #3: PII is not intrinsic when identity and activity artifacts are in separate repositories.

---

If the identity information and IoT activity artifacts are logically or physically separated into two or more repositories, correlation should be assumed nonviable in the face of legitimate controls. In other words, if multiple repositories must be correlated and there are auditable security programs in place to prevent unapproved usage and disclosure of the data, there is no assumption that PII exists. Especially if security has been controlled among repositories, and the custodian of the information is of good character.

## What About the Network?

Information and data exist in three primary states: (1) at rest (in storage of some sort), (2) in use (in active memory and being processed), or (3) in motion (within the network, moving among processing or storage).

Our earlier discussion about PII rules was centered around an assumption that data are most often accessed while at rest, in a repository. Information in use is also accessible but is far more complicated to gain access to, and a "viability" argument will rapidly come into play: accessing volatile memory used for processing requires highly specialized tools, skills, and privileges—and sometimes physical access to the guts of the system. But what about data in motion?

If you really want to know everything about someone, you tap their network connections. The ability to tap network connections is essentially the ability to watch everything. So does this mean that networks are the ultimate form of PII, being some form of "dynamic repository" subject to all the regulation and controls of PII? The answer is "no" and here are just two reasons why networks are not the ultimate vessels of PII.

First, within any given network, many of the data streams are specifically encrypted from source to destination. So understanding what is in the data stream is frequently not possible, although traffic pattern analysis remains possible even with encrypted data streams. So the PII is limited to the fact that a given network address (not "identity") communicated with a place on the Internet at a certain time and in a certain volume.

Second, most devices that originate substantial amounts of potential PII these days are mobile devices, like smartphones. Mobile devices tend to traverse many networks throughout the day. Mobile devices might start on the home Wi-Fi network, move to the 4G cellular network on the way to work, offload to the employer's office network, offload to the local café network at 10 a.m. and then again at lunch and then again at 2:30 p.m., back to the employer network, and then the 4G network, and finally the home network. All these networks are frequently, independently controlled. Also, the same device will be assigned unique, recycled IP addresses each time it jumps from network to network. Trying to track such devices and collect their traffic falls in the "nonviable" category for the National Security Agency, Superman, and probably God. Network-based correlation by default usually fails IoT Privacy Rule #1—"not viable," although exceptions will exist but must be proven rather than assumed.

# The Dawning of the Personal Information Service Economy

The Information Age, the service economy, and the ability to provide and derive value from personal information are combining like never before and, accordingly, a new class of services is unfolding; these new services are classified as "personal information services." There are currently at least two classes of personal information services. The first types of services are those that aspire to help individuals manage and protect personal information. Security tools, single sign-on/identity management services, "do not track" technologies and policies, and compliance solutions for managing web-based cookies are all examples of this kind of personal information service.

The second type of personal information service are services that use personal information to provide value—sometimes to the individual and often to the enterprise. Examples of such services are personalization tailored to individual wants and desires, device recovery, or data retrieval and cloaking services. Clearly, there is overlap between data management and value-based services and a near infinite possibility for combining value propositions for personal data in emerging business, cultural, and individual value scenarios.

As individuals contribute more about what they want to do and what they want their communities to do (either socially or economically), the combination of all these actions will impact the whole economy. Personal information services may become a pivotal economics resource that can drive or measure an economy.

## Data-Centric and Person-Centric Processing

There is a powerful movement toward data-centric and person-centric computing. Data centric implies that data and information processed from it are primary design drivers. Person centric implies that a person is also a primary design driver. Taken together data-centric and person-centric processing involves the processing of personal information (PI) and thus potential privacy concerns. Privacy engineering is a crucial competency when designing and implementing data-centric and person-centric systems. Data-centric and person-centric design and execution require a proactively engineered system architecture because:

- It takes data to protect data. We need to collect data from customers and those with whom customers may interact to determine whether privacy rules based on statutory or enterprise privacy policies apply.

- The scope of PI is expanding. What was once considered just "machine" data (i.e., not personal) is being recognized as something else.

- DV > DR = Success. A well-designed system ensures that data value (DV) exceeds data risk (DR)

- Privacy engineering is about user experience, brand definition and augmentation, and meeting customer satisfaction.

- Privacy engineering also translates into repeatable engineering principles rather than handcrafted one-off design and execution.

21

# PRIVACY CAN'T BE FIXED

By John Berard, Founder, Credible Context

Got your attention? Privacy is certainly a problem that can be solved. But first our mindset needs to change. Privacy—encompassing the transparent collection, secure storage, meaningful use and scheduled deletion of personally identifiable data—has no single right answer.

That's because privacy is not a single, static goal. Unlike the strength of a bridge, yaw of a yacht or recurring field in a relational database, privacy is a lock that opens with a combination, not a key. In designing systems to deliver on a commitment to privacy, the variables of time, place, platform and intended use are only a few of the constantly changing inputs that can overwhelm a more traditional, linear engineering approach.

Whereas a bridge needs to accommodate the weight of cars and trucks and a yacht must navigate the hull pressure of tide and wind and a database seeks to create order out of business chaos: privacy hopes to deliver on something even more challenging—the expectations of people. Worse, the need is to meet the expectations of people not in a group but as individuals. There is no engineering table for privacy.

This is guidance that can be drawn from former IBM executive Irving Wladawsky-Berger[29] who made a career of applying technology solutions to new classes of highly complex problems, "many based on disruptive innovations which we have not encountered before." Sound familiar? No development has been quite as disruptive as the Internet and the digital data stream it creates.

This is why many find "privacy by design" such a compelling concept. As described by the course catalog at Carnegie Mellon, which offers a privacy engineering degree, the emphasis of "privacy by design" is on "safeguards that can be incorporated into the design of systems and products from the very beginning of the development process."[30]

Rather than retrofit systems with data protection and privacy attributes, the notion is, "Wouldn't it be great to build *them* in at the start?" But is that the answer? The difficulty is in defining what "them" are.

To engineer a solution to meet the demands of consumers, business, and government for more transparent, informed, and value-driven use of data, we need to think holistically. Data protection and privacy engineering cannot only be about structured collection, hardened storage, authenticated access, and clear use, but must also accommodate the kind of variability that is human behavior.

---

[29]http://blog.irvingwb.com/
[30]http://www.cmu.edu/news/stories/archives/2012/october/oct15_privacymasters.html

We know that most existing systems running on data are designed as *point solutions*. The Internal Revenue Service (IRS) needs data to ensure the size of our refund, supermarkets need data to stock their shelves and colleges see social security numbers as a way to manage applicant and student files.

But what happens when the IRS can see new enforcement value in our data? What happens when the supermarkets see more value in selling our shopping preferences to advertisers? And what happens when college entrance decisions become based not on scores but on social context?

In each case the very best engineered solution to what had been the present problem did not have the ability to anticipate what insights might arise or the flexibility to cover whatever might come next—and something always comes next.

Data can now be connected, collated and queried in ways previously unimagined. The results can be of great benefit. But the dark cloud in all this is our inability to predict what stories our data will tell. This increases anxiety over who gets to tell them. Systems able to manage this uncertainty and unease are a tall order whose solution requires that we flip the engineering model on its head. To be blunt, we need to begin at the end rather than the beginning.

In many respects, the model for effective privacy engineering cannot be public works like the Hoover Dam, concerned with resistance, rebar strength and the heat of hydration of concrete, or a software program like Microsoft Word, built, in part, to correct spelling and grammar.

If the goal is to deliver on privacy, especially at the edge of the network as represented by the smartphone in the hands of its owner, a quite different model must emerge, one as fluid in its approach and design as it is hard and fast in its results. The one that comes most to mind was devised more than 60 years ago to solve the problem of the delivery of supplies to a constantly moving army. The result was the birth of Operations Research and an end to World War II.

As studied at Cornell University, Operations Research "deals with decisions involved in planning the efficient allocation of scarce resources to achieve stated goals and objectives under conditions of *uncertainty and over a span of time*."[31] That says pretty well what may be the best approach to delivering on a promise of privacy—contingent upon shifting variables of time, place, platform and purpose.

What is telling is that at the start Operations Research was not a single discipline but rather a matrix of many. The necessity of working together—manufacturing, transportation, topographic, finance and communications, to name a few—to solve a new problem on the battlefield may be the perfect metaphor for managing our privacy relationships today.

---

[31]www.orie.cornell.edu/news/spotlights.cfm?s_id=158

Although data are far from scarce, the usable insights they generate are exceptional; so much so that their pursuit has spawned whole new industries (e.g., Big Data). And if privacy, by its definition, is personal, then each transaction we make must be tagged at a different level of care and concern.

The implications for privacy engineering are as clear as they are counterintuitive. By focusing on the outcome of data use—less expensive health care, quicker oil and gas exploration, the most suitable advertising for an individual consumer—we can begin to design systems to be both focused *and* flexible.

# Conclusion

Privacy engineering in the intelligence stage is crucial because information provided by or gathered about individuals often determines:

- What we build

- How we build it

- How it works

- How our customers use it

- How well it protects our customer or other persons involved

- The risks it may pose to our business and to future markets

Privacy engineering uses engineering principles and processes to build privacy controls and measures throughout system and data lifecycles (development, production, and retirement). Privacy is important to people impacted by the systems; privacy protection encourages trustworthiness and other factors that people expect when working with an enterprise or with an enterprise's systems. Privacy engineering will further assist in:

- Protection of customers and other people impacted by our systems and their data

- Improving trust by the people impacted by enterprises and their systems

- Developing secure and respectful computing that may drive more data sharing and engagement

- Gathering better information that will help create better tools

- Greater innovation and opportunity in the marketplace

All of these areas will be examined in this book. We begin our journey in Chapter 2 with a look at the foundation concepts and frameworks of privacy engineering.

■ ■ ■

# Foundational Concepts and Frameworks

*From within the secret court of men's hearts, Tom was a dead man the minute Mayella Ewell opened her mouth and screamed.*

—Harper Lee, *To Kill a Mockingbird*, 1960

We cannot escape the secret courts within the hearts of men. Opinions, impressions, judgments and prejudices are formed, often instantly and subconsciously, based upon available data, context, and experience. The availability of greater and greater quantities of multimedia-enriched data makes more acute the imperative to manage and respect the power of information to impact individual lives as well as those of entire races and nation-states.

*There's a terror in knowing what the world is about.*

—David Bowie

This chapter addresses key definitions and concepts of privacy that anyone involved in engineering writ large (i.e., architecting, designing, developing, managing, and implementing components, products, services, processes, systems, or applications that process personal information) must understand to be successful as we enter a new stage in the Information Age—that of intelligence and data science. We also will define what privacy engineering is, what a privacy engineer does, and the goals of privacy engineering. In subsequent chapters, we will discuss how to apply these definitions and concepts to a privacy engineer's work, broadly defined as designing, creating, inventing, imagining, and building things that process personal information.

## What Is Privacy?

A great majority of the complexity this book addresses arises, in fact, from the imperfections and difficulty of defining this multifaceted thing called privacy. There are different forms of privacy. *Data privacy* (also known as *data protection* in Europe), which is the kind of privacy this book addresses, can be discussed at great length, but finding one, global, consistent definition can be elusive. This chapter will propose an operational definition of data privacy as it is most often conceived by organizations that consume and process data about people and the governments and institutions who wish to regulate its many aspects and uses. This is not a book about public policy, philosophy, religion, or advocacy other than for privacy engineering.

Data privacy is one form of privacy that is derived from substantive privacy. *Substantive privacy* describes the right and ability of an individual to define and live his or her life in a self-determined fashion. Other forms of privacy attempt to describe and define this basic human fact. Data privacy is a derivative of the substantive right to privacy in that it is about data that has been created about an individual (1) by him- or herself, (2) by others through observations and analysis, or (3) by the consumption or processing (i.e., use) of that data about an individual by others.

Some of the other forms of privacy, or ways in which substantive privacy may be broken down, are behavioral privacy, decisional privacy, and physical privacy. They all interrelate and overlap in various ways. For simplicity sake, throughout this book, whenever we refer to privacy or data privacy we intend them as one and the same (i.e., data privacy) and if another form of privacy is intended, it will be identified.

## THE DIFFERENT FORMS OF PRIVACY

There are different forms of privacy such as behavioral privacy, decisional privacy, and physical privacy.

*Decisional privacy* is really about being able to make decisions and choices without third-party inspection or intrusion. This may be thought of as self-determination within one's own private life. Not having to explain or justify one's behavior or share personal opinions or thoughts is an example of decisional privacy.

*Behavioral privacy* is about being able to act as one wants, free from unwanted third-party intrusion or observation (assuming no harm to others is incurred or laws broken). In this realm, people may dance in their living rooms or whistle in their cars or don various forms of dress or undress upon their own discretion.

*Physical privacy* is privacy about one's body or person. Modesty is another word for it. Some people are more sensitive to physical privacy than others.

Two things about the different forms of privacy should be noted. First, in many instances the examples overlap. Rarely is an example of one kind of privacy exclusive of another. Second, data privacy runs through all types of privacy because as soon as something about you or someone is observed or articulated (even just by you), you cantilever into the data privacy space. Data privacy is literally the language of substantive privacy forms whenever an action or behavior or even a stillness occurs. As such, as soon as any third party becomes involved in data that describe another person, data privacy becomes a fiduciary activity where access, sharing, or exchange of personal information is the corpus of the fiduciary trust.

# THE SUBSTANTIVE NATURE OF PRIVACY

By Stewart Room, Partner, Field Fisher Waterhouse LLP

The right to privacy has been described in many different ways. US lawyers often talk about the Fourth Amendment prohibition against unreasonable search and seizures as protecting private spaces. European Human Rights law says that the right to privacy protects our home life, family life, and correspondence from unreasonable interference by the state. Legislation that is commonly grouped together as privacy laws has focused on the topics of health, financial services, children, electronic communications, and data security breaches. Famous court cases have protected the image rights of celebrities, the chassis of cars,[1] and office computers[2] all in the name of privacy. Statutory regulators use consumer laws to prevent the misselling of home closed-circuit television systems and smartphones as being privacy enhancing.[3]

Two golden threads run through this diverse list of interests, creating a common and uniting bond among them: the concepts of substantive and informational privacy. Within a civilized society, it is the desire to protect substantive and informational privacy that unites the celebrity, the child, the consumer, the smartphone, the camera, the home, the workplace, and the car. All theories of privacy and all privacy laws will pay service to one or both of these concepts.

The idea at the heart of the concept of substantive privacy is that people should be free to make decisions about how they lead their lives, free from interference by others. The idea at the heart of the concept of informational privacy is that people should be able to control the use of information about themselves. Within a state of privacy, these concepts reinforce and support each other; substantive privacy needs and relies upon informational privacy, and vice versa.

In this day and age it is readily appreciated that the threats to a person's privacy do not flow only from the state—the Identity Theft bogeyman is as much an icon for privacy interference as Big Brother—yet the example of the malevolent state provides the easiest way to demonstrate the relationship between and the concepts of substantive and informational privacy and their interdependencies. And among the many sickening examples of state-level evil that have plagued mankind and shamed our history, Hitler's Nazi regime in Germany stands among the very worst.

---

[1] *US v. Jones*, 565 US __, 132 S. Ct. 945 (2012).
[2] See, for example, *Copland v. United Kingdom*, 62617/00 [2007] ECHR 253 (3 April 2007). See also the UK Information Commissioner's "Employment Statutory Code of Practice" (2008).
[3] See, for example, *US Federal Trade Commission v. HTC*, File No. 122 3049 (2013).

The Jew in Hitler's Germany was required to wear a yellow star. This badge said publicly "I am a Jew." The information it conveyed restricted the Jew to the ghetto and, later, it destined him to the gas chamber. The evil Nazi state controlled the information, and the substantive effects will never be forgotten. Shortly after the end of the war, Europe adopted the Convention on Human Rights, ensuring the right to privacy for all persons, so that these horrors could not be repeated. Yet even in the modern world, states still interfere with informational privacy to substantively maligning effects. The Internet is intentionally tapped in North Korea and China to gain information about dissidents, which creates a general appreciation of the presence of surveillance and creates fear, which causes modifications to substantive actions, decisions, and the way people live their lives.

But why is any of this important to the privacy engineer? Simply put, remembering the very real connections between information and substantive actions and decisions creates a mental knot in the handkerchief of the mind (not to be glib about the use of information and the design of information processing systems). Often the substantive effects of information mishandling are hard to see, fathom, or articulate. The connection between a yellow star and a gas chamber is nonobvious. The harms or distress that may result from a security breach can also be nonobvious, likewise those resulting from data profiling, data aggregation, or data monetization. The privacy engineer will understand, however, that adherence to the principles and disciplines of engineering will provide the best prospects of understanding the substantive risks that can flow from the processing of personal information, and that engineering gives the best prospects for risk mitigation.

A captain of the industry has famously stated that the boundary between lawful data processing and unlawful interference with privacy is a "creepy line," a statement that for good or bad will sustain along with "the right to be let alone" within the lexicon of privacy. If the boundary between lawfulness and illegality is to creep and shift, the risk of unwelcome substantive effects becomes embedded within the organization. A risky business may accept this, but the privacy engineer who understands the connections between information and substantive privacy will understand the truth of this fascinating area; the boundary cannot creep and change, but should be fixed. This can only be achieved by coding the boundary into the architecture of the processing system.

# Privacy Engineering

Too often the necessary controls and measures to protect personal information required by a process, application, or system are either ignored or bolted on at the 11th hour of development. When this happens, it usually results in poor user experience, with subpar protections, unnecessary overhead, and customer dissatisfaction.

This is not a wishful or hopeful book about the management of data centers or leadership. This is a practical and pragmatic book that charts out an approach allowing for innovation from many workbenches—legal, technical, political, artistic, or logical. We can call these disciplines, when they come together to create something that promotes the best of data privacy, the innovative and beneficial uses of personal information or those that chase out uncertainty and risk to data wherever possible: *privacy engineering*.

"Engineering" has been defined by the Engineers Council for Professional Development as the creative application of "scientific principles to design or develop structures, machines, apparatus, or manufacturing processes, or works utilizing them singly or in combination; or to construct or operate the same with full cognizance of their design; or to forecast their behavior under specific operating conditions; all as respects an intended function, economics of operation, and safety to life and property.[4]"

Privacy engineering as a discrete discipline or field of inquiry and innovation may be defined as using engineering principles and processes to build controls and measures into processes, systems, components, and products that enable the authorized, fair, and legitimate processing of personal information.

Privacy engineering may also be applied to the creative innovation process to manage increasingly more complex data streams and datasets that describe individual humans. Privacy engineering can be considered the gathering and application of privacy requirements with the same primacy as other traditional feature or process requirements and then incorporating, prioritizing, and addressing them at each stage of the development lifecycle, whether its for a process, project, product, system, application, or other.

The intent of privacy engineering is to close the gap between privacy policy and the reality of systems or technologies or processes. The greater the mismatch between the two, the greater the opportunity for needless inefficiencies, risk, or both.

The risk of failure to follow a privacy engineering approach will be discussed in greater detail in later chapters. In short, poor system design, poor policy requirement gathering, or poor communication (which are the hallmarks of design without privacy engineering techniques) may cause risk or harm to the inventors of such systems, the owners of them, and the individuals described or implicated by the data, or all of the above. Further, the monetary, reputational, organizational, or even criminal risks or harms will only increase for those who fail to recognize a privacy engineering approach as systems become more complex and personal data more valued.

Privacy engineering is not merely a call for mindful engineering where personal information is involved. The call for privacy engineering use and study is a call for leadership, innovation, and even a good measure of courage to change the status quo for design and information management.

Once every system owner, designer, and user expects and understands privacy engineering principles, we expect that privacy engineering will become so integrated into standard innovation cycles that there will be no need for reference to a discrete practice. Rather, the principles of privacy engineering will be an obvious and necessary part of engineering of any kind when personal information is involved or potentially involved.

---

[4]www.britannica.com/EBchecked/topic/187549/engineering

When privacy engineering becomes ubiquitous, individuals will not be treated as "inventory," and data about them will be viewed as a special asset, important, sometimes profitable, and always one with a fundamental ethical value. When this happens, systems that use personal information will be designed, implemented, and decommissioned accordingly.

However, to accelerate the arrival of this day and the ability to safely unlock the rewards of the Internet and the personal information service economy, there is an urgent need for leadership and for stakeholders to act expeditiously in adopting and extending the vision of privacy engineering as articulated throughout this book. Getting to privacy engineering ubiquity will require many acts of courage and cunning. But, as clearly articulated by Ford Prefect in Douglas Adams's *A Hitchhiker's Guide to the Galaxy*, "Don't Panic" and always carry a towel. Please consider this book your towel.

## WHAT ARE THE "REAL" PRIVACY RISKS?

So far, most of the individuals who have gone to jail for data privacy violations have been hackers, spammers, identity thieves, and peeping toms. Unless related to large or multimillion dollar operations, most of the convictions do not receive wide-scale coverage in the mainstream media attention. It is the same with data breaches, which, unfortunately, are increasingly commonplace and thus less newsworthy.

But jail isn't the only possible repercussion for misbehaving in the privacy space and getting caught. Increasingly, corporations and organizations are being cited for privacy violations and are being fined, given sanctions, being placed under regulatory supervision, or pilloried in the public square of opinion. Some of these fines have been in the multimillion dollar range, required recoding of software and data deletions, resulted in multiyear sanctions requiring biannual privacy audits being submitted to regulatory authorities for review, or caused a decline in shareholder value.

We propose that privacy engineers take responsibility for:

- Designing and constructing processes, products, and systems with privacy in mind that appropriately collect or use personal information

- Supporting the development, implementation, and measurement of privacy policies, standards, guidelines, and rules

- Analyzing software and hardware designs and implementation from a privacy and user experience perspective

- Supporting privacy audits

- Working with other stakeholders to ensure privacy requirements are met outside as well as inside the engineering space

We propose that privacy engineers, in addition to better protecting and ensuring the proper use of personal information in the things they design, build, and implement, will provide the following benefits to individuals, as well as government and business enterprises:

- Protection for customers, users, or citizens

- A more objective basis for a trusted data platform

- A foundation to drive more thoughtful and higher-quality personal information services, sharing, and engagement

These benefits can lead to better and more information from users, which in turn helps to build and inspire better user experiences, better applications, better services, better products, and greater innovation.

Before we get into the toolbox for privacy engineering or the implications privacy engineering has for organizational design, let's explore some key privacy concepts and frameworks.

# Personal Information

It is critical for privacy engineers to thoroughly understand how personal information is defined and how its definition evolves and shifts over time. Personal information is the asset protected by privacy rules, processes, and technologies. Traditionally, personal information has been defined as information that directly identifies or, in combination with other data, allows for the identification of an individual (i.e., basic examples are an individual's name, address, phone number, or national or tax identification number) or any otherwise-anonymous information that when combined can only be a single person. An example of this would be "the CPO of Sun Microsystems in 2005," because there is only one person who fits this description. An example of anonymous information would be "three of the thousand engineers carry laptops," because the characterization fits more than one person and, therefore, does not identify anyone in particular.

Traditionally, the term for these data elements has been *personally identifiable information* (PII) or, alternatively it could be called *personal information* (PI). Using different nomenclature can create unnecessary confusion due to unnecessary distinctions. The real issue is does the data alone, or in combination with other data, identify a single individual? The term PII is useful, however, in terms of determining which elements make a collection of information personal or identifying which data elements need to be removed to depersonalize or deidentify it. We will use PI as our convention throughout the rest of the book.

Some forms of PI are additionally considered "sensitive," either culturally, under the law, or both (e.g., the type of information that can be used to embarrass, harm, or discriminate against someone). Different cultures consider different categories of PI as sensitive PI, but the following are fairly common:

- Information about an individual's medical or health conditions

- Financial information

- Racial or ethnic origin

- Political opinions

- Religious or philosophical beliefs

- Trade union membership

- Sexual orientation

- Information related to offenses or criminal convictions

Largely due to the explosion of the Internet, mobile computing, and telecommunications technology, the definition of PI is evolving to include unique device and network identifiers such as the universally unique identifier (UUID) and Internet protocol (IP) addresses. The Federal Trade Commission effectively redefined PI to include certain types of what used to be considered machine data such as device ID and IP addresses when it stated in its 2010 report, "Protecting Consumer Privacy in an Era of Rapid Change," that:

> *the proposed framework is not limited to those who collect personally identifiable information ("PII"). Rather, it applies to those commercial entities that collect data that can be reasonably linked to a specific consumer, computer, or other device.*[5]

It should be noted that not all device IDs or IP addresses should be considered PI de facto. Some devices, just as some IP addresses, are not associated with an identifiable person or personal system.

## HOW TO THINK ABOUT DEIDENTIFYING OR ANONYMIZING DATA

One way to remove risk or potential harm in processing personal information is to only use what is needed. One strategy for this is to deidentify or anonymize the data before using it.

Anonymizing or deidentifying data begins when deciding what to collect or use.

If personal information is not needed, then it is better not to collect or use it.

Always ask (1) is the information needed to serve the purpose of the processing; and (2) what is the minimum amount of information that is needed?

Example: Birth date: Is the day and month of birth needed or the actual birth data (day, month, year)? If the purpose is to automate birthday salutation, then month and date of birth should be sufficient. If the requirement is to ascertain age as part of authorizing access to content on a web site, just ask month and year, or age, or better yet, ask the age in ranges of 5 years.

---

[5]Federal Trade Commission, "Protecting Consumer Privacy in an Era of Rapid Change: Recommendations For Businesses and Policymakers," p. 43.
www.ftc.gov/os/2012/03/120326privacyreport.pdf

Example: Geographic location: If the requirement is geographic, is GPS needed or will street address, ZIP code, or just city and state meet the need?

The second part of the discussion has to do with uses of the data. Some of the uses of the data may require the elements that make it personal information; others may not. So it becomes important to think about how to anonymize or deidentify data.

Does PI − P = I? In other words, if one removes the personal, is what is left just information? Well, technically yes; but this is something you may not want to be right merely on a technicality.

Consider the number of people in the data pool. For instance, although the information may be anonymous (because the personal identifiers have been removed), the data is still very distinct and the pool of possibilities so small that it might effectively reflect only three or four people. So, although the information does not truly identify a single person, the group is so small that an educated guess can easily be made as to whom is in it. You could say there are different levels of anonymization. One in 10 is different from one in 10,000.

Another vector to be considered is the methodology. How was the data anonymized? Were the unique identifiers removed completely from the dataset or were they merely replaced with a pseudonym?

If it was replaced with a pseudonym, does the pseudonym pass a reidentification test? Or can the data still be used to take action or contact a person? If it doesn't pass the reidentification test or it still can be used to contact a person or reasonably linked to a system, then it cannot be truly called "anonymized," perhaps deidentified, but not anonymized.

A third vector to consider is whether specific data elements are needed or whether ranges or categories suffice. In other words, using an executive income report as an example, one can remove name and titles, but even in large organizations, the actual income may be unique enough that it identifies an individual even though all other descriptors have been removed or genericized.

Finally, if the decision is to aggregate data, make sure it is anonymized as well. Aggregate data about a single individual is not necessarily anonymized.

# Privacy

*Merriam-Webster's Dictionary* defines privacy as:

1. a: the quality or state of being apart from company or observation: seclusion

   b: freedom from unauthorized intrusion one's right to privacy

2. archaic: a place of seclusion

3. a: secrecy

   b: a private matter: secret

According to Yael Onn et al. in *Privacy in the Digital Environment*:

> *The right to privacy is our right to keep a domain around us, which includes all those things that are part of us, such as our body, home, thoughts, feelings, secrets, and identity. The right to privacy gives us the ability to choose which parts in this domain can be accessed by others, and to control the extent, manner, and timing of the use of those parts we choose to disclose.*[6]

Privacy defined colloquially seems to be subjective rather than systematic or governed by objective or pragmatic requirements; privacy is certainly contextual, including cultural and time-sensitive contexts that introduce variability and complexity. What one person may feel is the appropriate level of privacy can change, based on the situation. One person's sense of what is the appropriate privacy level for a given situation may be different from another's. Further complicating this is the fact that across the world, cultural values and social norms vary widely. Finally, the same person's notions and sensitivities may change over time and context, which is to say, what one may want to share at one point in his or her life may change as life progresses, just as it changes based on the environment.

Consider, as an example, the act of wearing a bathing suit. An office worker would probably feel that his or her sense of privacy was being violated if a condition of employment was to wear a bathing suit to work; but this is not so for a swimming pool lifeguard. External social and cultural norms would also be violated in the former instance (contextual). However, even for a lifeguard, the type and cut of bathing suit is a factor to acceptability, social normative value, and sense of well-being (subjective).

The challenge of privacy engineering is to architect and design products, processes, or systems that are sufficiently configurable to allow this sort of control.

## An Operational Definition of Privacy

Data privacy may be defined as the authorized, fair, and legitimate processing of personal information. Much of the activity resulting from this functional definition will appear to focus on organizations' and the management's philosophies and policies from that

---

[6]Yael Onn et al., *Privacy in the Digital Environment*. Haifa Center of Law & Technology, 2005.

perspective, but it must always be remembered that the individual data subject—literally the *subject* matter of the information (i.e., the individual to whom the data applies)—remains the ultimate requirement-setting entity. To the extent feasible, flexibility built into privacy-engineered solutions will always be critical to properly govern that very human variability. Note, too, that it is not always possible to make everyone happy.

Although this operational definition may seem deceptively simple, we can break it down into its components to start to see this definition as the beginnings of a pragmatic framework to not only define data privacy but also to begin to build it from these foundations (Figure 2-1).

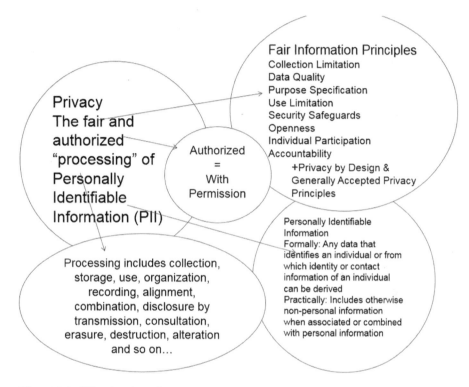

**Figure 2-1.** *What is privacy?*

We have already discussed and defined personal information, so now let's turn to what is meant by processing, authorized, and fair and legitimate.

## Processing of Personal Information

Data is processed upon any action or inaction that can be performed in relation to that data or dataset. Processing personal information includes, but is not limited to, collection, storage, use, sharing, organization, display, recording, alignment, combination, disclosure by transmission, copying, consultation, erasure, destruction, and alteration of personally identifiable information and any data related to it.

# DOES THE USE OF DATA FIT WITHIN A CULTURAL CONTEXT

By Martin Abrams, Executive Director and Chief Strategist for the Information Accountability Foundation

The slogan "Keep Austin Weird" works really well for that swinging Texas city, but the culture in Hebron, Texas, would likely not be associated with "weird," at least not in the same way. Local cultures are reflected in the way people interact with people. And privacy is one of those areas where culture is reflected.

Privacy scholars such as Alan Westin who established the basis for modern privacy management understood that privacy culture is a function of how a society balances the autonomy of the individual against the interests of the group, and then factors in the way a society defines a space reserved for the individual, free from observation from others. Although residents of both Hebron and Austin might have similar views on concepts of space, the balance between individual expression and community cohesiveness would be very different. Understanding cultural diversity and applying it to privacy is difficult enough when making decisions about what is an appropriate use in Texas, now think about looking at a global program that needs to work in Germany, Japan, weird Austin, and stern Hebron. How does an engineer begin building application requirements that fit the cultural context of diverse populations?

Let's use an example. Millions of smartphones are sold each year in places as diverse as Galesburg, Illinois; Bangalore, India; and Frankfurt, Germany. Each smartphone has a unique signature, just like each of us have distinct finger prints. All smartphones are designed to run on Wi-Fi networks. This design factor saves consumers money on their monthly mobile bills. It is no surprise that most consumers want to save money, so they set their phone to look for available Wi-Fi networks.

An innovative engineer quickly figured out that one can track a device through a physical space like a store by equipping the space with Wi-Fi. Furthermore, the engineer can see how much time the individual spends within a physical quadrant and can then link that information to the activities that take place in that quadrant. If it is a store, the activity is most likely shopping. For example, if the mobile device is in a home improvement store, the engineer now knows how long the device spends in the paint department and when it moves from paint to window treatments. Maybe he or she can even link the shopping activity to the items purchased and track what the device buys over time. It's not the device that buys the item, it is actually the individual holding the device; while the device might not have a cultural perspective, the individual does. It really doesn't make any difference whether we know the name of the individual. The actions we take based on tracking the device are particular to that individual. So the privacy question becomes: Is it appropriate to take actions based on the predicted behavior of the individual holding the device?

The answer is: It depends.

In the United States we have many conflicting values. First and foremost, we believe that we are free to observe what we are free to see and hear within the public commons. In the physical world, we, as a society, have defined the public commons: Pretty much, it is anything outside one's home. It is the public street, the shopping mall, front yard, and the courtyard, if one is flying over in an airplane. Furthermore, we are free to express ourselves based on how we process what we have observed. Making a sales offer is a form of expression. This value is captured by the First Amendment to the US Constitution.

The American people also cherish seclusion. That means, in our private space, we are free to do what we will do and think what we will think without fear of others observing and using what they hear and see. Our home is our castle, and it is not part of the public commons. You may watch me in my front yard, but you may not look in my window and invade my seclusion.

In the United States, the Wi-Fi-enabled store is the public commons. The observation of a device in a public space is probably okay, even if some might consider it obnoxious. Furthermore, we are free to think about what we have learned and apply that knowledge for practical ends such as increasing sales.

The preeminent nature of observation based on free expression doesn't have the same deference in other cultures. In those cultures, the sense that privacy as a fundamental right trumps the recording of what we observe and making use of that information. This is particularly so for most other Western cultures. In Germany or France, the collection of the device signature, if it is easily linkable to an identifiable individual, is probably subject to data protection law. Such a collection would be a processing of personal information that requires either permission from the individual or the law. Furthermore, any additional processing of that information, even storage, would also require permission from the law or the individual. We are talking about the same activity in different locations and having two different takes on whether the use is appropriate.

US culture puts a premium on free observation in the public commons, while societies with traditional data protection have no such deference for free observation. So, if an engineering team were to develop an observation model for a client that is dependent on observing devices in a physical space, the application would probably work in US stores but would be a violation of both societal norms and laws in stores in Western Europe. The analysis might be entirely different in Asia, where rights to seclusion are limited but where such observation might be seen as violating norms necessary for a crowded society where physical space is limited. The laws are different because the cultures are different.

These differences in privacy culture have impacted digital public policy for more than 30 years. Justice Michael Kirby, former chief justice of the Australia High Court, led the experts that developed the Organisation for Economic Co-operation and Development (OECD) Privacy Guidelines between 1978 and 1980. He said the most difficult issue he had to overcome in leading that group was the huge deference Americans give to free expression. Even though these differences are understood, we tend to default to what feels comfortable to each of us. Business concepts based on monetizing the fruits of observation have been developed in the United States, but when the same applications are applied outside the United States, we tend to see friction.

Ninety percent of the privacy issues that concern both individuals and regulators are the same no matter where the activity takes place. These include ensuring security, accommodating transparency, and not facilitating illegal behavior by others. If one deals with these issues, one can have a fairly high level of certainty that an application is okay. Moving beyond what is the same, one can anticipate key cultural markers. One such marker is at what age an individual reaches the age of maturity. This influences the consent children and adults are able to grant.

Lastly, one needs to be truly sensitive to cultural differences related to observation. You know when the technology tracks behavior, so tracking is an indicator that a cultural review is necessary when a technology is taken from one geographic market to another. Such applications probably require a privacy impact assessment (discussed in Chapter 10) with experts who understand the cultural frame. Lastly, there are cultural aspects to automated decision making. If applications make decisions without human intervention that impact the ability of an individual to gain employment, get credit or insurance, or travel, one should check cultural norms related to such decision making.

Just be sensitive to the fact that what is appropriate where you are doesn't mean it will be appropriate somewhere else; if you keep this in mind, you should be successful in your data-use initiatives.

# Authorized

Authorized processing of personal information only happens where the person or organization processing it has appropriate privilege for that processing. Additionally, there is a chain of custody and a sense of fiduciary responsibility that must follow the PI throughout the lifecycle of its processing. For example, those who can access a system containing PI must be authenticated to be the person he or she claims to be and that individual must also be acting within a role that would allow him or her to process the data within a system.

The type of data, the nature of the processing, as well as local laws and regulations will determine the nature and level of permission that may be required. The four primary protocols for permission gathering are:

- Opt out/Opt in

- Implied consent

- Informed consent

- Express consent

*Opt out* allows processing of PI unless or until an individual rejects data processing according to the context at hand. *Opt in* (the logical twin to opt out) is where no processing is allowed unless and until permission is granted. These concepts are relatively new in the comparative areas under the law, as discussed below, particularly in Common Law jurisdictions.

Context, narrowness of purpose, and transparency practices can make opt out or opt in relatively effective mechanisms.

*Implied consent* is a relatively straightforward concept where the context of collection and other processing is deemed so routine, obvious, and expected that permission for processing within this context may be implied by an individual's participation in the contextual relationship at all. An example of implied consent would be when PI is used for necessary processes (business or otherwise). When you give your name and telephone number for a reservation, the permission to use it to hold your table and for the maître'd to use it to call you is implied because it is necessary and within the scope of the function for which it is being used. However, if the maître'd chose to send text messages to the reservation number to solicit charitable donations to his favorite charity, he would be violating the implied consent to use contact information.

*Informed consent* relates to a very well-established and understood area of contract and tort law where a data subject has all relevant and timely facts to enable a reasonable choice of whether, how, how much, and for what purpose data will be processed. A good example of well-informed consent in a nondata context is the difference between giving consent or accepting the risks of skiing vs. receiving medical treatment from a trained doctor. In the former example, an individual is physically aware of his condition, standing on a snowy mountain, on two small skis. Yet there may be unexpected risks, and thus a disclaimer may be written on his ticket, but that disclaimer may be in smaller type and with no individualized explanations. In the latter example, however, the doctor and patient have very different levels of expertise, the procedures and risks may be unfathomable to the reasonable layperson, and the side effects may be unknowable without specific clarity. The type and depth of disclaimer and expository of risks and rewards are much different and far more extensive in this case.

Informed consent requires some responsibility and action on the part of the data subject and so may never become universally accepted as the standard for gaining or maintaining authorization, but its longevity in other fields of risk management and conflict resolution and the various aspects that allow breaking informed consent into measurable components make this form of consent particularly attractive to the budding privacy engineer.

*Express consent* is simply where a person takes a specific observable action to indicate and confirm that they give permission for their information to be processed. An example of this is checking a box that says, "yes" on an online form.

So that it does not go unrecognized, express consent and informed consent are both subspecies of the opt in.

The strength and validity of any of these permission forms and types depend on the clarity, conspicuousness, and proximity of data processing intended to be governed by authorization. It must be clear that the user knew what was being accepted to make the permission valid when permission was granted. Similarly, permission must be freely given and not under duress for data processing to be authorized to the appropriate degree.

The other key ingredient is, for all these different forms of permission, they must be presented before personal information is collected and before it is processed. For example, there has been much debate about the ability for web site operators to use cookies on the first page of a web site where notice is presented about the possibility of data collection through electronic means. In fact, the difficulty in ensuring that data subjects know and understand the potential and actuality of data privacy in a clear, conspicuous, and proximate fashion is one of the many reasons that those processing the data, governing bodies, and users are skeptical that a governance and enforcement regime focused on "Notice and Consent" is effective in today's data-enriched environment.

Permission is only one component of ensuring that PI is processed with authorization. In addition to ensuring that one has permission to use the data, one also has to be able to manage and prevent unauthorized use or access to the data. This requires using controls and measures to ensure PI and related data is processed in an authorized and legitimate manner. These controls and measures can take the form of administrative, logical, technical, and physical routines or a combination of all of these, which will be discussed later in this chapter and in Chapter 6.

# THE EVOLUTION OF CONSENT

By Eduardo Ustaran, Data Protection Lawyer and author of *The Future of Privacy*

Is individual choice still the essence of data privacy law? In the early days of data protection as a regulated activity, putting people in control of their information was thought to be what mattered the most. From the 1980 OECD Guidelines to the latest version of the EU e-privacy directive, consent has been a cornerstone across legal regimes and jurisdictions. European data protection law is based on the principle that an individual's consent is the most legitimate of all legitimate grounds to use information about people. But does this approach still hold true? Can we—as individuals—attempt to have a meaningful degree of control over the vast amount of information we generate as we go about our lives?

Information about who we are, what we do, what we are like, and how we behave is captured every single second of the day. From the moment we turn on the light (or the Blackberry or our smartphone) in the morning to the moment we turn it off in the evening, every action that involves using technology is recorded somewhere.

The Internet has maximized this in such an unprecedented way that the value of the information we generate by simply using it makes other more traditional identifying factors look trivial. From a legal perspective, this phenomenon has entirely distorted the meaning and scope of personal data, but the point is that information about us is constantly flowing around the world without our knowledge, let alone our consent.

Let's face it, attempting to put people in control of their own information by giving them the power to consent to the uses made by others is simply unachievable. The concept of consent should not be underestimated. The ability to make choices is what makes people free. However, pretending that we can take a view in any meaningful way as to how information about us is gathered, shared, and used by others is wishful thinking. We cannot even attempt to recognize what personal information is being made available by us in our daily comings and goings, so how could we possibly decide whether to consent or not to every possible use of that information? Consent might have been a valid mechanism to control data handling activities in the past, but not anymore.

So what now? Is data privacy dead? I hope not. But in the same way that our ability to control our own information is moving away from us, our responsibility to decide what others can know about us is also receding. Our privacy is less than ever in our own hands because the decision-making power is not really ours. Any legal regime that puts the onus on individuals (who are meant to be protected by that regime) is bound to be wrong. The onus should not be on us to decide whether a cookie may reside in our computer when hardly anyone in the real world knows what a cookie does. What the law should really do is put the onus on those who want to exploit our information by assigning different conditions to different degrees of usage, leaving consent to the very few situations where it can be truly meaningful.

The law should regulate data users, not data subjects. Like it or not, individuals have a limited role in the data-handling decision-making process. That is a fact, and regulation should face up to that fact. Technology is more and more complex, while our human ability to decide remains static. Feeding us with more detailed and complex privacy policies does not change that. In the crucial task of protecting our personal information and our privacy, consent can only have a residual role. Continuing to give consent a central role in the protection of our privacy is not only unrealistic, but also dangerous because it becomes an unhelpful distraction for individuals, organizations, and regulators. The emphasis must simply be put elsewhere.

## Fair and Legitimate

Of all the concepts that underpin the notion of data privacy, the ability to provide information handling that is "fair and legitimate" is probably the most complex and difficult to reduce to a scientific rule or even an approximate measurable metric.

The concept of *fair and legitimate* processing is not limited to the organizational view of fair as "necessary" (or, more often, "desired") processing. However, a series of principles called the Fair Information Practice Principles (FIPPs)as embraced by the OECD in the OECD Privacy Guidelines, is a useful prism through which to look at the notion of fairness and legitimacy.

# Fair Information Processing Principles and the OECD Guidelines

The original FIPPs were developed by the Department of Health, Education, and Welfare in the 1960s in reaction to and concerns over implementation of large government databases containing information on US citizens. As mentioned earlier, the principles were then extended by the OECD in 1980 in a document titled "The OECD Guidelines on the Protection of Privacy and Transborder Flows of Personal Data."[7] These principles, commonly know as the OECD Principles, have since become the foundation for much of the existing privacy legislation and thinking throughout the world. More important, they continue to be a cornerstone in grounding governments, businesses, and consumer advocates in their approach and dialogues on privacy and the use of personal information. In other words, they form the common vocabulary in which privacy is discussed. As we detail later in this chapter and elsewhere in Part 2, most privacy laws and regulations (and thus privacy policies and the privacy rules) are derived from the FIPPs and the OECD Guidelines.

## Collection Limitation Principle

The OECD Guidelines, published in 1980, state that "There should be limits to the collection of personal data and any such data should be obtained by lawful and fair means and, where appropriate, with the knowledge or consent of the data subject."[8] This means before PI is collected or processed in another fashion, the processor must obtain permission to process the data. There are rare exceptions to this requirement, including certain types of law enforcement practices and for "national security" purposes.[9]

Given the increasing reality of law enforcement requests and requirements from around the world, it is imperative that privacy engineers contemplate such uses and their potential conflict with the "Collection Limitation" principle for their processing.

---

[7]An outgrowth of the Organisation for European Economic Cooperation (OEEC), which was formed in 1948 and chartered to run the Marshall Plan, the OECD, established in 1961, consists of 34 countries who work collaboratively to "to help governments foster prosperity and fight poverty through economic growth and financial stability."

[8]The OECD Guidelines on the Protection of Privacy and Transborder Flows of Personal Data. http://www.oecd.org/internet/ieconomy/oecdguidelinesontheprotectionof privacyandtransborderflowsofpersonaldata.htm#part2. All quotes from the OECD Guidelines come from this source.

[9]Even those cases are not consistent from jurisdiction to jurisdiction and, in those cases, there must be other control processes in place to ensure that individual rights are not being violated and that the data is collected in a manner that allows law enforcement to use them for policing or security.

# Data Quality Principle

From the OECD Guidelines: "Personal data should be relevant to the purposes for which they are to be used, and, to the extent necessary for those purposes, should be accurate, complete, and kept up-to-date."

There are two key ideas in this principle. The first is "relevancy" (i.e., the data collected/used must be genuinely pertinent to the purpose and proportional, that is, only the appropriate amount and type of data to suit the purpose for its collection or processing). The second idea is accuracy. This is important because it creates obligations on behalf of the entity that controls the data to ensure data integrity. This requirement has evolved to also require giving data owners the ability to access their data and correct or update any errors.

It should be noted that data "integrity" is one of the core principles and goals for the security practitioner as well. For security, confidentiality, integrity, and availability are key markers for success and planning security requirements. Throughout this book we will note where synergies and common goals exist such as the case of *data integrity*. In doing so, the building and maintenance requirements for privacy engineers should be viewed as additive to other requirements rather than competing or negating "compliance" post facto requirements.

# Purpose Specification Principle

From the OECD Guidelines: "The purposes for which personal data are collected should be specified not later than at the time of data collection and the subsequent use limited to the fulfilment of those purposes or such others as are not incompatible with those purposes and as are specified on each occasion of change of purpose."

This principle provides guidance regarding the type and quality of transparency or notice. From an innovator's perspective, creators of systems or services should carefully consider how PI will be used throughout the lifecycle of the current situation and should plan ahead as carefully and fully as possible to ensure that enough flexibility for data processing is introduced into the system and any contextual cues, including notice leading to transparency and understanding of data use.

# Use Limitation Principle

From the OECD Guidelines: "Personal data should not be disclosed, made available or otherwise used for purposes other than those specified in accordance with Paragraph 9 [Purpose Specification Principle] except:

> a) With the consent of the data subject; or
>
> b) By the authority of law."

This principle qualifies both the limits for data processing and the expectations of the data subject and also suggests conditions for potentially adding to the type, kind, and timing of data processing when that processing was not included in the initial authorization. As discussed previously, some legal enforcement should be contemplated and presented in the original "Purpose Specification of the Notice."

## Security Safeguards Principle

From the OECD Guidelines: "Personal data should be protected by reasonable security safeguards against such risks as loss or unauthorised access, destruction, use, modification or disclosure of data."

Any entity controlling PI must protect it from unauthorized access or processing. This principle clearly invokes the wide and complicated discipline of security for all types of data but focuses the requirement to specifically protect personal data. This is one of the overlaps between privacy and security that will be discussed later in this chapter.

## Openness Principle

From the OECD Guidelines: "There should be a general policy of openness about developments, practices and policies with respect to personal data. Means should be readily available of establishing the existence and nature of personal data, and the main purposes of their use, as well as the identity and usual residence of the data controller."

Publication of privacy policies and statements is one means to achieve a level of openness in and about an organization.

## Individual Participation Principle

From the OECD Guidelines: "An individual should have the right:

> a) to obtain from a data controller,[10] or otherwise, confirmation of whether or not the data controller has data relating to him;

> b) to have communicated to him, data relating to him within a reasonable time; at a charge, if any, that is not excessive; in a reasonable manner; and in a form that is readily intelligible to him;

> c) to be given reasons if a request made under subparagraphs(a) and (b) is denied, and to be able to challenge such denial; and

> d) to challenge data relating to him and, if the challenge is successful to have the data erased, rectified, completed, or amended."

This principle describes an individual's right to update, correct, and know which data has been collected about them from a given entity. It is closely related to the accuracy principle. Much innovation is required for this principle, in particular in a world of vastly dispersed and complex data sharing and processing even to achieve relatively simple goals.

---

[10]Author note: A data controller is the entity that is responsible for determining how data is processed. The data controller gives direction to the data processor. Sometimes the data controller and data processor are one in the same; sometimes not, such as in outsourcing. In such as situation, the service provider is the data processor.

An example of some of this complexity may be the fulfillment of an online contact lens service where an individual may be described by a common carrier, an ophthalmologist, a fulfillment center, a manufacturer, and more. For any one individual to possibly glean where and when his data changes hands among all of these specialized and related steps is a daunting task indeed.

## A PRACTICAL APPROACH TO DETERMINING IF DATA COLLECTION AND USE IS "FAIR AND LEGITIMATE"

Here is a two-tiered process to determine if data is needed.

The first tier is to ask the question. Is this data needed? Not wanted, needed.

If they answer is yes and all other design and architectural reviews and options (such as not collecting at all, truncating or de-identifying the data) have been exhausted, then run each data element through the following set of formulas:

I need X to do Y

Without X I cannot do Y.

If the answer to the first two equations is true, proceed to the third:

Y is a subset of uses for the data for which Z has given permission (Y < ?).

If the answer to this equation is true, then ask, does it pass the smell test (fit the spirit of the permission, as well as the letter). If the answer to this is yes, then proceed.

If the answer is no, then based on the data and the use (i.e., the risk), explore what level and type of notice and consent are required and consider who best to expand the existing permission to cover the contemplated use.

If there is reluctance to go back to an individual for permission, then someone has to ask what is the locus of that discomfort. It usually is because the benefit is not so much for the person but for the organization or because there is a lack of proportionality between the risk to the privacy of the individual vs. the benefit to him or her. Knowledge of this will help the real goals and purpose of the processing to surface, which will then lead to a more productive discussion of how to address and manage the risks.

## Accountability Principle

From the OECD Guidelines: "A data controller should be accountable for complying with measures which give effect to the principles stated above."

This principle means whomever is controlling the data, that is, in charge of determining how they are going to be used and processed, is the party who will be held responsible for ensuring the data is processed in an authorized and fair and legitimate manner and will bear the consequences if they are not.

# THE INTERSECTION OF PRIVACY, UNIQUE IDENTIFIERS, AND COLLECTING TELEMETRY

*Telemetry* is the collection of information about machines and systems. It is often collected remotely to monitor how a system is functioning so that issues can be detected and resolved in advance or in order to provide services. Sometimes it contains unique identifiers. The most obvious of these were IP address, but there were also things like machine name, media access control (MAC) address, and so on.

Although collection of telemetry was not considered in the past the same as collecting personal information now, there have always been privacy concerns with it. These concerns were mainly whether the collection of it was authorized or not and thus whether it was a form of spyware or not (think industrial espionage).

However, with the widespread adoption of smartphones, PDAs, and other devices, the quantum leap in the ability to collect, parse, and understand patterns (i.e., Big Data or Data Science) and the ability to act on those patterns and push communications to devices (or take other actions) based on what was once just considered machine data has all changed.

Now unique identifiers such as those collected as part of collecting telemetry need to be examined and considered. The important thing to remember in evaluating whether a unique identifier falls under the definition of PI is that not all unique identifiers are equal. Below is a list of characteristics to consider when evaluating unique identifiers to see if any one of them is something that can reasonably be linked to a person or a person's device (vs. a system that front ends a network):

Uniqueness

Reidentification (correlating an identifier with other data that leads to the ability to identify the user)

Using as an "anchor" to aggregate and analyze information from one or more sources

Permanence

Frequency of change

Ease of change

Reachability (can it be used to contact or track)

# Other Governance Standards of which to be aware

In addition to the OECD Guidelines, there are other frameworks such as the Generally Accepted Privacy Principles (GAPP), the 1995 EU Data Directive (also known as Directive EU 95/46/EC), the Federal Trade Commission's version of the FIPPs, the Asia-Pacific Economic Cooperation (APEC) Privacy Principles, and International Organization for Standardization (ISO) Standards that will inform how personal information and privacy issues are managed and governed. In the previous section, the OECD Guidelines have been highlighted to explain the notion of fair and legitimate processing of personal information. These other frameworks help one get to a more granular and comprehensive view of *data governance*, which will be discussed in Chapter 3.

# Privacy Is Not Confidentiality and Security Is Not Privacy

Confidentiality is about protecting designated nonpublic information (often information that is either a trade secret or proprietary) (Figure 2-2).

## Confidentiality ≠ Privacy

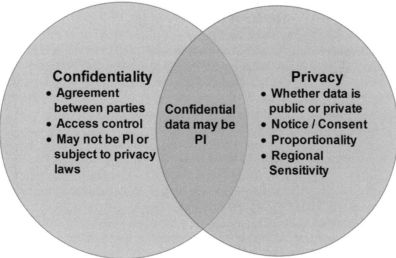

**Figure 2-2.** *Confidentiality is not privacy*

Confidentiality rules only apply to what is designated by agreement as confidential.

Sometimes confidential information is also personal information. For example, some information relating to the private lives of individuals may be confidential, such as medical records or family secrets. Sometimes, actually often, confidential information contains no PI.

This is the first difference between confidentiality and privacy. Confidential is an imposed label that signifies access control. PI is an organic label; it speaks to the substance of the information. Just as with that famous line in Shakespeare's immortal play *Romeo and Juliet* "A rose by any other name would smell as sweet," so it goes with PI. PI is always going to be personal information when it identifies an individual.

Another difference is that rules that govern or protect the PI apply whether the personal information is public or not. Just because PI is public does not mean it can be used or "processed" for one's own purposes. One example of this is e-marketing lists. Many of our e-mail address are publically available, but that does not mean they can be wantonly maintained on e-marketing lists without our permission.

A third difference, and perhaps the most important, is that when the PI is nonpublic personal information, keeping it "confidential" only addresses the access requirement and not the use or any of the other requirements of the OECD Guidelines.

So, although there is overlap between the safeguards used to protect personal information and the safeguards used to protect confidential information—most of the overlap is in terms of access control—protecting one is not the same as protecting the other.

Just as privacy and confidentiality overlap but are not the same, privacy and security overlap in that each is about data protection, but they are not the same (Figure 2-3).

## Security ≠ Privacy

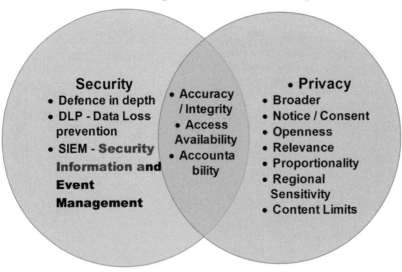

*Figure 2-3.* *Security does not equal privacy*

Information security has three areas of focus, known as CIA:

Confidentiality (i.e., preventing unauthorized access)

Integrity (i.e., ensuring the data is not altered without approval)

Availability (i.e., ensuring the data is accessible)

It uses logical, administrative, physical safeguards to ensure the CIA of the data is maintained. Aspects of security that do not overlap privacy include:

- *Defense in depth:* A sophisticated firewall structure can protect personal information.

- *Data loss prevention (DLP):* Discovering and monitoring the location and flow of sensitive data such as customer credit card data, employee PI, or corporate intellectual property.

- *Security information and event management* (SIEM)

# The Overlaps

The safeguards enable the "authorized" in the "authorized access and use" element that is a cornerstone the operational definition of privacy. This is the first overlap between privacy and information security.

In addition to the fact that both "information security" and "privacy" are data protection regimens, other areas of overlap are:

Integrity (information security) and accuracy (privacy)

Availability (information security) and access (privacy)

Accountability (both)

Confidentiality (when the data is both personal information and nonpublic)

Information security's focus on data integrity overlaps with privacy's accuracy requirement in that both target ensuring the data is not altered with authorization.

Information security's availability requirement supports privacy's access requirement because if the data is not available, they cannot be accessed.

Both information security and privacy doctrines require data owners and custodians to be responsible for protecting the data in accordance with the respective protection regimen, which is a form of accountability.

And when the information is both nonpublic and personal information, confidentiality supports privacy because nonpublic data need to be kept nonpublic.

## The Disconnects

The reason there is not a complete overlap between privacy and information security is threefold.

First, privacy has a wider set of obligations and responsibilities than information security does, such as:

Collection limitation

Openness

Relevancy

Use limitation

This means there are things privacy addresses that information security does not.

The second disconnect is confidentiality. Because PI is not always nonpublic (consider the phonebook), the notion of confidentiality does not apply. Also, in a resource-constrained world, if the data is not considered confidential, they are not always "valued" and the necessary measures to ensure authorized access and use will be overlooked.

Third, and perhaps most important, while information security techniques can be privacy-enabling technologies (PETs) (which means they are tools that enable privacy) and are often necessary, these PETs can also become "feral" if applied incorrectly (i.e., in an invasive manner). This is why you can have security without privacy, but you cannot have privacy without security. This will be discussed further in Part 2.

# Conclusion

The purpose of this chapter is to enable you to understand the nature of privacy and privacy engineering.

This is the foundation and context for the guidance—the explanation of tools and techniques—that makes up the remainder of this book.

If you follow the guidance in this book, you will be poised for success and you will have a set of tools you can use and configure to enable privacy, but the actual success will ultimately depend on how you tailor the guidance that follows to specific situations (i.e., the data, the processing, whose data, and specific jurisdiction, regulations, or best practices that apply) and how you configure the tools we are providing. Chapter 3 will discuss privacy and data governance concepts.

# CHAPTER 3

■ ■ ■

# Data and Privacy Governance Concepts

*Computers are magnificent tools for the realization of our dreams, but no machine can replace the human spark of spirit, compassion, love, and understanding.*

—Louis Gerstner

This chapter will look at the relationship among privacy frameworks and data management, data governance, and data stewardship, highlighting how frameworks such as the OECD Guidelines and GAPP are used for personal information management. Included in this discussion will be a look at Privacy by Design (PbD), which supports and complements privacy engineering (Figure 3-1).

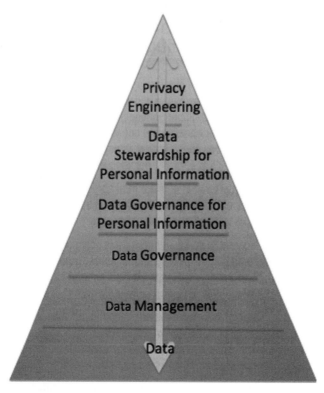

*Figure 3-1.* Good privacy engineering is built on a foundation of data management and governance

# Data Management: The Management of "Stuff"

The raison d'etre of any organization, whether a corporation, a nonprofit, or a governmental entity, is to do "stuff;" doing "stuff" requires managing "stuff." Data represents this stuff. Examples include:

- Customers
- Suppliers
- Money
- Resources
- Products
- Customer orders
- Customer order line items
- Inventory

- Policies

- Business rules

- Privacy rules

- Roles

- Intellectual property[1]

The administration of the data that represents the "stuff" of an organization is the science and art of data management, or as it is defined in the DAMA Data Management Body of Knowledge: "Data management is the development, execution, and supervision of plans, policies, programs and practices that control, protect, deliver and enhance the value of data and information assets."[2]

In a structured data management program, data stewards, who are domain or subject matter experts for each of these classes of data, work with data management experts to ensure that procedures, processes, standards, guidelines, and business rules for using such information support the goals and objectives of the enterprise. This is called data governance.

# Data Governance

*Data governance* is a strategic, "top-down" program for data management in which an organization's leadership communicates the core value of data quality and integrity to stakeholders. It includes the development and enforcement of standards and procedures. It requires broad understanding of data entrusted to the organization, the value and use of data, upstream and downstream stakeholders, systems, and processes for all decisions and issue resolution. To be effective, data governance requires data stewardship and data stewards. It also requires executive sponsors and support.

Stewardship is not ownership. A *steward* is a custodian who is responsible for managing something that belongs to someone else. *Data stewardship* is the managing of information on behalf of the "owners" of the data. The data steward is in effect "the feet on the ground," ensuring the data governance standards are adhered to and evolve as necessary.

---

[1]For any enterprise, we would expect to find over 20 different data models containing at least five unique classes or data entities and the relationships between these classes or data entities. We have built these types of enterprise data models for a number of pharmaceutical companies, communications companies, oil companies, hospitality companies, and government agencies, among others.
[2]"DAMA-DMBOK Guide (Data Management Body of Knowledge) Introduction & Project Status." www.dama.org/files/public/DI_DAMA_DMBOK_Guide_Presentation_2007.pdf.

An effective data governance program requires that:

- Data is created, recorded, and distributed in compliance with standards

- An established metadata gathering process clearly describes requirements and characteristics of the data to be maintained (discussed in Part 2 of this book, and Appendix A contains a variety of metadata)

- There is a metric-driven adherence of all data definition standards

- There is a feedback or notification system to identify inadequacies in the data

- There is a data quality assurance process that monitors the integrity of information within the system

- There is a data management structure that includes data stewardship, a data governance panel, and an executive layer

There are two data steward roles: data producer stewards and data usage stewards. Data producer stewards are responsible for:

- Appropriate data content creation and maintenance of quality.

- Appropriate business rules related to all data elements and attributes for which the data steward has responsibility. A data attribute is a fact or characteristic about a data element or entity.

Data usage stewards are responsible for:

- Appropriate data usage quality, including screens and reports

- Appropriate business rules, including privacy

- Appropriate presentation:

  - Method

  - Design

  - Architecture

  - Aesthetics (ugly user interfaces are avoided)

In addition to the role of the data producer and data usage steward, there is the role of data administrator.

Data administrators are those responsible for:

- Data analysis

- Data acquisition design

- Data organizing or classifying

- Data storage and distribution design

- Data archiving

- Ensuring the implementation of business rules

- Data management (metadata) tool administration (as a data dictionary)

Depending on the size and volume of the data being managed, these roles may be combined or staffed by more than one person.

# Benefits of Data Governance

Data management programs that have implemented data governance have benefited from features such as:

- *Common names and definitions:* If existing data is not well named, they cannot be found and therefore cannot be shared.[3] In order to determine whether a data object already exists, common names, based on a standard naming convention, speed the analysis. Common names imply that there is a readily understandable business name and an abbreviated short physical name, based in part on a standard abbreviation list.

- *Consistent data:* A consistent business definition of the data is important so that the knowledge worker can determine whether a data object with a name similar to his or her data requirement is in fact the same data object.

- *Consistent reports:* If data attributes are well named or well defined, then the reports resulting from the analysis or use of the elements are apt to be more consistent because the underlying data is consistent.

- *Less duplication of data:* Consistent names and definitions will facilitate the discovery of redundant data. Data modeling normalization is a process for eliminating duplication.

- *Trust by the business users:* Well-executed data governance and data stewardship should improve quality and reliability, which, in turn, should increase accuracy and trust in the data analysis process.

- *Less data correction:* Better managed data should be more accurate and require less correction.

However, the most important feature and benefit of data governance is that the data is being governed and that there are structured, mindful controls and measures in place to manage the data and ensure that its use is in alignment with the organization's overall goals and requirements. In short, the data is being viewed as an asset and is appropriately and meaningfully curated.

---

[3]B. Van Halle and C. Fleming, *Handbook of relational database design*, Addison-Wesley, 1989, p. 16.

# The Privacy and Data Governance/Stewardship Connection

Although it is not often articulated this way, data privacy is a key part of data governance for personal information. In this context, privacy engineering is engineering data governance for personal information into the design and implementation of routines, systems, and products that process personal information. An enterprise's privacy policy (including rules, standards, guidelines, etc.) "governs" the processing of personal information by an enterprise (and in Chapter 4, the privacy policy is not only viewed as a governance concept but also the meta-set of personal information data protection use-case requirements for privacy engineering).

Understanding how data management frameworks (such as data governance and data stewardship) fit with privacy frameworks (such as GAPP and the OECD Guidelines) is key to organizational development. Such frameworks and guidelines help to create the necessary roles and responsibilities to build and maintain a privacy-aware and ready enterprise. Such understanding will also help to recognize and understand privacy policies at meta-use-case requirements for privacy engineering.

Although the connection between data governance and privacy frameworks should be very close, the closeness is not often recognized nor leveraged by either domain. Too often data privacy teams sit outside enterprise-wide data governance and stewardship initiatives. This is unfortunate. File this under the opportunity not realized category. Ultimately both groups should have a shared goal of ensuring data is curated and cared for as an asset whose value is recognized and cultivated within defined parameters.

# Data Privacy Governance Frameworks

The OECD Guidelines, that were discussed in Chapter 2, is one of the better-known privacy governance frameworks. In addition to it, are other global and regional frameworks such as the 1995 EU Data Protection Directive (also known as Directive EU 95/46/EC), the Federal Trade Commission's version of the Fair Information Privacy Principles, (FIPPs), the ISO 2700x series of security standards, and the Generally Accepted Privacy Principles (GAPP), which were created by the American Institute of Certified Public Accountants (AICPA) and the Canadian Institute of Chartered Accountants (CICA) Privacy Task Force.

All these and others are worth knowing and learning about to perfect a privacy engineering tradecraft.

## HOW THE FRAMEWORKS ALIGN

You can see from Table 3-1 how the various frameworks cited align. One of the most comprehensive is GAPP, which was designed to create a set of principles that would encompass the key points of the existing frameworks.

*Table 3-1.* How Key Privacy Frameworks Align

| GAPP | OECD Guidelines | FTC FIPPS | EU Directive | ISO 27002 | APEC |
|---|---|---|---|---|---|
| Management | Management | | | Operations Management | Preventing Harm |
| Collection | Collection Limitation | | Proportionality | Information Acquisition | Collection Limitations |
| Quality | Data Quality | | | | Integrity of Personal Information |
| Notice | Specification of Purpose | Notice/Awareness | Transparency | | Notice |
| Use, Retention, Disposal | Use Limitation | | Legitimate Purpose | Asset Management | Uses of Personal Information |
| Security for Privacy | Security Safeguards | Integrity/Security | | Security | Security Safeguards |
| Access | Openness | Access/Participation | | Access Control | Access and Correction |
| Choice/Consent | Individual Participation | Choice/Consent | | Asset Management | Choice |
| Monitoring and Enforcement | Accountability | Enforcement/Redress | Supervisory authority | Compliance | Accountability |
| Disclosure to Third Parties | | | Transfer of personal data to third parties | | |

# Generally Accepted Privacy Principles (GAPP)

According to the American Institute of Certified Public Accountants (AICPA), which developed the Generally Accepted Privacy Principles:

> *Generally Accepted Privacy Principles (GAPP) have been developed from a business perspective, referencing some, but by no means all, significant local, national and international privacy regulations. GAPP operationalizes complex privacy requirements into a single privacy objective that is supported by 10 privacy principles. Each principle is supported by objective, measurable criteria that form the basis for effective management of privacy risk and compliance in an organization.[4]*

The following are the 10 GAPP:

1. *Management:* The entity defines, documents, communicates, and assigns accountability for its privacy policies and procedures.

2. *Notice:* The entity provides notice about its privacy policies and procedures and identifies the purposes for which personal information is collected, used, retained, and disclosed.

3. *Choice and consent:* The entity describes the choices available to the individual and obtains implicit or explicit consent with respect to the collection, use, and disclosure of personal information.

4. *Collection:* The entity collects personal information only for the purposes identified in the notice.

5. *Use, retention, and disposal:* The entity limits the use of personal information to the purposes identified in the notice and for which the individual has provided implicit or explicit consent. The entity retains personal information only as long as necessary to fulfill the stated purposes or as required by law or regulation and thereafter appropriately disposes of such information.

6. *Access:* The entity provides individuals with access to their personal information for review and update.

7. *Disclosure to third parties:* The entity discloses personal information to third parties only for the purposes identified in the notice and with the implicit or explicit consent of the individual.

---

[4]See www.aicpa.org/InterestAreas/InformationTechnology/Resources/Privacy/Generally AcceptedPrivacyPrinciples/DownloadableDocuments/10261378ExecOverviewGAPP.pdf

8.  *Security for privacy:* The entity protects personal information against unauthorized access (both physical and logical).

9.  *Quality:* The entity maintains accurate, complete, and relevant personal information for the purposes identified in the notice.

10. *Monitoring and enforcement:* The entity monitors compliance with its privacy policies and procedures and has procedures to address privacy-related complaints and disputes.

We will show in later chapters how frameworks like the OECD Guidelines and GAPP are used as a basis for developing the enterprise's privacy policies, processes, procedures, standards, guidelines, and mechanisms.

## ISO2700X: HOW SECURITY STANDARDS SUPPORT PRIVACY

By Joel Weise, Director of Security and Compliance, Hootsuite

The ISO 27001:2005 "Information technology—Security techniques—Information security management systems—Requirements" and the complementary ISO 27002:2005 "Information technology—Security techniques—Code of practice for information security management" standards provide a very good framework for defining, creating, and managing a comprehensive security architecture and governance framework that supports not only security but also privacy. Some of the primary advantages are that these are mature standards, internationally recognized and well harmonized with other local and national standards such as the US NIST Special Publication 800-53 "Recommended Security Controls for Federal Information Systems and Organizations." Further, when utilized, the standards can enable compliance to privacy laws, demonstrate an organization's commitment to privacy and minimize, or limit the opportunity for breaches that could affect security and privacy of data, people as well as supporting technology and governance.

The overall value of the standards is to elaborate an information security management system (ISMS) as noted in ISO 27001:2005 and based on the security control objectives as noted in ISO 27002:2005. The ISMS uses a continuous improvement approach so that it is flexible and can change as new laws, technology, and threats emerge. The standards further allow for the foundation of a framework that can be audited so that its effectiveness can be measured. Such a foundation is critical to supporting security and privacy efforts in an organization. According to the standards, "The ISMS is designed to ensure the selection of adequate and proportionate security controls that protect information assets and give confidence to interested parties." This goal is fundamental to how the ISMS functions and addresses both security and privacy. The overall benefit of the standards is that they are used to enable the design, configuration, implementation, and use of controls that reflect best practices, and, most important, it allows for interoperability and a lingua franca so that different organization, security, and privacy professionals as well as auditor and legal authorities can analyze the use of those controls.

When considering security and privacy controls, one must always consider the costs of such controls. It is important that controls be balanced against their actual and intangible costs. For example, it would not be reasonable to implement a $100 control to address a risk that is only worth $10. A security practitioner must always evaluate controls within the business context of the environment in which they will be implemented. In addition to an actual value, one must consider the intangible costs of controls. For example, even if a $100 control is used to address a risk valued at $1,000, the security practitioner must consider intangible costs such as the impact the moral, productivity, and general perception of security. If a control negatively impacts the organization, even in such intangible ways, those should be taken into consideration.

The ISO 27002:2005 standard has 11 different sections. Table 3-2 outlines each of these areas as they apply to privacy.

***Table 3-2.*** *Standards that Apply to Privacy*

| Standard Topic Area | Overview | Privacy Objective |
|---|---|---|
| Policy | The policy is a high-level statement about information security and privacy. It lays down the key information security and privacy directives for an organization. | The policy should reflect the privacy compliance objectives of the organization and reference applicable standards, legal and regulatory mandates, and relevant industry-best practices. |
| Organizing Information Security | An information security governance structure should span the entire business and technical components of the organization. | The organizational governance structure should include specific individuals and functions that have privacy as their primary mandate. |
| Asset Management | Asset management is a means for an organization to identify, organize, and manage their information resources. | The maintenance of privacy for data assets is an organizational imperative because many assets include a privacy component. |

(*continued*)

*Table 3-2.* (*continued*)

| Standard Topic Area | Overview | Privacy Objective |
|---|---|---|
| Human Resources Security | The organization should manage user access rights as well as undertake suitable security awareness training and educational activities. These are all necessary to ensure the human element actively participates in the overall security effort. | In order to ensure employee personal information is secure, protected, and used appropriately, privacy needs to be instilled in an organization's culture through training and awareness activities. |
| Physical and Environmental Security | Valuable IT equipment should be physically protected against malicious or accidental damage or loss including damage or loss due to environmental factors such as an inadvertent loss of power or overheating. | Maintaining privacy in an organization's physical space is also important as is security and privacy of data assets. |
| Communications and Operations Management | Controls for systems and network management include a broad range of capabilities from network management to operational procedures. | In the IT world, privacy can only be enabled when appropriate system and network controls are utilized to ensure the security, availability, and reliability of operational resources. |
| Access ControlCommunications and Operations Management | Access control includes user access controls for IT systems, including, operating systems, networks, and applications and data. | Access control is critical for the support of privacy in any environment where data and processing resources may contain personal information. |

(*continued*)

*Table 3-2.* (*continued*)

| Standard Topic Area | Overview | Privacy Objective |
|---|---|---|
| Information Systems Acquisition, Development, and Maintenance | This section details the policies covering everything from cryptography to processes for specifying, building or acquiring, testing, implementing, and maintaining IT systems. | Maintaining the privacy of data is predicated upon implementing and supporting an IT infrastructure that works as advertised. Without that assurance, it is not possible to state that an organization is capable of maintaining the privacy of data. |
| Information Security Incident Management | Incident management covers procedures required to manage incidents consistently and effectively. | Knowing that intrusions can exacerbate vulnerabilities, maintaining the privacy of data relies upon a comprehensive incident management function. It also alerts you to breaches so you can remedy them as quickly as possible. |
| Business Continuity Management | This section describes the relationship between IT disaster recovery planning, business continuity management, and contingency planning. | To the extent that personal information is retained in backups, then disaster recovery and business resumption processes must ensure the continued control over those assets. |
| Compliance | Compliance includes not only compliance with legal requirements, but also with security and privacy policies and standards. | Compliance to relevant security and privacy policies is integral to ensuring privacy as this enables users a means to validate adherence to those policies. |

# Impact of Frameworks on the Privacy Engineer

Privacy engineers must understand the OECD Guidelines, GAPP, and the other frameworks, as well as their organization's own privacy policies, standards, and guidelines sufficiently to understand their purpose and limitations. In doing so, any creative innovation should have a tie into a rationalized set of existing requirements. This will, in turn, make it easier to implement such an innovation or manage change effectively as a logical leap forward in achieving the ultimate goal of efficiently, effectively, and ethically protecting information about people.

If data is processed in a way that honors or adheres to the OECD Guidelines or GAPP, or one of the other frameworks, then chances are, under most data privacy regimes, it will likely be considered to be fair and legitimate processing as most privacy laws are based on the FIPPs in some fashion (and these other frameworks essentially follow the FIPPs). However, as noted later, each specific case or legal regime can and often does interpret the FIPPS, adherence, and individual level of competency differently.

In Part 2 of this book, we will discuss how privacy rules are developed based on privacy policies, processes, procedures, standards, guidelines, and best practices that are derived in part from these frameworks. These privacy rules will be used to implement mechanisms that are used within systems satisfying privacy requirements.

# Frameworks Are Not the Same as Laws

How each enterprise addresses privacy requirements at a deeper more granular level is a decision that is based on many factors such as size, jurisdiction, risk profile, internal policies and public positions, and, most important, what kind of personal information is involved (i.e., how much and how sensitive) and whose data it is.

To get to this level of granularity in understanding requirements, you should work with legal resources with privacy domain expertise and look at the specific laws and regulations that govern the space in which you are working, as well as applicable internal policies and requirements.

For this reason, the techniques for privacy engineering that will be discussed in this book and the issues that they will address are going to be characterized at a framework level, not based on a specific statute or regulation level.

## UBIQUITOUS COMPUTING REQUIRES GLOBAL PRIVACY LAW AWARENESS

By Francoise Gilbert, Founder and Managing Director of IT Law Group and author and editor of *Global Privacy and Security Laws*

As citizens, we might feel allegiance to a particular region where our ancestors were born and our family roots were formed, but these boundaries are artificial. When looking at the earth from the 10,000-foot level, states merge into one another seamlessly. Clouds that fly over country borders ignore the passport control booths.

Like their geophysical cousins, the clouds in which our electronic files are stored and processed know no borders. Our smartphones, tablets, laptop computers, smart watches or glasses and the underlying technology into which we plug our equipment allow us to be connected at all times, from anywhere to, to anyone.

Data, like the genie, have jumped out of their bottle. They are taking a path of their own that does not stop at the edge of the device that was used to collect them or at the political border of the country in which that device is operated. With interconnectivity and ubiquitous computing available to us, we can, while seated on a bench in the middle of Golden Gate Park in San Francisco, access or modify files that are processed in Argentina by a payroll service established in France. These files may be simultaneously backed-up in Singapore and replicated for disaster recovery purposes in New Zealand. They may pertain to the employees of an Australian company who telecommute to work from South Africa.

This might look like a law school exam hypothetical. It happens increasingly in the 21st-century world of virtual companies or virtual employees where intangible intellectual property is frequently the most valuable asset of a business. Which privacy or data protection law applies to this hypothetical? Which state or country has jurisdiction over a particular dataset?

Ask five different judges, and you are likely to receive five different answers. The laws of several countries might apply, and more than one court could assert jurisdiction: That of the country where the data controller is located; that of the countries where the servers that process or store the data are located; that of the country where the data subject is physically located, or where his employer is established to do business, or where his payroll is generated.

Countries are very protective of their citizens and want to apply their laws—or are asked by plaintiff to apply their laws—to matters that may take place within their boundaries or affect their citizens. See, for instance, the current Article 3—Territorial Scope-- of the draft EU Data Protection Regulation, which is expected to supersede the 1995 EU Data Protection Directive. This provision might allow the application of the EU Data Protection laws to the hypothetical above, due to the fact that the payroll company is established in the EU, even though the data subjects are located in South Africa and their employer in Australia. Article 3 provides in part (emphasis added):

> This Regulation applies to the processing of personal data in the context of the activities of an establishment of a controller or a processor in the Union, *whether the processing takes place in the Union or not.*

> This Regulation applies to the processing of personal data of data subjects residing in the [European] Union by a controller or processor *not established in the Union,* where the processing activities are related to:
> (a) the offering of goods or services, irrespective of whether a payment of

the data subject is required, to such data subjects in the Union; or (b) the monitoring of such data subjects.

This Regulation applies to the processing of personal data by a *controller not established in the Union*, but in a place where the national law of a Member State applies by virtue of public international law.

We cannot rely on the law of a single country as the framework in which to develop policies, practices, and procedures or evaluate the risk to which data might be exposed. Ubiquitous computing, business process outsourcing, and cloud computing are available to all companies. Size no longer matters. The proverbial flower shop around the corner may have its accounting or payroll data processed or stored on another continent, in the same manner as a Fortune 10 company can.

Privacy professionals must be aware, and keep abreast of, the legal developments regarding information privacy or security laws in all the countries in which the personal data in their clients' custody are or might be located. It is only with this global knowledge and legal awareness that they will be able to properly evaluate and anticipate the legal constraints to which these data might be subject.

Although most of the world's data protection laws take an approach to the protection of personal information, personal space, and intimacy that is loosely based on similar fair information privacy principles (whether they are expressed in the OECD Guidelines, the APEC Privacy Framework, or other document), the devil is in the detail. Each country's legal framework is different. When these principles are implemented, each country has its own view and its own sensitivity to a particular topic.

Keeping abreast of these developments is difficult and time consuming. It is not that simple to know and appreciate a country's vision of privacy and what is necessary to achieve compliance in that particular country. It is a major mistake to take a one-size-fits-all approach or ignore the legal and cultural nuances among countries, even neighboring ones, or the historical foundation that have resulted in a certain legal system or certain local customs or behaviors. A formality that does not exist here may be required there and may be attached to prison terms elsewhere in cases of delinquency.

Privacy is a cross-functional and complex concept. Unlike tax, real property, or corporate law, privacy laws do not have hundreds of years of history in the making. Nevertheless, all over the world, there is more to privacy than what judges or legal scholars have designed. The social aspects and the individual, cultural, or ethnic sensitivities are also part of the foundation. Before becoming regulated, privacy has evolved in great parts outside courts, being shaped slowly by reactions to significant or traumatic events.

Privacy concepts and privacy laws may result from societal pressures, changes in mores and habits, reaction to government abuses, or may respond to technology advances. In each country, they are a reflection of the country's culture, history, and sensitivity. At times, the religious and philosophical beliefs of its citizens may have also influenced the way in which a country designed and implemented (or not) data protection principles and protected (or not) the privacy rights of its citizens. Developing a global privacy program requires an appreciation and understanding of these nuances and sensitivities.

The world of privacy and data protection is uniquely complex. As the field evolves, and, concurrently ubiquitous computing is becoming the norm, it is indispensible to take a global approach to privacy and data protection while remaining aware of the significant discrepancies between the laws, regulations, guidelines, and sensitivities that exist and will remain at the micro level in each country or state.

# Privacy by Design

Privacy by Design (PbD) is a concept popularized by Ann Cavoukian, the commissioner for information and privacy for the province of Ontario, Canada. It was developed to ensure that privacy was protected and that people gained control over their information and the information of their enterprises. In 2011, at their 32nd annual conference, the international Data Protection and Privacy Commissioners recognized PbD as an "essential component of fundamental privacy protection."[5]

It teaches the following seven "Foundational Principles":[6]

1. *Proactive not* Reactive; *Preventative* not Remedial

2. Privacy as the *Default Setting*

3. Privacy *Embedded* into Design

4. Full functionality—*Positive-sum,* not *Zero-sum*

5. End-to-End Security—*Full Lifecycle Protection*

6. *Visibility and Transparency*—Keep it Open

7. *Respect* for User Privacy—Keep it *User-Centric*

---

[5]Resolution on Privacy by Design, 32nd International Conference of Data Protection and Privacy Commissioners, Jerusalem, Israel. www.justice.gov.il/NR/rdonlyres/F8A79347-170C-4EEF-A0AD-155554558A5F/26502/ResolutiononPrivacybyDesign.pdf
[6]Foundational Principles, Privacy by Design. www.privacybydesign.ca/index.php/about-pbd/7-foundational-principles/

# NEXT-GENERATION PRIVACY FOR A NEXT-GENERATION WORLD: *PRIVACY BY DESIGN* RESOLUTION

By Ann Cavoukian, PhD, Information and Privacy Commissioner, Ontario, Canada

In October 2010, a landmark resolution was unanimously passed by the International Privacy Commissioners and Data Protection Authorities at their annual conference, recognizing *Privacy by Design* (PbD) as an "essential component of fundamental privacy protection." The Resolution also:

> Encouraged the adoption of the principles of *Privacy by Design* as part of an organization's default mode of operation; and

> Invited Data Protection and Privacy Commissioners to promote *Privacy by Design*, foster the incorporation of its Foundational Principles in privacy policy and legislation in their respective jurisdictions, and encourage research into *Privacy by Design*.

Since then, PbD has become a global operation, having been translated into 35 languages. Public policymakers in the United States, Europe, and Australia have issued proposals to express PbD in reformed information privacy governance and oversight regimes. More than a concept, PbD has become a legal and regulatory requirement in major jurisdictions around the world. With the world evolving so rapidly, privacy protections must also evolve in equal measure.

## Evolving Privacy Contexts

Privacy is often said to be in "crisis" today as a result of numerous developments:

> Leapfrogging information and communications technology developments;

> The advent of social, cloud, mobile, and ambient computing;

> Evolving cultural norms; and

> A global patchwork of outdated privacy laws.

The information privacy solution requires a combination of data minimization techniques, credible safeguards, meaningful individual participation, and robust accountability measures, informed by an enhanced and enforceable set of universal privacy principles adapted to modern realities.

PbD evolved from early efforts to express Fair Information Practice principles directly in the design and operation of information and communications technologies, resulting in *Privacy Enhancing Technologies* (PETs). Over time, the broader systems and processes in which PETs were embedded and operated were also considered. These include organizational practices and networked information ecosystems. PbD principles emphasize proactive leadership, systematic methods, and demonstrable results.

## Proactive Not Reactive; Preventative Not Remedial

PbD principles have changed the global privacy conversation by shifting emphasis away from reactively detecting and punishing privacy offenses after they occur to minimizing risks and preventing harms *before* they occur. "Build it in early" is now a common message from data protection authorities around the world.

PbD principles aspire to the highest global standards of practical privacy possible—to go beyond compliance and achieve visible evidence of leadership, regardless of jurisdiction. Good privacy doesn't happen by itself; it requires proactive leadership and continuous goal setting at the earliest stages.

Global leadership begins with explicit recognition of the benefits and value of adopting strong privacy practices, early and consistently (e.g., preventing data breaches and harms from arising). This implies:

A clear commitment, at the highest levels, to prescribe and enforce high standards of privacy, generally higher than the standards set out by global laws and regulation;

A demonstrable privacy commitment that is shared by organization members, user communities, and stakeholders in a culture of continuous improvement;

Establishing methods to recognize poor privacy designs, to anticipate poor practices and outcomes, and to correct any unintended or negative impacts, well before they occur, in proactive, systematic, and innovative ways; and

Continuous commitment and iterative processes to identify and mitigate privacy risks.

The preventative and systematic approach to engineering privacy is often associated with privacy-enhancing technologies, particularly in Europe. Although PbD is often best illustrated through specific technologies (the more user-centric the better), it is the *organization* that has become a more central and effective focus for applying PbD Principles, especially in view of the requirement to comply with privacy and data protection laws.

Being proactive and preventative requires a clear understanding of the strategic risks, challenges, and rewards of applying strong privacy throughout an organization and across information systems, in a comprehensive manner.

# Privacy Embedded into Design

Privacy promises are not enough—they must be implemented in systematic and verifiable ways. Information and communications technologies, systems, and networks are highly complex and dynamic in nature. Data processing is interdependent and tends to be opaque in nature, requiring more trust than ever from stakeholders and users for sustainability. These are not ideal conditions for ensuring that accountability, data protection, and individual privacy will thrive.

Privacy commitments and controls must be embedded into technologies, operations, and information architectures in holistic, integrative, and creative ways:

Holistic, because broader contexts must be considered to properly assess privacy risks and remedies;

Integrative, because all stakeholders should be consulted in the development dialogue; and

Creative, because embedding privacy rights and controls, at times means reinventing the choices offered because existing alternatives are unacceptable.

A systematic, principled approach to operationalizing privacy should be adopted, one that relies on accepted standards and process frameworks, amenable to external reviews and audits. All fair information practices should be applied with equal rigor, at every design step.

Wherever possible, detailed privacy impact and risk assessments should be carried out, documenting the privacy risks and measures taken to mitigate those risks, including consideration of alternatives and the selection of metrics.

The privacy impacts of the resulting technologies, processes, and information architectures should be demonstrably minimized and not easily degraded through use, misconfiguration, or error.

In the United States, the Federal Trade Commission (FTC) has begun to require some organizations to put in place comprehensive, auditable privacy programs. In the European Union, "prior checking" and other due diligence requirements are becoming mandatory for organizations to demonstrate compliance with privacy laws.

## Full Functionality: Positive-Sum Not Zero-Sum

Privacy is not an absolute value. To design practical, yet effective, privacy controls into information technologies, organizational processes, or networked architectures, privacy architects need to acknowledge many legitimate (and, yes, sometimes competing) goals, requirements, and interests and accommodate them in optimized, innovative ways.

The PbD Principle of *Full Functionality* requires going beyond privacy declarations and best efforts to *demonstrate* how data processing and other objectives have been, and are being, satisfied in a doubly-enabling, win-win model. External accountability and leadership are enhanced by applying this principle, which emphasizes transparency and measurable outcomes of multiple functionalities:

> When embedding privacy into a given information technology, process, system, or architecture, it should be done in such a way that full functionality is not impaired, and that all legitimate interests are accommodated and requirements optimized;

> Privacy is often positioned in a zero-sum manner; that is, having to compete with other legitimate interests, design objectives, and technical capabilities in a given domain. PbD rejects this approach; it embraces legitimate non-privacy objectives and accommodates them in an innovative, positive-sum manner; and

> All interests and objectives must be clearly documented, desired functions articulated, metrics agreed upon and applied, and unnecessary trade-offs rejected, in favor of finding a solution that enables multi-functionality.

Additional recognition is deserved for creativity and innovation in achieving all objectives and functionalities in an integrative, positive-sum manner. Organizations that succeed in overcoming outmoded zero-sum choices demonstrate global privacy leadership.

This principle challenges policymakers, technologists, and designers, among others, to find ways to achieve better privacy in a given technology, system, or domain than is currently the case and to document and demonstrate achievements that become best practices.

There are many examples of positive-sum "transformative" technologies that achieve multiple objectives in tandem in a privacy-enhancing manner. For example, Biometric Encryption (BE) achieves positive identification without the need for centrally stored templates. BE has been successfully deployed across Ontario gaming facilities to identify gamblers requesting to be barred from entering the premises. The positive-sum PbD principle has also been successfully applied in a wide range of areas: road toll pricing, smart meters, whole-body image scanners, RFID-enabled systems, geolocation-enabled services, and many other technologies and services.

The creation, recognition, and adoption of PETs as a means to achieve PbD operational goals is being actively promoted by the European Commission, not only as a major ongoing research funding initiative under the Framework Programme, but notably in the context of the EU review of, and proposed amendments to, the Data Protection Regulation.

Current work by international data protection authorities to define accountability is also establishing common definitions and best practices that help advance organizational PbD practices. Similar work is also under way in international standards groups to define privacy implementation, assessment, and documentation methods. The preparation, use, and publication, whether mandatory, contractual, or voluntary, of privacy impact assessments and privacy management frameworks are also on the rise. We are seeing the growth of standardized privacy evaluation, audit, and assurance systems, innovative co-regulatory initiatives, certification seals and trust marks, and other criteria. Enhanced diligence and accountability measures are consistent with the PbD emphasis on demonstrating results. The publication of successful case studies adds illustrative and educational value for others to emulate. Perhaps the most exciting chapters on achieving PbD results have yet to be written, as public policymakers on both sides of the Atlantic Ocean actively propose weaving the PbD framework and principles into the fabric of revised privacy laws, and in strengthened systems of regulatory oversight—the best is yet to come.

Like privacy engineering, PbD teaches that privacy is also a business issue. The building of consumer trust will provide a competitive advantage. Just one data breach interferes with this trust. PbD, like privacy engineering, recognizes that both physical design and information technology design are crucial to develop an effective privacy program. The privacy designer needs to carefully construct physical security to protect the privacy of both data facilities and paper records. Information technology design can enhance privacy by the use of PETs (discussed in detail in Chapter 6) like a uniqueness identifier with no specific meaning and by utilizing encryption correctly. Security and privacy work together and do not work at cross purposes. It is important that privacy be embedded into the IT system as part of the design process, baked in so it will not interfere with the business purpose of the system but will actually enhance the business objectives.

## How Privacy Engineering and Privacy by Design work Together

Privacy engineering is a concept for which PbD is a facilitator. PbD provides valuable design guidelines that privacy engineers should follow. In turn, privacy engineering adds to and extends PbD. It provides a methodology and technical tools based on industry guidelines and best practices, including the Unified Modeling Language.

In the rest of this book, we will discuss the methodologies and the various modeling processes to develop privacy mechanisms that can be used independently or can be plugged into new and existing enterprise systems to enhance their ability to implement enterprise privacy policies.

# Conclusion

This chapter explained how privacy and other data management frameworks overlap and can be leveraged as an overall governance framework for personal information. Data management teams and privacy functions have common goals: the health, hygiene, and well-being of the data under their respective custodianship. While there may be different approaches to data management and different privacy frameworks, there are strong points of similarity that can be harmonized to arrive at a functional set of policies and requirements for an enterpise. Chapter 4 will discuss how these Privacy Policies are developed and how an organization's privacy policy can be coordinated as the "meta" document for use case requirements.

# PART 2

# The Privacy Engineering Process

# CHAPTER 4

■ ■ ■

# Developing Privacy Policies

*If at first the idea is not absurd then there is no hope for it.*

—Albert Einstein

Don't skip this chapter because the information presented seems obvious or is something you might feel you want to pass off to your legal team. The search for solid engineering requirements starts with solid policy. By policy, we mean the rules that govern, not the Privacy Policy we associate with the web site that is never read.

This is not a chapter about traditional policy creation. The Privacy Policy is the "silk road" (in the classic sense of the ancient Asian Silk Road, not the contemporary online black market web site). It leads the organization to this new world of innovation and privacy engineering. It brings multidisciplinary actors and actions together and combines the best of legal, technical, and process-oriented teams for fair and legitimate processing of personal information (or privacy). This Privacy Policy becomes the basic map or blueprint for the build out. It ultimately should be viewed as the "meta" set of use-case requirements.

This chapter covers the development of policies that will be used as the basis for development of the controls and measures to protect personal information (i.e., privacy standards, guidelines, business rules, and mechanisms). When we discuss policy creation in this context, we are talking about starting with business requirements (a task or series of tasks needed to serve a goal) and functionality goals. Once defined for goals and basic functions, we add requirements driven by applicable law. We then fit and bend our requirements to view the policies we must create through a lens of *functionality* (i.e., each action taken or demanded may be viewed as a requirement specification that must be included in a *system*). That system may be an enterprise, a subunit, end-to-end processing cycle, application, an element of functionality, a person-managed governance activity, among others. There is no exclusive list of what constitutes a system.

Every discussion in this chapter must be considered in this operational, requirement-driven context otherwise it will be easy to slip into traditional "policy" mode. This is *not* a discussion chief privacy officers (CPOs; or whomever is leading the privacy function) will have with every privacy engineer; however, every CPO *must* consider the output of his or her labor in terms of the concrete and measurable requirements and the outcomes discussed here.

Following chapters will show Unified Modeling Language (UML) and systems creation techniques for metadata as a methodology for taking the requirements derived from privacy policies and other technical sources and creating solutions that reflect those requirements. Where neither systems nor features nor privacy enhancing technologies can meet the requirements set forth, governance, training, and leadership "systems" involving the human players in the privacy engineering drama are discussed.

# Elements of Privacy Engineering Development

Privacy engineering is the discipline of developing privacy solutions that consist of procedures, standards, guidelines, and mechanisms. Part 2 covers the process of developing privacy solutions, as depicted in Figure 4-1.

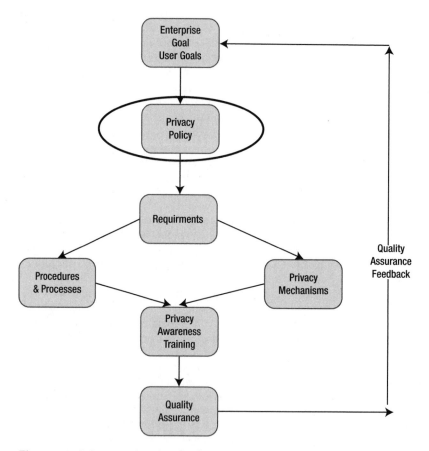

*Figure 4-1.* *Privacy engineering development process*

The elements of the process of developing a privacy solution, based on a set of privacy policies, are:

- *Enterprise goals*: They must be reflected and aligned with privacy engineering solutions, including their privacy policies, standards, and guidelines. To make this happen, a privacy development team[1] must first understand the goals and objectives of the enterprise in which the solution will operate. For the purposes of this book, "enterprise" includes organizations large and small that manage or otherwise process data. This definition would, of course, include government entities that may be governed by specific or additional rules and regulations and the organizing principles will still apply.

- *User/individual goals*: These must be incorporated to develop effective and flexible privacy policies that will be accepted by the end user and individuals. The team members must understand the goals and objectives (and privacy sensibilities) of the end users and individuals who will participate in the system or become the data subjects for PI managed by the system.

- *Privacy policy*: Development of a privacy policy is discussed in Chapter 4. The policy plays a key role in guiding how privacy engineering is applied.

- *Privacy requirements*: Requirement gathering is critical for effective policy creation and solution development. Chapter 5 describes the application of use cases for requirement collection and introduces a unique use-case metadata model.

- *Privacy procedures and processes*: These are the overall privacy activities (procedures) and their human or automated tasks (processes). Chapters 5 and 6 cover developing and using these as part of the privacy engineering discipline. Mandated standards and recommended guidelines factor into the creation of procedures and processes. It is procedures, processes, standards, and guidelines that translate "policy" into reality.

- *Privacy mechanisms*: These are the automated solutions built with software and hardware to enforce privacy policies. Examples are created for illustration in Chapters 7, 8, and 9 using the development process presented in Chapter 6, including a privacy engineering component and how it can fit within an application system environment.

---

[1]This team will consist of members from a formal privacy function, business-oriented data stewards, privacy engineers, security analysts, and IT data analysts. Data governance was discussed in Chapter 2. Organizational aspects of privacy engineering will be addressed in Chapter 11.

- *Privacy awareness and readiness preparation*: As part of developing a privacy engineered solution, the team will engage with various stakeholders so they are aware of what the Privacy Policy is and what it does. The privacy team works together with these stakeholders to address how the privacy-engineered solution could affect their roles and responsibilities. This subject is addressed in Chapter 10.

- *Quality assurance*: This is required to ensure that the privacy engineering solution functions properly, as well as satisfies enterprise goals, user goals, and accepted privacy standards within the context they are to operate. Quality assurance for privacy solutions is discussed in Chapter 10.

- *Feedback loop*: This will ensure that the privacy engineering solution is improved continuously as it will periodically quality assess or audit the solution and build in the ability to do so as a technical and procedural requirement.

After reading Part 2, whether you are a privacy professional or an engineer without a privacy background, you should have an understanding of how privacy is engineered into systems.

# Privacy Policy Development

Balanced with the enterprise requirements (where the data value of the solution should always exceed its risks when used in context), individual or "user" goals must be considered as part of the final articulation of the "enterprise" goals. The mission, goals, and objectives of the enterprise must be recognized, understood, and analyzed to determine a privacy-engineered solution's requirements. From these, the privacy policies that will govern the privacy engineering solution can be determined. The privacy policy development should be done at two levels: a general level, relevant to all parts of the enterprise, and at an enterprise-specific level, which will often be more specific and detailed than an "enterprise-wide" policy.

Although drafting privacy policies can be the subject of entire legal or organizational tomes, this chapter will go into enough depth so that the principles that comprise privacy policies are sufficiently understandable as the foundational layer of privacy engineering and use-case requirements. These policies enable the management of the principles *as a framework*, which in turn can also lead to:

- The development and deployment of privacy engineered systems

- The exciting missing beast—the framework to build and innovate the privacy engineered data-centric networks, tools, and solutions of the future

## What Is a Good Policy?

A policy is considered good based on the manner in which it functions as well as its contextual fit (i.e., how well it balances the needs and objectives of the enterprise with the objectives of the users or customers or employees whose data ultimately flows through that organization). A good policy:

- Arises from well-articulated enterprise goals, which are based on a clear statement of belief or purpose

- Describes what is wanted or intended by the various parties of interest impacted by the enterprise

- Explains why these things are wanted

- Provides positive direction for enterprise employees and contractors

- Provides transparency to the users of systems or individuals interacting with the enterprise

- Is flexible enough so there can be adjustments to changing conditions without changing the basic policy itself

- Is evaluated regularly

- Can be readily understood by all

Policy statements should be written in clear, concise language. A privacy policy should contain everyday words and short sentences and avoid the use of acronyms. If actions are compulsory, "must" should be used. If actions are recommended, "should" should be used. The policy must be practical and easy to implement.

# Designing a Privacy Policy

Some organizations begin taking action on mitigating business risks before an official Privacy Policy is published, but defining the policy should be a high priority. Sadly, many enterprises copy policies they find on other companies' web sites and post what amounts to an ad hoc policy of their own before any due diligence has been exercised with regard to knowing their personnel's, process's, or technology's requirements. It's a sad fact, but a vast majority of enterprises own what we call "complianceware"—stuff that they purchase, license, or otherwise "acquire" just in case there is a data breach or a regulatory inquiry at a later date but that they never actually completely deploy.

An example of this is where an enterprise purchases an identity management suite of products and sets the roles to "employee" or "nonemployee" without regard to a good policy that would illuminate why individuals required access to process data or how the roles or employees themselves should be protected and governed. A good privacy policy should be linked closely to this type of deployment. It will set its requirements before deployment or, better yet, before purchase or development if the identity solution is homegrown.

The next section describes the key considerations for crafting an effective privacy policy as well as how to maintain it.

# What Should Be Included in a Privacy Policy?

Policies must be designed to meet a complex set of competing needs:

- Local and international legal, jurisdictional, and regulatory necessities, depending on the scope of the enterprise

- Organization or business requirements

- Permission for the marketing–customer relationship for management or business intelligence

- Brand identity

- Industry standards

- Usability, access, and availability for end users of information systems

- Economic pressure to create value through efficient sharing or relationship building

- Enforceability and compliance

- Ethical obligations

- Realistic technology capabilities and limitations

Everything with a digital heartbeat is connected through dynamically formed relationships governed by privacy, security, and trust policies. This means there may be multiple interactive or cascading privacy policies based on the role of the various parties of interest:

- Customers

- Employees or contractors

- Third parties impacted by the enterprise

- Intellectual property owners

- Data types

Each privacy policy should start with the data type and its anticipated lifecycle and be aligned with the enterprise brand and the enterprise standards of conduct. The policy should add value by managing data:

- Respecting and managing regulatory and industrial standards compliance

- Using personal information and confidential data related to it safely and ethically

- Reconciling differences and leveraging synergies between overlapping or competing enterprise policies and goals for other areas, such as audit or litigation data preservation, records management, and physical and IT security

- Establishing a basis for objective respect and trust between an enterprise and its customers, employees, and other impacted groups

As discussed in Chapters 2 and 3, there are several sets of external standards and guidelines defining privacy requirements, including the OECD guidelines for the protection of privacy and transborder flows of personal data, GAPP, PbD, sectorial and competition laws in the United States, APEC privacy accountability frameworks, and the European Union (EU) Data Protection Directive (and member-states implementation of its requirements).[2] These external guidelines and principles can provide a framework for ensuring that the Privacy Policy will offer compliance within the related jurisdictional area.

It should, of course, be noted in the privacy requirements that:

- Not all laws are granular enough to provide one objective interpretation that must be instantiated

- All rules and regulations can always be harmonized to be free of directly conflicting standards and so-called best practices

What is possible is an objective working framework that will become the policy for the enterprise and, ultimately, the basis for process and technology policies, as described in the sidebar.

## INTERNATIONALIZATION: DEVELOPING A GLOBAL PRIVACY POLICY

By Dr. Mark Watts, Head of Information Technology Law, Bristows

Europe is not a country. It isn't. And while this will be blindingly obvious to most people reading this book, it's surprising how often I hear it assumed that Europe is essentially a country, with a single, homogenous data privacy law that sets out the rules applicable across the entire region (50 or so countries). If only life were that simple. If only European privacy rules were *that* simple. Sadly, they're not. And the point here is not to ridicule anyone's understanding of European geography or laws, but rather to make the point that, although when working "internationally" in privacy we all make assumptions—we have to, to rationalize the almost overwhelming legal complexity involved—making the wrong assumptions can quickly cause a project to go astray.

---

[2] OECD Guidelines on the Protection of Privacy and Transborder Flows of Personal Data are available at www.oecd.org/document/18/0,3343,en_2649_201185_1815186_1_1_1_1,00.html. A downloadable version of the Generally Accepted Privacy Principles (GAPP), along with additional information about the development and additional privacy resources, can be found at www.aicpa.org/privacy. Information about the European Union's Directive on Data Protection is available at http://ec.europa.eu/justice_home/fsj/privacy/index_en.htm.

Perhaps the most common working assumption I see crossing my desk is that the data privacy laws of a particular country are either (i) completely and utterly different from those that apply at "home" (usually the country of the parent company) so none of our existing data privacy policy can possibly apply, or (ii) absolutely identical to those that apply at home and so we don't need any special consideration or handling in the privacy policy; in other words, the international privacy policy can simply be the same as a domestic one. Unfortunately, most of the time, neither "working" assumption works particularly well. A sensible, well-drafted data privacy policy written to meet, say, North American legal requirements will contain much of relevance and application to Europe and beyond because good information handling practices, such as transparency, data quality, and security, are just that—*good* practices that should transcend country borders. But equally, to assume that that's all there is to it and that, say, North American laws can be exported globally would be complacent and would be to ignore significant cultural differences and priorities, not to mention historical sensitivities. Many an international company has come unstuck making this assumption.

For example, assuming the laws that relate to monitoring employee communications in, say, Finland are the same and so just as permissive as those in the United States (an assumption we see a lot) could easily land a company in hot water. Equally, for a European-headquartered company to assume that there are no security breach notification laws in the United States simply because there are so few at home in Europe at the moment can be just as problematic. A privacy policy built on shaky, overly broad assumptions can put a company, even a company that is trying very hard to do the right thing, in breach of applicable law, despite it following its privacy policy to the letter. Perhaps more worryingly, sometimes a breach can occur precisely *because* a company followed a privacy policy—admittedly, a poor privacy policy—to the letter.

Shaky assumptions can lead to another, more subtle but equally problematic risk—the risk of unnecessary overcompliance. Now, this isn't to suggest that companies should develop policies requiring only the minimum amount of compliance required by local law (essentially as little as the company can get away with) but would a company really want to apply the highest common denominator—the strictest standard anywhere—to all of its operations worldwide? Surely not. For example, would it really be wise to export the highly restrictive Finnish laws on monitoring employee communications to every country where a company does business? Most unlikely, because although this approach would ensure compliance with the communication monitoring laws of almost all other countries where the company has employees, it could seriously hamper its business operations in countries with more permissive regimes. This isn't a risk of noncompliance; it isn't a risk of breach. It's a risk of overcompliance that can fetter existing business processes, potentially inhibit sales, and, just as importantly for the privacy professional and privacy engineer, can damage their internal credibility within the company. All in all, overcompliance can be as much of a problem for the company as undercompliance.

The problem here is not that broad "international" assumptions are being made. They have to be. A global company with operations subject to the data privacy laws of hundreds of different countries cannot realistically be expected to identify every last detailed requirement of every last applicable law because, at least from a regulatory point of view, the world is still a very big place. So developing an international privacy policy (including all procedures, consent statements, contracts, and other supporting documents that go with it) has to involve making certain assumptions. It's just that they have to be the *right* assumptions. You have to know when it's safe to assume (or indeed, force) conformity between countries at a privacy policy level and when to leave enough room to accommodate important local differences in countries' laws.

Where does one start? As good a place as any for most companies is to think carefully about what it actually wants its international privacy policy to do. Is it meant to be some all singing, all dancing document that seeks to set out the various compliance requirements for each of the countries where the company does business? Or is it intended to be something with less lofty ambitions, merely a common set of requirements that will improve compliance everywhere while accepting that in certain countries there will be a "delta" between the requirements of the policy and those of applicable law?

Well-advised companies adopt the second approach, prioritizing the simplicity of a common, global policy that leads to a "good" (and hopefully even "very good") level of compliance everywhere over the more comprehensive and unwieldy, not to mention expensive, approach directed at full compliance everywhere, at least on paper and most likely only on paper. By adopting the second approach, companies are recognizing that there will inevitably be some specific (but hopefully minor) country legal requirements that are not covered by the policy in detail and which may not be complied with to the letter and only in spirit. In an attempt to plug the most significant of any known "gaps" like this, companies often develop country-specific annexes or sections in their privacy policy. An example of this would be a section specific to data collected in Switzerland that extends the privacy policy's requirements to information about legal entities (e.g., companies) as well as individuals (i.e., human beings). To include such an onerous requirement in the main body of the data privacy policy would be to export the Swiss requirement globally unnecessarily, requiring all companies to apply the policy in full to information about legal entities even though it is not legally required where they operate. Including the obligation in an additional annex to the policy and restricting it to data collected in Switzerland enables compliance with the local requirement while limiting its impact geographically.

But—tweaking the facts slightly—what if the parent company developing the privacy policy is, say, a Swiss bank? In this case it may be desirable or even essential to require its global operations to handle data about legal entities as if they were all subject to Swiss data privacy law. This would suggest that the "Swiss" provision should be included in the body of the privacy policy rather than being buried in an annex limited to data collected in Switzerland.

And this is how international privacy works; there are few if any invariably true assumptions that can be built into any global privacy policy. They always have to be considered and reconsidered on the particular facts for the company developing the policy. Done well, the result can be a robust privacy policy with a good degree of conformity from country to country, capable of generating clear technical requirements that give the privacy engineers a chance of coding "privacy." Done poorly, the result can be a policy that's unnecessarily strict, or with too many exceptions, or which is simply too vague to be useful, any one of which can require last minute changes to the Privacy Policy (and consequently any technical requirements based on it), something which, in my experience, coders really don't seem to like.

# General-Level Privacy Policy Development

One of the first things to be determined when drawing up privacy policies is which geopolitical regions or jurisdictions impact the enterprise. Privacy policies for a global enterprise, for example, can start the foundational development process by basing a strategy on the OECD Guidelines and GAPP. In some cases, other localized articulations of fair information processing may be the foundational basis for policy creation. For whatever framework is chosen, the policy creators will need to be able to translate how the various principles are managed if the policy is going to be an effective tool for process and privacy-enhanced systems and features in a privacy engineering context.

For example, a policy statement might require that data be collected relevant to services provided by the current enterprise. The general policy would require a well-defined privacy notice to provide for transparency between the collector of data and the data subject as well as to build an enforceable governance structure where the data asset is known as it enters and moves through its predicted lifecycle. An enterprise must be able to articulate and document how much personal information would be collected for specific purposes according to proportionality principle.

A policy statement should cover proportionality requirements: the benefit derived from the processing of the data should be proportional to its impact to privacy of the individual whose data is being processed. To achieve data proportionality at the time of collection, the data subject's perspective needs must be balanced within the enterprise's objectives.

The Privacy Policy should require a storage and archiving strategy. Encryption, obfuscation, or other security tactical requirements should be covered in the Privacy Policy and have associated standards and guidelines for operational implementation.

Allowances for revisions and exceptions should be included in privacy policies to address the fact that policy needs will change. There are occasions when a customer's, employee's, supplier's, or other party of interest's feedback or requirements may lead to the need to modify privacy policies or grant exceptions.

When an enterprise operates internationally, privacy policies should address the transfer of data among various jurisdictions. The underlying strategies should be people-process and technology oriented and include governance mechanisms that must be designed and executed to follow the data wherever they travel.

This is the point at which many initiatives often fail due to the lack of coordination and integration of effort. The lawyers head off to draft elaborate legal documents neatly tucked away behind a small link that says "Privacy Notice" at the bottom of a web page or buried in the terms and conditions statement of an application. The technical teams can rush off to buy products that obscure or encrypt enough data to satisfy the annual return of the audit team and so on among the teams. An institutional anthropologist could build an entire career analyzing the fascinating and often divergent goals of these now forever-parted teams. Anthropologic observations aside, the course of behavior that should be charted is an ongoing dialogue between the key stakeholders so that a privacy policy (i.e., requirements for processing personal information) can evolve and continue to meet the needs of individuals and the organization and keep pace to aid and not hinder innovation.

# Enterprise-Specific Privacy Development

The nature and culture of an enterprise business impacts privacy policies and the creation process. For instance, in the United States, the legal approach is often sectorial governed. An example of this is health care in the United States, where the Health Insurance Portability and Accountability Act of 1996 (HIPAA) policies and privacy rules should be incorporated. This type of enterprise will always be extremely open with many third parties, operating in a nonstop high-stakes context (in some cases, life and death). Getting the balance between use, sharing, access, and accuracy will be a supreme consideration. The rights and sensitivities of the data subjects within this context are highly subjective while also the subject of extensive regulation. Although other jurisdictions may not have standalone health data protection statutes, this type of context, and health data specifically, is governed as a protected class—or even an enhanced protected class, as in the European Union, a "sensitive" data class of data worldwide.

A health care-, financial-, or politically sensitive type of context is actually the proving grounds for many other types of businesses. These enterprises require personalization and intimate knowledge of personal information, but also value a certain level of autonomous innovation with data and financial models based on data. Innovating for high-risk data is a bit like the lyrics from the song "New York, New York": "If I can make it there, I'll make it anywhere."

A similar illustration can be drawn for financial data in the United States where the Gramm-Leach-Bliley Act requires financial institutions—companies that offer consumers financial products or services like loans, financial or investment advice, or insurance—to explain their information-sharing practices to their customers and to safeguard sensitive data. These types of data are covered by other comprehensive global laws such as the Personal Information Protection and Electronic Documents Act (PIPEDA) in Canada or under the Argentine Data Protection Laws but may not be called out under a specific law or called out as "sensitive" data calling for enhanced protections beyond the comprehensive requirements. The point here is that although not all data is created equal (nor do they call for exactly the same type of privacy policy treatment), personal information should be considered a controlled substance, and close partnerships and legal considerations are certainly necessary before we innovate on top of the foundational policy.

# Internal vs. External Policies

Data protection standards such as the OECD Guidelines and GAPP, among others, require that privacy policies should be published both internally in enterprises and externally (actually, externally, it is usually a statement or notice of an enterprise practices that is posted, not the actual policy) to give notice to users of systems, customers, or other data subjects interacting with the enterprise. Failure to comply with the enterprise public notices can lead to:

- *Dissatisfied customers*: Customers and other users will expect compliance to the privacy protection actions as indicated within the notice. It may be considered an implied contract. If there is a breach, users will tend to look to safer sites. If a user discovers identity theft that seems to have come from personal information collected by an enterprise, that user will take it out on the enterprise maintaining the site that failed them.

- *Regulatory investigations*: Where an enterprise has not lived up to its notice commitments, regulators from one or more jurisdictions will likely investigate the problems and may take either criminal or civil actions or both against both the enterprise and, conceivably, against employees within the enterprise.

- *Bad publicity*: Forty-six US states, the District of Columbia, plus other US territories have security breach notification laws that involve personal information. There are comparable laws throughout the world. The media keep a lookout for such notifications and determine when breaches are significant. Any breach scares people, and serious breaches equal bad publicity.

- *Litigation*: Potential liability in privacy-related lawsuits has been increasing steadily in recent years. This expanding legal exposure has been fueled by plaintiffs' class action lawyers targeting privacy litigation as a growth area. Moreover, federal and state government agencies, as well as data protection agencies throughout Europe and Asia, are becoming increasingly aggressive in their efforts to investigate and respond to privacy and data security concerns and incidents. The Federal Trade Commission (FTC) is imposing stricter standards on businesses, while state attorneys general are pursuing enforcement actions and conducting high-profile investigations in response to data breaches and other perceived privacy violations.

- *Harm to brand*: For most enterprises, the equity invested in their brands is an invaluable but fragile asset. When privacy protection problems occur, the reaction of the enterprise is crucial to the maintenance of a very positive brand.

- *Weak innovation*: Effective innovation comes from making improved products that deliver what people want. To find what customers and potential customers want requires the collection of data. An enterprise that does not protect the privacy of data will weaken the ability to collect the data needed to determine where innovation is required.

- *Employee distrust*: Just as customers can be turned off when privacy notice failures occur, employees can begin to distrust their enterprise when their data is not protected as the privacy notice promise.

An enterprise should consider creating training based on internal privacy rules that are more granular, specific, and more restrictive than externally posted notices. These internal policies should be coordinated with a human resources policy team to ensure that staff and business partners know exactly what to do, how to get help when they need it, and how and when these may be enforced and encouraged.

These policies must all be reflected and are instantiated in product and systems development as discussed further in Chapters 5 and 6.

# ENGINEERS AND LAWYERS IN PRIVACY PROTECTION: CAN WE ALL JUST GET ALONG?

By Dr. Annie I. Antón, Professor in and Chair of the School of Interactive Computing at the Georgia Institute of Technology

Peter Swire, Nancy J. and Lawrence P. Huang Professor, Scheller College of Business, Georgia Institute of Technology

In March 2013 we participated in a panel titled "Re-Engineering Privacy Law" at the International Association of Privacy Professionals Privacy Summit. The topic of the panel closely matches the topic of this book, how to bring together and leverage the skill sets of engineers, lawyers, and others to create effective privacy policy with correspondingly compliant implementations. As a software engineering professor (Antón) and a law professor (Swire), we consider four points: (1) how lawyers make simple things complicated; (2) how engineers make simple things complicated; (3) why it may be reasonable to use the term "reasonable" in privacy rules but not in software specifications; and (4) how to achieve consensus when both lawyers and engineers are in the room.

1. *How lawyers make simple things complicated.* A first-year law student takes Torts, the study of accident law. A major question in that course is whether the defendant showed

"reasonable care." If not, the defendant is likely to be found liable. Sometimes a defendant has violated a statute or a custom, such as a standard safety precaution. More often, the answer in a lawsuit is whether the jury thinks the defendant acted as a "reasonable person." The outcome of the lawsuit is whether the defendant has to pay money or not. We all hope that truth triumphs, but the operational question hinges on who can prove what in court.

The legal style is illustrated by the famous *Palsgraf* case.[3] A man climbs on a train pulling out of the station. The railroad conductor assists the man into the car. In the process, the man drops a package tucked under his arm. It turns out the package contains fireworks, which explode, knocking over some scales at the far end of the platform. The scales topple onto a woman, causing her injury.

From teaching the case, here is the outline of a good law student answer, which would take several pages. The answer would address at least four issues. For each issue, the student would follow IRAC (Issue, Rule, Analysis, Conclusion) form, discussing the issue, the legal rule, the analysis, and the conclusion: (1) Was the man negligent when he climbed on the moving train? (2) When the railroad conductor helped the man up, was the conductor violating a safety statute, thus making his employer, the railroad, liable? (3) When the man dropped the fireworks, was it foreseeable that harm would result? (4) Was the dropping of the package the proximate cause of knocking over the scales? In sum, we seek to determine whether the railroad is liable. The law student would explain why it is a close case; indeed, the actual judges in the case split their decision 4-3.

Engineers design and build things. As such, they seek practical and precise answers. Instead of an IRAC form, engineers seek to apply scientific analytic principles to determine the properties or state of the "system." The mechanisms of failure in the *Palsgraf* case would be analyzed in isolation: (1) The train was moving, therefore, the policy of only allowing boarding while the train is stopped was not properly enforced, thereby introducing significant safety risk into the system. (2) The scales were apparently not properly secured, thus a vibration or simple force would have dislodged the scales, introducing safety risk into the system. Is the railroad liable? An engineer would conclude the compliance violation and unsecured scales means that it would be liable. The engineering professor would congratulate the engineering student for the simple, yet elegant, conclusion based on analysis of isolated components in the system. In engineering, simplicity is the key to elegance.

---

[3]*Palsgraf v. Long Island Railroad Co.*, 248 N.Y. 339 (N.Y. 1928).

The lawyer may agree in theory that simplicity is the key to elegance, but law students and lawyers have strong reasons to go into far more detail. The highest score in a law school exam usually spots the greatest number of issues; it analyzes the one or two key issues, but also creates a research plan for the lawyers litigating the case. For example, the railroad has a safety rule that says the conductor shouldn't help a passenger board when the train is moving, but surely there are exceptions? In the actual case (or the law school exam), the lawyer would likely analyze what those exceptions might be, especially because finding an applicable exception will free the railroad from liability. The good exam answer may also compare the strange chain of events in *Palsgraf* to other leading cases, in order to assess whether the plaintiff can meet her burden for satisfying the difficult-to-define standard for showing proximate cause.

In short, lawyers are trained to take the relatively simple set of facts in *Palsgraf* and write a complex, issue-by-issue analysis of all the considerations that may be relevant to deciding the case. The complexity becomes even greater because the lawyer is not seeking to find the "correct" answer based on scientific principles; instead, the lawyer needs to prepare for the jury or judge, and find ways, if possible, to convince even skeptical decision-makers that the client's position should win.

2.  *How engineers make simple things complicated.* A typical compliance task is that our company has to comply with a new privacy rule. For lawyers, this basically means applying the Fair Information Privacy Principles (FIPPs), such as notice, choice, access, security, and accountability. The law is pretty simple.

The engineer response is: How do we specify these rules so that they can be implemented in code? Stage one: specify the basic privacy principles (FIPPs). Stage two: specify commitments expressed in the company privacy notice. Stage three: specify functional and nonfunctional requirements to support business processes, user interactions, data transforms and transfers, security and privacy requirements, as well as corresponding system tests.

As an example, some privacy laws have a data minimization requirement. Giving operational meaning to "data minimization," however, is a challenging engineering task, requiring system-by-system and field-by-field knowledge of which data are or are not needed for the organization's purposes. Stuart Shapiro , Principal Information Privacy & Security Engineer, The MITRE Corporation, notes that an implementation of data minimization in a system may have 50 requirements and 100 associated tests. Input to the system is permitted only for predetermined data elements. When the system queries an external database, they are permitted only to the approved data fields. There must be executable tests—apply to test data first and then confirm that data minimization is achieved under various scenarios.

For the lawyer, it is simple to say "data minimization." For the engineer, those two words are the beginning of a very complex process.

3.  *Why it may be reasonable to use the term "reasonable" in privacy rules.* Swire was involved in the drafting of the HIPAA medical privacy rule in 1999–2000. Antón, the engineer, has long chastised Swire for letting the word "reasonable" appear over 30 times in the regulation. Words such as "promptly" and "reasonable" are far too ambiguous for engineers to implement. For example, consider HIPAA §164.530(i)(3): "the covered entity must *promptly* document and implement the revised policy or procedure." Engineers can't test for "promptly." They can, however, test for 24 hours, 1 second, or 5 milliseconds. As for reasonable, the rule requires "*reasonable* and appropriate security measures"; "*reasonable* and appropriate polices and procedures" for documentation; "*reasonable* efforts to limit" collection and use "to the minimum necessary"; a "*reasonable* belief" before releasing records relating to domestic violence; and "*reasonable* steps to cure the breach" by a business associate.

The engineer's critique is: How do you code for "promptly" and "reasonable"? The lawyer's answer is that the HIPAA rule went more than a decade before being updated for the first time, so the rule has to apply to changing circumstances. The rule is supposed to be technology neutral, so drafting detailed technical specs is a bad idea even though that's exactly what engineers are expected to do to develop HIPAA-compliant systems. There are many use cases and business models in a rule that covers almost 20% of the US economy. Over time, the Department of Health and Human Services can issue FAQs and guidance, as needed. If the rule is more specific, then the results will be wrong. In short, lawyers believe there is no better alternative in the privacy rule to saying "reasonable."

The engineer remains frustrated by the term "reasonable," yet accepts that the term is intentionally ambiguous because it is for the courts to decide what is deemed reasonable. If the rule is too ambiguous, however, it will be inconsistently applied and engineers risk legal sanctions on the organization for developing systems not deemed to be HIPAA compliant. In addition, "promptly" is an unintentional ambiguity that was preventable in the crafting of the law. By allowing engineers in the room with the lawyers as they decide the rules that will govern the systems the engineers must develop, we can avoid a lot of headaches down the road.

4.  *How to achieve happiness when both lawyers and engineers are in the same room.* Organizations today need to have both lawyers and engineers involved in privacy compliance efforts. An increasing number of laws, regulations, and cases, often coming from numerous states and countries,

place requirements on companies. Lawyers are needed to
interpret these requirements. Engineers are needed to build
the systems.

Despite their differences, lawyers and engineers share important similarities. They
both are very analytic. They both can drill down and get enormously detailed in
order to get the product just right. And, each is glad when the other gets to do *those*
details. Most engineers would hate to write a 50-page brief. Most lawyers can't even
imagine specifying 50 engineering requirements and running 100 associated tests.

The output of engineering and legal work turns out to be different. Engineers build
*things*. They build systems that work. They seek the right answer. Their results are
testable. Most of all, it "works" if it runs according to spec. By contrast, lawyers
build *arguments*. They use a lot of words; "brief" is a one-word oxymoron. Lawyers
are trained in the adversary system, where other lawyers are trying to defeat them
in court or get a different legislative or regulatory outcome. For lawyers, it "works" if
our lawyers beat their lawyers.

Given these differences, companies and agencies typically need a team. To comply,
you need lawyers *and* engineers, and it helps to become aware of how to create
answers that count for both the lawyers and the engineers. To strike an optimistic
note, in privacy compliance the legal and engineering systems come together. Your
own work improves if you become bilingual, if you can understand what counts as
an answer for the different professions.

We look forward to trying to find an answer about how to achieve happiness when
both lawyers and engineers are in the room. Antón presumably is seeking a testable
result. Swire presumably will settle for simply persuading those involved. However,
we both agree that the best results come from collaboration because of the value,
knowledge, and expertise that both stakeholder groups bring to the table.

# Policies, Present, and Future

Policies have to be living documents that can be readily changed as a business changes or
as the regulatory environment changes; however, they should not be changed lightly or at
whim. There is overhead associated with policy changes, especially in the privacy space.
For instance, a change in policy may indicate a change in use of data, which then may
require an enterprise to provide notice of the change to whomever's data is affected and
get permission for the new uses of the data. Even without a pressing need for change, it is
important to review policies on a regular basis, perhaps annually, to determine if change
is necessary.

A good policy needs to be forward looking and, at the same time, accurate to the
current state. It should be sufficiently detailed as to give direction and set parameters,
but not so detailed as to be overly specific or to require excessive change. Each enterprise
will need to find the balance between what is communicated as "policy" and what is

communicated as an underlying standard or guideline for meeting the requirements of the policy. Key stakeholders should review policies and practices at least annually to see if revisions are warranted.

Engineered privacy mechanisms can ease the change and improvement of the policies, especially with the specific procedures, standards, guidelines, and privacy rules that need to change if there are policy revisions. The privacy component discussed in Chapters 6, 7, 8, and 9 addresses this crucial need.

# Conclusion

Privacy policies are powerful tools in the overall privacy engineering process. Privacy professionals, lawyers, and compliance teams can use them to communicate expected behaviors and leverage them to create accountability measures. In the process of policy creation, internal and external—including systems' users and regulators—requirements and expectations must be gathered. These same requirements and expectations in the traditional lexicon can also be leveraged as engineering requirements in the privacy engineering model and execution sense. We will explore how such requirements fit into a system's model in Chapters 5 and 6. In the remaining chapters of Part 2, we will continue to call on these policy requirements in the context of discrete tools and features that rest in the privacy engineering toolkit.

■ ■ ■

# CHAPTER 5

# Developing Privacy Engineering Requirements

*The expectations of life depend upon diligence; the mechanic that would perfect his work must first sharpen his tools.*

—Confucius

*I should live my life on bended knee; If I can't control my destiny. You've gotta have a scheme; You've gotta have a plan.In the world of today, for tomorrow's man.*

—David Bowie, "No Control"

This chapter begins with a discussion on the topic of requirements gathering. If a business or other enterprise is required to be responsible for personally identifiable information, it'll need to develop strong policies for managing that responsibility, and the entire process begins with determining the crucial requirements for internal and external policy development.

Requirements engineering use cases that leverage an industry-recognized approach will be introduced and applied to personal information (PI) and other data related to it. The data protection-driven fair processing principles will be leveraged to determine requirements, and a use-case metadata model that is unique to privacy engineering will be introduced.

Third-party service providers and unique distribution channels (such as cloud computing or mobile technology) for personally identifiable information can impact the engineered privacy solution. One should anticipate tumult, digital earthquakes, and continental shifts in the data protection landscape over time and build accordingly. The value in the methodology that is proposed in this chapter is in its inherent flexibility. The tools themselves are flexible as well so that, for example, if the privacy component is developed, it could be plugged into numerous applications so that any privacy rule changes will be reflected in all applications invoking the privacy component.

This chapter introduces three scenarios to be used throughout the book to illustrate the tools, techniques, methodologies, and sometime pitfalls of the requirements-driven privacy engineering discipline. The requirements use case-driven models to illustrate how a privacy framework may be fitted to a known system's development model to suggest a privacy-driven solution.

# Three Example Scenarios

These use-case examples (each explained in detail in Chapters 7, 8, and 9, respectively) should be considered expository workshops rather than a definitive formula that would extend to every data protection context. Different scenarios may require different use cases, and different use cases and policies may require components with different functionality. Nonetheless, the methodology defined in this book is designed to work in all circumstances.

## Example Scenario 1: The Privacy Component

Example scenario 1 will show how a privacy management team can develop or acquire a software privacy component (mechanism or tool) that supports and maintains the privacy rules derived from the privacy policies developed to meet the requirements of the enterprise and the people impacted by the enterprise systems. (See Chapter 4 for privacy policy and notice requirements.)

The resultant privacy component can be used independently or invoked by enterprise applications where privacy rules need to be enabled. This example scenario will be discussed in more detail in Chapter 7. The implications and a few potential benefits of an interoperable privacy component will be further explored in Chapter 14 that imagines "A Vision of the Future."

## Example Scenario 2: A Runner's App

Example scenario 2 will present a mobile application for which we developed a use case with Traver Clifford (grandson and nephew to two of the three manifesto authors). Traver was 17 years old and participating in an app development internship. He is one of the first to be trained and recruited as a young privacy engineer and to leverage the privacy engineering methodology. He was also a member of a high school cross-country team and we used his interest area for a case study. The runner's app invokes a simplified privacy component that may be used for mobile and smaller enterprise feature development. The runner's app will be discussed in more detail in Chapter 8.

## Example Scenario 3: Hospitality Vacation Planner

Example scenario 3 will assume that the privacy component has been developed, tested, and implemented. A large hospitality company required a system to help its customer community plan a vacation at one of their hospitality sites. The system supported both a telephone call center and a web site. The privacy component was invoked by this new system to ensure that privacy policies were enforced. Further, the hospitality vacation planner example shows the privacy requirements and fair information privacy principles as they operate as functional requirement specifications and quality control measures. This example scenario will be discussed in detail in Chapter 9.

# Privacy Requirements Engineering

To link the existing landscape of privacy—people, process, and technology—techniques as they exist today with the innovations that are required to manage privacy requirements of an increasingly complex world, we start by reexamining privacy policy creation as a means of requirements gathering as well as a basis for rules setting. The next step is to put those requirements into a dynamic creative cycle, as presented in Figure 5-1.

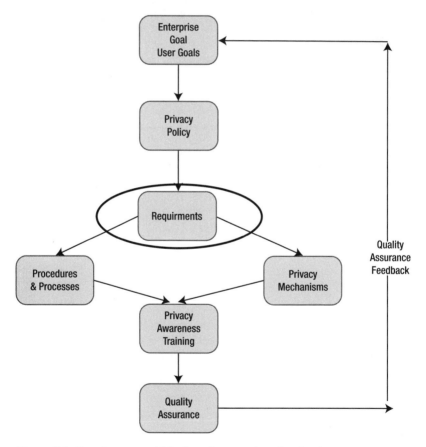

***Figure 5-1.*** *Requirements within the privacy engineering development structure*

*Requirements engineering* is the process of determining user needs or expectations for a new or modified solution. A solution in this context can be considered as broad as an enterprise-wide processing system architecture or as small as the addition of a new capability into one small and dedicated process. These features, called requirements, must be quantifiable, relevant, and detailed. In *software* engineering, such requirements are often called *functional specifications.*

For privacy engineers, requirements gathering and development can follow the same development path as for other functional specifications, with a twist. The art of privacy policy creation for the enterprise or for the government affairs professional is often stated in aspirational or behavioral terms: reasonable, proportional, no harm options and choices. Here, policy serves as a critical requirements-gathering source or end state upon which to draw certain functional requirements.

The policy must be explored and deconstructed to look for action words and decision trees that lead to the desired outcome. For example, a typical privacy policy may begin with the sentence "Company X respects your desire for privacy and so herein follows the way Company X will manage the personal information that it collects." Out of this very first seemingly boilerplate or throwaway sentence arises certain possibilities for the makers, owners, or users of systems. Some such systems requirement possibilities are:

- Company X requires certain accountability or measurement or testing to determine that it is providing information protection.

- Company X requires processes to collect information.

- Company X requires collection or awareness mechanisms regarding the desires of its users with respect to data processing in order to judge how to balance protection or collection against this desire.

- Company X requires data management processes.

- Company X requires a granular definition regarding who within Company X and its partners, affiliates, and vendors will carry the ultimate task of managing these requirements throughout the expected lifecycle of any data collected. In other words, Company X requires a specific "who" to manage now granulized "what" assets that will flow through "how" systems.

So, with the very first sentence of a public-facing policy, taking a requirements approach begins to turn nonsystems, noncomponent, nongovernance seeming legalese into functional requirements that may be implemented in a people-, process-, and technology-driven systematic fashion. The privacy engineer is a distinct practitioner because he or she may indeed be teaching the policy teams about the impact of their craft as much as they dictate aspirational requirements to them. Pretty cool stuff.

Requirements engineering involves frequent communication with system users to:

- Determine specific feature expectations

- Resolve conflict or ambiguity in requirements, as demanded by the various users or groups of users

- Avoid *feature creep*

- Document all aspects of the project development process from start to finish

Energy should be directed toward ensuring that the final system or product conforms to the client's needs rather than attempting to mold user expectations to fit the requirements.

# Privacy Requirements Engineering

Historically, in many organizations, requirements for systems to process personal information were set by inherent limitations, such as technical systems limitations or the lack of configurable features across applications or systems. Any data were forced to fit a system or series of systems rather than the systems adapting to reflect the user's and management's actual desired requirements for a task or use case.

The exponential rate of systems' capabilities and choices that have been developed in recent years can allow the privacy engineer to flip that equation and lead with person requirements first, data second, and technical limitations third in priority for design.[1] The evolution, or indeed revolution, of data-centric and person-centric processing vs. machine-limited data-processing design potentially creates a rich and creative environment for innovation and downstream economic benefits based on new business models. In fact, a person-centric design may be a way forward beyond the buying or selling of ads or other content-independent schemas to create "value" from new algorithms and person-first services.

Additionally, many hours of frustrating double talk have transpired where a legal team member asks a development team to ensure that there are "reasonable" controls included in the system before it can launch, only for both teams to discover that neither had the foggiest idea what was really expected from the other, another oft-occurring potential pitfall. If nothing else, privacy engineering models and techniques should provide an earlier and more productive conversation starter (or finisher). The launch party for new business models and systems may even enjoy a mutual clink of the glass for the legal, design, technical, customer advocacy, compliance, risk, and other business teams—the mind reels at the remote possibilities. "Legal" becoming a friendlier term for the enterprise is, unfortunately, beyond the scope of this book.

Thus, requirements engineering must be considered a team effort that demands a combination of hardware, software, human factors, privacy knowledge, and system design engineering expertise as well as skills in interpreting and communicating with other people with differing perspectives and lexicography.

## Use Cases: A Tool for Requirements Gathering

One form of requirements documentation is called a *use case*,[2] which is a complete course of events initiated by a primary actor. Actors may be people, functional roles, or

---

[1] This addresses a potential pitfall. So often both businesspeople and IT will think in terms of technology first and user later. This is a shortcut to user unhappiness.

[2] We will see later that the class or data model is another form of requirements documentation.

interfacing systems that interact with the enterprise (or system) under study. One or more use cases are developed for each actor to allow for scenario development and testing under different conditions. There are two levels of use cases: Business use cases describe the business process, and system use cases describe the interaction of one or more actors and the system to be developed.

Use cases are valuable to allow business personnel and technical creation teams to define and refine requirements in terms that are understood by all stakeholders. (At a large telecommunications company, we taught the businesspeople to write use cases and thus the use cases were understandable to both other businesspeople and the IT development team with few questions.) Use cases specify the interaction that takes place between the actor and a business process[3] (whether automated or not).

The use-cases technique is designed to capture user needs early and fast. Enterprise requirements are captured in a form both businesspeople and developers find engaging. They can also serve as a chain of evidence from requirements to value delivered and are useful in consensus building, training, and quality testing, as discussed in Chapter 10.

## Use Cases within Privacy Engineering

Another added benefit of employing use cases to add to the privacy engineering methodology is that management teams and developers can readily understand them and, in fact, have more than likely created use cases in other contexts. Here, we apply privacy requirements to this type of systems' engineering lifecycle methodology.

In addition to creating a cohesive design plan with integrated requirements, use cases can also be used to start to understand how system interfaces actually function and perhaps how a "feature" may act as a bug in practice to introduce unwanted risk or faulty controls according to the privacy policy requirements based on FIPPS/ISO or other relevant standards.

It should be noted that the development of use cases in this context also acts to lower the probability that bad data risk will have significant overall impact. Employing use cases allows the design team to role play potential risk and value scenarios and test various game theories to create policy requirements, education, and processes, thus avoiding another pitfall. Here, the expected people, process, or technology running within the use case should reveal where the anticipated design or feature leaves a gap *or* creates an unexpected value. Regulators will also be looking for documented scenario testing or gaming to determine where risks are contemplated and planned before data collection and processing. [A UK example: Fines pursuant to breaches found by the ICO[4] where no scenario testing or game play was undertaken by the data controller.]

---

[3]Here, business process is any activity performed in furtherance of the goals or objectives of an enterprise. Business processes operate in any type of system or organization and are not limited to private commercial businesses.

[4]The Information Commissioner's Office (ICO) is the United Kingdom's independent authority set up to uphold information rights in the public interests, promoting openness by public bodies and data privacy for individuals. Each European Union member-state has a similar body to enforce the country-level requirements implemented after the 95/EC/ Data Protection Directive.

# Privacy Requirements Derived from Privacy Frameworks

In Chapters 2 and 3, we explained how the privacy frameworks provide guidance as to which privacy requirements should be included in the requirements statements, be they in a use case, in the user-experience definition, or in the data-model metadata. The following outline provides some privacy requirements to be considered:

- *Purpose:* Collect and process for purposes that are relevant to the services being provided. PI must not be collected or used for purposes that are materially different from the original purpose for which the data were provided:

  - What purposes do the PI data perform?

  - Does each data attribute, related to personal information, have a direct relationship to the purpose for which it was collected and processed?

  - What privacy rules are needed to ensure that the purpose principle is satisfied? Are there other metadata that support the purpose principle?

  - Is there a chance that a data subject, whether an individual or an enterprise, would be embarrassed or damaged by the processing or publication of the personal data?

- *Notice:* System creators, owners, and fiduciaries must explain to users how their information will be used, collected, protected, retained, kept accurate, accessed, corrected, or otherwise processed before any processing occurs:

  - Does the requirements statement define a complete notice that satisfies the notice principle?

  - Is the intended processing included in the notice (some types of processing may require supplemental or just-in-time notices)?

  - How and when will the notices be presented to the user (and how or if will the user need to acknowledge or accept these notices)?

  - Are there statutory or common law requirements concerning notice in all jurisdictions wherever the system impacts?

  - Is the notice clear, consistent, relevant, and current?

  - Can innovative presentation techniques be used to explain the notice requirements in a way that encourages review and facilitates understanding (for instance, would animation or a pop-up video make the notice more appealing and clearer)?

- *Choice/consent:* Data subjects must consent to the collection and use of their personal information:

  - Choices must be shown clearly.

  - Choices must not be easily bypassed or ignored.

  - Defaults most be explained clearly.

  - Prechecked boxes should be avoided.

  - Defaults should be set to either lessen the sharing of PI or that default must be so clearly tied to the notice and the context so that the only reasonable expectation any user would have would be that the information is shared (a form of implied or informed consent).

  - Tools for the privacy engineer regarding choice should be considered during all phases of the data lifecycle of PI so that choices made by the data subject may be recorded, audited, and corrected along the way.

  - Limit the types of data allowed to be collected and segmenting more sensitive PI (or disassociating identifying attributes from aggregate data) are technical, managerial, as well as policy and legal decisions.

- *Transfer:* Data should not be transferred to third parties for their own use without the data subject's permission:

  - Data transferred to and from a third party must be "adequately protected" by contract, administrative, technical, logical, and physical means.

  - The transfer of data to different geographic areas, such as member-states of the European Union, may require an additional legal mechanism (such as Safe Harbor Certification or Model Contracts) to make the transfer legitimate.

  - PI should not be transferred to third parties without the proper procedures included as part of the overall architecture. Are the proper procedures in place for all types of third-party transfers and all impacted jurisdiction?

  - No PI should be transferred to a third party or geographic area without appropriate agreements and approved security provisions that detail how the data will be processed and how they will protected. As part of vendor management and the sourcing or procurement process, ensure third parties are vetted from a privacy and security controls perspective before data feeds are enabled.

- Encryption and obfuscation techniques are the obvious tools to leverage when a system owner wishes to prevent an attack of data in motion.

- *Access, correction, deletion:* Data subjects must have a means of accessing the personal information that has been collected about them. They also are entitled to delete or amend false or inaccurate data:

  - Can data be segmented (group together) so that different segments can be handled with different privacy, encryption, or security rules?

  - Can roles be defined so that privacy risks can be managed by means of privacy rules?

  - Are rules concerning correction and deletion in compliance with the laws or regulations of all jurisdictions impacted by the system or process or by the enterprise policies?

  - Although there is currently heavy debate over proposals to include a yet to be defined "right to be forgotten," a right of deletion is not absolute as of this date. (We will approach this subject again in Chapter 14 in our discussion of how the future may look on a broad scale.[5]) For the privacy engineer, engineering tactics that allow for search and removal of common media such as photos or video and some ability to add metadata would be a wise addition as this debate widens.

- *Security:* Use appropriate technical, logical, and administrative measures to ensure only authorized access and use of data:

  - Do you leverage ISO and other standards for information and physical security (see ISO framework as discussed in Chapter 3) and work with information security teams within your enterprise?

  - Are the security and encryption rules defined for each data attribute?

---

[5] It should be noted that there is not yet any proposal to notify victims of the behavior of the unintelligent or those who intend evil which now seems to dominate the hearts of legislators catapulting the legal discussion into historical data revision. To be fair, they do so with innocent intent to remove silly or youthful indiscretions. From an engineering perspective, it is worth a thought of creativity as to how a system would react to a picture or court filing being removed from public view where that media or filing specifically impacts the victim or other third-party beneficiary. Perhaps having a metadata attribute cataloging those individuals identified in the media so that the person requesting removal would have to document approval of impacted parties before holders of valid information were forced to remove it is needed. This is worthy of debate *and* a great deal of design before a notion like this would be enacted into law.

- Are security rules covered for data transfers, especially across jurisdictional lines?

- *Minimization:* Collect and process the minimum necessary data to achieve the identified, legitimate intended purposes. The minimization principle is closely related to the purpose limitation requirement where only the necessary PI is collected and processed to achieve a legitimate purpose:

    - For each piece of personal information data being collected, the following statement must be true: Without X data attribute, I cannot do Y legitimate task and I need no less than X to do Y. Is each personal information data attribute being collected needed to accomplish the solution being designed or is it being collected "just in case"?

    - If data are being collected for potential big data purposes, can big data analysis be used to identify a person, thus raising a potential privacy issue?

- *Proportionality:* Data collection should be legitimately proportional to need, purpose, and sensitivity of data. This requirement can be one-step further abstracted to connect those data to quality and value:

    - As with minimization and purpose, can collection be limited wherever possible to only what is required?

    - Think in terms of a Venn diagram that parses the proposed data, asking what is the minimum data needed that is proportional to the purpose intended?

    - Is the amount of data and the character of data itself proportional to the purpose, the sensitivity of the data, or the risk to a data subject should it be compromised?

    - Do the data subject and data fiduciaries keep a common perspective where risk and value are balanced? The following formula for proper weight of data comparison may be considered for overall data protection and governance efforts, but it also fits well into the discussion regarding proportionate collection and use, where Data Value (DV) > Data Risk (DR) = Success.

- *Retention:* Retain data only as long as they are required:

    - Are archiving rules for each data attribute well established?

    - Instead of determining how long data can be kept, determine how soon (in whole or in part) it can be deleted and act accordingly; wherever possible, define controls to automate deletion. If this is not feasible from a business or technical perspective, have data inventory review and deletion processes been created (archiving rules)?

- • Have data destruction tactics such as degaussing, permanently encrypting, and destroying keys or overwriting data after specific deadline been considered?

- • *Act responsibly:* Put a privacy program in place:

  - • Is the privacy team included on the project team?

  - • Has a privacy-oriented data governance or data stewardship program been established?

---

## DEFINING PRIVACY REQUIREMENTS IN AN EVER-CHANGING WORLD

By Peggy Eisenhauer, Founder of Privacy & Information Management Services— Margaret P. Eisenhauer, P.C.

In 2008, my son received a fun game, Fluxx, for his birthday.[6] Fluxx calls itself "The Card Game with Ever-Changing Rules!" It could also call itself "The Card Game that Provides a Perfect Metaphor for Privacy Requirements!"

Fluxx game play is quite simple. There are four kinds of cards: Actions, Rules, Keepers, and Goal. The Basic Rule says that, on each turn, you draw one card from the deck and play one card. To win, you collect the Keepers and meet the requirements of the Goal.

---

[6]Fluxx is a product from Looney Labs, available online at www.looneylabs.com/games/fluxx or at local retailers.

The twist with Fluxx is that everything can change while you're playing. Players take Actions, such as stealing a Keeper. Players change the Rules. Instead of draw 1, you have to draw 3. Or play all the cards in your hand. One possible Rule prevents you from winning unless you meet the Goal *and* have the Radioactive Potato card. Some of the Actions change the Rules. For example, one Action card lets you "Trash a Rule." Any player can change the Goal as well. Instead of needing the "Milk" and "Cookies" Keepers, now you need the "Rocket" and the "Moon." And nonplayers can join game at any time by picking up three cards from the top of the deck.

The ever-changing nature of Fluxx illustrates the challenges that we face in defining privacy requirements. When setting privacy requirements, we consider the data elements and proposed processing activities and establish rules to address four sets of mandates: (1) specific legal requirements for privacy and security, (2) requirements driven by internal policies, (3) requirements driven by industry standards, and (4) requirements that likely exist as a matter of stakeholder expectations for appropriate processing. At a particular point in time, the first three types of requirements can be objectively known. The fourth type of requirement (addressing consumer and regulator expectations for appropriate use) is subjective. For example, consumers generally feel that processing to prevent fraud is appropriate, but they disagree as to whether it is appropriate for companies to scan all the data off their driver's licenses in connection with a retail product return. Nonetheless, privacy professionals can collaborate with their product design teams to document a solid set of privacy requirements for any proposed activity.

As is always the case with requirements engineering, however, the requirements change over time. This is especially true for privacy requirements, due to the rapid evolution of legal standards and industry codes, mercurial consumer and regulatory views about privacy, and the dynamic nature of internal policies (which have to keep up to date with at least the laws). Privacy requirements are also challenged by changes within the business itself. Within any given company:

> Business objectives constantly evolve, creating new goals. Companies want to wring every last ounce of value from their data, leading to new uses for existing databases, novel types of analytics and business intelligence processes, and increasing pressure to leverage customer or consumer data assets to benefit partners and create incremental revenue streams.

> Business requirements evolve, requiring new rules. Companies move from controlled technology deployment to BYOD (bring your own device) programs. Customer and consumers are increasingly empowered to engage via social media platforms and mobile apps.

> Routine actions have consequences. Companies outsource, requiring new rules for vendor management and data transfers. They enhance data and create inferred data, pushing the boundaries of what may be considered appropriate by consumers and requiring new rules for notice, choice, and access.

Companies have security breaches. Even the actions of other entities can have consequences, as we know from revelations about government programs that demand access to consumer data.

Privacy professionals and product designers also need to recognize that some business attributes hinder achievement of some privacy objectives, and even privacy objectives sometimes compete. Let's consider a real-life scenario: a company may be committed to providing more transparency, but this may trigger an expectation that consumers will have additional choice. For example, the company may disclose that it is using cookies to recognize consumers' devices, but consumers will then want the ability to opt out of having the cookies placed. However, providing additional choice may make it more difficult to meet security requirements, for instance, if the cookies are used as part of a multifactor authentication process.

Additionally, as in Fluxx, the actions of various stakeholders (and the orders of actions) are not predictable. Nonplayers (such as regulators) routinely take actions that affect the business. Nonplayers (especially regulators) can also change the rules. It is thus critical to have a deep understanding of not only the legal requirements for data processing but also the more subjective opinions about appropriateness of the processing held by the myriad stakeholders: employees, consumers, industry groups, regulators. Because the rules are rapidly changing, companies must anticipate new requirements so they can implement new rules effectively and efficiently.

Consider, for example, the legal requirements for collecting children's data. The "Basic Rule" in the United States under the Children's Online Privacy Protection Act (COPPA) required verifiable parental consent in order to collect personal information from children under 13 years old via a commercial web site. COPPA regulated web sites that targeted kids as well as general interest web sites, if the site operators knew that kids were submitting personal information. Although COPPA was one of the most effective (and enforced) privacy laws, concerns persisted about the collection of personal information from children. These concerns intensified when studies revealed that web sites targeting children were collecting vast amounts of data via passive technologies, such as cookies, without triggering COPPA requirements.

In 2012, the Federal Trade Commission revised COPPA rules to add new requirements. The new rule expands the definition of "personal information" to include persistent identifiers, device IDs, geolocation data, and images. It also expands the definition of "website or online service directed to children" to clarify that a plug-in or ad network is covered by the Rule when it knows or has reason to know that it is collecting personal information through a child-directed web site or online service. All web sites that appeal to children must age-gate users. Companies operating general interest web sites online are now playing a very different game.

Like every great game, Fluxx has expansion packs and variant versions, such as Eco-Fluxx, Zombie Fluxx, and (our personal favorite) *Monty Python* Fluxx.

Expansion packs for "Privacy Fluxx" should be coming as well. Information security requirements are constantly evolving and becoming more prescriptive. The "InfoSec Monster Mandate Fluxx" will require very specific types of security controls and impose even stricter liability for data breaches. We can see this trend today in jurisdictions such as Russia and South Korea.

"Consumer Protection Fluxx" is already imposing new rules based on evolving concepts of privacy harm. Expect new purpose limitation requirements and "minimum necessary" standards as well as opt-in consent for secondary uses of personal information. Additional limits on the collection, use, and disclosure of personal information based on the nature of the technology used (such as cookies) are also featured in this version.

Companies that operate in a multijurisdictional environment know the challenges associated with "Global Data Protection Fluxx" quite well. These companies will face exponentially greater complexity as they define privacy requirements for systems and processing activities that touch data from multiple countries. These companies must account for all possible local requirements and implement controls to meet the most restrictive requirements. As in the United States, international data protection authorities are focused on data security and consumer protection. International regulators seek to achieve privacy goals by limiting data retention periods and cross-border data transfers.

# Develop Privacy Requirement Use Cases

Use cases reflect the requirements of business processes, and business processes are supported by information systems and automated business processes. Figure 5-2 shows a simple set of privacy use cases that could be used to develop a privacy engineering program.

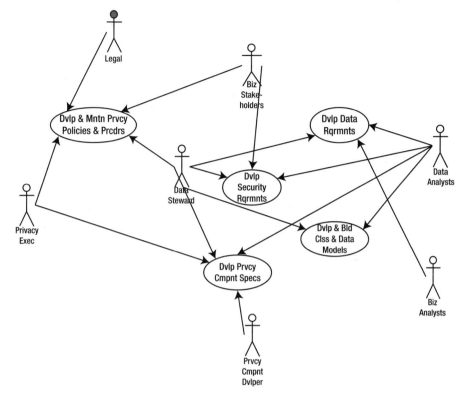

***Figure 5-2.*** *Privacy requirements use cases*

These use cases may contain explanatory elements that may be developed into use cases themselves, for instance, to:

- Determine and maintain privacy policies and procedures:

  - Develop privacy policy

  - Develop privacy procedures, standards, and guidelines

  - Design privacy notice

  - Develop archiving rules

- Determine security requirements:

  - Develop authentication rules related to privacy

  - Develop authorization rules related to privacy

- Determine data requirements:

  - Determine proportional PI and related data collection and maintenance requirements

- Determine privacy processing requirements
- Developed backup strategy
- Develop third-party transfer rules
- Develop and build class and data models:
    - Include privacy indicators in the model metadata
    - Include encryption indicator in the model metadata
- Develop privacy component specifications, including:
    - Enter privacy rules
    - Test for authorization rules
    - Present privacy notice
    - Enter opt-in/opt-out rules
    - Allow user to opt in or opt out depending on rules
    - Test for privacy indicator in database metadata
    - Test for encryption indicator in database metadata
    - Test for privacy rules
    - Test or third-party transfer rules

Use cases will usually be used to gather requirements as part of a project system's engineering development lifecycle. The information gathered as a part of use-case development should be entered into use-case metadata.

## USE CASES AS THE UNIVERSAL TRANSLATION TOOL

By Virginia Lee, Senior Attorney, Privacy and Security Legal, Intel Corporation

Engineers and lawyers may be speaking the same language, but you wouldn't know it when it comes to communicating about privacy. Imperfect communication leads to enmity between the two groups. It is as if they were living on opposing alien planets. Successful communication can be achieved between these seemingly disparate factions. It's not rocket science, but it may feel as difficult. It comes down to peeling back the jargon and teasing out the essence of what is being communicated.

What are the issues that crop up when engineers and lawyers try to communicate over privacy issues? The first critical impediment to good communication between the two are the perceptions held by each. Engineers have the perception that lawyers only say no. Lawyers believe that engineers don't really care about privacy. These perceptions are rooted in some truths. There are relentless calls from legislators and regulators about the need for more restrictions around the collection and use of consumers' data. All of us are bombarded by news articles about how some app developer surreptitiously collected a user's personal information without any concern as to whether the user would approve. So it is no wonder that there is a disconnect between the two groups.

Another roadblock to a mutual understanding are the concepts used by each. Engineers are accustomed to working in a deterministic environment. Most things are black or white for an engineer. On the other hand, lawyers tend to deal in the gray spaces. The issues they deal in are much more "squishy," lacking clear definitive answers. Additionally, both sets of concepts tend to be very complicated to outside parties.

There is hope for developing a middle ground where engineers and lawyers can meet and dialogue. To do this, both lawyers and engineers should more frequently use plain spoken language. A tool in the engineer's toolkit can accomplish this task. Use cases can provide a bridge for reaching this plain spoken middle ground without using technical or legal jargon.

Engineers are adept at creating use cases for defining the features and functionality in a product release. These same use cases can be drafted to describe to a lawyer what the flow of events is for a user. Use cases can also be used in defining how privacy legal concepts or rules can be applied to the functionality of a product or service. Lawyers need to understand how the user's information will be collected, used, and shared. The user flow described in a use case is a great tool for providing this information.

One major benefit of use cases is that they make difficult concepts more concrete and comprehensible. Scenarios can be created that define privacy issues in a manner that is understandable by both parties. With these more simple descriptions comes a clearer view of the user interaction that lawyers can more easily grasp.

Another advantage is that use cases help create a shared glossary. Engineers and lawyers should develop a shared privacy glossary that aligns with the company's privacy policies and principles. This glossary needs to be based on the company's own business practices. A shared glossary will provide the necessary definitions that can bridge the language gap. For example, what does the company mean by the term "personal information"? There are numerous definitions of this term used in rules and regulations, as well as by companies in their privacy policies. A company's definition of "personal information" will impact the way information is collected from users. Engineers and lawyers should work together to develop an appropriate definition through use cases and provide guidelines that are used throughout the company's development cycle.

Use cases move teams to speak a shared language. Lawyers need to limit the legalese and try to distill the legal concepts into more understandable concepts.

Engineers need to limit the techno jargon to more simple concepts. So often the legal rules or regulations are written so obtuse that it can drive an engineer crazy. Working with the lawyer, this "legalese" can be deciphered into something more palatable. As an example, the phrase "data only used for the purposes for which it was collected" crops into rules surrounding the appropriate collection of personal information from users. Translated this means only using the information collected from the user for the reason you told the user you were collecting it. As an illustration, an app developer collects a piece of data to provide recommendations to a user but then decides to use the information for serving targeted ads, without letting the user know beforehand. Lawyers can provide these types of real-world examples through use cases to better describe confusing legal concepts.

Ultimately, use cases help to develop rapport and understanding between the two factions. The best way to develop affinity with an opposing side is to find ways to interact using less formal methods. In order to work in harmony, engineers and lawyers need to develop rapport with each other. We all tend to face similar challenges and can find solidarity.

A successful privacy engineering engagement between an engineer and a lawyer is possible. Engineers and lawyers will always look at privacy issues differently due to how they frame the issues. However, by developing use cases to define concepts, these differences can be lessened. Both sides need to be cognizant of the other's point of view and approach any engagements with a jargon-free approach. Engineers and lawyers working in unity to mitigate the privacy issues will make for a successful and privacy-enhanced product.

## Use Case Metadata

Metadata is business information that information technology needs to design and develop databases and the systems that satisfy business objectives and requirements. Whereas, *mathematics* is the language of science, *metadata* is the language of data, business, application, and technology architecture. Metadata is the *who, how, where, when,* and *why* of things we manage and the activities performed in managing them. Metadata is crucial to quality solution design and to maintain data quality and consistency in the operational environment.

The following are pieces of information (metadata)[7] gathered during use-case development:

- For each use case:

  - Use-case name

  - Use-case description

---

[7]The use case metadata collected is the same for both business and system use cases. The differences are in the level of detail and the language used considering the audience.

- PI involved in use case:
    - Intended uses
    - Related use cases
- Expected use-case results
- Measures of success
- Primary actor performing the use case
- Support actor(s) performing the use case
- Location of the use case
- Frequency of the use case
- Related use case(s)
- Ideal course of action:
    - Event name and description (iterated for all events):
        - Decision 1 name and description
            - Business rule 1 description (If . . . Then . . . Else)
                - Business rule data entities/attributes required
        - . . . (iteration)
            - Business rule and description (If . . . Then . . . Else)
        - Decision and name and description
            - Business rule 1 description (If . . . Then . . . Else)
            - . . . (iteration)
            - Business rule and description (If . . . Then . . . Else)
    - Business processes triggered by event
        - Process data entities/attributes required
- Alternative courses of action (extension use case)

For privacy engineering, use cases are key to understanding which events or behaviors have privacy impacts. By including privacy indicators and related privacy rules in the use-case metadata, the privacy engineer can easily index issues and understand where to focus attention.

| WHEN IS METADATA NOT METADATA? |
| --- |

The answer is "when it's not."

Metadata can be defined as business information that information technology needs to design and develop databases and the systems that satisfy business objectives and requirements. Others give an even more terse definition: Metadata is data about data. Both definitions define metadata as something that is descriptive of other data. But when data initially identified or initially collected and processed as metadata are used not to describe other data but *as data itself*, such data may be considered content and not metadata, that is, either proprietary as in trade secret or other confidential data or personal data where it identifies an individual human. The fact that such collections of metadata may not name an individual by his or her legal surname is *not* determinative for legal and process based consideration.

For example, the US National Security Agency (NSA) collects telephone call and e-mail envelope metadata so it can more easily access large databases to determine end points where possible terrorists may be calling within the United States. This would be a correct use of the word "metadata." Where such data are used to create analytics and patterns to show anomalies or help predict known threatening behavior, they may also be used to build a case of probable cause for further individual inspection. Due process principles and protections apply under existing law to prevent further message content inspection without such process. Where this process is not followed or where overcollection of metadata capable of individual identification takes place, an inevitable political and social backlash is unleashed.

But what if this so-called metadata is analyzed as data itself to gain an understanding of calling patterns or some purpose other than that described to a court or other reviewing body that allowed the correction of the data? Then the metadata itself may be considered content (and is not metadata) and thus is separately subject to data protection and other cyber security rules and regulations. In other words, the expectation of privacy in the United States and in other countries may be broader than initially considered by law enforcement agencies and international policing requirements. Metadata, like all other forms of raw data, is subject to the reengineering and new protection requirements implied by the jargon "big data."

## Use Case Metadata Model

Figure 5-3 presents a metadata model showing the metadata that needs to be collected for any use case being developed (see also Appendix A).

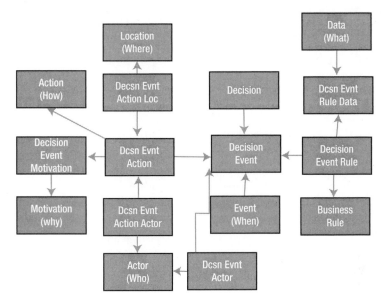

***Figure 5-3.*** *Use-case metadata model*

As discussed previously and later in Chapters 6, 7, 8, and 9, it is helpful to understand the various elements that need to be covered in each use case:

- An *event* (the when) may require one or more *decisions* to be made.

- Each decision event pairing may have a *decision event actor* (the who) who is involved in making the *decision*.

- A *decision event* may be governed by one or more *decision event rules*, including one or more *privacy rules*, which are a type of a business rule, as discussed later.

- Each *decision event rule* will require one or more *data attributes* (the what) needed to determine the decision criteria. For example, if the *decision event rule* is IF role name = Guest THEN invoke Guest Privacy Rule processing, "role name" is a data attribute used as part of the rule.

- Once the *decision event rules* have been processed, a *decision event action* (the how) may be taken by the system.

- This *decision event action* may impact a *decision event action actor*.

- The *decision event action* may be motivated by a goal or objective (the why) form of *motivation*.

- A *decision event action* will take place in a *location* (the where).

All this information that has been gathered within the use cases would then be put into a metadata repository based on this metadata model.

# The Privacy Engineer's Use of Use Case Metadata

In this section, we show an example of use-case metadata. This use case will be repeated in Chapter 7, as it reflects the requirements of what we call the privacy component (example scenario 1)

- *Motivation (Why):* How does the project, procedure, or process address issues concerning privacy that involves the authorized, fair, and legitimate processing of personal information?

- *Actors (Who):*

  - *Decision event actors:* Which parties of interest are making decisions and which decisions are made concerning personal information and information related to it?

  - *Decision event action actors:* Who is impacted by actions taken within the project, program, and process and how is their personal information impacted by the actions taken?

  - Privacy team, including legal advisor(s)

  - Data stewards

  - Business stakeholders

  - Developers

  - Data analysts

- *Events (When):*

  - Is a Privacy Notice needed? If so, who are the data subjects from whom personal information will be collected? How will personal information be used? Will personal information be shared within or outside the enterprise? How long will the data be kept?

  - Where is encryption needed?

  - What are the data archiving rules, especially related to personal information?

  - Which data, especially personal information and data related to it, are collected? How are these data protected? Is it proportional to the data need? How are the data to be processed? How will the data be backed up?

  - Will data, especially personal information and data related to it, be transferred to third parties? How will such data be protected? Are there jurisdictional issues concerning transfer?

- What are the authentication and authorization security rules? Are there any special rules due to personal information?

- *Behavior (How):*

  - When the system is invoked, authenticate the user and determine whether the role of user allows authorization.

  - Display the Privacy Notice, if needed or requested.

  - Collect only data, especially personal information or data related to it, proportional to need.

  - Allow maintenance of data, according to privacy principles and regulations.

  - Present data for use and for reporting reasons, according to privacy principles and regulations.

  - Archive data, according to privacy principles and regulations.

- *Data classes (What):*

  - Privacy Policy

  - Privacy rules

  - Role

  - Individual person

  - Organization

  - Data classes, as needed for the application that is covered by the project

- *Location (Where):*

  - Where are the users? Are there any jurisdictional problems?

  - Where are the data being processed? Are there any jurisdictional problems?

  - Where are the data being transferred? Are there any jurisdictional problems?

# USER EXPERIENCE REQUIREMENTS AND PRIVACY ENGINEERING REQUIREMENTS: MAKING THE TWO MESH

Privacy engineering requirements and decisions will inform, influence, create, and determine user experience requirements and vice versa. Therefore, it is important to review privacy engineering requirements from a user's experience perspective, as well as to review and understand the impact of user-interface design and user-experience requirements on privacy engineering, and in both cases resolve disparities where detected.

This issue extends from the idea of what is being engineered to the fine points of user-interface design and packaging and requires a high degree of interactivity between the engineering team and the user experience team.

The comparison starts with the notion of transparency. Will the user of the application, system, or process understand how and in what context his or her personal information will be used and processed?

One example is notice and choice. Decisions to collect and process certain types of data may require notice and consent. The question then becomes when such notice should be presented and how consent is collected. This is both an engineering issue and a user experience or design issue. What is easiest from an engineering perspective may not be best or the most satisfactory from a user experience or design point of view.

Another fair information factor is consideration of proportionality or relevancy. Are the data being requested from the user proportionate to the required use or truly relevant to the service being provided, or is the collection just opportunistic or assumptive? An example of this would be collecting geolocation information through a mapping app on a mobile device. It may be easiest from an engineering perspective to begin routing as soon as a destination is entered into the system. However, in reality, someone might be just looking to see where a street address is—not how to get there. If this is the case, then turning on and collecting location information from the device falls into the assumptive or opportunistic bucket, and it may be neither necessary nor relevant to the task being contemplated. Think how the issues might be seen differently if the button the user clicked to find the location of the address said "locate and route" and not "find"? Although the functionality is privacy engineering, the labeling of the buttons is user-experience design.

For this reason, it is important to review both privacy engineering requirements and how those requirements are being met from user-experience and user-interface perspective using such things as privacy policies, privacy governance frameworks, and common sense so that how a process, products, or system uses personal information does not come as a surprise to a user, is perceived as invasive or creepy, or creates an air of mistrust or uncertainty.

# Determining Data Requirements

As we will be discuss in more detail in Chapter 6, a business data model reflects the data requirements complementary to the use case. The model shows the items managed by the enterprise and the relationship between the classes and the data entities.

As an example, a high-level business model focusing on privacy (Figure 5-4) shows that more than one *privacy rule* may be derived from each *privacy policy* (the diamond icon in UML indicates an aggregation or one to many). Each of the various *roles* that a *party of interest* plays may have multiple *privacy rules*. In Chapter 6, the fact that detailed (logical) data models will be derived from the business data models and that the database will be designed from the detailed data model will be explained. In Chapter 7, the detailed class or data model derived from this privacy business data model will be shown and explained as the class or data model for the privacy component.

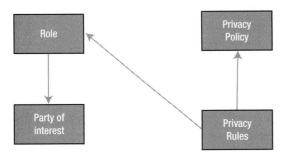

***Figure 5-4.*** *Privacy business data model*

# How Does the Distribution Channel Impact Privacy Engineering Requirements?

The privacy component may be an app within a mobile app, a web service invoked by a system, or a component object included within a database or cloud-utilizing system. The privacy component will be programmed with a programming language able to be run on a broad range of platforms. The privacy code will be encapsulated with an input/output interface that can be adapted to the file or database system on which the PII and the data related to it are stored. In this regard, the cloud has become a very significant distribution channel.

## Cloud Privacy Requirements

*Cloud computing* is the practice of using a network of remote servers hosted on the Internet to store, manage, and process data rather than a local server. There are a number of privacy issues in the cloud:

- How does the cloud provider handle encryption and encrypted data?

- Does our user have exclusive access to his or her data?

- Do our data get commingled with other people's data?

- Can our user access all of his or her data whenever needed?

- Does the cloud provider satisfy all compliance requirements including OEDC, FIPPS, and GAPP, specific statutory regulations for all jurisdictions or all enterprise privacy policies?

- Are data stored so as to be physically protected?

- Can data be transferred without the knowledge of the cloud provider?

- Are the laws of all relevant jurisdictions satisfied?

- Can our archiving strategies be enforced within the cloud?

- Can we be assured that appropriate data are deleted wherever they are stored so as not to be subject to a subpoena or a search warrant?

- Does the cloud provider mine the data that it stores for its own or someone else's purposes?

- Is the cloud provider fully auditable?

- Does the cloud provider provide breach notification according to our privacy policies as well as statutory requirements of all jurisdictions affected?

- Is the overall cloud provider security sufficient?

- Can a cloud provider provide data transfer capability and sufficient security to satisfy data transfer?

All relevant questions and the appropriate answers to each may be considered requirements and thus covered or implicated by privacy policies or other processing rules as well as business use cases. Privacy components may be designed for these environments at the cloud provider as well as the recipient of the cloud services following the privacy specific UML models and architectural approach. In this particular data use case, contractual, procedural, and additional roles at the organizational and individual levels may be considered and leveraged as part of the overall solution where, in a single organizational or single purpose cloud environment or structure, technology components may have sufficed alone. In other words, distributed computing techniques such as cloud computing may create additional modeling requirements, but the techniques underlying the premise of privacy engineering as a practice remain relevant and quite powerful.

# Conclusion

This chapter introduced *use cases* as a vehicle for defining and documenting overall requirements, including privacy requirements. This is a form of requirements engineering. We presented detailed use-case metadata, which answered the who, what, where, when, how, and why questions regarding the privacy component. We then covered user experience and distribution channel requirements. We began introducing the Unified Modeling Language (UML) Class Model showing a simple business data model. We will discuss use of the class model in chapters 6, 7, 8, and 9.

You might be concerned that this process is too time consuming or too difficult to accomplish, but if you develop your requirements, especially the privacy requirements, with care, you'll have a smoother development and testing process. You'll also be able to deal with auditors and regulators with much greater ease. Actually, the requirements process does not have to be time consuming or difficult, as we will show with our runner's app scenario in Chapter 8. Chapter 6 will discuss the Privacy Engineering Methodology.

■ ■ ■

# A Privacy Engineering Lifecycle Methodology

*"They always say time changes, but you actually have to change them yourself."*

—Andy Warhol

This chapter discusses a systems engineering methodology that can be adapted to privacy engineering. The methodology presented should be followed throughout development of a project for a privacy solution. It involves interactive models that provide pictorial documentation as well as business language use cases that together present requirements, analysis, design, and test cases in a readable form. The models work together to provide an understandable information and application architecture that satisfies business requirements, including, of course, privacy and security.

Executives may wish to glide through this chapter to get a feel how their teams work toward a project solution. Engineers, designers, and consultants will want to dig in deeper to perform their function more effectively.

The requirements use cases, the class model and supporting metadata, the user experience requirements, and any supporting requirements, as discussed in Chapter 5, are the basis for developing an architectural solution.

## Enterprise Architecture

This section discusses an enterprise architecture approach that actuates these requirements into an architectural solution. The privacy engineering methodology is based on concepts derived from enterprise architecture.

An enterprise has been defined as an association consisting of a recognized set of interacting functions that are able to operate as an independent, stand-alone entity. There are enterprises within enterprises. For instance, a business unit within the overall corporate entity may be considered an enterprise as long as it could be operated independently.

Architecture provides the underlying framework, which defines and describes the platform required by the enterprise to attain its objectives and achieve its business vision. Architecture is an amalgam of engineering art and engineering science; there is no single enterprise architecture. Instead, the overall architecture can be considered to consist of four interrelated architectures or architectural views (Figure 6-1).

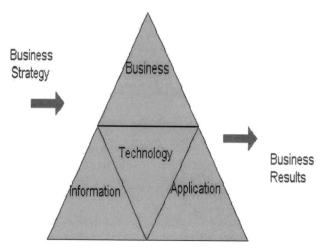

***Figure 6-1.*** *Enterprise architecture views*

# Architectural Views

The suggested architectural approach[1] envisions four architecture views: business, information, application, and technology architectures. These may contain levels of detail that are used to describe the elements of a privacy engineered architecture, but are not the processes themselves that will be built using these defined architectures.

In the privacy engineering methodology, the underlying architectural views have specific privacy opingcharacteristics:

- *Business architecture*: Models the business enterprise to show how business is to be done.[2] The use cases, activity diagrams, and supporting metadata documenting the business architecture privacy requirements are enterprise requirements that must be enforced.

- *Information architecture*: Enables the enterprise to develop a common, shared, distributed, accurate, and consistent data resource that is based on the various data models and supporting metadata. Some of the key factors in information architecture are privacy requirements. Data stewards[3] indicate that there are privacy requirements that need to be enforced based on their knowledge of the data for which they are responsible. This will take the form of a metadata indicator that shows that privacy rules need to be followed or that the data should be encrypted.

---

[1]The enterprise architecture section is based on two much-quoted papers: "Enterprise Architecture: What and Why" by Tom Finneran (www.tdan.com/i007ht03.htm) and "Enterprise Architecture: The What's And How's" by Tom Finneran (www.tdan.com/i018ht02.htm).
[2]Again, this is applicable to for-profit, nonprofit, and governmental enterprises.
[3]The privacy team will work with the data stewards to ensure that they are familiar with legal and enterprise privacy policies, procedures, and privacy rules.

- *Application architecture*: Links the information and business architectures to reflect applications and how they are used and distributed. The UML sequence diagram and the component diagram are application architecture documents. During the application architecture process, the architect determines whether to invoke privacy component rules or requirements from within the system or to use it as an app. The application architecture also reflects what privacy enabled technology (PET) components, if any, will be included in the design. PETs are discussed later in this chapter.

- *Technology architecture*: Links up with the application, business, and information architectures to provide interoperable technology platforms that meet the needs of the various user roles (actors) at identified work locations. In developing the technology architecture, decisions regarding which automated solutions can be employed and whether to build or buy them are made.

In addition to the four enterprise architecture views shown in Figure 6-1, there is another that can be considered.

- *User interface architecture*: Links up the information, business, application, and technology architectures with the user facing design and controls. The user interface architecture provides the user experience, as discussed in Chapter 5 and below. This type of architecture must provide a way to incorporate privacy requirements into the architecture and design of the user interface.

## Solution Architecture

The solution architecture (Figure 6-2) is developed from a system engineering methodology that consists of joining a user interface architecture design, information architecture (reflecting data modeling and big data analysis), and an application architecture. Thus, the privacy engineer can draw from a known engineering design and build techniques to add fair processing requirements and standards in a manner that is readily understood. The first new step on the journey to privacy innovation begins on a well-trodden path.

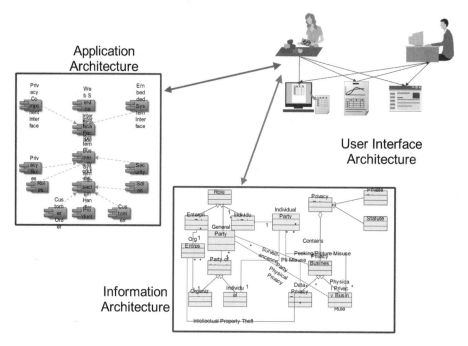

**Figure 6-2.** *Solution architecture*

Given the understanding of the business architecture, information architecture, and application architecture, the design team, including privacy engineering representatives, apply the appropriate technology architecture.

# Develop Procedures, Processes, and Mechanisms

Privacy policy development is discussed in Chapter 4 and requirements development in Chapter 5. This chapter describes the methodology used to develop privacy procedures, processes, and mechanisms, focusing primarily on the latter (Figure 6-3). Note that mandated standards and recommended guidelines based on privacy policies heavily influence the end solution.

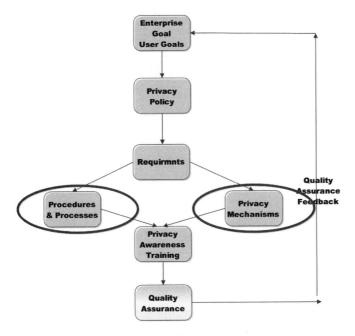

***Figure 6-3.*** *Privacy engineering development process*

# Methodology
## System Engineering Lifecycle

Although the focus of this chapter is development of automated privacy mechanisms, the creation of processes and procedures will follow the same system engineering lifecycle (Figure 6-4). The system engineering lifecycle is a methodology that has commonly been used for at least 30 years. Some of the terminology has varied but the concepts remain the same. The familiarity of the design methodology makes it an excellent known best practice to leverage when adding in privacy specific requirements that may not have been raised at early phases of requirements gathering, planning, designing, and execution at the technical level.

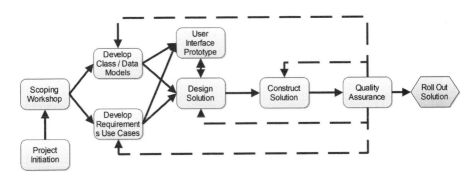

***Figure 6-4.*** *System engineering lifecycle*

The system engineering lifecycle is composed of six stages in which the project team adapts the tools and methods to the environment in which they are working:

1. The project initiation and scoping workshop stages look at policies and best practices surrounding the enterprise and the expected project or projects being considered (see Chapter 4).

2. The development of requirement use cases and class or data model states defines the enterprise and seeks to understand the business requirements sought to be addressed (see Chapter 5).

3. The solution design stage includes prototyping the user interface for the project.

4. The implementation stage includes solution construction.

5. The quality assurance stage includes testing and user acceptance.

6. The final stage is solution rollout.

The lifecycle, at first glance, seems to be a "waterfalls approach," where one step is completed and then handed off to the next step until the project comes to completion, but the dashed feedback lines in Figure 6-4 show that the process is actually iterative. Incremental improvements will be made to project deliverables throughout the lifecycle. This methodology has been combined with Agile techniques on many successful projects. (See the sidebar "Privacy Engineering and Agile Development" to understand how this approach and Agile techniques can be integrated.)

It should also be noted that inclusion of privacy principles in the technology and governance frameworks early and continuously through the system engineering lifecycle returns added important utility. The governance framework or policies must be updated or managed as policies change. The resultant systems will be better understood and documented.

## PRIVACY ENGINEERING AND AGILE DEVELOPMENT

Rich Schaefer - Director Technical Alliances, Good Technology

Various aspects of Agile development make it a very good fit for privacy engineering. A primary Agile tenet is to address customer needs by continually delivering working software that often must meet changing requirements. The customers for privacy engineering projects include internal and external stakeholders. Chapter 5 identified several actors present in use cases. The context diagrams in Chapters 7, 8, and 9 explicitly identify parties involved in the three scenarios. Notable are business stakeholders, especially the data stewards introduced in Chapter 3. As key members of the privacy team, they are both customers specifying privacy requirements and participants in development. The original Agile principles[4] include a requirement that businesspeople and developers work together on a *daily* basis. Data stewards are the embodiment of the need for this type of collaboration. Their responsibilities include working directly with data analysts and database designers to develop data models.

Collaboration is inherent to privacy engineering, bringing together a wide variety of experts from different disciplines within business, privacy, information technology, and development. Agile project management approaches such as scrum can be used to bring effectiveness to such diverse teams. Agile scrums are mentioned as a best practice for coordinating privacy teams and their stakeholders to create and review metadata models in this chapter. Additionally, scrum meetings and sprints allow for timely adaptability to change. The need for flexibility to change is a recurring theme throughout this text. Privacy requirements can change due to factors external to the enterprise, including legal, consumer, and regulatory reasons. Within the enterprise, new business objectives, requirements, practices, and technology uses can have effects as well. Privacy engineering teams and their projects must be able to incorporate new requirements at nearly any point in their schedules. Agile processes enable the teams to prioritize changing requirements and even exploit such change for customer benefit.

The incremental delivery of working software via Agile sprints not only tries to guarantee that customers or their representatives receive what they desire, but also gives the opportunity for ensuring quality as the project progresses.[5] Regression testing at the end of each sprint may detect flaws that can be fixed within the following sprint(s). This practice avoids a shortcoming of traditional software approaches where quality assurance teams perform regression testing after development is completed and bugs are most costly to fix.

Given the general discussion above, one may ask how Agile engineering practices relate specifically to the formal techniques espoused in this text and depicted in the system engineering lifecycle (Figure 6-4). Use cases were introduced in Chapter 5 as the foundation for developing requirements for the system. They describe the needs of a user or actor and their answers to why, who, when, what, where, and how in describing the interaction within the system. Use cases can be seen as an agreement between customers and the development team.[6] Sufficient detail is provided for developers to understand what is required by the system and to embark on design.

*User stories* are a tool originating from the extreme programming (XP) Agile community for describing user needs and the planning of releases and iterations (their version sprints). Each consists of a few sentences, written in language a

---

[4]"Manifesto for Agile Software Development" at Agilemanifesto.org.

[5]The prototyping approach in this chapter is an example of incremental development.

[6]In fact, as mentioned in this chapter, first-cut use cases can be written by business users, with scrum interactions and a scrum review. This is not merely theory but fact at a major telecommunication company. These first-cut use cases could be considered user stories.

user could understand, expressing a single user's need representing an amount of work small enough to be reasonably well estimated. They serve as the basis for conversations with customers to flesh out more detail. Hence, use cases and user stories serve somewhat different purposes. However, accompanying user stories are acceptance criteria or tests that describe the conditions for their correct implementation. It has been noted that use cases and user stories plus their acceptance criteria are essentially equivalent. For much deeper comparison of use cases and user stories, see "Use cases vs. user stories in Agile development."[7]

UML models, also introduced in Chapter 5 for class and data models, give structure to the solution being developed throughout the system engineering lifecycle and provide an explicit communication tool among internal and external stakeholders. They have been applied for large enterprise teams and complex projects that have formal modeling methodology and documentation requirements. The Agile Manifesto values the interaction of individuals and working software over tools and comprehensive documentation. This apparently less formal approach has often led to the attitude that Agile methods are better suited to smaller projects and will not scale. However, significantly sized projects are referenced by Kent Beck (40 person-years)[8] and Scott Ambler (several hundred person-years).[9] Additionally, Agile modeling for scaling has been advocated by the latter, the developer of "Agile Model-Driven Development" based on Agile principles from XP.[10]

Agile proponents have had mixed reactions to the use of UML. Some say the practices within Agile development user stories and acceptance criteria supplant the need for UML. The most positive seems to be that UML should be used to work through specific issues where it is useful rather than in an end-to-end, comprehensive fashion. Martin Fowler's often-quoted article "Is Design Dead?"[11] discusses traditional planned design vs. evolutionary design employed by XP. He includes recommendations for the use of UML diagrams alongside "Class-Responsibility-Collaboration" cards typically used in XP. He emphasizes their use is for communication and can be used effectively for design exploration and documentation.[12]

---

[7]"Use Cases vs. User Stories in Agile Development" and the links within this article at www.boost.co.nz/blog/agile/use-cases-or-user-stories/.

[8]Kent Beck, "Test-Driven Development: By Example" (www.eecs.yorku.ca/course_archive/2003-04/W/3311/sectionM/case_studies/money/KentBeck_TDD_byexample.pdf).

[9]At a large-information-provider-over-200-person project, we used a combination of Agile and the UML-based approach discussed in this chapter. Chapter 9 is another example; well over 100 people were involved. Compare Chapter 8, where an intergenerational scrum was used along with UML modeling.

[10]"Agile Model Driven Development: The Key to Scaling Agile Software Development" at www.agilemodeling.com/essays/amdd.htm.

[11]"Is Design Dead?" at http://martinfowler.com/articles/designDead.html.

[12]The modeling, using UML, proposed throughout Part 2 of this book, is most effective where scrum-like modeling sessions and model review sessions, modelers, data stewards, privacy team, and other business stakeholders are held. In fact scrums have been used for good modeling before Agile and scrum terminology was being used.

Later in this chapter, creation of test cases from UML diagrams is described. A potential use of modeling, UML based or otherwise, has been proposed for the generation of test cases for tests-as-specification or test-driven development (TDD), a technique from XP.[13] TDD is iterative and proceeds by writing tests first and then developing code to pass the test. It produces simple code and is followed by continual refactoring or restructuring to avoid complexity and increase maintainability. TDD alone could be a good development process to employ in privacy engineering, because policy rules (e.g., in the privacy component) could be embedded in the tests driving the development and acceptance tests.

The software engineering lifecycle can incorporate either the formal use case or UML-based methodology in the text, employ Agile process management (e.g., scrum), use Agile engineering practices (e.g., from XP), or possibly a combination of these.

## The Use of Models within the Methodology

The methodology utilizes a series of interrelated UML models, as shown in Figure 6-5.

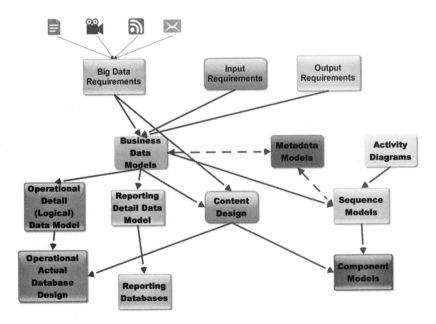

***Figure 6-5.*** *Architectural model relationships*

[13]"Modeling in an Agile World" at www.nyu.edu/classes/jcf/CSCI-GA.2440-001/handouts/ modellinginanagileworld.pdf.

Models and modeling best practices[14] focus first on the progression from an enterprise view of the business data model, through the more detailed logical data model, and finally to a database design based on these models. Likewise, from the business data model, a reporting model is derived for the reporting database.

*Requirements models*: Input and output data requirements gathered from a system interface, from a web site, or from a mobile source, together with the big data requirements must be modeled within the business data model, here using the UML class modeling diagram.[15] Figure 6-5 shows how the need for information from a document, from a video, from an audio file, from an e-mail, or from any other big data source comes together as big data requirements.

*Business data model*: The business data model is an integrated view of all of the data requirements within the enterprise. The business data model contains business-level (not necessarily normalized[16]) data classes. It may contain many-to-many data relationships and may not contain information about the optionality of data relationships. It should contain all super-type data classes but not necessarily all subtype data classes.[17] It will contain only those data attributes that are easy to find and define that are particularly interesting or important. It will refer to corporate data classes and relationships where possible and will raise data issues and ambiguities early.

*Operational (logical) data model*: The logical data model (see Figure 6-9 as an example) should contain all of the business data requirements within the problem domain under study (here, privacy information data processing). The conceptual data model subject areas, high-level data classes, and high-level relationships are used as the starting point for developing the logical data model. More detailed data classes are developed as well as data classes, which are the product of normalization. Subtype classes will also be derived from the high-level business data classes.

---

[14]See *Handbook of Relational Database Design* by B. Van Halle & C. Fleming (Addison Wesley, 1989), pp. 18–24; *Data Base Management* by F. McFadden and J. Hoffer (Benjamin Cummings Publishing, 1985), pp. 272–299; "The Bottom Line: Data-oriented Deliverables," by T. R. Finneran, in *Handbook of Data Management* (Auerbach Press, 1993), pp. 289–298.

[15]Other data modeling tools can be used. We recommend UML so that you can use one consistent toolset throughout the whole lifecycle.

[16]Normalization is a well-known data analysis process of organizing the data attributes to minimize redundancy and inconsistency. The business classes will not contain all of the data attributes and therefore normalization is not applicable. The logical data model will use normalization.

[17]Classes can be arranged in hierarchies so that concrete classes (subtypes such as persons or organizations) inherit attributes, relationships, and operations or methods from more abstract classes (super-types such as parties of interest).

The logical data model is different from the less-detailed business data model in that the former is normalized and does not contain many-to-many data relationships. Instead, it contains information about the optionality of data relationships and contains both super-type data classes and subtype data classes. It contains all data attributes relevant to the enterprise and refers to corporate data classes and relationships as much as possible.

As part of the data modeling process, the enterprise data model as well as legacy databases not represented in the enterprise data model will be examined to ensure that redundant data are not created and that the enterprise data models are complete.

*Operational database*: The detailed operational data model is used to develop the actual operational database. The reporting data models are used to develop the reporting databases, which could be the data warehouse, one or more data marts, or one or more big data analytic data structures. Big data requirements may also contribute to any required content handling or presentation.

*Metadata models*: All modeling metadata are based on a series of metadata models.[18] To ensure that models and modeling best support the corporate enterprise, best privacy engineering practices require that all models and modeling metadata be readily available to business users and to information technology personnel. All data administrators and database administrators should collaborate to ensure an enterprise view of all information required by the enterprise and to ensure that the best practices concerning shared data are followed.[19]

Best practices that support data sharing include data naming and data identification standards, the collection of integrity rules, the collection of security rules, and management of information in all of its forms. One way that works well in gaining collaboration among businesspeople, the privacy team, and the information technology development team is to hold Agile scrums. These scrums are often called first thing in the morning for the very detail-oriented people. Management scrums would be held weekly in some cases and biweekly in others.

---

[18]More than 20 metadata models comprise the database design of a typical metadata repository. Appendix A shows data attributes of some of these models.

[19]It must be noted that such collaboration does not require the mythical, monolithic data mapping and classification exercise of old where millions of dollars were expended, and consultants were sent swarming across the enterprise to arrive—perhaps—with a set of already outdated binders of data. Instead, data privacy principles define privacy information and a common understanding of how and where and by whom those data may be processed becomes a discovery methodology to evaluate existing data patterns.

*Activity diagram, sequence model, and component model*: The activity diagram showing the business process combines with the various data models to define a sequence within the system and then to the component design. The component design model and supporting metadata will contribute to the component design. Therefore, the various models and modeling efforts interact to provide a well-engineered, data-centric design.

*Content Design*: The user experience of the system and its user interface are based on the content design that takes inputs from the visualization aspects of the big data requirements and the business data model. The content design also impacts the actual operational database design and the component models by determining how users interact with them.

The steps of the methodology are described in detail in the following sections to illustrate how the system engineering lifecycle applied to privacy is effectively deployed.

## INNOVATING WITH PRIVACY STANDARDS

By Dawn N. Jutla, PhD, Board Director, OASIS, and Professor, Sobey School of Business, Saint Mary's University, Halifax, Nova Scotia, Canada

Consumer and privacy legislators are working to understand new online business environments that exploit personal data outside of citizens' working knowledge and control. The Office of the Privacy Commissioner of Canada, the 27 different data protection agencies in the European Union, the US Federal Trade Commission, and senators in the US Congress now regularly question major innovators about their business practices concerning their handling of personal data. Associations such as the Electronic Frontiers Foundation and the Electronic Privacy Information Center also regularly highlight new online privacy violations. Media reports openly criticize marketers, raising awareness of personal data collection practices, as in the *Wall Street Journal's* "What They Know Series": "Marketers are spying on Internet users—observing and remembering people's clicks, and building and selling detailed dossiers of their activities and interests."[20] VentureBeat, a technology news website, identifies a key privacy issue:

The fact of the matter is that most end users are ignorant of how much they expose about themselves when they authorize through Facebook or Twitter or any other sign-on process—and that this information would be shared to entities outside just the app developer.[21]

---

[20]"What They Know" (November 25, 2013). *Wall Street Journal*. Retrieved from http://blogs.wsj.com/wtk/.

[21]I. Mosquera (August 27, 2011). "Why Mobile Apps Need to Have Privacy Policies." *VentureBeat*. Retrieved from http://venturebeat.com/2011/08/27/why-mobile-apps-need-to-have-privacy-policies/.

To respond to this situation, can companies integrate privacy standards into Internet products and services to achieve an online environment that both protects privacy (as with user-permission-based models) and allows for commerce? OASIS (Organization for the Advancement of Structured Information Standards) is a leader in the Internet identity management and trust elevation standards space. Its OASIS Privacy Management Reference Model and Methodology[22] (PMRM) Technical Committee (TC) has created a committee specification draft as a standards track product.

The advantages of privacy standards are manifold. They include building a common and widespread understanding of privacy governance among adopting organizations at an international level and creating consistent compliance, auditing criteria, and user expectations across industries. Privacy standards can promote better system design, facilitate information interchange and interoperability, and foster innovation through multi-stakeholder collaboration. Some organizations may leverage the resulting privacy-enhanced products and services for market differentiation.

However, people don't usually think of standards as vehicles of innovation, even though numerous examples exist of new standards leading to new markets and technologies. Rather, standards are sometimes seen as the outcome of long political processes that are way too slow for young Internet innovators. These same innovators are busy with the newest commercial technologies, such as Big Data plays, the emerging Internet of Things, and attendant new business models focused on aggregating, interlinking, and monetizing personal data. Meanwhile, the tension between these new business models and the user's privacy rights is increasing with each passing day. Indeed, there is a growing sense among experts that many Internet companies, renowned for innovation and high levels of experimentation with new services, are not well versed in best practices for privacy governance. These relatively young companies, and many others, would benefit from more comprehensive privacy governance guidelines from the executive to the unit software testing levels. Here is where the patient process of standards can pay off to play a catalyst role in spurring responsible innovation and competitive advantage for many.

Upcoming privacy standards should foster another entire level of protection for consumer rights, as well. Privacy consultants praise the OASIS PMRM standards-track specification for codifying the processes for specifying privacy requirements. One excitedly said, ". . . it's better than the ad-hoc processes that are in my head. Now I have an explicit reference methodology that my clients are willing to invest in."

Certainly, the PMRM is valuable for its step-by-step guidelines and clear and concise identification of privacy domains, controls, and critical touch points—or leakage points—through which data flow. Privacy stewards and other stakeholders may use the PMRM to create a privacy management analysis for use cases. PMRM's methodology

---

[22]Privacy Management Reference Model and Methodology (PMRM), Ver. 1.0, March 2012, OASIS Committee Specification Draft. Retrieved from http://docs.oasis-open.org/pmrm/PMRM/v1.0/csd01/PMRM-v1.0-csd01.pdf.

extends to helping software engineers understand complex privacy requirements inherent in today's collaborative web-based systems. Indeed, stakeholders can use the methodology to perform thorough privacy management analyses in a wide variety of contexts, from executive management to unit-level software testing for privacy compliance.

Focusing entirely on the software engineering space is the work of an even newer standards committee, the OASIS Privacy-by-Design Documentation for Software Engineers Technical Committee[23] (PbD-SE TC), which I convened and co-chair with Dr. Ann Cavoukian, the founder of Privacy by Design, and Ontario's Information and Privacy Commissioner. The PbD-SE TC members are collaborating on a future standard that will help software engineers visualize privacy requirements and operationalize Privacy by Design principles. As a first step, the PbD-SE TC has accepted the PMRM specification to help organizations create use cases that embed privacy requirements as functional requirements. In addition, this TC is currently debating a new hybrid method of using software engineering modeling languages and spreadsheets to represent integrated privacy requirements in tabular and diagrammatic forms. Together, these approaches represent richer privacy models for our increasingly socially responsible software engineers.

As shown in this timely book, professional software engineers in industry use Unified Modeling Language (UML) diagram models for sharing vision, giving visual representations of (sub)-systems, influencing code generation, and documenting software requirements and design. The Object Management Group (OMG)'s UML is an International Standards Organization (ISO) software engineering industry modeling standard. Because of UML's ubiquity, OASIS PbD-SE leverages UML and may offer new extensions to it to support privacy.

Software engineers use UML to understand and collaborate on building software. UML abstracts away confusing details and allows software developers to more easily examine a system's behavior, data, and process models more quickly compared to textual documentation. However, while UML is a commonly used communications medium, it has different degrees of adoption and use. For some large systems, UML use may be quite formal, while for users of agile methodologies, software engineers may sketch out a quick UML-like diagram that allows them to share and easily refer to requirements and design. Today, requirements analysis takes up the largest proportion of time in agile software engineering efforts. Any aid in reducing the amount of time an engineer spends in understanding and embedding privacy requirements is a bonus for productivity. Hence, the work of the OASIS PbD-SE is positioned to provide such a productivity boost to the field.

---

[23]OASIS Privacy by Design Documentation Technical Committee (PbD-SE) Charter. Retrieved from www.oasis-open.org/committees/pbd-se/charter.php.

In summary, organizations participating in online privacy standardization efforts today provide valuable leadership in shaping tomorrow's privacy-preserving societies. Software engineers, from business analysts and software developers to unit testers, can use the current OASIS PMRM 2013 committee specification draft and the OASIS PbD-SE standards-track approaches to promote high quality privacy engineering and responsible governance.

Author's Note: The Privacy Engineering methodology described in this book is based on a system's engineering methodology used for over 30 years and therefore developed independently from PMRM and PbD, but when we reviewed these approaches, we found that privacy engineering is consistent with these approaches. We have been using UML from its early days. When Jonathan and Michelle presented their privacy assessment approach, we adapted it to UML using existing UML icons without extending UML. Dr. Jutla will be reviewing our proposed approaches as part of the OASIS PbD-SE TC analysis.

# Stage 1: Project Initiation and Scoping Workshop
## Project Initiation Defines Project Processes

During project initiation, the project team will develop project mechanisms for:

- Developing a first-cut project plan, including a statement of project objectives and scope. It should also include project tasks, resource roles, task start date and duration, and task dependencies.

- Defining the method for monitoring milestone deliverables.

- Reporting project status, including reporting period accomplishments, next period plans, problems or issues, and suggestions.

- Managing change or service requests.

- Release to management.

Change management is critical to the success of a project and must be fully formalized, approved, and promulgated via service requests. The change management process should be tracked and documented from the receipt of the first service request to the final implementation. Service requests should:

- Trigger all system development activities

- Be made for all scope changes that could affect a project's objectives

- Be made for all scope changes that will affect a deliverable's completion date

- Be analyzed in regard to impact of the project on the entire enterprise

- Have a measurable business benefit stated

Release management should provide a formal process for authorizing the movement from development and test into the production environment. Changes should be scheduled as releases, as much as possible, and the scope of next releases should be made available to all interested parties. The following steps should be performed:

- *Track problems and issues*: Issue number, related project, task problem or issue description, responsible team member, date reported, resolution, date closed, status, priority, reported by whom

- *Hold analysis, design, and development walkthroughs*: Management and technical team

- *Measure success and design metrics*: Process engineering metrics (mean time to failure, repair, and extend), deliverables delivered, resources to deliver

- Obtain user signoff on preagreed to measure of success

# Requirements Definition Within the Scoping Workshop

*To win a race, the s wiftness of a dart availeth not without a timely start.*[24]

Fred Brook's classic article "The Mythical Man Month" begins with the following profound observation: "More software projects have gone awry for lack of calendar time than for all other causes combined. Therefore it is important to get a project off to a running start."[25]

John Zachman has stated that the beginning phase of any project is scoping objectives.[26] During the first week of any project, a scoping workshop is in order, during which a variety of business users, the privacy team, and information technology (IT) participants meet, preferably out of the office, to develop a project mission statement. A mixture of user executives, managers, the privacy team, and workers along with knowledgeable IT persons works best, but a less diverse group will be successful as long as the participants understand the business. The scoping workshop participants then develop a context diagram (see examples in Chapters 7, 8, and 9) that shows the suppliers and recipients of information from the engineered solution.

---

[24]Jean de La Fontaine, 1621-1695, *Fables* as quoted in L. D Eigen and J. P Siegel, *The Manager's Book of Quotations* (AMACOM, 1991).

[25]F. B. Brooks, Jr., *The Mythical Man-Month* (Addison-Wesley Publishing Company, 1975), p. 14.

[26]J. A. Zachman, "A Framework for Information Systems Architecture," in *Handbook of Data Management* (Boston: Auerbach Publications, Warren Gorham Lamont, 1993), pp. 3–22.

Next, the scoping session identifies major business classes, major business events, major business processes, major business rules, and major business objectives.

The participants then review and set study priorities on major business events, processes, or business classes. Typically, the events, processes, or business classes will be designated either as being a primary focus item, a secondary focus item, or out of scope. For primary and secondary focus items, stakeholders and subject matter experts are identified. The stakeholders and subject matter experts will be use case participants, those interviewed, or both.

## Scoping Deliverables

The following deliverable may be developed[27] from the scoping workshop:

- List of business drivers
- Scoping mission statement
- Context diagram
- List of context actors
- List of actor locations
- List of triggering events
- List of information flows
- List of business classes
- List of business processes
- Potential privacy requirements
- Use case schedule using identified subject matter experts

# Stage 2: Develop Use Cases and Class or Data Models

Chapter 5 discussed use cases in detail. This is the step in the methodology where use cases should be developed. In the following chapters, other use case examples are presented.

## Develop Business Activity Diagrams

The business activity diagram in Figure 6-6 shows the events and processes and decision making between the various business processes involved in supporting vacation planning (Chapter 9 discusses the vacation planner example in scenario 3).

---

[27]These things come to the surface during the scoping workshop and may or may not be formally documented depending upon the time available.

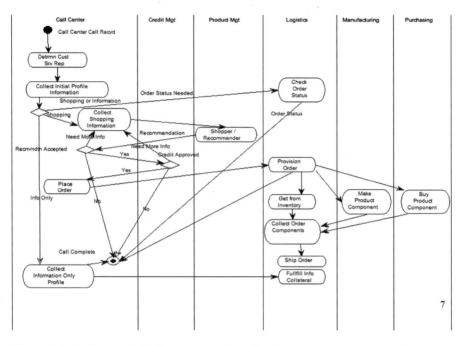

*Figure 6-6.* *Business activity diagram: vacation planning*

## Using the Business Activity Diagram for Privacy Assessment

Some privacy professionals have proposed using the business activity diagram as part of the privacy requirements assessment. The privacy team works with business stakeholders, including data stewards, to identify key data attributes, especially identifiers, within the business processes and decisions, as represented in Figure 6-7. Privacy rules will be developed for these and other attributes as found and entered in the metadata.

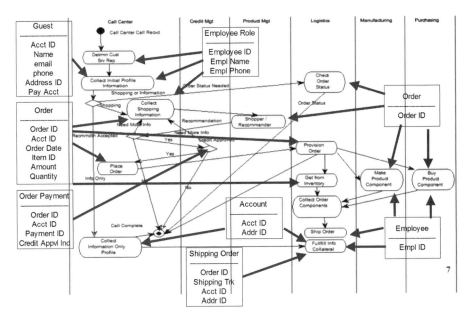

***Figure 6-7.*** *Business activity diagram with key data attributes*

# Defining Business and Privacy Data Classes

A *class* is a person, place, thing, concept, or event deemed to be of significance to an enterprise. Classes deal with attributes, behaviors, and message passing. A class has a name and a definition of its purpose and it has knowledge properties ("Data") and action properties ("Event Handlers and Processes").

Data classes can also be persons, places, things, concepts, or events of interest to the enterprise. Both class and data modeling approaches look at classes of things and how they are related to each other. During the business-level (conceptual) stage, methods (action properties) are not defined and the class model and data model may be congruent.

Where data required are contained within a document, such as a graphic, an audio input, web site content, something from e-mail, or from any other big data source, the data may be either processed as an object reflected in the data model as a data block or the data may be extracted within the program and stored as a data entity or data table. A data block shows the data attributes of the data class and would be processed using a NoSQL or a Hadoop system component. The scenario 3 vacation planner data model (in Chapter 9) shows an example of a big data data block within the data model.

The business data requirements are, perhaps, the most important requirements to be evaluated. If data are available in the database, a query can be developed to access it. If required data are not there, then significant customization is required. Business data modeling leads to a strong, well-designed, and flexible database.

Use cases identify classes and data attributes within the class. Class and data modeling support use case analysis. Class and class relationships are represented as UML class diagrams. Data and data relationships are represented as entity relationship diagrams.[28] Metadata document all aspects of class and data modeling. Data-oriented business and privacy rules are documented as metadata. (See Appendix A for examples of data-oriented metadata.)

## Using the Unified Modeling Language Class Model as a Data Model

The class model, much like a data model, shows the information we manage and the relationships among the various classes. A data model reflects the data requirements and is the basis for the design of the database used to support the system meeting these requirements.[29] Each data item can have rules, identifiers, and universal truths that will become tables and columns within a database or otherwise processable data structure. These are the "things" we manage—policies, rules, people roles—when they turn into software or hardware. For consistency throughout the methodology, the UML class model is used for the data model.

One example class model is the party of interest model, which can be any individual or organization that is of interest to any enterprise. Figure 6-8 shows a more detailed piece of the class model that would be developed. The party of interest would have a uniqueness identification number, name, primary address, ZIP code, and primary telephone number. The relationship lines[30] indicate that persons and organizations are the most common types of party of interest and inherit the data attributes and the operational attributes (often referred to as methods). So person would have the attributes of party of interest as well as its own attributes. It would also have create, read, update, deactivate, and archive methods available.

---

[28]We use the UML class models for both class and data modeling. See the example below.
[29]We discuss a database here because it is in common use, but data models may be used in designing other data structures. Even in the case of unstructured data, data modeling helps organize the data elements extracted from the unstructured data into a "big data" data block. In the *Trillions* book (**Trillions: Thriving in the Emerging Information Ecology** by Peter Lucas, Joe Ballay, MickeyMcManus Wiley Press (2012)), the authors describe data storage containers that will implement a so-called internet of things. Understanding the various data entities, and the relationships of other data entities to it, is a condition precedent for the successful use of data.
[30]The arrow-like icon on the relationship lines indicates that there is an inheritance relationship between the super-type party of interest and the subtypes individual person and organization.

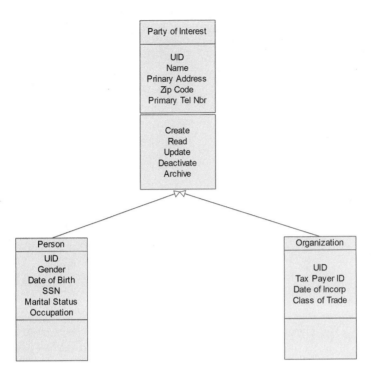

***Figure 6-8.*** *Detail class model*

## Example: Privacy Component Class Model

The party of interest is a class of the privacy component class model. Figure 6-9
shows *classes* that represent thing                by the enterprise and the data privacy
requirements. Each class represe                        hing, concept, or event deemed
to be of significance to an enter                              on realm. Classes deal with
attributes, behavior, and mess                                and a definition of its
purpose and other attributes                              ass. This class model will be
described in more depth in (

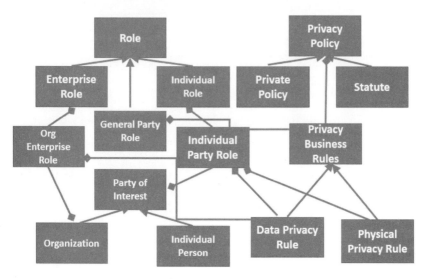

*Figure 6-9.* *Privacy component class model*

## Data Modeling Steps

The following data modeling steps should be performed:

1. Identify major classes

2. Identify big data requirements (documents, videos, audios, web downloads, e-mails)

   a. Find where the useful data are located. In the case of big data, the same data may be scattered within and across different sources.

   b. Determine how to pull the data into a "single source of the truth" to consolidate, cleanse, and centralize the data.

3. Identify one or more data block(s) in which data attributes should be placed (e.g., a vacation plan data block in the scenario 3 vacation planner data model in Chapter 9).

4. Identify attributes of each class and big data data blocks

5. Determine relationships between classes and data blocks

6. Identify uniqueness identifiers (part of data modeling)

7. Validate classes through normalization and big data analysis

8. Attach business and privacy rules to classes, data blocks, data relationships, or data attributes

9. Integrate with existing class and data models

10. Analyze for stability and growth

11. Record in a metadata repository throughout process

# Stage 3: Design an Engineered Solution

Once the analysis of business requirements has been completed, the project team works with the system developers to support the design of system solutions. The team will perform the activities in the following checklist, some of which are described in more detail in the following sections:

- Recommend redesign of business processes, where needed: Existing business processes that need to be revised and improved

- Define automation boundaries: Which business processes can be automated by technology and which processes are administrative

- Develop and utilize the system activity diagrams

- Expand system use cases and class models and supporting metadata

- Design the operational and reporting databases and big data analytics, from logical class or data model and expanded data models, including big data data blocks

- Perform dynamic modeling

- Define service components and supporting metadata, including big data handling components

- Perform system evaluation and prototyping (as needed)

- Define design units based on use cases

- Design presentation layer (user interface), including any content handling or presentation

- Perform development and proof of concept prototyping (if needed)

- Design batch program modules

- Finalize the solution (application and technology) architecture

# User Interface Design
## Basic User Interface Design Steps

There are several user interface (UI) design best practices that should be followed:

1. Understand your users' requirements:

   a. What are they trying to accomplish?

   b. How experienced are the users?

   c. What interfaces are they used to?

   d. What data attributes to be collected or reported upon require special privacy rules?

2. Use UI patterns that are as familiar as possible to the users.

3. Recognize a data hierarchy. For instance, an order with descriptive information about the order and one or more items should be shown as the order description with a list of clickable items that, when clicked on, will give a description of the selected item.

4. Interact with the user:

   a. Be as self-descriptive as possible

   b. Provide feedback

   c. Help users and forgive mistakes

   d. As the user becomes more used to the system, allow the user to select a more powerful, sophisticated interface

   e. Keep interactions conversational

   f. KISS (Keep It Simple, Stupid)

## Mapping Business Class Objects to System and Technology Objects

The UI can be designed by mapping the business class objects to the system and technology objects.

There are various types of business class objects

- *Elemental business object:*[31] Class and related components and relationships

- *Complex business class object:*[32] User view and related components and relationships, including big data object.

- *Atomic business object:* Data attribute and related components and relationships

System objects are business objects viewed from a system's perspective. There are various types of system objects:

- *Elemental presentation objects:* Forms, lists, reports, or graphics of elemental business objects

- *Complex presentation objects:* Forms, lists, reports, or graphics of complex business objects, including privacy notices

- *Action selection mechanisms (controls):* Icons, pop-up or pull-down menus, pop-up or pull-down lists, action buttons, radio groups

- *Specific functional object modules:* Ad hoc reports and queries, security, configuration management, privacy notice presentation mechanisms, and consent mechanisms (opt-in or opt-out).

# User Interface Prototype

A crucial part of rapid application design and development is development prototyping, which is performed by the development team, consisting of IT personnel and business personnel. At the minimum there should be a team leader, prototype developers, and a modeler, along with representative business knowledge workers. In the case of a privacy-related project, the privacy team should be represented. It cannot be overstated how important the role of a great user interface designer who is skilled in aesthetic, functional, and technical aspects of user based interfaces can be. Because privacy engineering is relatively new and certainly rarely practiced, the more user centric and less opaque or "creepy" intrusive the interface, the more acceptable and the more data or person centric the system end product will be.

Larger functional areas will require more people. Starting with the demonstration (analysis) prototype, the online system is developed interactively with the business knowledge workers, along with further reports and functionality invoked by means of the system's presentation layer. Analysis and development prototyping are similar in

---

[31]Elemental objects or classes may be considered analogous to data classes. Elemental objects are analyzed utilizing an approach called "fact-based normalization."
[32]Complex objects are objects comprising or using information from more than one elemental object.

method. Development prototyping is more design-oriented and, thus, more detailed. The development prototyping deliverables are:

- A working prototype of the online application system

- A portion of the system design

- Detailed information required to transform the logical data model and the system use cases into the implementation system and the implementation database

## Prototyping Caveats

Prototyping is inherent in the design approach described previously. However, no matter how good the development team's efforts are and no matter how good the prototype looks and acts, *the prototype is NOT the production system.*

- The team does not take time to tune the prototype for performance.

- Entity and referential integrity protection may not be completely developed.

- Although some of the security features may be developed in order to demonstrate how security might work, the security system, especially security administration, will not be completely developed.

- Although some of the help screens may be geared toward the business knowledge workers, the help system and screens will not be complete.

- Although the most important exception processing will be developed and demonstrated to the business knowledge workers, not all exception processing will be completed.

- Some of the system administration functionality, especially crucial reference tables, will be designed and geared toward the business knowledge workers, but not all system administration will be completed.

- Some stress testing experiments will be carried out in regard to the server and the network as a part of proof of concept prototyping. The remainder of stress testing will take place once production development is completed.

# Component Design
## What Is Component Architecture?

A component architecture[33] is a representation of the underlying set of interrelated components that define and describe the solution domain required by the business to attain its objectives and achieve its business vision.

---

### COMPONENT ARCHITECTURE HISTORY

By Tom Finneran

In this book, we propose using a component architecture approach. There might be some concern that designers might try a noncomponent architecture approach. However, one might make the case that all programmers make use of components and component architecture.

From the beginning of computer programming, we programmer designers have grouped our code into modules or subroutines. We might have an input code module, a process module, and an output module. In the 1830s, Ada Byron Loveless, studying the Babbage Differencing Engine, developed an algorithm for calculating a sequence of Bernoulli numbers. The algorithm contained an input module, a processing of the numbers module, and a resulting list of numbers. Even back then, we can consider the modules a type of component, and Ada's approach was an early form of component architecture.

---

A component is a self-contained, reusable building block that can be used independently or assembled with other components to satisfy software requirements. A component handles a specific event, or related set of events, and provides a particular function or group of related functions through a well-defined and stable interface. All components consist of one or more component interfaces, component decision event handlers, and component behavior activators. The component interface may send or receive data from a file or may be a user interface. The decision event handler utilizes business rules to determine which component behavior should be activated.

It is important to understand that from the beginning of computer programming some form of component identification and architecting was done, although the terminology was developed later. Things like routines, subroutines, macros, and subsystems can be considered forms of a component.

---

[33]See "A Component-Based Knowledge Management System" by Thomas R. Finneran at www.tdan.com/i009hy04.htm.

## INVENTION METHODOLOGY

By Tom Finneran

I was approached by a team of engineers who had an invention idea. It was a network interface card (NIC) based on a standard network protocol that would greatly increase the power of a local area network (LAN). We started with a scoping workshop, as discussed above. We then worked up a set of use cases and then developed a component architecture, based on the component architecture metadata model. This gave us an engineering spec from which we could designed both the card and supporting software, but also having engineering documentation, which made a favorable impression on the companies to which we were presenting our invention. The documentation was mapped right on to the patent application, including the patent claims, which are the basis for any patent.

So the methodology led to a hardware/software solution and a very straightforward patent approval process. See Patent #60/029,902.

# Example: Privacy Component

We can understand how the privacy component, or any component, might work by interpreting the component metadata model (Figure 6-10). The privacy component may be embedded in a system or as a mobile app or web service or program subroutine. It may invoke a more broad-based system in the Cloud.

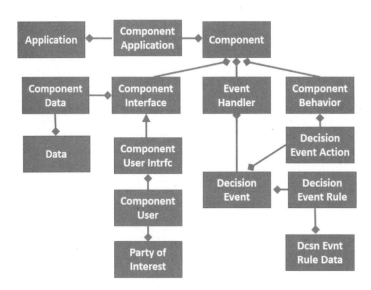

***Figure 6-10.*** *Component metadata model*

The component interface may utilize a database based on a data model and, in most cases, it may utilize the database for the system it is embedded within (e.g., the simplified customer order data model in scenario 3 in Chapter 9). The component interface may also have a user interface for interacting with the actors shown in a context diagram.

The component event handler will process the events listed as the triggering events in the use case requirements (see Chapter 5). Each event implies one or more decision to be made. For instance, the UI will ask the user if he or she wishes to see the Privacy Notice.[34] When the user answers, an affirmative answer invokes one set of privacy rules and a negative answer invokes another set of privacy rules. Thus, each event triggers one or more decisions, and each decision requires a set of privacy rules as the criteria for making the decision. Each decision will then invoke a process or behavior that may trigger another event, and its decision sets or may invoke another behavior, all in accordance with the business rules. Each of the rules may require access to a database related to the component.

## Privacy Rules

A *privacy rule* is a type of business rule. A *business rule* is a written statement in natural language that functions as a communication tool to express a rule, decision criteria, or a policy common practice as a statement that relates to a decision involving business information or business processes. A business rule is represented as an IF . . . THEN . . . ELSE pattern.

For example, IF Privacy Notice is clicked THEN invoke Privacy Notice routine ELSE check user role routine. These privacy rules will be derived from the privacy policies and the privacy procedures, standards, and guidelines as discussed herein.

## Develop a System Activity Diagram

A system activity diagram shows how the various actors impacted by the system interact with the system processes, which are program modules with components and subcomponents. In the privacy engineering methodology, we have added a new feature, using a UML Note icon, to show which module satisfies the various FIPPS or GAPP principles. Chapter 7 presents an example of a system activity diagram with the privacy engineering enhancement.

## Dynamic Modeling

For event-triggered activity identified within each system use case, a UML sequence diagram is used to model implementation details of the various activities or transactions of the system. The sequence diagram represents an interaction, which is a set of messages exchanged among objects within a collaboration to effect a desired operation or result.

---

[34]FIPPS/GAPP requires that a Privacy Notice that defines the enterprise's privacy policies be made readily available to a system user.

A sequence diagram shows objects involved in the activity by vertical lines, which are called object lifelines or swim lanes. Horizontal vectors between the object lifelines represent the messages passed between the objects. The messages are drawn chronologically from the top of the diagram to the bottom; the horizontal placing or spacing of objects is arbitrary.

A message from one object to another can be defined by the method called, or invoked, by the sending object on the receiving object. The method called must belong to the definition of the class instantiated by the receiving object.

During dynamic modeling, methods are included in classes in the class model.

Figure 6-11 presents a simplified UML sequence diagram showing the entry of a scenario 3 order that shows use of the privacy component.

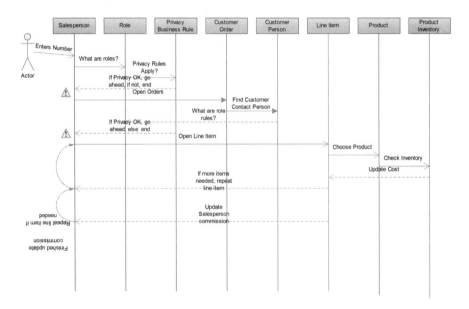

**Figure 6-11.** *Customer Order Sequence Diagram*

# Define Service Components and Supporting Metadata

A service component is a self-contained, reusable building block component. It can be used independently or assembled with other components to satisfy an enterprise's requirement(s). A service component may implement one or more class objects and handles a specific event or a related set of events. It provides a particular function or group of related functions. A service component has a well-defined and stable interface(s).

UML defines a component as a software module (source code, binary code, executable, DLL, etc.) with a well-defined interface. The interface of a component is represented by one or several interface attributes that the component provides.

Components are used to show compiler and runtime dependencies as well as interface and calling dependencies among software modules. Components also show which component implements which specific class(es). Both business service classes (e.g., the customer class and the customer credit class) and controller classes (e.g., system business workflow class) may be considered part of a component within the component model (Figure 6-12). A UML component might not be a service component, in that the UML component may not meet the more rigorous service component definition stated previously.

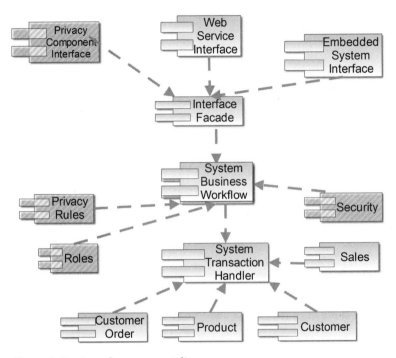

***Figure 6-12.*** *Sample component diagram*

The privacy component can be seen as a component containing subcomponents. For instance, although Figure 6-12 would reflect a simplified component design for example scenario 3 (the vacation planner in Chapter 9), that scenario contains the embedded privacy component (for example scenario 1). The privacy component interface, the privacy rules, the roles, and the security components on the diagram are actually subcomponents of the privacy component.

151

# Privacy Enabling Technologies

There is no uniform definition of PET; but it typically refers to the use of technology to help achieve compliance with data protection legislation or privacy policies. Many of the technologies referred to as PETs can protect corporate confidential information and protect revenues by securing the integrity of data. There are many PETs, and their benefits are both technology-specific and application-specific. The privacy component is itself a PET (Figure 6-13). The following concepts have been identified as PETs:[35]

- *Encryption*: Encryption may be implemented as a piece of code included in an information system or as a component invoked by the privacy component or by an embedded system.

- *Digital rights management*: Digital rights management (DRM) is a systematic approach to protect an enterprise's content and intellectual property. DRM technology focuses on making it impossible to steal content in the first place, a more efficient approach to the problem than the hit-and-miss strategies aimed at apprehending online poachers after the fact. Like encryption, DRM may be implemented as a piece of code included in an information system or as a component invoked by the privacy component or by an embedded system.

- *Privacy rules within application programs*: As discussed previously, privacy rules should be developed in conjunction with data stewards. System developers will implement those rules within the programs they develop. With the privacy component, privacy rules can be maintained easily and, if invoked by the various application programs, roles will be consistent throughout the enterprise. If the privacy rules change, those changes may be made within the privacy component and reflected within all of the various application programs. The changes are made in one place as opposed to individual changes made to all of the application systems.

- *Identity management*: Enterprises may develop identifiers for the various individuals impacted by their systems. Thus, they can develop a set of security components for authenticating their system users. There will also be authorization components that answer the question whether the user has the right to perform the action he or she is attempting. This may be based on security rules, privacy rules, or both. Authentication should be consistent throughout the enterprise. Therefore, including the authorization and authentication component as a part of the privacy component is often a prudent design decision.

---

[35]See "An Introduction to Privacy Enabling Technology" by Steve Kenny–Privacy Advisors, at https://www.privacyassociation.org/publications/2008_05_introduction_to_ privacy_enhancing_technologies.

- *Engineering and architecture*: A well-architected system that utilizes the privacy engineering approach can be considered a form of PET.

- *Privacy information services*: As discussed previously, privacy information services can be considered a PET that can be plugged in wherever personal information functionality is needed.

***Figure 6-13.*** *PETs does not equal privacy*

Some feel that just by using PETs, they are protecting privacy. Although this can be partially true, it is not completely true. There is more to it than that. As discussed, a privacy solution may include PETs, for example, encryption, as one or more component within a component's architecture design. Even if the design is full of PETs, privacy will not be fully protected without well-written policies, standards, procedures, guidelines, and a notice presented in a readable form, among other things. PETs are enablers, but they are not substitutes for privacy engineering. PETs can be just one of many design components but alone are not a privacy solution.

# BIG DATA: WHAT'S NEW? WHAT'S NOT? WHAT IT MEANS TO YOU: 10 THINGS YOU NEED TO KNOW

Leslie K. Lambert

Chief Security & Strategy Officer for GuruCul Solutions

1. **What is Big Data, *Really*?** Big Data is a term recently coined within the information technology field to describe tremendously large amounts of unstructured, or partially structured data that has been collected. Data is typically considered to rise to the level of "Big Data" when the amount of data that's available would take too much time and would cost too much money to load and process in a traditional manner via a relational database. The quantity of data that is presumed to imply Big Data is petabytes or more.

2. **Big Data is Evolving Faster As a Concept Than As a Working Infrastructure** The problems we've experienced in the past with storing, securing, sharing and making meaning of data are exacerbated in the current world of Big Data. Issues and struggles we experienced are magnified in the world of Big Data, accompanied by a growing set of data collection and storage technologies that are not yet up to the task of being able to properly protect the sensitive data contained therein. Older security models may not be enough or sufficient to properly care for the Big Data that is being collected.

3. **Hadoop is Big and Getting Bigger** New information technology that originates from the open source software world has been developed to work with Big Data. This new technology, called Hadoop, is capable of enabling the processing of very large quantities of data. Hadoop has created incredible opportunity to reveal more of the unknown in Big Data through the ability to bring so many more pieces of the puzzle together and serve it up ready for analytics engineers. One downside to Hadoop is that Hadoop databases typically have very slow processing rates, an artifact of current architectures. However, there are many powerful Hadoop-specific analytical tools that have been developed that are capable of processing and gleaning innovative meaning from these hoards of Big Data in a faster way.

4. **We May Need New Models for Database Security** Past models of secure schemes for entire data bases may be too costly for today's Big Data. However, the same theories, rules, and technologies apply to data today, even though the quantity of data has grown exponentially. We need to remind ourselves of the basics of data protection, both for security and privacy's sake, and that if they are performed well "in the small", they can be performed well "in the large" i.e. in the new world of Big Data. As is typical for technology that rises from within the open source community, the functional capabilities to work with Hadoop databases have developed far more quickly than the associated technology to control or protect the security and privacy of this data. If we did not perform these data protection tasks well in the past, didn't take proper care of our earlier data stores, how are we to secure and care for the Big Data we have in hand today, in a less mature, open source technology framework?

5. **Big Data Requires More Protection** Given the current state of technology and controls available today, it is easy for Big Data to quickly become a big problem with a really big price tag. Current issues we see today, where companies already do not sufficiently protect their data, lead to law suits, negative publicity, brand damage, and, possibly, regulatory fines and other fees. The more data that exists, the MORE data protection is required. Big Data requires newer security and privacy models that scale with Big Data, including both the ability to control access to data that is held within your networks, and providing protection to data that is leaving your networks.

6. **Surgical Application of Better Protection** In the current world of Big Data, secure practices and technologies may need to be applied in a more surgical manner to maintain the cost of implementing and maintaining the protection. There are costs to acquire the data, costs to maintain the data, costs to secure the data, as well as the cost to use and get value from the data. At the same time, there is an even stronger need to handle data and perform the basics of identifying, authenticating, authorizing and controlling access to data in the Big Data world. Applying strong data protection for all of your data can be very costly and cumbersome, with limited extra value or return on your investment. A need exists to implement stronger data protection for Big Data exactly where and when it is needed and to accept the costs of that stronger data protection.

7. **Know the Value of Your Data** It is vital that we truly understand the nature and sensitivity of the data in hand. Not all data are created equal. Some data is more liable to place an organization at risk, some data is more sensitive than others. Encryption of data can slow down performance, increasing latency and time-to-value on the data. This is even truer with the current state of Big Data technology. Hadoop technology is inherently slow, and imagine placing the additional burden of encryption into this same mix. Encryption can be applied to Big Data, and it's recommended to encrypt only the most sensitive data components within your Hadoop infrastructure—to not encrypt non-sensitive Big Data. As well, Big Data system back-ends, need to be protected in the manner of permitting only limited or no access to raw data by applications or services. For more real-time analysis, utilization, or reporting of data, it is recommended to use a relational database on the front-end of your Big Data back-end.

8. **Investment Drives the Need to Derive Meaning** Given the expense that businesses have likely invested to collect and store their tremendously large amounts of data, pressures to produce answers build within business organizations as they attempt to derive meaning from their data through analyzing their Big Data stores, looking for meaningful relationships via analytical tools to reveal correlations or repeatable patterns.

9. **New Old Career Opportunities** Gleaning meaning from Big Data means greater investment in decision-making algorithms and correlation engines. Data science, once an old career, is suddenly new again, and job candidates are sought with high priced compensation packages. It is a new model for "mentalists" who can see all by drawing meaning from mega data stores.

10. **Privacy Engineers are Vital** Remember, data is still data. You must know your data, the credibility of sources and frequency of update of your data. And, with Big Data, the value of data is growing at the same logarithmic rate as its size. It is important to focus on what truly needs to be protected, and at what level. To manage both cost and performance degradation, it is recommended that the

> Privacy Engineer spend energy on protecting the data within the Big Data store that is related to true risk or compliance. We need to mega-protect only what needs to be mega-protected. There are new technologies to facilitate the handling, correlation and making of meaning of Big Data. However these new technologies have grown and expanded far more quickly than the controls to maintain the protection of the data. It is vital to balance prudence, care, fiduciary obligation, and enablement. Just because we can, doesn't mean that we should.

# Stage 4: Complete System Development

The development team will take the approved development prototype and complete the system development as soon as the prototype becomes accepted as a basis for the production system. The prototype caveats can provide elements of the completion criteria.

# Stages 5 and 6: Quality Assurance and Rollout
## Develop and Execute Test Cases

Test cases are developed for each use case, based on the activity diagram, the use case metadata, the sequence diagrams, and the class model. The supporting metadata test cases contain the following information:

- The application name

- The use case name

- The use case code (ID)

- Hardware or software

- The tester name(s)

- The date completed

- Test scenarios

- Within each test activity, test cases, and test conditions

The FIPPS/GAPP or similar principles will be used as test case criteria, along with other use case requirements. Chapter 10 contains a privacy question and answer checklist.

As construction builds are developed, the various components are integrated. The quality assurance project team members utilizes test cases, as described previously. As defects are found, they should be systematically documented.

## Testing and Rollout Deliverables

Rollouts may be pilot operations or incremental implementations. Testing and rollout deliverables are:

- Test cases or scenarios based on data metadata business rules

- Test cases or scenarios based on use cases; activity, collaboration, and sequence diagrams; and supporting metadata

- Onsite and remote tests

- Defect list, including resolutions

- User acceptance tests

- Incremental rollout plans

## Knowledge Transfer

Knowledge transfer to client personnel is critical for the effective transition of the application to the deployment and maintenance teams. It facilitates quick system problem resolution when issues arise in production and ensures system extensibility when additional functionality is needed.

Concerning the privacy component delivered alone, the training will be technical for most direct users. Business stakeholders and management will need to be made aware of the functionality and the potential impact of the privacy component.

For scenario 3 Vacation Planner Application, the training would focus on the functionality of the embedding system. The development team will need to be made aware of the functionality of the privacy component and its interface with an embedding system. The business team and management will need to understand the privacy rules enforced within the specific system.

For the scenarios, the use case requirements' specifications will provide the basis for the content of the subject matter within the training materials. This content may be presented as a white paper or an online training class or within a classroom setting. The students will be made aware of the privacy requirements being satisfied by the solution along with the business and technology aspects of the solution.

A key to implementing a successful privacy program is empowering employees and stakeholders of the organization to assist the company in preventing privacy problems. If privacy education and training are provided to the entire population within the organization, they will come to understand the fundamentals of privacy so they can help protect against privacy vulnerabilities. More advanced instruction can be provided to key people within the organization whose duties involve more exposure to systems or processes that implicate privacy information implementation.

Internal communications such as published guidelines, FAQs, and other documents are good ways to leverage the resources within the privacy team so that a broad audience can be reached efficiently. These published communications also provide a good starting point for new employees who need to quickly understand the important elements of the privacy policy. Ongoing internal training events can provide another way to educate many at the same time. Problem-solving exercises involving practical scenarios can be very effective in getting active learning participation in internal training events.

## Conclusion

This chapter has presented a systems engineering lifecycle methodology adapted to implement privacy engineering. This methodology has been used successfully for over 30 years, with the privacy adaptations being used in recent years. The use of models and modeling is crucial to intelligent systems design. The international standard UML was selected because it is a widely used standard and it covers object, data, and process modeling. Chapters 7, 8, and 9 will provide practical examples using this methodology and discussed in more detail.

# CHAPTER 7

■ ■ ■

# The Privacy Component App

This chapter describes a primary tool in the privacy engineer's toolkit, the privacy component, originally introduced in Chapter 5. The privacy component is a self-contained, reusable software building block module developed to satisfy the privacy requirements derived from the use case discussed below. It is recommended that this component be developed as a module that can be used standalone or plugged into another enterprise program or mobile app, as will be discussed later in this book.

The privacy component should be developed according to the privacy engineering methodology, as described in Chapter 6. It will ensure that personal information is collected according to privacy policies and will be used to maintain the Privacy Notice as per the use case. The privacy team, along with the data stewards, will enter and maintain the privacy rules. The privacy component will determine the role of the person impacted and then execute the appropriate privacy rules. Encryption and security subcomponents are invoked, as appropriate, by the privacy component, according to the privacy rules.

## Privacy Component Context Diagram

Figure 7-1 presents a context diagram for the privacy component.

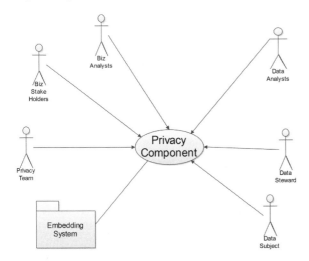

*Figure 7-1.* *Privacy component context diagram*

Privacy team members ensure that the privacy rules are entered into the metadata repository according to the privacy policies established, as discussed in Chapter 4. The business analysts and business stakeholders utilize the data governed by the privacy rules. The data analysts may analyze the data but also support the data stewards in adding privacy-oriented metadata. The data subjects are both impacted by the privacy component and use the privacy component directly via the user interface. The embedding system interacts with the privacy component via an application program interface (API).

# Use Case Requirements to Build a "Privacy Component"

A use case can be used to gather and document privacy requirements, as discussed in Chapter 5. The privacy component will satisfy the requirements as discussed in this section. These requirements will be documented in the use case documentation or documented in a metadata repository.[1] When developing the requirements, six analytical questions are asked:

- *Why*: The privacy component mission based on the requirements developed in this section

- *Who*: The privacy stakeholders, as depicted in the context diagram in Figure 7-1 (organizational aspects of the roles are discussed in Chapter 12):

    - Privacy executives and other privacy team members, who should ensure the requirements of the enterprise's privacy policy are understood and met, including requirements based on relevant laws and regulations

    - Business stakeholders, who, along with data stewards, must represent the end-user community (e.g., employees and parents) as well as business interests

    - Business analysts

    - Data analysts

    - Data stewards, who represent and may also be data subjects or advocates themselves

    - Data subjects, who share or are the subject of data collection and processing

- *When*: The privacy component triggering events:[2]

    - Data subject events:

        - Need to provide the data subject's data to the subject

---

[1]See further discussion of this in Chapter 6 and Appendix A.
[2]A triggering event is one that causes decision processing that uses business rules, including privacy rules, as decision criteria and triggers a behavior.

- Need to allow a data subject to correct his or her own data according to privacy rules

- Privacy notice needed

- Ability to gain the consent needed and manage changes within the model

- PI-related events:

  - Need to collect PII and related data to maintain, store, test, or deactivate these data

  - PI and related data to be presented to user

  - PII need to be transferred or transformed with metadata

  - Machine or other non-PII to be transformed to PII upon combination with other data elements or combinations with additional systems

- Privacy component internal events:

  - Need to create or update privacy rules

  - Need to transfer data to third party

  - Need to determine archive rules

  - Need to invoke encryption or obfuscation or other data limiting or masking technology solution

- *How*: The information privacy component behavior processes invoked by triggering events

  - Data subject related:

    - The Privacy Notice should be presented by means of an interactive user interface so that the end user can choose whether to read the notice.

    - Data subject must be able to agree to the storage of his or her data and needs to understand how these data will be used.

    - Data subject must be able to review his or her data.

    - The data subject should be able to correct any incorrect data.

  - Data collection related:

    - Must be the minimum relevant requirement needed to support the services provided

    - Must be proportional to the need

- Privacy component internal behaviors:

  - The user interface must contain a security component, including authentication and authorization.

  - Archiving rules need to be executed.

  - Encryption must be available as needed.

- *What*: The information privacy component data:

  - Privacy policies reflecting legal, cultural, and enterprise requirements (as discussed in Chapter 4)

  - Privacy business[3] rules

  - Individual role

  - Enterprise role

  - Organization

  - Individual person

  - Interface mechanism between the privacy component and an embedding system that may be used for adding or updating privacy rules. Another use is to present the Privacy Notice and allow an end user to choose whether his or her data are collected.

- *Where*: Locational aspects, depending upon where the enterprise operates and how distributed the enterprise network is. These considerations are particularly important for transborder data flows, where multijurisdictional rules or policies may apply, or where end users or other third parties may require an audit or limitation on data flows.

# The Privacy Component Class Model

We use the UML class model as both a class model and a data model, as mentioned in Chapter 6. A UML class model is *not* a data flow diagram. Instead, a class model shows the relationship (or association) of the classes to one another. In Figure 7-2, the arrow-like symbol shows class inheritance. For instance, an organization and an individual person are subtypes of persons of interest and inherit attributes from the person of interest super-type. The diamond-like icon indicates an aggregation, whole-part, or one-to-many association. For instance, each role can have one or more privacy rules relationships, and the various rules may have overlapping origins as well.

---

[3]In this case, "business" rules cover any type of organizational activity rules. These are not exclusive to commercial enterprises.

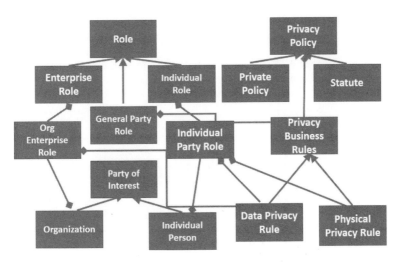

**Figure 7-2.** *Privacy component class model*

A class also has knowledge properties (data) and action properties (event handlers and processes). Each of these classes will have both class and operational metadata attributes. Class attributes are data elements that describe aspects of that class. A class that describes one of the privacy policy requirements may have a uniqueness identifier, a name, and a text description. Operational metadata attributes are names of operations that are also the names of code modules or services to be invoked according to embedded rules implied by requirements.

# Developing the Unified Modeling Language Class Model

The class model, like a data model, shows the data that will be managed and the relationships between the various classes.

The privacy component class model graphic in Figure 7-2 shows *classes* that represent data managed by the enterprise and the data privacy requirements. The privacy component is composed of parties of interest, roles, policies, and rules. The party of interest subcomponent (lower left corner of Figure 7-2) was described in detail in Chapter 6.

Roles (upper left corner subcomponent) may be defined as the nature of work performed by an individual person or organization with regard to enterprise functions. General party roles, as opposed to individual or enterprise roles, may be relevant to a party of interest whether they are an individual person or an organizational entity. An individual can have one or more individual roles as mapped through the individual party role and an organization can have one or more enterprise roles as mapped through the organization enterprise role.

Privacy policies (upper right corner) may be statutory or a policy developed and enforced by private entities, as described in Chapter 4. Privacy policies contain the basis for privacy business rules or requirements.

Privacy business rules can be defined as written statements in natural language that function as a communication tool to express a rule, decision criteria, policy, or a common practice in relation to a decision involving business information or business processes. They can be data or physical privacy rules. Privacy rules are mapped across the diagram to the individual party, organization enterprise, and general party roles. Note that general party roles may be related to surveillance or other aspects of party of interest physical privacy as well as data privacy per se, but it is the data about that protection that will require policy creation, execution, and monitoring for both individuals and organizations.

# Privacy Component User Interface Requirements

The privacy component and the system or application in which it is embedded will need to protect the integrity and security of the data subject's data. Some aspects of the user experience may be balanced with the requirements under privacy legal and regulatory schema to protect information with security techniques. Often, in development environments, additional steps or required processes may be deemed a diminution of overall user experience. When the overall architectural aspects are managed in a privacy engineering data and user-centric environment, security protocols are also managed and contextual cues and other aspects of user experience design are utilized to effectively engage the user.

A Privacy Notice describes to the user a summary of enforcement and redress relevant to the privacy-oriented information related to the system. The user experience and Privacy Notices can themselves be deemed privacy-enhancing technologies. They may set and expand context and set a tone of expectation for the user. They also may function to provide clear guidance to the privacy governance professional who will serve as the fiduciary of data processes within the architecture. This is where an innovative animated notice enhances both the user experience and the data subject protection.

The system user, whether of the standalone privacy component or of an application that invokes the privacy component, interacts with the privacy component. If the privacy component is invoked, the user should not have to know that the invocation has occurred. Instead, a seamless transition should happen between the overall system and the privacy component.

The data steward, supported by the privacy team and the data analyst, ensures that the privacy rules are entered. The privacy team representative enters and maintains the Privacy Notice. The user of the system will interact with the system invoking the privacy component, utilizing that system's functionality. The privacy component will mostly operate behind the scenes.

# Design the Privacy Component Solution
## The Privacy Component Solution Architecture

The privacy component use case lays out the requirements for developing a privacy component that can be invoked by an enterprise application to ensure that privacy policies are enforced, as discussed in Chapter 5 and previously in this chapter. The privacy component class model provides the basis for the information architecture (Figure 7-3) and defines a series of events requiring a user interface architecture.

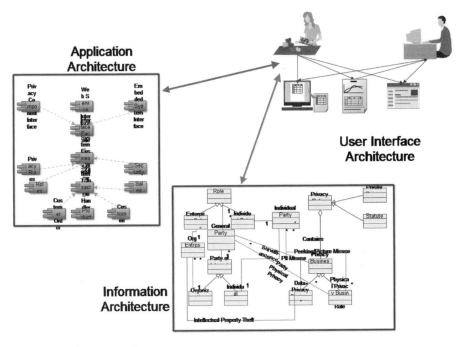

***Figure 7-3.*** *Solution architecture*

Examples of user interface requirements include:

- The ability to request the Privacy Notice

- The display of the notice, if requested

- The ability to add and maintain privacy rules related to the roles shown in the metadata model

The application architecture is developed by following the component design methodology, as described in Chapter 6.

# The Privacy Component Class Structure

We can best understand how the privacy component might work by analyzing the component metadata model (Figure 7-4). The privacy component may be embedded in a system (as a component within an application), as we discussed regarding scenarios 2 and 3, or as a mobile app (itself) or program subroutine (code within the application), or it may invoke a more broad-based system in the Cloud.

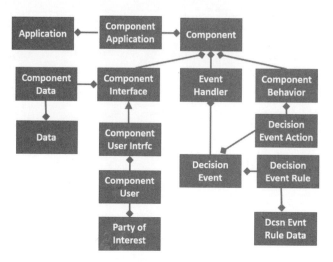

***Figure 7-4.*** *Component metadata model*

The component interface may utilize a database (component data) based on the privacy component data model shown in Figure 7-2, and, in most cases, it may also utilize the database for the system it is embedded within (e.g., the simplified customer order data model [scenario 3], as discussed in Chapter 9). The component interface has a user interface for interacting with the privacy component actors shown in the context diagram in Figure 7-1.

The privacy component event handler will process the events listed as the privacy component triggering events in the privacy component use case requirements. Each event implies one or more decision to be made. For instance, the user interface will ask the user if he or she wishes to see the Privacy Notice.[4] When the user gives an affirmative answer, it invokes one set of privacy rules, and a negative answer invokes another set of privacy rules based on the role of the user.

Thus, each event triggers one or more decisions, and each decision requires a set of privacy rules as the criteria for making the decision. Each decision will then invoke a process or behavior that may trigger another event, and its decision sets or may invoke another behavior all in accordance with the privacy rules. Each of the privacy rules may require access to a database related to the privacy component.

# Privacy Component System Activity Diagram

The system activity diagram in Figure 7-5 shows where the major actors interface with the privacy component system functionality as defined by the use case and implied by the data requirements. The functionality is grouped into modules or subcomponents: The first subcomponent may be considered administrative in nature; the second subcomponent is for initiation and data collection; the third subcomponent handles third-party transfers; the fourth subcomponent manages data correction; and finally, there is the archive rules subcomponent.

---

[4]FIPPS/GAPP requires that a Privacy Notice that defines the enterprise's privacy policies be made readily available to a system user.

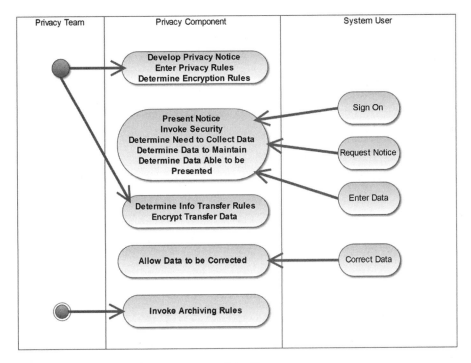

***Figure 7-5.*** *Privacy component system activity diagram*

Figure 7-5 shows that the privacy team begins the process by developing the Privacy Notice, developing and entering the privacy rules, and determining and causing implementation of the third-party transfer rules and the encryption mechanism. The system user uses the privacy component to make a Privacy Notice decision and to enter, maintain, and correct personal information according to privacy rules managed within the privacy component. The privacy component will periodically run the archiving rules under the direction of the privacy team.

## Privacy Assessment Using the System Activity Diagram

The system activity diagram is useful for documenting the design of the system. But just as important, the diagram can be used to assess how well the system satisfies the privacy principles' requirements. Figure 7-6 shows the system activity diagram with the FIPPS/GAPP principles designating which subcomponent satisfies each privacy principle. This assessment will also be useful as a tool for quality assurance and privacy impact assessment.

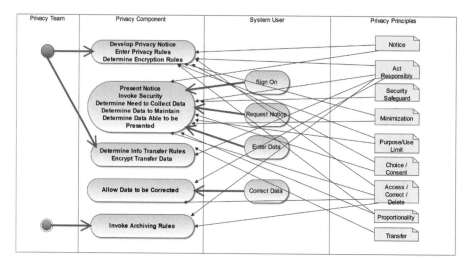

**Figure 7-6.** *System activity diagram of the privacy component with a tie to privacy principles*

# Develop the Privacy Component Design

Figure 7-7 shows that the privacy component should have its own interface. The privacy component may be a web service whose user interface may be a web site. The embedding system often collects data and then passes the data through an API. These various data sources are passed through a well-known program pattern, the interface facade that allows data from the various sources to come into the component. The component may have a workflow manager that controls the privacy rules engine, a security subcomponent, and role data that are related to the privacy rules. The various transactions run by the privacy component will reach out to the various databases holding personal information and manage those data. Thus, the privacy component consists of a series of subcomponents and will be both data-centric and person-centric.

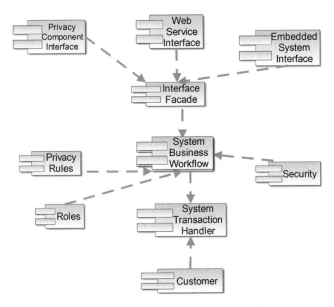

***Figure 7-7.*** *Component model for the privacy component*

# Using the System Development Methodology for the Privacy Component

A project to build a privacy component begins with project initiation. The privacy team and the system's engineering team who are knowledgeable in privacy engineering should first hold a short scoping workshop. The use case requirements should be developed along with the class and data modeling. Using both use case and the data model, the user interface will be designed. The development team will determine whether a user interface prototype will be necessary. A combination of the class model with the methods needed to support each class, the use case requirements, and the system activity diagram should be used to develop the component design and dynamic modeling sequence diagrams. From this documentation, the test cases are developed, including the system activity diagram showing the relationship of the privacy principles to the various subcomponents. Once the privacy component is developed and tested, an incremental rollout is recommended.

# INTUIT DATA STEWARDSHIP – AND DATA USE GUIDANCE – GIVING PRODUCT DEVELOPERS, MANAGERS AND DATA SCIENTISTS THE ABILITY TO IMPLEMENT ETHICAL PRIVACY DECISIONS.

By Barb Lawler

Chief Privacy Officer, Intuit

Data Stewardship Principles articulate a broad mission and guide product teams to use customer data to help customers improve their financial lives, while being clear that it is the customer's data, not ours. The principles were crafted less than three years ago with input from the highest levels of the company, including the CEO and a Co-founder. The principles define Intuit's role as a trusted steward of customers' data, specifically state that Intuit will give customers choices about Intuit's use of data that identifies them, and give open and clear explanations about how Intuit uses their data. Most importantly, the principles state that Intuit will not, without explicit permission, sell, publish or share entrusted customer data that identifies the customer or any person. Our customers have a basic expectation of privacy – but they have told us **they also expect us to find new ways to make their data to benefit them and help empower them** to improve their financial lives. There are dual consumer interests that need to be taken into account: consumer protection AND economic empowerment. At Intuit, we call this "Big Data for the Little Guy" – we give our small business customers the tools they have never had access to before, to harness the power of their data to deliver practical benefits for their business.

But how can the product manager, engineer or data scientists take action on these important concepts?

What if a product manager wants to use data to improve an offering or develop a cool new feature – can he do it, and if so how? Data scientists explore and test different theories to identify a breakthrough benefits and services, but they don't want to unintentionally misuse the customer data. Whatever the scenario, Intuit business unit and data services teams often have questions. Are they using the customer data in line with Intuit values, privacy policy and compliance requirements? Have other employees at Intuit used data in similar ways?

The Data Use Guidance Tool was developed to provide an interactive, automated tool developed to provide fast, consistent guidance for dozens of data use scenarios – taken from actual product usage, and to enable product teams to move quickly and with confidence. It also provides examples of best practices for informing and involving Intuit customers in the use of their data. Built using html on an Intuit QuickBase foundation, the Data Use Guidance tool is a rules-based engine drawing on no fewer than 500 "rules" behind the scenes. A group manager in analytics told us, "It makes gray, black and white. I know what my team can do with data."

The tool gives specific guidance to engineers in three easy steps. They select how they want to use customer data (e.g., direct marketing, share with a third party, etc.), check the type of data they want to use (e.g., business relationship, product usage, etc.) and choose the source of the data (e.g., desktop or mobile, SaaS or online service, etc.). Based on the selections made, the tool leads employees to one of three types of guidance: 1) Appropriate use – good to go; 2) Need to confirm and then go; and 3) Let's talk. At each step, the employees sees on-screen a summary of the steps he's taken. And with just one more click, he can navigate to a pattern library, with real examples of Intuit and external best practices for in-context transparency and choice. "Examples are so, so beneficial. I can develop and test quickly," commented a PM leader.

About half of all data use scenarios the tool will give developers the green light to move ahead without further consultation with the privacy team. At any time using the tool, they can request a consultation at the click of a button. This generates a confirmation e-mail, and the privacy team follows-up within one business day.

Example 1: A product manager would like to help a small business customer offer her employees a health benefit using a health payment card. Small Business owners have told us they want to be in control of the use of her employees' data and communication about the offer. The Tool guides the product manager to know that the customer would be involved and participate in the decision to share her employees' information with the third party delivering the Card. It shows the PM examples of how to describe the value and choice options to the Small Business owner and messaging to communicate to their employee about the offer within the product screen flows.

Example 2: A group marketing manager wants to conduct a direct marketing campaign that offers GoPayment, a mobile payment app and secure mobile device swiper to all QuickBooks Online customers using their business relationship data. The Tool shows the marketing pro that when he uses business relationship data to conduct this offer is an acceptable use of customer data which does not require additional action on his part (beyond applying relevant marketing preferences to the campaign mailing.

Example 3: A data scientist wants to evaluate a potential new business opportunity based on anonymous consumer financial transaction data from Mint and Quicken. The data scientist believes that this unique set of data, when combined with certain 3rd party data sets will create a unique perspective on consumer behavior which will be attractive in helping Small Business customers acquire new customers. The tool walks the data scientist through the type of use – a breakthrough benefit, the type of data – user entered in the products that is anonymized and 3rd party data. In this scenario, the Tool informs the data scientist that a consultation with the privacy team is required.

Example 4: Product developers use specific mobile privacy-by-design guidelines for smartphone and tablet applications. The Tool will take the mobile app developer directly to these guidelines, including mobile device patterns, which encourage the development and operation of mobile apps to reflect sound data privacy and protection policies that put customers first. The guidelines help developers understand:

- What data a mobile app may collect or access,

- How the data will be used and shared and for what purposes

- How the data will be stored and retained

- What choices the customer has over the collection and use of his/her data

An example is how to effectively implement Geo-location. Customers will say 'yes' when the benefit is clearly stated and in context of the mobile applications operation and user flow.

Geo-Location: Access, Collection & Use

We are transparent and provide choice if we access, collect, and use or store geo-location data.

Only access and/or collect geo-location data if it is required for the App's functionality and provides a clear benefit to the customer (e.g.,, facilitates local sales tax calculations or locates merchants).

**Collection.** To access and use geo-location data, we must notify the customer, describe how it will be used, and obtain customer consent before his or her geo-location data is accessed or used by our App.

- Notification and consent should be in real-time

- Consent should be affirmative, and not based on pre-checked boxes or preset defaults

- Notification should: alert customer to the collection of geo-location data, describe the purpose or benefit of the collection, and explain how the consent may be withdrawn (e.g., through a settings feature)

- Customer should understand whether collection or use of geo-location data is a one-time event or ongoing (e.g., whether agreeing once to permit a geo-location feature causes this feature to remain on, until settings are adjusted)

**User Alerts.** Methods for alerting the customer to ongoing collection of geo-location data could include: (1) A symbol can be used to indicate an app is actively accessing and using geo-location to alert and give the customer access to geo-location data use and settings, or (2) A periodic email or push-notification can be sent reminding the customer that geo-location is enabled and how it may be disabled.

EXHIBIT B – Geo-Location

(*continued*)

For Apple iOS, use the "Purpose" field to provide transparent notification of how the location data will be used.

**User Control.** If the geo-location consent is for ongoing use, and not a one-time use:

- Provide a means to alert the customer of the continued ongoing use of geo-location.

- If an application is closed, do not collect or use geo-location data unless the customer has specifically agreed to it.

- Provide easy to find and use settings that allow the customer to easily turn off geo-location tracking.

**Retention.** The retention period for geo-location data should be no longer than is necessary for the purposes for which the data were collected or for which they are further processed. Unless there is a valid, approved business reason, geo-location data should be retained no longer than 24 hours unless it is anonymized.

Anonymized location data should not be re-identified, or maintained in a manner that allows for re-identification.

# Conclusion

This chapter discussed the privacy component, which is a unique aspect of this privacy engineering approach. It allows the privacy rules based on privacy policies to be added and maintained in one place. It can be used as a standalone application or as a web service. As a standalone app, the Privacy Notice can be maintained and privacy rules can be entered and maintained. When the privacy component is embedded in a system or app, the database designed from the privacy component data model may be maintained in whole or in part within the privacy component portion of the system. The key business purpose of the privacy component is to ensure that the required privacy policies are enforced in a uniform manner. Chapters 8 and 9 will discuss applications where the privacy component may be used.

The sidebar discusses a wonderful program that developed in parallel to the writing of this book. It provides a practical example of a rule-based program and a proof of the privacy component concept.

■ ■ ■

# CHAPTER 8

# A Runner's Mobile App

*"I'm an instant star. Just add water."*

—David Bowie

This chapter describes the process of designing a small mobile app using privacy engineering methodology. This example scenario shows how these methods can be used for small apps and systems. The runner's mobile app began, as discussed in the sidebar, as a discussion between grandfather and grandson concerning the usefulness of the privacy engineering methodology for designing an app.

---

### MY GRANDSON, CODESLINGER AND PRIVACY ENGINEER IN THE MAKING

by Tom Finneran & R Traver Clifford

My grandson, Traver, was looking forward to his summer internship at the end of his junior year in high school with a company that builds apps for smartphones. I asked him if he knew how to design an app. He wasn't sure. So we sat down to discuss app design. He wanted a runner's app. We went through the who, what, where, when, how, and why as pertains to a runner's app using the requirements gathering for UML systems engineering lifecycle planning. The next step was to create a context diagram (shown below) showing potential users of the app, including the runner, the coach, and other runners as stakeholders. We then leveraged various UML diagrams and the other aspects of our methodology. His draft runner's app could be created and implemented with a data-centric, privacy engineered architecture. His component diagram is also shown below.

The modeling and planning processes are as appropriate for a single developer acting as a part-time summer worker for a large and complex global enterprise. Privacy engineering is not too cumbersome for the small or the cash strapped. No excuses and, in this case, gain with no pain.

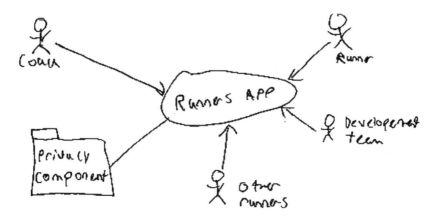

*Traver's context diagram*

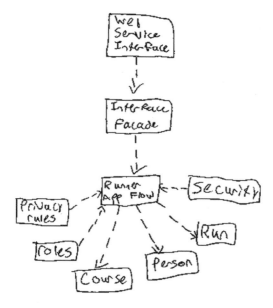

*Traver's component diagram*

The runner's mobile app could use a simple version of the privacy component, as will be discuss in this chapter. It will be used to track cross-country race results as well as practice runs. The original intent of the runner's app was use as a smartphone or tablet app. The runner's app could be a web application that uses a PC, a school server, or could run in the Cloud as well.

The development team, including a privacy team representative, will add a Privacy Notice and privacy rules tied to the roles, and a simplified privacy component can be invoked by the runner's app. The coach, runner, and other runner will be able to interact within the runner's app (Figure 8-1).

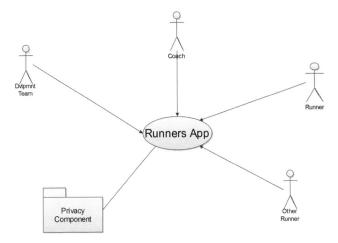

***Figure 8-1.*** *Runner's app context diagram*

# The Runner's Mobile App Use Case

The runner's mobile app design began with the development of a use case, as discussed in Chapters 5 and 6. One important requirement that needs to be considered within the runner's app is compliance with the requirements for collecting personal information from minors. Many countries have restrictions on collecting and using personal information from children and what is necessary to consider the processing fair and legitimate. For instance, in the United States, the Children's Online Privacy Protection Act (COPPA), among other things, requires verifiable parental consent before one can collect data from children under 13 years old. If your app will collect or process personal information from children, make sure you understand the associated requirements and use cases.[1]

These are the answers to the six use case questions, as outlined in Chapter 7:

- *Why*: Record a runner's runtime on a given cross-country course against an appropriate standard. The app will be used by the runners on a team and by their coaches.

---

[1]COPPA requires a Privacy Notice that describes the type of information collected, how parents can give permission, how information collected from the child will be used, whether it would be distributed to other third parties, and how the parents can contact the web site operator by phone or e-mail. The Federal Trade Commission provides a guide to COPPA on their web site.

- *Who*:
  - Individual person:
    - Runner role
    - Coach role
    - Other runner role
    - Development team
- *When*:
  - Application of data-related events:
    - Need to enter/maintain courses
    - Need to enter/maintain standard for courses
    - Need to enter/maintain runner information
    - Need to enter/maintain run
    - Need to present run history
    - Need to correct data
    - Need to enter/maintain archive rules, for all data, including privacy rules
  - Privacy-related events:
    - Privacy Notice needed
    - Need to enter and maintain privacy rules
    - Need to enter/maintain roles
    - Need to encrypt
- *How*:
  - Application related:
    - Maintain courses
    - Maintain course standards for each runner level
    - Enter runner information
    - Enter run on course
    - Present run history report
    - Run archiving rules

- Privacy related:
    - Maintains a Privacy Notice
    - Which data are collected
    - Which roles and how date are used
    - Which rules, including children's privacy requirements, if needed
    - Who can see what
- Maintain privacy rules for each role
- Request notice
- *What*:
    - Privacy rule
    - Runner role
    - Other runner role
    - Coach role
    - Individual person
    - Course
    - Run
    - Run history
- *Where*:
    - Mobile:
        - Smartphone
        - Tablet
    - School server
    - Cloud

# The Runner's App Class or Data Model

In developing the runner's app class or data model, take into account the team requirements and a simplified privacy component data model.

In Figure 8-2, the various *roles* may have one or more *privacy rules* related to them. The *runner role* is related to one *individual person* at a time, whereas the *other runner roles* and the *coach's role* may be related to more than one *person*. An *individual* may make multiple *runs* on multiple *courses*. The *run history* consists of information about multiple *runs*.

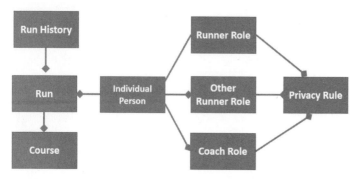

***Figure 8-2.*** *Runner's app class or data model*

---

## ADDITIONAL REQUIREMENT

After the fact, as a part of our book review process, an additional requirement surfaced. A *team* class should probably be included in the data model. This would enable the app to be used for more than one team at the same time. This is just one example of how as you progress within the methodology new requirements surface.

---

# The Runner's App User Experience Requirements

The development team is supported by a privacy expert who develops a Privacy Notice that contains:

- Which data are collected

- Which roles the data benefit and how they are used

- Which rules are applied

- Who can see what

The development team and the privacy expert enter the privacy rules for each role. The coach enters information about each course, both practice courses and competitive courses. Course information contains course standards for rookie runners, junior runners, and senior runners as determined by the coach. The runner can enter his or her times and review runs and the run history against the appropriate course standard. The coach can review runs and the run history for all runners on his or her team and can correct any data-entry mistakes. Runners may be allowed to check other runners' times if those runners allow that. A runner can run the run history report for his or her runs and for other runners' runs when he or she has been granted permission. The coach can run archiving rules at the end of the season.

# Design the App Structure

The runner's app will be structured according to the component metadata model discussed in Chapters 6 and 7. Thus, it will have a user interface that takes in data from both the app's database, designed from the data model, and from data entered by the various actors. It will have an event handler for events contained in the use case and behaviors listed in the "how" section of the use case.

The coach, the runner, and the other runners will be able to use the component user interface for adding data, correcting data, and requesting information. Run, course, and individual data will be drawn from the database that may be stored on the device, on the school server, or in the Cloud. Event handling and behavior execution may be done on the device, on the school web site server, or in the Cloud. The technical design team makes those platform decisions once the design is completed.

# The Runner's App System Activity Diagram

The runner's app system activity diagram (Figure 8-3) shows the development team, consisting of the designer or developer and a privacy expert, utilizing an administrative module for setting up the app. All system users have to sign on regardless of their role. The runner adds the data into the data collection module. The runner, other runners, and the coach may all perform queries or run the history report as long as they are given permission. The coach will perform data correction in the data correction module and will work with the development team on handling archiving.

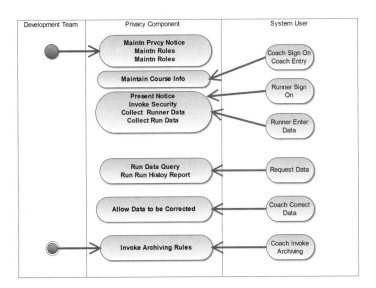

***Figure 8-3.*** *Runner's app system activity diagram*

185

# Privacy Assessment Using a System Activity Diagram

Figure 8-4 shows the privacy principles satisfied by the various runner's app modules.

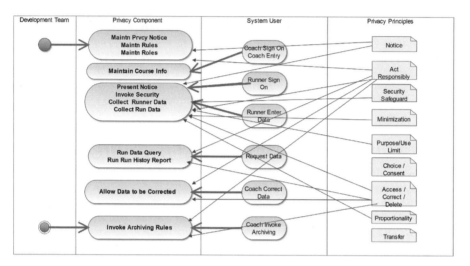

***Figure 8-4.*** *Runner's app system activity privacy assessment*

# Develop the Runner's App Component Design

Figure 8-5 shows the runner's app interface subcomponent, which may be implemented by means of a smartphone, tablet, or web site. The interface facade accepts the data from whichever source and presents it in a common format to the runner's app flow handler. We could simplify the design by deciding what the user interface source is and eliminate the interface facade pattern. This is a design decision. The runner's app flow handler controls the flow of the privacy rules subcomponent, the security subcomponent, the individual person subcomponent, the roles subcomponent, the course subcomponent, and the run subcomponent.

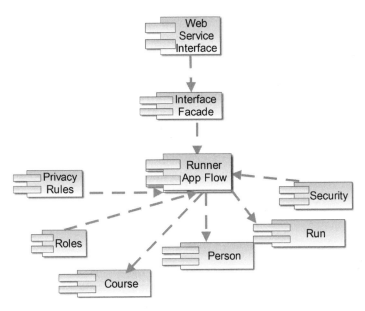

**Figure 8-5.** *Runner's app component diagram*

# Using the System Development Methodology

For an application as simple as the runner's app, the steps described in Chapter 6 should be followed but in a less formal manner. Project management can be simpler, although there should be a simple project plan and project status measurements. In the case of the runner's app, our scoping workshop and the initial use case development was a 2-hour discussion. The modeling approach recommended in this book provides simple but extremely useful documentation that facilitates a correct, well-designed, maintainable application.

# Conclusion

This chapter included the runner's app design because it was a fun, interesting incident that happened while in the process of writing this book—using its methodology to help a teenager understand how to design an app. More important, the app development process shows you how the privacy engineering methodology can be used for small individual applications as well as for large enterprise applications, as will be discussed in Chapter 9. A small application may not have a privacy component available or may not even need a privacy component. However, an app like this, especially where younger children may be involved, does require privacy protection. Any small app requires a disciplined design and development methodology with sufficient documentation so maintenance and future changes are facilitated.

■ ■ ■

# Vacation Planner Application

*"The patterns are simple, but followed together, they make for a whole that is wiser than the sum of its parts, Where Good Ideas Come From: The Natural History of Innovation*

—Steven Johnson

This chapter presents a vacation planner application that utilizes a privacy component that has already been developed, tested, and implemented. A large hospitality company requires a system to help its customers plan a vacation at one of their hospitality sites. The system will support both a telephone call center and a web site. The privacy component will be invoked by this new system to ensure that privacy policies are enforced. Additionally, this example will explain the privacy requirements and fair information privacy principles as they operate as functional specifications and quality control measures. The privacy engineering methodology steps are followed and the process of development is shown in more detail. This example scenario is based on a major project at a well-known hospitality company.

## Requirements Definition

As a result of a scoping workshop, the first step would be to draw up a context diagram (Figure 9-1). Although the focus would be on the order entry portion of the system, the context diagram shows the major actors of the system as a whole.

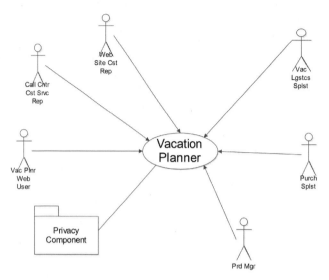

*Figure 9-1. Vacation planner context diagram*

# Use Case Metadata for Hospitality Vacation Planner Enterprise Application

The privacy engineering methodology steps, as described in Chapter 6, are followed to start production on the vacation planner app.

- *Why:* Motivation—Vacationer wishes to order a planned vacation package.

- *Who:* Actors:

  - Vacation planner web user

  - Call center customer service representative (vacation planner)

  - Web site customer service representative

  - Vacation logistics specialist

  - Purchasing specialist

  - Customer credit specialist

  - Product manager

- *When:* Events:

  - Customer interface related:

    - Customer call

    - Customer selects vacation package

- Customer enters order on web site
- Customer receives credit approval
  - System related:
    - Customer service enters credit information
    - Credit check system invokes privacy component
    - Customer order system invokes privacy component
    - Order provisioned
- *How:* Processing or behavior:
  - Update customer credit data
  - Privacy component processing (see Privacy Component Use Case in Chapter 7)
  - Update customer order database
  - Process order
- *What:* Data:
  - See Customer Order data modeling, including Big Data Data Block (Figure 9-5)
  - Privacy component data model (Figure 9-4)
- *Where:* Location:
  - Call center
  - Hospitality locations

Additionally, in this example the enterprise business rules, including the privacy rules, are required for consistent integration with the enterprise:

- Customer call center business rules
- Web site business rules
- Credit check business rules
- Customer order business rules
- Customer credit check privacy rules
- Customer order privacy rules
- Customer order provisioning rules

# Develop Business Activity Diagrams
## Business Activity Diagram for Scenario 3: Vacation Planning

The business activity diagram in Figure 9-2 shows the events, processes, and decision making for the various business processes involved in supporting a vacation planning app. The diagram shows the call center's functionality, but the web site would also have that same functionality.

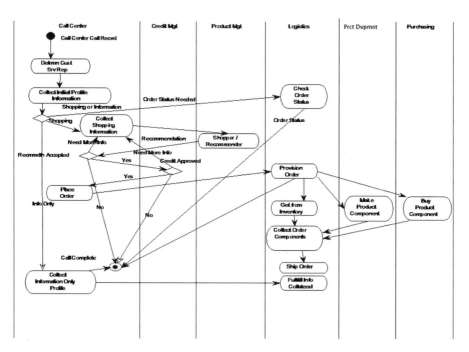

*Figure 9-2.  Business activity diagram for the vacation planning app*

## Activity Diagram Used as a Part of Privacy Assessment

The privacy team works with business stakeholders, including data stewards, to identify key data attributes, especially identifiers, within the business processes represented on the business activity diagram (Figure 9-3). Privacy rules will be developed for these and other attributes as found and entered in the metadata.

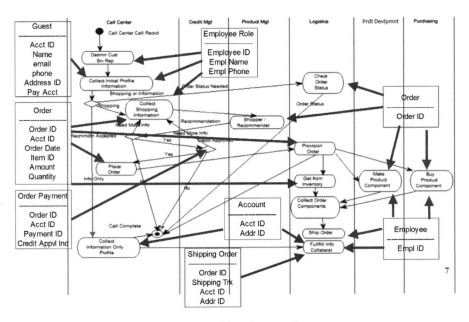

*Figure 9-3.* Business activity diagram with key data attributes

# Privacy Component Class and Data Model

The privacy component class and data model (Figure 9-4) contains the overall data requirements for the vacation planner application. For illustration purposes, an additional, simplified portion of the vacation planner data model focusing on customer order entry is shown in Figure 9-5.

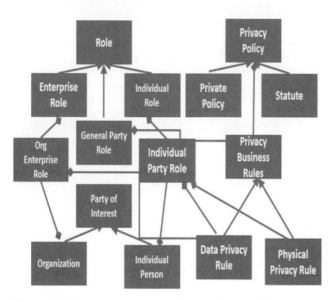

***Figure 9-4.*** *Privacy component class and data model*

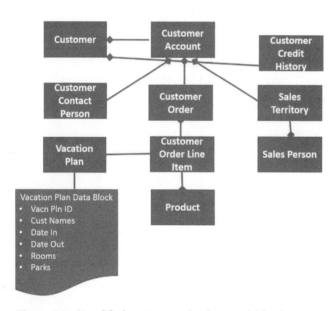

***Figure 9-5.*** *Simplified customer order data model for the vacation planner app*

As discussed in Chapter 7, the privacy component class data model is used to design the database for both the privacy component (scenario 1) and as a part of the database in the vacation planner (scenario 3). The model shows the various roles played by parties of interest, whether that is an organization entity or an individual person. The privacy rules are based on privacy policies that are related to the various role types. The vacation planner application invokes the privacy component as it deals with roles such as a customer or perhaps a contact person, sales person, or employee.

The data model presented in Figure 9-5 will be used to design the system database. The *Customer Person* is an *individual person* playing the *Individual Party Role* of *Customer* (or in the hospitality company, *Guest*). The *Customer Order* will contain a combination of *products* within a *Vacation Plan* developed from unstructured vacation planning data organized into a big data data block contained in one or more *Customer Order Line*. The *Sales Person* is another *individual person* who serves as a customer service representative. As a part of the order processing, a *credit history* check is performed.

# Vacation Planner User Interface Requirements

The *customer*, also called *guest* at some hospitality companies, would either call into a call center or sign on to a web site. The *customer* can then decide whether he or she wishes to review the Privacy Notice. The *customer* would indicate what *vacation plans* he or she wishes to have. The *customer* would then enter information about him- or herself and the other members of his or her party. In this case, *privacy* rules may apply and the privacy component would be invoked. Once the *vacation plan* is fully defined, the *customer* will be asked to pay for the package. The *customer's credit history* will be checked and *privacy* rules may apply. If the customer passes the credit check, the *vacation plan order* will be entered. The *vacation plan* will go through a provisioning process. When the plan is provisioned, the *customer* will get a notice of approval and the *vacation plan* is made available for saving or printing.

---

## HOSPITALITY GAMES

By Tom Finneran

Let's say that a hospitality enterprise develops a game based on their attractions, rides, shows, and movies. If the game appeals to children who are under 13 years of age, the Children's Online Privacy Protection Act (COPPA) applies in the United States. (There may be similar laws in other jurisdictions.) COPPA provisions regulate web sites upon which personal information of children under 13 years of age is likely to be collected. Therefore, if our hospitality enterprise wants to offer games to potential young *guests,* a set of privacy rules will need to be entered into the privacy metadata model so that our privacy component can enforce rules required by COPPA. The rules would require that:

- The clearly written privacy policy must be included in the Privacy Notice. Access to the Privacy Notice must be on the web site's home page and at each area where the site or online service collects personal information from children. The Federal Trade Commission (FTC) encourages that a privacy policy for a mobile app be posted by the Internet store at the point of the app download.

- There must be a description of the kinds of information collected from children, for example, name, address, e-mail address, hobbies, and age. This requirement applies to all information, not just personal information.

- There must be an explanation of how the data are collected, whether directly from the child or behind the scenes through "cookies."

- There must be an explanation how the web site operator uses the personal information, such as marketing to the child or notifying contest winners, and whether personal information is disclosed to third parties.

- Parents are given the web site operator's address, phone number, and e-mail address, including anyone who would be collecting or maintaining the children's personal information.

- There must be the capability for the parent to give consent before collecting, using, or disclosing personal information about a child.

- If parents don't consent to their child's personal information being processed, there must be the capability to search and delete the child's information from all systems under the enterprise's control.

- There must be the capability for parents to review and delete information about their children collected by such services.

- There must be reasonable procedures "to protect the confidentiality, security, and integrity of personal information collected from children."

COPPA is a very complicated law. This summary is insufficient for developing a complete set of privacy rules. The FTC maintains updated guides to COPPA on their web site.[1]

Other privacy rules over and above COPPA would be needed to complete the privacy engineering of these game applications.

---

[1]Available at www.business.ftc.gov/privacy-and-security/childrens-privacy.

# Design the Vacation Planner Solution
## The Vacation Planner Solution Architecture

The vacation planner use case along with the data identified in the overall vacation planner data model and the vacation planner user interface requirements should be used to develop the user interface architecture. The complete vacation planner class and data model, including the information outlined in Figures 9-4 and 9-5, constitutes the information architecture. We'll discuss the development of the application architecture in the next sections, but Figure 9-6 provides an overview.

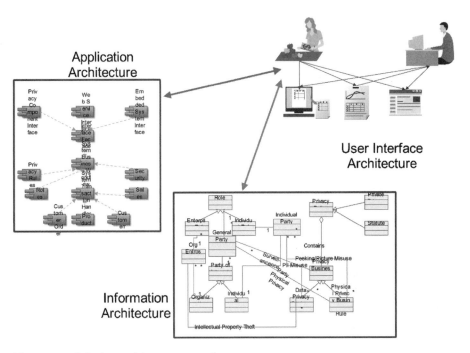

***Figure 9-6.*** *Solution architecture example*

## The Vacation Planner Component Architecture Structure

The vacation planner app can be developed using the component architecture approach discussed in Chapter 6. The component interface utilizes a database designed from the information architecture discussed previously. The component interface will also have a user interface that is used either by a call center representative or by the customer accessing the web site. The vacation planner use case shows several events and behavior processes that the event handler and the behavior processing will execute.

# Develop System Activity Diagrams

The UML activity diagram is a workflow diagram used to model sequential aspects of a business process or system and the parallel and sequential interactions between use case actors. The activity diagram shows the interaction of the various role actors with system actors within each use case.

Figure 9-7 shows that the development team, including the privacy team, begins the process by developing the Privacy Notice and privacy rules that are entered into the privacy component. They also determine and implement the encryption mechanism. The system user invokes the privacy component to make a Privacy Notice decision and to manage security. The call center representative or the web site user enters, maintains, and corrects personal information according to privacy rules managed within the privacy component. The user will then review the vacation plan alternatives, choose a plan, and buy it with a credit checked card. The provisioned plan will then be submitted. The privacy component will periodically run the archiving rules. The diagram in Figure 9-7 is also used to ensure that all privacy principles are covered by the vacation planner system.

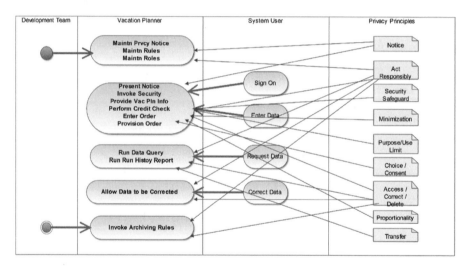

***Figure 9-7.*** *System activity diagram of vacation planner app with tie to privacy principles*

# Dynamic Modeling

Figure 9-8 is a simplified UML sequence diagram showing the entry of an order for the vacation planner using the privacy component.

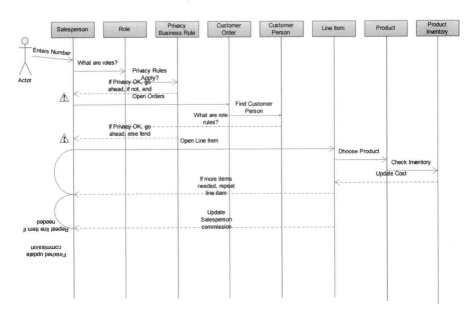

***Figure 9-8.*** *Customer order sequence diagram*

Figure 9-9 is a zoomed-in version of part of Figure 9-8, drawn larger to improve readability. The actor, who is either a call center customer service representative or the web site application component, enters an order number identifying the order. The role of the actor is determined and verified. Next, it must be determined whether privacy rules apply. The privacy component is invoked using the privacy component data model. If privacy rules are satisfied, the flow goes forward. Otherwise, an error is flagged. If the flow goes forward, the order is opened. Next, the customer contact person and his or her role is determined. Privacy rules' analysis is invoked to ensure that privacy rules for the customer are protected. If so, the process moves forward and the transaction sequence is completed. Otherwise, an error is flagged.

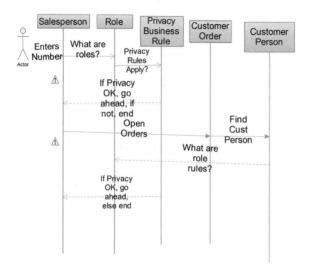

*Figure 9-9. Entering customer orders and related privacy rules in a vacation planner transaction*

Before the privacy component can be used, privacy rules for each role type need to be entered by privacy team members working with data stewards from the various business units and information technology system administrators. As stated before, these privacy rules are based on privacy policies and policy processes, procedures, guidelines, or standards.

Farther along in the vacation planner transaction, the actor will need to enter the names of persons who will play the role of guests. The guest role will have one or more privacy rules included as metadata including creation rules. When entering an order, it must first be determined whether any of the named persons who will be guests at the hotel(s) or park(s) already appear in the enterprise database. If a customer is a returning customer, the system would display the data currently held about the person and give the user the chance to make any corrections. FIPPS/GAPP suggests that a person should have the ability to make such changes. "Maintain Guest" business and privacy rules (examples of customer order business and privacy rules) should govern. They are rules that cover changes to Guest information.

If the person is new to the system, he or she is assigned the role of "Guest" with this order. This event will trigger decisions using the "Create Guest" privacy rules. According to FIPPS/GAPP, the privacy component should offer the ability to review the Privacy Notice. Once the Review Privacy Notice processing is completed, the Enter Guest Information processing begins. If the input is through the user interface, the call center guest representative, whose authorization has been verified, enters the guest data. When the data have been entered through the hospitality enterprise's web site, it will be entered by the guest or the guest's representative.

Both enterprise and statutory influenced policies govern the gathering of the data being entered. Under FIPPS/GAPP, the hospitality enterprise must:

- Ensure that there is a reason for every attribute of data being collected.

- Ensure that the guest or the guest's representative can consent to the personal information being collected. If the guest or guest representative does not consent, the guest has made an implied choice to not place the order.

- Be accountable for the process and procedures that may process the data.

- Collect only the minimum amount of data necessary to achieve the legitimate purpose of the hospitality enterprise. This includes the use of these data for ongoing marketing purposes. The use of data for these purposes should be explained in the Privacy Notice.

- Limit data collection wherever possible proportionate to the need, purpose, and sensitivity of the data being collected.

- Retain the data only as long as it is useful. This implies there is a reasonable archiving strategy.

- Adequately protect any data transferred to third parties for uses explained in the Privacy Notice to create an implied consent for such transfers. Encryption may be used as part of this process. Authentication and authorization are other parts of the process.

In the case of the hospitality enterprise mentioned, there was an enterprise business privacy rule that data would be encrypted when stored and whenever transferred to third parties. Therefore, when the guest data were entered, an encryption indicator would be set. If the guest being entered is a child, additional rules, both private and statutory, must be taken into account.

Once all of the guest's data have been entered, the guest representative or the web site will ask if there is another guest to be covered under this order. If this is the last guest to be entered for this order, the remaining data needed to complete the order will be entered. If, however, there is an additional guest, the Create Guest process will be repeated.

# Define Service Components and Supporting Metadata

The privacy component can be seen as a component containing several subcomponents. For instance, although Figure 9-10 would reflect a simplified component design for the vacation planner app, that scenario does contain the embedded privacy component. The privacy component interface, the privacy rules, the roles, and the security components on the diagram are actually subcomponents of the privacy component.

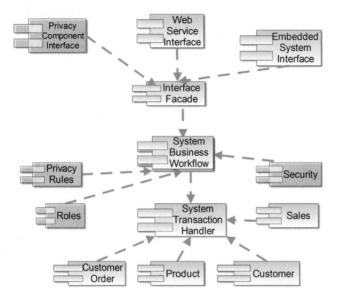

***Figure 9-10.*** *Sample component diagram*

# Using the System Development Methodology

It is recommended that the steps described in Chapter 6 should be followed completely. This methodology with an Agile overlay was used with great success on a similar project.

# Conclusion

This chapter discussed the vacation planner application as an example of the complete use of the privacy engineering methodology for an enterprise system that invokes the privacy component. When the privacy component is used, enterprise system modifications for privacy rule alterations, whether due to statute, regulation, or enterprise policy changes, will be made in a single component and available to the entire embedding system. Chapter 10 discusses Privacy Engineering quality assurance.

■ ■ ■

# Privacy Engineering and Quality Assurance

*If you don't have time to do it right, you must have time to do it over.*

—Unknown

This chapter will look at best practices for managing privacy issues within the process of quality assurance (QA) for developing and deploying products, systems, processes, and applications that involve personal information. Quality assurance is done continuously throughout the development process.

Privacy impact assessments (PIAs) will be presented as a tool for both identifying where privacy controls and measures are needed and for confirming they are in place. The benefit of a PIA for the many stakeholders in protecting personal information will also be discussed.

## Quality Assurance

Similar to the creation of privacy policies, there already exists a fairly extensive body of literature regarding QA as a discipline, a process, and an art form. So this book will not go into extensive detail on the concept of QA other than to say that it is the planned and systematic set of activities in the development process of a product or service ensuring that quality requirements are consistently met. In practice, QA is making sure that what is produced works how it was designed to work and whether it meets an enterprise's requirements. The privacy development structure for QA is presented in Figure 10-1.

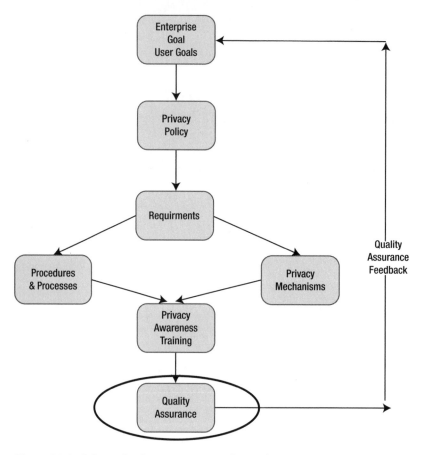

*Figure 10-1.* *Privacy development structure for quality assurance*

In many engineering programs, these underlying QA activities are part of each phase of the development lifecycle with a final QA check, including testing, as the last phase of development before deployment or release (Figure 10-2).

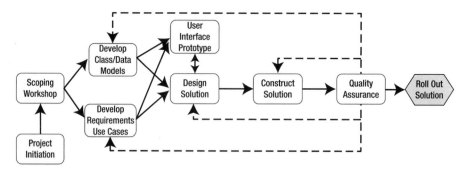

*Figure 10-2.* *Systems' engineering Lifecycle*

# Using Frameworks to Create a Privacy Quality Assurance Checklist

As in any other type of change management, using existing frameworks and standards hastens adoption of the new desired state. They provide a home base for known ways of doing things and thinking about things where appropriate and open the possibility to tackle positive change. The most well-known and accepted frameworks for fair information governance are understood by the data privacy community, but they may be less known or understood by the technical or management actors in an enterprise. When these time-tested governance principles are leveraged to create design and feature development requirements,[1] they are joined to well-known and time-tested basic technical practices and a new but grounded framework emerges.

In each step in the system engineering lifecycle (Figure 10-2), a privacy engineering QA checklist, like the one outlined in the following sections, should be referred to.

## Purpose

While answering the following questions, the use case and data model, including the metadata, should be considered:

- Are the purposes of this project (and uses of personal information) clearly defined? Are they legitimate and known to the user?

- Does each data element and attribute, related to personal information, have a direct relationship to the purpose for which it is collected and processed?

- What privacy rules are needed to ensure that the purpose principle is satisfied?

- Are there metadata that support the purpose principle?

- Is there a chance that a data subject, whether an individual or an enterprise, would be embarrassed or damaged by the processing or publication of the personal information?

- Should the data be segmented?

- Are the types of information allowed to be collected limited?

---

[1]The concept of policy that is created and leveraged for systems and governance requirements is covered in Chapter 4.

# Notice

While answering the following questions, the use case and data model, including the metadata, should be considered:

- Does the requirements statement define a complete notice that satisfies the notice principle?

- Does the notice accurately describe the processing?

- Is the notice(s) presented to the user in a timely manner?

- Are there statutory or common law requirements concerning notice in all jurisdictions wherever the system impacts?

- Is the notice clear, consistent, and relevant to the intended reader?

- Does the technique used to meet the notice requirement encourage review and facilitate understanding? For instance, would animation or a pop-up video make the notice more appealing and clearer?

- Is the notice context based or discoverable?

# Choice or Consent

While answering the following questions, the use case and data model, including the metadata, should be considered:

- Are choices clearly shown to the user throughout the design?

- Does expressing choice require action by the user? Can choices be missed or easily overlooked?

- Are defaults explained clearly? Do they put privacy at risk?

- Are defaults set to either lessen the sharing of PI or so clearly tied to the notice and the context that the only reasonable expectation for a user would be that the information is shared?

- Are tools used so that choices made by the data subject may be recorded, audited, and corrected along the way?

# Transfer

While answering the following questions, refer to the use case, data model, including metadata, and database design:

- Is data transferred to and from a third-party protected by contract, administrative, technical, logical, and physical means?

- Does the transfer of data from or to different geographic areas, such as member-states of the European Union, require a legal mechanism (such as Safe Harbor Certification or Model Contracts) to make the transfer legitimate?

- Are the proper procedures in place for all types of third-party transfers and all impacted jurisdiction?

- Are encryption and obfuscation techniques used both appropriately and effectively?

# Access, Correction, or Deletion

While answering the following questions, refer to the use case, data model, including metadata, and database design:

- Has the requestor been authenticated?

- Is the segmented appropriately so that different segments can be handled with different privacy or security rules?

- Can roles be defined so that privacy risks can be managed by means of privacy rules?

- Are rules concerning correction and deletion in compliance with the laws or regulations of all jurisdictions impacted by the system or process or by the enterprise policies?

# Security

While answering the following questions, check the use case, data model, including metadata, and design documentation:

- Has the data been classified so appropriate controls can be determined?

- Are ISO and other standards for information and security leveraged to ensure the necessary confidentiality, integrity, and availability of the data?

- Are the information security teams within your enterprise included on the project team?

- Are the security rules (including encryption) defined for each data attribute?

- Are security rules covered for data transfers, especially across jurisdictional lines?

# Minimization

While answering the following questions, check the use case, data model, including metadata, and design documentation:

- Is each personal information data attribute being collected needed for the solution being designed or is it being collected "just in case"?

- If data is being collected for potential big-data purposes, can big-data analysis be used to identify a person, thus raising a potential privacy issue?

# Proportionality

While answering the following questions, check the use case, data model, including metadata, and design documentation:

- Is the data being processed proportional to the purpose of the processing?

- Are risk and value balanced? Is the risk to an individual's privacy outweighed by the benefit (to the individual or society at large) and if not, what are the compensating controls?

# Retention

While answering the following questions, check the use case, data model, including metadata, and design documentation:

- Are archiving rules for each data attribute well established?

- Have data destruction tactics such as degaussing or permanently encrypting and destroying keys or overwriting the data after a specific deadline been adequately considered?

# Act Responsibly

- Is the privacy team included on the project team? Has a data governance or data stewardship program that include privacy been established?

This checklist is comprehensive and can be used throughout the system development process.

# Privacy Concerns During Quality Assurance

At a conceptual level, QA for privacy-engineered products, systems, processes, and applications is no different from other engineered products especially since the privacy requirements should have been factored into the design and the development from the early stages of planning. What needs to be emphasized, however, is the operational level, which has three vectors:

- The first vector concerns making sure the very act of QA doesn't create privacy issues.

- The second vector is the use of the privacy impact assessment (PIA) tool to determine whether the processing of PI in a given situation meets (or surpasses) an enterprise's privacy requirements and hence its quality requirement.

- The third vector is the importance and value a PIA has for a variety of stakeholders from internal and external regulators to the wide range of roles associated with developing products, systems, and processes that use personal information.

## Vector 1: Managing Privacy During Quality Assurance

To ensure a product, system, or process works, it needs to be tested and the results examined, diagnosed, reported, and shared. For products, systems, or process that use personal information, this presents a potential privacy conundrum: How do you test that the proper thing is happening without unnecessarily or improperly exposing the underlying data?

Best practice is to conduct QA of a system, product, service, or process that involves personal information with fake or dummy data. This data can be made up whole cloth or at least suitably deidentified from a real dataset. The reason for this approach is threefold:

- First, during system testing data often gets manipulated and changed. You don't ever want changed data corrupting production or live data should it ever migrate back into the live system by accident before deployment (e.g., in the case of system or process upgrade or migration). Also, you don't want to create an incident or breach due to real data not being properly deleted and later being "found."

- Second, data is provided for specific purposes and are supposed to only be used for such purposes. Therefore, it is not proper for data from one system or process to be used to test or model another system without permission from the owner of the data.

- Third, using real data for testing may expose it to people who, under normal circumstances, would not have had access or reason to see the data. Although the type of data may not necessarily be the kind contemplated by data breach notification legislation and regulation, this may be considered unauthorized use and access may be a violation of most organization's privacy policies.

Unfortunately, this practice is increasingly difficult to regulate with mobile apps and large, complex enterprise applications and systems, especially when it comes to replicating errors or testing new functionality.

Therefore, there are some steps that can be taken to manage privacy during the QA of systems, products, processes, or applications that contain "live" personal information. Below are some things to consider:

1. Test in read-only mode.

2. Test in a secure environment with tightly controlled access.

3. If testing requires any manipulation of data, ensure the test file is destroyed at the end of testing.

4. Mask data whenever possible.[2]

5. Do not give testers greater access than they would have as system users under normal circumstances.

6. Perform a PIA on the testing environment and QA test plan (more about PIAs below).

# PRIVACY CAN BE A COMPONENT OF DATA QUALITY

Data quality has been defined as creating and maintaining data that consistently meets knowledge worker and end-customer expectations.

To implement data quality, an enterprise needs to develop a data quality strategy, and to develop this, in conjunction with the data stewardship working team, the project must devise:

- An enterprise-wide data quality policy and procedures regarding the move to production activities

- A data governance charter as a part of data governance

- Data quality controls

- Data quality reviews and sourcing analysis methodology as a part of the architectural reviews during development

- Enterprise standards on unique identifiers and reference attributes

- Error logging and tracking

- An integration plan with the metadata strategy

---

[2]Masking data is hiding or deidentifying actual data to protect the actual data while having a functional substitute for occasions (like testing or prototyping) when the real data is not required.

The controls and measures, policies, standards, and guidelines listed above support and align with the goals of data privacy provided they factor in privacy requirements.

From Table 10-1, it is easy to see how the characteristics of data quality and the associated benefits align with privacy. However, many data quality programs do not factor in privacy. If an organization has a data quality program, it does not necessarily mean that it has factored in privacy. However, an enterprise cannot consider its data of highest level of data quality unless privacy concerns are fully addressed.

***Table 10-1.*** *Benefits Related to Data Quality Characteristics*

| Quality Characteristic | Benefit |
|---|---|
| The right information | Timely information from the right source |
| With the right completeness | All the information I need |
| In the right context | Whose meaning I understand |
| With the right accuracy | I can trust and rely on it |
| In the right format | I can use it easily |
| At the right time | When I need it |
| At the right place | Where I need it |
| For the right purpose | I can apply it |

# Vector 2: Privacy Impact Assessment: A Validation Tool

The second vector of QA for privacy engineering is to ensure the necessary privacy controls and measures are in place by using the PIA tool. The PIA tool can be used during the design and development phases of a project to determine which controls and measures are needed. It can also be used to validate that the prescribed controls and measures are in place or that suitable alternative risk management activities have been implemented.

The PIA provides a living document that becomes the "system of record" for how, within a given activity, personal information is collected and managed; where risks exist to the data, the enterprise, and the people impacted; and which controls and measures are used to mitigate the risks and legitimize the processing of the personal information. It is an interactive process that looks at business, operational, and technical issues.

The PIA is a five-phase process, as shown in Figure 10-3.

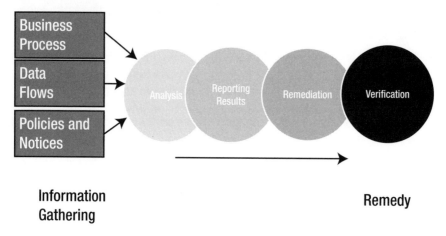

**Figure 10-3.** *The privacy impact assessment has five phases*

- *Phase 1:* Information gathering—Business and technical stakeholders will be interviewed; appropriate use cases and class and data models will be reviewed; and privacy policies, procedures, standards, guidelines, and best practices will be assessed.

- *Phase 2:* Analysis of the information gathered—The privacy team will analyze the information gathered.

- *Phase 3:* Reporting results—The PIA report will be developed containing controls and processes currently in place, an identification of the gaps between the current state and desired state, controls and mitigations where needed, and recommendations.

- *Phase 4:* Remediation needs are determined.

- *Phase 5:* Verification that privacy requirements have been met.

As data flows and usage of controls and measures change as products, systems, processes, and applications evolve, information will need to be regathered, reanalyzed, rereported, and possibly reremediated and definitely reconfirmed. The PIA process does not end until the data is disposed of or deleted.

In addition to being interactive, PIAs are iterative. Until the development stage (and even then) not all the controls and measures are always known or fixed. It is the same with usage of data. The development and functional specifications process, especially in the age of Agile development, can be quite fluid. Depending on where in the development cycle the PIA is being conducted, the PIA can serve as a tool to indicate what is needed or a tool to confirm what is in place or planned.

# 10 BEST PRACTICES FOR CONDUCTING PRIVACY IMPACT ASSESSMENTS

By Denise Schoeneich, CIPM, CIPP/IT, CISA, PMP, IT Risk, Compliance, and Audit Professional at Resources Global Professionals (RGP)

1.  *Craft an elevator pitch:* Do not assume that everyone has the same level of understanding of the definition for personal information and the objectives and requirements for a PIA.

2.  *Request a demonstration:* A demonstration of the process, product, application, or technology (system) will help provide an understanding of how personal information is processed.

3.  *Engage the right people:* Identify the system's business and technical owners responsible for each process related to the flow of personal information. Documenting a PIA is usually a progression; be prepared to contact additional system owners as the processing of personal information becomes clearer. Have another member of the privacy team review the PIA through fresh eyes to identify privacy impacts not previously recognized.

4.  *Conduct PIAs in real time:* Guide system owners through the steps of completing a PIA by scheduling working sessions; completing a PIA can be daunting the first time. Blocking out time to walk through the PIA rather than waiting for the system owners to respond is a good way to ensure timely completion.

5.  *Describe the "big picture":* In the description, broadly describe the system and include whether any personal information will be processed. The description should identify any links with other systems or processes.

6.  *Right size the PIA:* No one size fits all; the PIA effort should be commensurate with the complexity of the system and the level of privacy risk identified. For complex systems, separate PIAs with detailed process narratives and flowcharts should be created for each major component. The PIA documentation should be brief for a system with minimal privacy implications.

7. *Document the system's personal information flows:* A process narrative is a high-level description of the system's personal information process flows and identifies how the processing of personal information complies with GAPP. By documenting and understanding the personal information flows, the controls, or absence of controls, will stand out.

8. *Map the data flow of personal information:* Illustrating the data flows using diagrams that identify all key processes in the information's lifecycle can provide a clear picture that pinpoints where information is collected, used, stored, transferred, and retained and visually depict the risks, controls, and gaps.

9. *Be aware of scope:* Consider all the uses of personal information including those that may be expected but are uncommon such as administrative use of data and customer and technical support.

10. *Trust but verify:* Obtain and review database schemas, integration documentation, system guides, and architectural diagrams to confirm the accuracy of information provided by the system's owners.

# Who Is Usually Involved in a PIA?

The roles involved in a PIA vary from organization to organization. Therefore, it is better to discuss the functions or areas of activity that are usually involved:

- Business

- System development

- Engineering

- User experience representatives

- Data governance

- Legal

- Privacy team members

Why so many? The short answer is that a PIA looks at the entire lifecycle of the personal information in a system, product, process, or application. Rare is the case in which one or two individuals have a sufficient functional or operational understanding to perform the PIA. Just as it takes a village to raise a child, it takes a team to design, develop, and launch a product, system, process, or application.

# PRIVACY ENGINEERING REQUIRES BOTH QUALITY AND SECURE CODE (PART 1)

By James Ransome, PhD, CISSP, CISM, Senior Director, Product Security at McAfee

## Quality and Secure Code

Privacy engineering requires both quality and secure code, but quality and secure code need to be understood and work together. I will start by defining what quality software is and then move on to the differences and synergies and differences between quality and secure code and then the importance of privacy in the security development lifecycle (SDL).

## Quality Software

Software quality refers to two related but distinct concepts:

1. How well its functional aspects comply with or conform to a given design, based on functional requirements or specifications.

2. How well the structural aspects comply with the nonfunctional requirements that support the delivery of the functional requirements, such as robustness or maintainability.

The structure, classification, and terminology of attributes and metrics applicable to software quality management are typically derived or extracted from ISO/IEC 25010:2011—*Systems and software engineering—Systems and software Quality Requirements and Evaluation* (SQuaRE)—*System and software quality models.*[3] The initial Consortium for IT Software Quality (CISQ) version of the CISQ Software Quality specification was first published in 2012. The software quality characteristics included in this specification were selected in the CISQ Executive Workshops held in Washington, D.C.; Frankfurt, Germany; and Bangalore, India. These quality characteristics include:

- Reliability
- Performance efficiency
- Security
- Maintainability

---

[3]www.iso.org/iso/iso_catalogue/catalogue_tc/catalogue_detail.htm?csnumber=35733

The current version of the CISQ quality standard is version 2.1.[4] This specification is currently being prepared in the formats required by the Object Management Goup (OMG) and will be submitted into the OMG approval process in early 2014. When finalized, OMG will submit these specifications through their fast-track process to ISO.

I believe one of the most relevant descriptions of software quality for this article is that provided in *Juran's Quality Control Handbook*:

> The word quality has multiple meanings. Two of these meanings dominate the use of the word: 1. Quality consists of those product features which meet the need of customers and thereby provide product satisfaction. 2. Quality consists of freedom from deficiencies. Nevertheless, in a handbook such as this it is convenient to standardize on a short definition of the word quality as "fitness for use."[5]

In general, producing quality software is the degree to which software meets its specifications and satisfies its intended purpose and that the customer is satisfied with the product. It is generally accepted that the customer is satisfied with the quality of the software when they believe the product has delivered exactly what was promised, their product experience does not result in any negative consequences, and they believe the product meets or exceeds their expectations.

Many software quality practitioners describe quality as the elements that can be built into the software development process. If this is a reflection of customer needs and expectations, then the software can be deemed good quality. It is important to meet the needs and expectations of the customer. In order to do so, the elements of software quality must be built into your software. Elements of quality include:

- Capability
- Flexibility
- Maintainability
- Portability
- Readability
- Reliability
- Reusability
- Testability
- Understandability
- Usability

---

[4]This can be found at: http://it-cisq.org/wp-content/uploads/2012/09/CISQ-Specification-for-Automated-Quality-Characteristic-Measures.pdf
[5]J. M. Juran, *Juran's quality control handbook*. New York: McGraw-Hill, 1988.

The software developer has not completed the process of developing a software program of good quality until the customer has declared satisfaction with the product delivered. Although much of the quality is focused on end-user requirements, it also includes nonfunctional and system function requirements.

Ultimately, security, privacy, and reliability issues are quality bugs. The relationship between security, privacy, and reliability as elements of quality can overlap. For example:

- Security mechanisms can be used to mitigate privacy concerns.

- A security issue can result in a reliability issue. Security bugs that lead to reliability issues could mean reduced uptime and failure to meet service-level agreements, and security bugs that lead to disclosure of sensitive, confidential, or personally identifiable information are privacy issues and can have legal ramifications.

- Reliability and security issues can result in a failure of the software to protect PI, which in turn becomes a privacy issue.

Reliability, security, and privacy can also be independent of quality and fall out of that overlapping relationship. For example:

- An employee may neglect to shred paper print-out copies of a database containing PI in a software program and it is found by a cybercriminal in the local dumpster; this is not a security/privacy–quality issue but rather a security/privacy issue outside the purview of quality software.

- A power outage may occur that results in downtime of a software product because the affected machine doesn't have a UPS; this is not a software reliability/quality issue but rather an operational reliability issue unrelated to the design of the software.

Overall, security and privacy should not be considered separate tasks but approached in a holistic sense intersected with reliability and quality. To be effective, the principles of quality must be ingrained in the software developer's mindset so that it becomes second nature and part of the process by which they correctly develop code on a daily basis. As you will see later in this chapter, the attribute of quality also includes security and privacy. Although all three may be dealt with separately in the development process, they must be dealt with in a coordinated fashion with equal importance.

One of the key challenges in producing quality software is the desire to keep costs down and meet aggressive schedules which exacerbate the inconsistency in the application of quality requirements in the software development lifecycle, even for mission-critical and human-life dependent systems. The speed of delivery required by Agile development processes has made this even more challenging. Another key challenge is that the practice of software quality is still an art form, and it is costly and hard to find those who are talented with an ability to create software that can meet the ever-changing challenges we face in today's cyber environments.[6]

## What Should a Privacy Impact Assessment Document Contain?

The PIA report acts as a record of compliance for OECD Guidelines, GAPP, or other regulatory or corporate privacy requirements as reflected in the privacy policies. A PIA acts as a tool to surface risk and drive risk acceptance or mitigation. Specifically, the PIA report will contain:

- A baseline of controls and processes currently in place

- Identification of the gaps between the current state and desired state

- The framework for implementing controls and mitigations where needed

To get sufficient answers about product, system, process, or application, the following list of areas must be delved into and explored. These are pretty much the same as those discussed in terms of setting requirements, but now the purpose for examining them has changed. It is not which controls and measures should be designed or requirements set, but rather what was actually done and does it meet or exceed the requirements

- *Data:* What data is involved? Are they sensitive? Are they proportional? Do they constitute the minimum necessary?

- *Purpose:* How and why is the data being processed? Is the data being collected in alignment with the services for which the data is being collected? Is the need and reason for each data element documented?

- *Means of collection:* How was the data acquired? From the individual? From another system? From a third party? Were they legitimately collected with notice and choice?

---

[6]Portions of this article are reprinted from *Core Software Security: Security at the Source* by James Ransome and Anmol Misra. © 2014 CRC Press. Reprinted with permission. www.crcpress.com/product/isbn/9781466560956

- *Notice:* Where was notice presented? What was in the notice? Did it adequately explain how the personal information would be processed? Was it a just-in-time notice or via a link to a privacy notice?

- *Choice/Consent:* What kind of choice is the owner of the data given? Is the use of the data an option? Is consent to process the personal information required? If check boxes were used, was there a prechecked box?

- *Transfer:* Is it possible to transfer the data to third parties or another system? For what and whose purpose? Are contracts in place with the third parties? Has a privacy review been conducted? Is the data protected during transfer? Are there cross-jurisdictional issues?

- *Access, Correction, Deletion:* Does the user have a means of accessing his or her personal information and the ability to correct or delete it should it be false or inaccurate? How is the data segmented to facilitate this? Is it a self-service model? Is there a process documented and tested?

- *Security:* Is the data secure at rest or in motion? Are both required? Is the means of authentication and authorization process sufficient? Is the security mechanism overly invasive?

- *Minimization:* Is the data collected the minimum necessary to achieve the intended purpose? Has the data passed the "minimization test" (as discussed earlier in this chapter)?

- *Proportionality:* Is the processing of the data proportional to the need, purpose, and sensitivity of the data? If the purpose of the processing were to be reported in the media, would it be "embarrassing" to the enterprise?

- *Retention:* Is the deletion strategy defined and enforced within the system or the enterprise? If so, how?

- *Third parties:* If third parties are involved, what is the relationship? Has a contract been signed? What is in the contract? Is a separate PIA required? Has a security review of the third party been completed?

- *Accountability:* Are responsibilities defined and the internal enforcement mechanisms in place? What are they? Who "owns" the program? How is it managed?

Based on an enterprise's specific privacy policy, there may be additional items explored, but for most, this is the basic framework. Also, depending on how detailed or complex the PIA, there may be multiple layers to these questions, and sometimes, additional PIAs are required. For instance, if the subject of an initial PIA is an application that transmits data back to the enterprise, then a PIA is required on the application and the backend system or systems to which the data is transmitted.

Many of the answers to questions the PIA asks can be found in the requirements documentation, such as use case, activity diagrams, use-case metadata, data models, and so on. The difference is that these are source documents and the PIA is a structured analysis of the source material. The PIA is meant to provide a focused discussion of how the privacy requirements of product, system, process, or application are being met within the context of its functionality and data flows.

A set of improvement or remediation recommendations will be included in a PIA. The status of each recommendation will be tracked and reported. Thus, as mentioned earlier, the PIA is a living document. As shown in Figures 10-1 and 10-2, a feedback loop will ensure that goals, policies, processes, and procedures and privacy mechanisms are kept up to date.

---

## PRIVACY ENGINEERING REQUIRES BOTH QUALITY AND SECURE CODE (PART 2)

By James Ransome, PhD, CISSP, CISM, Senior Director, Product Security at McAfee

### Quality vs. Secure Code

Although secure code is not necessarily quality code, and quality code is not necessarily secure code, the development process for producing software is based on the principles of both quality and secure code. You cannot have quality code without security or security without quality, and their attributes complement each other. At a minimum, quality and software security programs should be collaborating closely during the development process; ideally, they should be part of the same organization and both part of the software development engineering department. The organizational and operational perspective is discussed further in my latest book, *Core Software Security: Security at the Source.*

"The foundation of software applications, and the development processes that produce them, is based on the common best principles of quality code and secure code. These principles are the driving force behind the concepts and design of industry best practices. To produce secure code that will stand the test of time, you must learn how to incorporate these principles into the development process." Remember that secure code is not necessarily quality code, and quality code is not necessarily secure code.[7]

---

[7]J. Grembi, *Secure software development: A security programmer's guide.* Boston: Course Technology, 2008. p. 58

*Secure code does not mean quality code:* You must know how to write quality code before you can write secure code. A developer can write very secure code that authorizes and authenticates every user transaction, logs the transaction, and denies all unauthorized requests; however, if the code does not return expected results, then even this very secure code may never see the light of day. Software quality characteristics are not the same as security. Quality is not measured in terms of confidentiality, integrity, and availability, but rather in terms of ease of use and whether it is reusable and maintainable.[8]

*Quality code does not mean secure code:* A developer can write efficient code that is easy to maintain and reusable, but if that code allows an unauthorized user to access the application's assets, then the code is of no use. Unlike software quality, software security is not subjective. Sensitive information is either exposed or it is not, and there is no second chance to get it right. Ultimately, quality, security, and maintainability are the three primary goals the industry considers to be of the upmost importance in any secure software development process.[9]

You cannot have quality without security or security without quality. These two attributes complement each other, and both enhance overall software product integrity and market value. Good developers should be able to identify what quality factors are in software and how to code them. Likewise, good developers should know how the software they develop can be attacked and what the weakest areas are in the software; if the code allows an unauthorized user to access the application's assets, then that code is either exposed or it's not, and there is no second chance to get it right.[10]

## Privacy and the Security Development Lifecycle

Protecting users' privacy is another important component of the SDL process and should be considered a system design principle of significant importance in all phases of the SDL. Just as with a failure in security, a failure to protect the customer's privacy will lead to an erosion of trust. As more and more cases of unauthorized access to customers' personal information are disclosed in the press, the trust in software and systems to protect customers' data is deteriorating. In addition, many new privacy laws and regulations have placed an increased importance on including privacy in the design and development of both software and systems. As with security, software that has already progressed through the development lifecycle can be very expensive to change; it is much less expensive to integrate privacy preservation methodologies and techniques into the appropriate phases of the SDL to preserve the privacy of individuals and to protect personally

---

[8]Ibid, pp. 58-60
[9]Ibid. p. 60
[10]Ibid. p. 72

identifiable information data. Some key privacy design principles included in an SDL are the ability to provide appropriate notice about data that are collected, stored, or shared so users can make informed decisions about their personal information; enable user policy and control; minimize data collection and sensitivity; and the protection of the storage and transfer of data.[11]

It is imperative that privacy protections be built into the SDL through best practices implemented within the SDL. Ignoring the privacy concerns of users can invite blocked deployments, litigation, negative media coverage, and mistrust. In my recent book Core Software Security: Security at the Source, my co-author and I have incorporated privacy protection best practices into our SDL.[12]

## Vector 3: The Importance and Value of Privacy Impact Assessment to Key Stakeholders

A PIA also serves as a tool that provides confirmation of:

- *Accountability:* External regulators—Should there ever be an inquiry from external regulators, such as data protection authorities, a PIA shows that the organization has a proactive program in place and takes responsibility.

- *Compliance with internal guidelines:* Internal regulators—Should there be a question from an internal regulator such as for an internal audit, a PIA is a quick reference for answering questions. It also shows internal regulators that controls and measures were determined through an analytical process and deliberate steps were taken to avoid risk.

- *QA and continuity:* Product team—A PIA acts as a document from which the product team validates and confirms that the required controls and measures are in place and meet the enterprise's requirements. A PIA acts as a central document so that as requirements and functionality change, privacy requirements are not lost, obscured, neglected, or overlooked, especially as the project moves between teams.

- *Quick reference:* Data incident response teams—In the event of a data incident, a PIA acts as a quick reference to the potential scope of it.

---

[11]Microsoft Corporation. Microsoft Security Development Lifecycle (SDL), Version 3.2. 2012. www.microsoft.com/en-us/download/details.aspx?id=24308
[12]Portions of this article are reprinted from *Core Software Security: Security at the Source* by James Ransome and Anmol Misra. © 2014 CRC Press. Reprinted with permission. www.crcpress.com/product/isbn/9781466560956

- *Data maps:* IT and data governance team—Because PIAs usually contain data flow diagrams and maps, they can combine to form a "data" atlas for the IT and data governance teams.

- *Peace of mind:* For all—A successful PIA will give all involved peace of mind that the necessary controls and measures are in place and are the result of a structured analysis (as opposed to happenstance).

## QUALITY ASSURANCE DOESN'T END AT LAUNCH

By Jules Polonetsky, Executive Director, Future of Privacy Forum

One of the most useful privacy engineering tips that I have picked up over my years as a privacy professional is a very simple concept: Make sure you only get what you intend to get. In the messy world of data, this is easier said than done. It can be hard to know which data a system will eventually need, and it is often easier to collect and log and then figure out what should be used. But consider the backlash over revelation that Google Streetview cars logged the content of Wi-Fi transmissions as they drove by homes to understand the intense criticism and liability that can flow from logging more than is intended.

I first learned the lesson of limited collection by design early in my career. From 2000 to 2002, I served as chief privacy officer at DoubleClick, a new job title that had recently emerged at companies that want to show they were serious about privacy. I found myself running around like a madman, trying to educate employees, get privacy clauses into contracts, and support consumer-friendly policies.

One problem that plagued ad serving companies then and still today was a privacy snafu that occurs when ad tags or tracking pixels were placed on web pages that collected sensitive information. A company might wish to learn which ads were leading to consumers actually purchasing or registering and would set a tracking pixel on a page where a consumer typed in a credit card number or provided an e-mail address.

If the tags were implemented improperly, sensitive personal information would be sent by web sites to DoubleClick's adservers. Now we didn't want these data, we didn't use these data, and we didn't even know when they were being sent to us. Log files are often messy and adserving backend systems would analyze the adserving log files to pluck the fields that the adservers needed to track and target ads. Our policies promised that we served ads anonymously.

It turned out that it was trivial for critics to scan web sites and "discover" that companies were sending sensitive data to DoubleClick. I responded by educating our web site clients, warning them, cajoling, and inserting contract language barring them from sending DoubleClick personal information. All to no avail, as news headline after headline appeared, exposing the latest "data leak." Policy couldn't solve the problem, contracts couldn't solve the problem, and promises that we didn't use the data or even know we were getting them didn't restore the faith.

I was finally able to persuade the engineering team to implement a system that ensured that the adservers truncated on the fly any personal data before we logged them. We continued educating clients not to "leak data" to us, but only when I could show that our system was engineered to only do what we said it would do—serve ads anonymously—could we show that our code backed up our promises.

I wish I could say that the industry took this lesson seriously and future companies avoided making the same mistake. But every year we read of new versions of this type of data leakage at companies that promise that they do not collect or use or share sensitive data. It is against their policy! Unfortunately, policy doesn't trump technology and companies continue to be castigated as data continues to leak. As I write this, the Affordable Health Care web site is being criticized for leaking sensitive health registration data to analytics companies, a blow that this already troubled web site didn't need.

"Privacy by design" has become the mantra of many of us who practice at the intersection of data, policy, and technology. To succeed at privacy by design, privacy professionals need to think like engineers and engineers need to think like privacy professionals. Doing any less leaves the privacy professional subject to the failings of technology and leaves the engineer frustrated with the constraints of policy. In a fast changing world of data innovation, getting policy and technology to align can be the difference between success and failure.

# Resources for Conducting Privacy Impact Assessments

There are a number of resources available on the Internet regarding PIA that are worth reviewing:

> Privacy Impact Assessments: The Privacy Office Official Guidance. June 2010: www.dhs.gov/xlibrary/assets/privacy/privacy_pia_guidance_june2010.pdf

> Privacy Impact Assessment: Towards Best Practices. http://ehealthrisk.wikispaces.com/file/view/PIA%20Best%20Practices%20Guide_PSCIOC.doc/389845494/PIA%20Best%20Practices%20Guide_PSCIOC.doc

> Privacy Policy Appendix B Privacy Impact Assessment Template: www.novascotia.ca/just/IAP/_docs/Appendix%20B%20PIA%20Template.pdf

Privacy Impact Assessment (PIA) Guide: `www.sec.gov/about/privacy/piaguide.pdf`

Privacy Impact Assessment Guide: `www.oaic.gov.au/privacy/privacy-resources/privacy-guides/privacy-impact-assessment-guide`

---

## THINK WHOLE SYSTEM WHEN DOING QUALITY ASSURANCE

By David Mortman, Chief Security Architect, Dell Enstratius, and Contributing Analyst, Securosis

When hearing about penetration testing, people usually think "security" and not "privacy," but the fact is that testing your application to make sure your privacy controls are effective is just as important. Many security vulnerabilities will lead to privacy failures as well. Any time you have an attack that leads to a data disclosure you have a potential privacy issue as well. So in a very real sense, privacy vulnerabilities are a subset of security vulnerabilities. This is yet another example of the truism that security doesn't require privacy, but privacy requires security. When your security team plans the application penetration test, work with them to identify the areas of the application that contain privacy-related data so the pen-test team can prioritize those areas. Remember when performing the assessment to focus not only on the web frontend, but also on any mobile apps, administrative interfaces, and APIs that are exposed as they are also vectors of unintentional disclosure.

---

# Conclusion

Quality assurance and conducting privacy reviews go hand in hand. The PIA is the tool that enables the privacy engineer to discerns issues and characterize where they fit into the puzzle of privacy compliance. It acts as a map for the privacy engineer to understand historical aspects of a product and it acts as a headlight to show the future. The next chapter will will discuss how to access and ready your organization for Privacy Engineering.

# PART 3

# Organizing for the Privacy Information Age

# CHAPTER 11

■ ■ ■

# Engineering Your Organization to Be Privacy Ready

*Action springs not from thought, but from a readiness for responsibility.*

—G. M. Trevelyan

This chapter provides a methodology for assessing and implementing privacy awareness and readiness in the enterprise as a whole. It also discusses the privacy roles and responsibilities typically found in nonengineering groups throughout the enterprise and their contribution to an organization's privacy awareness and readiness.

Some may think the term engineering cannot cover organizational structure, input, and expected output. Nonetheless, an organization, like a series of hardware and software elements, can also be considered a "metasystem" and, as such, it needs to be designed and tooled (and in some cases, retooled) to function properly. This type of engineering work (i.e., organizational or industrial engineering) is instrumental in establishing an environment and cultural context in which privacy engineering can flourish and one in which data is recognized as an asset and is respected as a matter of ethical as well as financial importance.

It is just as important to engineer an organization for privacy as it is to engineer processes, products, systems, and services for privacy. In fact, the effectiveness of privacy engineering systems or programs depends on the privacy readiness of the overall organization. This is because processes, products, services, and systems are not built, licensed, deployed, implemented, or supported in a vacuum.

All tasks within an enterprise are ultimately performed against a backdrop powered by personal information use and management. This is true regardless of the percentage of PI related to employees vs. customer data processed by an enterprise or a subunit of an enterprise. In other words, almost anything requires uses of personal information throughout an enterprise.

This organizational engineering includes establishing privacy governance (which will be discussed in detail in Chapter 12) and creating privacy awareness and readiness throughout the organization (i.e., communication and training), functional alignment, and staffing. This staffing includes new and emerging privacy-focused roles, as well as more established roles such as the chief privacy officer (CPO)[1] and chief information security officer (CISO).

A good example of emerging privacy roles may be drawn from the experience of many CPOs in the early 2000s when the notion of organizational privacy roles was in its infancy. Many early CPOs first established a privacy council. This virtual organization consisted of business owners of required datasets (i.e., marketing and human resources), IT representatives, disaster recovery staff, legal representatives from outside the privacy function, business continuity, mergers and acquisitions groups, and risk and dedicated privacy professionals. The group would bring intelligence and best practices together on a regular basis and would be the central sharing point for information or workflows that required coordinated efforts from different owners. The levels of individuals on the privacy council often varied wildly to include security savvy junior programmers as well as high-placed officers who commanded large budgets and resources but who also were dependent on a constant flow of sanctioned and safe data. In many cases, a privacy council acted collectively in the enterprise system where distributed technologies and authority would not or did not exist.

Making an organization privacy ready is not solely the domain of privacy engineering teams any more than making sure an organization is ready to release a new product or deploy a new system is solely the domain of product engineering.

# Privacy Responsibilities in Different Parts of the Organization

Every organization's strategy for addressing its coordination and improvement requirements to become more data and person centric will be a bit different. These differences evolve as the privacy programs mature and as metrics for success become more ubiquitous. As such, there is no one-size-fits-all answer to what roles and areas of focus different departments will have in tuning an organization for privacy operational readiness; however, there are some typical roles and functions that are more than likely to appear in any organization.

Table 11-1 provides an overview of the high-level responsibilities of data privacy professionals in nonengineering departments (i.e., not IT or product development).

---

[1]We are talking about the CPO role. The job title may be different.

**Table 11-1.** *Privacy Responsibilities Throughout the Organization of Nonengineering Groups*

| Organization/Function | High-Level Privacy Responsibilities |
|---|---|
| Legal | Provide support for contractual documents and help privacy engineering staff stay current on new legislation and regulations, including assessing laws as they relate to privacy policies. |
| Marketing or business development and sales | Manage and safeguard customer data to protect its privacy and help ensure that customers' personal information is accessed and used only as authorized. Build trust in the organization so customers are comfortable sharing their data. Plan and address sales team playbooks for selling privacy engineered products or services or demonstrating to potential customers how their data will be subjected to high levels of protection and respect. |
| Vendor management | Ensure that if vendors collect, manage, or use PI on behalf of the organization, that the PI is accessed and used only as authorized and that appropriate safeguards are maintained. |
| Audit | Help develop a privacy compliance audit model as well as identify and track privacy risks during the audit process. Conduct audits in a privacy-compliant manner. |

# Privacy Awareness and Readiness Assessments

Awareness starts with an assessment. Those concerned with an enterprise's privacy preparedness must determine what is already in place (if anything) and what needs to be put in place for the enterprise to be privacy aware and ready. If an enterprise has engaged a CPO, this effort should be led by that CPO. If the enterprise does not yet have a privacy accountable executive such as a CPO, we recommend any one of these options:

- Create and staff the role as soon as possible as a permanent position with funding and executive support and buy in

- Fill the role temporarily until the assessment is completed and then fill it as a permanent chartered position based on the results of the assessment project

- Get the tasks, requirements, and responsibilities integrated into each relevant function

The process for making this assessment is called a *privacy awareness and readiness assessment* (it could also be called a Proactive Assurance Review [PAR], in internal audit terms). A privacy awareness and readiness assessment is similar to a privacy assessment of a process, product, or system, which is done through a Privacy Impact Assessment (PIA) (as discussed in Chapter 10).

The difference between a PAR and a PIA is typically one of horizontal vs. vertical scale. Where a privacy awareness and readiness assessment (the PAR) covers the organization as a whole, a PIA typically covers a system, a process, or a particular tool or feature.

A good privacy awareness and readiness assessment requires focused leadership, a budget, executive buy in, and a lot of finesse to convince stakeholders that they are, indeed, stakeholders and to gain an understanding of a data asset that may have gone unnoticed and uncurated for years.

In the experience of many privacy officers, one of the grumpier members of any executive staff may be the loveable yet cynically analytical chief financial officer. At first blush, the CFO should be the most excited and engaged in the notion of unearthing unleveraged assets and identifying potential liabilities, after all, this is the crux of his or her job. In reality, the CFO may consider a discussion of data risks and outcomes as the exclusive domain of the CIO and his or her only concern, the now well-trod notion of risk under the financial controls requirements.[2] Reaching and teaching teams that calculate financial worth in a world where data asset values are not yet competently reported can be a challenge. Be patient with them. The CFO and his or her team will ultimately report and leverage data valuation and risk for data assets, including personal information.

Nonetheless, performing a privacy awareness assessment and leveraging its results can create a significant contribution in building a sustainable privacy-ready enterprise. Think of a preliminary assessment as gathering the "requirements" for the enterprise metasystem as any good privacy engineer would also do for a product, process, or system.

A privacy awareness and readiness assessment provides the means to accurately map out an organization's current situation and understand how well the organization is currently executing the necessary controls and measures to mitigate risk or to create opportunity. It includes identifying organizational roles that are present or missing and defining the level of data utilization, privacy awareness, and readiness throughout the various functions involved in utilizing, managing, or manipulating data as well as those involved in developing products and services.

Remember that risk should always be compared with the value to the business, so the real objective here is to determine the current state of the controls and measures used to manage and protect (i.e., process) personal information so that unacceptable risk can be managed. The ultimate goal, however, is to make sure that risks taken before collecting, processing, or sharing data are all proportionally lower than the value of what is being assessed or achieved by processing those data. After all, if the costs to mitigate data-related risks are greater than the ultimate asset value, processing will not be a good business proposition, nor will the incentive to maintain and protect that data remain at the appropriate level.

A good privacy awareness and readiness assessment should not only define and document the existing situation but should also identify steps for remediation where unacceptable risks and opportunities for innovation are discovered.

---

[2]The Sarbanes-Oxley Act of 2002 is the most notorious legal requirement for publicly traded companies in the United States, but nearly every jurisdiction worldwide has similar requirements to protect financial reporting from fraud and shenanigans.

# Define Existing Systems and Processes

Because the use of personal information in an enterprise can be so vast and pervasive, it is rare for any one individual to understand it all. Many organizations have no map that defines the existing data flows for all personal information. Those that do have some mapping often proudly produce a spaghetti-looking diagram of existing databases and data markets and, perhaps, a key to identity management systems and corresponding role definitions. Rarely, if ever, do data elements have corresponding policies dated and marked to reflect timing and processing requirements for data within the enterprise map.[3] Rarer still are data element maps created for data flowing to and from third-party systems and vendors.[4] The privacy engineer should dance an unseemly and ungainly privacy jig if he or she encounters such a map, as the basic assessment and privacy readiness of such an enterprise would then be much easier.

The first step in a privacy awareness and readiness assessment is to define the current business processes and data flows as well as the existing privacy policies and notifications in use. The idea behind this first step is to document the current situation for analysis from a strategic perspective and to identify where additional controls might be needed. This step also allows the privacy professional to discover exemplars to hold up as models for emulation by others—competition is a strong cohesive force in most organizations.

This can be accomplished with a succession of high-level interviews with stakeholders that will culminate in sufficient information to chart activity diagrams or use-case diagrams that take into account the elements in the enterprise management lifecycle, as shown in Figure 11-1.

---

[3]Note the activity diagrams showing privacy requirements (Figures 9-3 and 9-7) in Chapter 9. There will often be enterprise data models in well-managed enterprises.

[4]An encrypt and forget legacy is a strong one that actually represents some of the more advanced organizations' early attempts at proactive data protection. This type of scenario is the likely result of a strong IT security group or an unfunded CPO who has been assigned under the CISO organization where the best-case protection for personal data has been deemed encryption for any suspected regulated data.

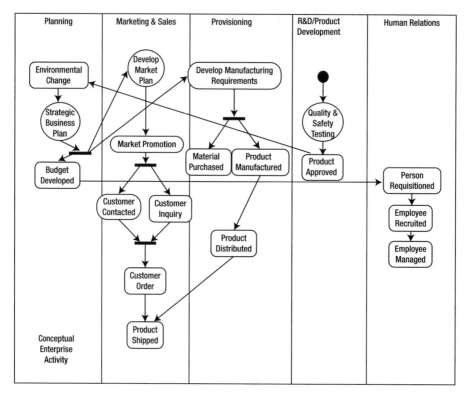

**Figure 11-1.** *UML activity diagrams can be used to document the existing high-level process flows and data flows*

Such activity diagrams capture a snapshot of how personally identifiable information flows within and between the existing processes products, services, and systems. They show how the information is currently being used, managed, collected, controlled, and safeguarded throughout the organization. Such diagrams also provide a good management snapshot to show where resources and tasks are owned and where more resources may need to be deployed.

## HIGH-LEVEL PRIVACY IMPACT ASSESSMENT QUESTIONS

Here is a sample set of questions you can use to interview key stakeholders and collect information about the data-processing activities of a group or division of an enterprise. The idea is to start at the executive level and begin to travel down the chain of responsibility until sufficient information has been collected and stakeholders at the management and execution levels have been interviewed.

Date:

Name:

Business Unit (BU):

Department:

1. Please describe the general functions of your department or group.

2. How much annual revenue is driven from this BU or supported by this BU?

3. Is there a product or services breakdown of the revenue?

4. What is the overall "value" of the information that is used or processed as part of this BU?

    a. Is there another way that you measure value for information (Example: churn, subscriptions/newsletters subscribed to)?

5. What is the volume of the information your team manages?

6. What are the elements, types, or categories of data? (i.e., customer e-mail addresses, credit card numbers)

7. What information is critical to your BU for success?

    a. What information helps with product or services or business development?

    b. What information, if not delivered on a timely basis, creates risk?

    c. What information, if not properly managed or stored, creates unwanted risk?

8. Which data elements are important (i.e., highly valued, but not critical) to your business?

9. What are the sources of the data (i.e., internal human resources, payroll systems, products, end users)?

10. Is the source of the data internal, external, or both?

11. What are the systems, applications, interfaces, or other tools your BU uses in performance of its functions?

12. Who are the data subjects?

13. With whom is the data shared?

14. What is the source of the data (i.e., systems, applications, APIs from which the data is gathered)?

15. Where do you see [insert name of company]'s information risk overall?

16. Who at [insert name of company] is doing a great job of data protection?

17. What type of training would be best for your team?

18. When you think about information and data, what worries you most?

To get started creating activity diagrams and enterprise data models, first engage with key stakeholders to understand the "stuff" that is managed[5] and the business processes, their purpose(s), and their value. Then as the business data flows are clarified and are ready for more granular information, begin to work with the IT organization to create activity diagrams and data models. An enterprise IT organization may already have an inventory of the majority of existing systems and may also have a starting point for defining data flows between systems and within business processes. They may not have the contents of various systems documented down to the data element (although they should), but knowing the type and ownership of systems is a great place to begin.

## MAPPING DATA FLOW HAS MULTIPLE BENEFITS

In every enterprise, everyone is busy. Everyone has their own set of goals and deliverables. Often, getting resources for a project is not easy, even when everyone realizes it is the right thing to do. Finding resources to map data flows may be similarly challenging and often requires working across multiple groups (at a minimum two—IT, who can tell you what data, and the business owners or data stewards of the systems, who can tell you how the data is used[6]).

Here are some benefits that mapping data flows provides IT, which can be useful in building the business case for IT resources and IT involvement:

- Clear picture of where the enterprise's information assets actually reside and a groundwork for data value assessments

- Quick understanding of risk in the enterprise

- True picture of which IT systems require more or less protection

- Fast analysis of issues when systems are updated or end-of-lifed

- Opportunity to remove redundancy in systems and reduce storage overhead

---

[5]The class or data models discussed throughout Part 2 are often available for most systems.
[6]Between IT and business organizations, it may sometimes seem that IT is the hardest to get involved. Sometimes this is because IT leadership falsely believes that the mission is complete after encryption of some of the incoming data or, more tragically, they do not believe that the stores of data they do collect, process, and manage is personal information. Perhaps a holiday gift of *The Privacy Engineer's Manifesto* may help with this common quandary!

Equally important, if not more important, is gaining an understanding of the data flows, models, and activities that involve service providers or are hosted at third-party facilities or data centers. When mapping data, it is important not to put blinders on and assess only what is within an enterprise's physical control. All the data flows and activities connected to the enterprise should be considered part and parcel of the same. This is particularly true for small to medium organizations where many off the shelf cloud instantiations or applications may be used to manage a business or organization or just a process. The data models in these cases may not be as complete on the backend, but even the smallest teams can understand which data they use for value and where they send them initially.

## Consider the Context

As part of the analysis, it's a good idea to consider the context in which a privacy initiative will operate. What are the aspects of data control that already exist and what is the understanding of privacy from the most senior management to middle managers, functional departments, and administrative personnel? Just getting a handle on the basic concepts and an understanding of privacy at these different levels of the organization will indicate the point from which a privacy awareness and readiness campaign must start.

Another critical factor in establishing context is the organization's overall bias toward risk. If the organization has a high tolerance for risk,[7] then making the business case to close gaps, protect data, and developing internal enthusiasm to do so will be more difficult. However, if the tolerance to undertake risk is low, then creating a business case and developing internal enthusiasm may be easier to engender.[8]

Ultimately, if privacy programs are perceived as providing value to the business or if an organization has made a strategic decision that embedding privacy controls into all of its systems and processes will improve its brand image or provide a competitive advantage, then IT, human resources, product marketing, engineering, legal, leadership, and other teams will likely be quite supportive of the overall privacy initiative.[9] An initial assessment can provide adequate detail to begin this effort.

If, on the other hand, senior management has mandated a privacy initiative to mitigate risk but lower levels of the organization are not yet onboard with the idea, then much more upfront effort will be required. In this example, the privacy professiona would need to spend more time educating engineering and marketing teams about what their risks are and how implementing better controls can provide value.

---

[7]This type of "risk" is risk that is not based in fact and data. A true risk-based organization would ideally take in relevant facts and then take action. This type of idealized organization can, arguably, make broader leaps forward because the risk is taken with data and not exclusively chest-bumping bravado.

[8]It should be noted that an excessive desire for too much detailed data or an overly conservative appetite for risk may also cause decision paralysis, and unnecessary paralysis can transform once innovative organizations into sleepy dinosaurs.

[9]This is more about corporate values and views of risk. Google and Facebook, for instance, have high thresholds for privacy risk and thus it has taken FTC sanctions for them to beginning toeing the privacy line. Whereas a bank like RBC has always understood privacy risks and implementing and managing privacy controls have always been relatively more straightforward.

Privacy awareness and readiness can also have implications for a business strategy. For example, where there is limited awareness and readiness in marketing and the business strategy depends on consumers opting in to an online community, there will be a need to bring greater maturity to the marketing team's privacy awareness and readiness. Without such readiness, it will be necessary to alter the business strategy to avoid the risk that marketing will not properly protect consumer data or will misuse that data to create whole-enterprise risk rather than a risk of a failed marketing campaign.

An organization's strengths and weaknesses with regard to privacy awareness and readiness should be documented so this knowledge can inform privacy strategy, help prioritize tasks in the privacy initiative, and can serve as a benchmark and starting point for improvement for the entire organization.

# Skills Assessment

The skills component of the privacy awareness and readiness assessment is a review of where these various responsibilities are currently hosted in an organization and to what degree skill sets currently meet or are capable of meeting desired objectives.

In most cases, there will be holes, meaning that some of these responsibilities are not currently being carried out in the organization or may not even have an assigned responsibility. Several factors can affect how well the responsibilities are carried out. The most common reasons for poor execution of privacy responsibilities include:

- *Lack of awareness and readiness:* The responsible party may not fully understand privacy risks or how to alleviate them. In this case, privacy awareness and readiness education is needed.

- *Lack of resources:* The responsible party will often be wearing multiple hats, and if there are limited resources to properly perform the privacy duties and responsibilities, they can fall by the wayside. Similarly, a lack of financial resources can stymie efforts to get proper local legal counsel, hire vendors for efficiency and outside perspective, and limit face-to-face communication, which is necessary for a strong (often virtual or matrixed) team.

- *Lack of incentive:* Other tasks that are more directly related to the charter of the department in which the person resides are likely to get more attention unless there are explicit incentives for privacy engineering support work.

Organizational alignment can fill these gaps through a matrix organizational structure or by getting buy in from management to assign goals and objectives related to privacy engineering.

In summary, the skills assessment identifies and documents the responsibilities that are currently unfulfilled as well as those that are already being carried out. It also identifies opportunities for improvement in how the existing responsibilities can be executed more efficiently or more effectively.

More detail about specific roles needed for successful privacy engineering can be found in Chapter 12.

# Building the Operational Plan for Privacy Awareness and Readiness

Based on the findings from the privacy awareness and readiness assessment, an implementation strategy and operational plan can be built.

Goals and objectives for privacy awareness and readiness can be organized to provide short-, medium-, and long-term focal points. They should include quantifiable metrics for success so that the privacy professional can measure progress of the program. The goals and objectives should take into consideration the existing business risks from known privacy vulnerabilities as well as the levels of privacy awareness and readiness throughout the organization.

The general level of understanding about privacy throughout the organization is a key factor in deciding which can be accomplished and the proper timeframe for goals and objectives. The initial data-gathering phase of the privacy awareness and readiness assessment should uncover the existing level of awareness and readiness in the organization. During this analysis phase, the privacy team should come up with a prioritized list of actions to improve privacy awareness and readiness.

## SAMPLE PRIORITIZED ACTION LIST

Here is a sample list of prioritized actions paired with the associated finding to which the action is a response.

Overall Awareness or Understanding of Personal Information

- General awareness communication and training across the organization to help apply clarity and consistency to how PI is defined

- Specialized or targeted training efforts to support specific roles (i.e., product development, human resources, sales and marketing)

Documenting Knowledge or Expertise

- Continued coordination between privacy and engineering teams to complete PIAs and translating results to formalized policies and procedures to guide the business on how to handle PI

Developing Data Lifecycle Model

- Coordination with corporate strategy or BU teams to help build a model on how to monetize the data utilized across the enterprise

- Company-wide effort to establish data retention and deletion requirements

Privacy Engineering

- Privacy teaming with engineering, IT, and operations to put in process gates or assessments to ensure privacy-related areas are considered in product development or project implementations

- Development of standards or guidance that will be business enabling and not business stifling

- Align roles and responsibilities with counterparts at parent company and other subsidiaries

Marketing Privacy-Related Products

- Privacy collaborating with corporate development, strategy, portfolio or product management, professional services, and go-to-market teams to segment out privacy-related products as a separate part of product solutions

- Focus on both organic and inorganic growth for privacy-related solutions

Privacy awareness and readiness are only two components of an overall privacy program that must make efforts toward improvements across a broad array of people, process, and technology issues. However, there is always some need to improve privacy awareness and readiness before other factors can be properly addressed. For example, if there are myths about privacy that have proliferated throughout the organization, these must be dispelled before the organization can successfully adopt the right privacy practices. Privacy awareness and preparedness are ongoing processes for the enterprise to remain strategically positioned and resilient in the face of changing legal requirements, external events, customer and business changes, and overall enterprise resilience.

## FIVE BIG MYTHS ORGANIZATIONS HAVE ABOUT PRIVACY AND THE RESPONSE SHOULD BE TO DISPEL THEM

Myth 1: We don't have any personal information to worry about.

Response: If you have employees or customers, you have PI.

Myth 2: Security has it covered.

Response: Security's focus is ensuring confidentiality, integrity, and availability of proprietary information, not all that privacy requires. Security can be, but is not always, a help. (See Chapter 3 for a discussion of this.)

Myth 3: No one gets in trouble if we screw up.

Response: Facebook, Google, Microsoft, and Eli Lilly are all currently under 20-year consent decrees from the FTC and need to submit to biannual audits. Fines and sanctions are growing every day. It may not always make headlines, but people and organizations are both getting into trouble. The recently passed European Regulation calls for a downside 5% of worldwide turnover for privacy failures with few specific guidelines regarding how individual member-states may attempt to assess such a fine. Even if this law and others like it do not stand, legal costs battling even speciously assessed fines will be the future for many years to come. Trouble.

Myth 4: Privacy people always say no to fun business ideas.

Response: This is the one myth that may be grounded in some truth and a failure of imagination. Unless the fundamental premise of that which is proposed is against the law, a good privacy person will answer: Yes, it may be done and here is how, or, at least, here are a few ideas. Although the hoops that must be jumped through to get something done may equal "no" in terms of a risk vs. reward calculation, the decision not to move forward with a bright shiny object is a sound business risk decision.

Myth 5: Privacy gets in the way of marketing or connection.

Response: In the era of customer engagement and e-marketing, it has been proven time and again that privacy-based permission and context-based marketing provide *better* results and return on investment.

---

Common approaches for building privacy awareness and readiness include internal publications, newsletters, custom apps, employee-specific goal setting, and formal training for specific audiences.

An operational plan should include a prioritized list of action items intended to advance privacy awareness and readiness. This prioritized list should be accompanied by a schedule for execution and an associated budget.[10]

---

[10]Ordering multiple copies of this book would be a good idea!

The privacy awareness and readiness operational plan should also include success metrics for each step of the plan as well as descriptions of the planned review processes that will help determine if additional steps are needed as time goes on.

# Building a Communication and Training Plan for Privacy Awareness and Readiness

To create awareness and build readiness into the enterprise, there must be a "there" there. For this reason, privacy policies must be defined, written, and communicated to employees. They also should be extended into standards and guidelines that are practical and both directional and instructional as needed. All such policies must be effectively communicated throughout the enterprise. Communication and training are crucial to building awareness and ensuring readiness and ownership.

---

### IT'S ALL FUN AND GAMES UNTIL SOMEBODY LOSES PI (PERSONAL INFORMATION)

By Ruby A. Zefo, Chief Privacy and Security Counsel, Intel Corporation

Does your enterprise have a bring-your-own-device (BYOD) program? If you work for a sizable company, the answer is likely "yes," whether you know it or not. Chances are that if you do not launch an "official" BYOD program, savvy employees who prefer using their own smartphones and other mobile devices will launch their own. When that happens, your intellectual property and your employees' PI could be at risk. BYOD programs should not be the reason you suddenly dust off your processes for data breach management or trade secret loss. Proper cross-company planning and maintenance of BYOD programs can make all the difference between a cherished employee and employer benefit vs. rogue devices and networks, employee complaints, and employee data loss.

Prohibiting employees from bringing their personal devices to work is not the answer. History shows that Prohibition didn't work the first time; alternative compute options only become more tantalizing if a company is overzealous in prohibiting their use. A recent study found that one of three respondents said they would gladly "contravene a company's security policy that forbids them to use their personal devices at work or for work purposes."[11] Many younger employees view using their own mobile devices at work as a right, not a privilege. An employer may find it difficult enough to stay ahead of the curve when it purposefully launches a new BYOD program, no less when the program "starts itself."

---

[11]InfoWorld report on Vision Critical study, "Young employees say BYOD a 'right' not 'privilege.'" www.infoworld.com/d/consumerization-of-it/young-employees-say-byod-right-not-privilege-195901

Embracing BYOD programs is the right answer. These programs are not only about employee convenience and satisfaction; BYOD programs can also provide corporate benefits, such as increased employee productivity. Right or wrong, employees use mobile devices to work while on vacation, in bed, during travel, on weekends, and while they are multitasking on the phone with old Aunt Marge who is droning on about the neighbor's barking dog. Managed properly, these programs can be a win-win for employers and employees.

So, you wisely decide to launch a BYOD program. What could go wrong? It's all fun and games until somebody loses PI. Even a company attempting an effective plan to launch a new BYOD service can get it wrong by failing to understand employee preferences and device usage habits, privacy and data security impacts, culture, environment, law, and so forth. When that happens, a company may see history repeating itself in the form of bootlegging: more rogue behaviors, networks, and devices.[12]

Even initially cherished implementations may grow stale; a company may erroneously expect a properly launched BYOD service to thereafter "run itself," and that it will remain static and rarely need changes in how it is administered. That can lead to a lack of funding and program management, gaps in security as technologies, user behaviors, and devices change, and increased risk.

Without a well-organized cross-functional launch plan, BYOD programs can create insecure devices, networks, apps, and behaviors that all risk company assets and create privacy problems, including:

- Lost, stolen, or misused PI, including sensitive PI—people store all kinds of sensitive data on their mobile devices

- Lost or stolen intellectual property

- Malware or intrusions that can impact the corporate network and assets and provide a route for illegal access to third-party data and assets connected to the corporate network

- Employee escalations over personal data loss and resulting harm

- Data protection authority or enforcement agency inquiries

- Lawsuits, including class action lawsuits can occur

---

[12]According to an iPass Mobile Workforce Report, nearly 25% of mobile workers say they bypass IT controls to access corporate data, claiming IT is slow in responding, they needed to do something immediately and could not wait for IT, and so forth. "BYOD mobile workers thumbing nose at IT security." www.zdnet.com/byod-mobile-workers-thumbing-nose-at-it-security-7000003519/

What can a company do to properly prepare, launch, and maintain a BYOD program? BYOD programs are more of an art than a science. So while in the BYOD context one size never fits all, a company can still prepare for the inevitable privacy issues that can Creating a cross-functional team that will gather data on employee preferences, beta test the services prior to broader launch, address any gaps in service and data protection, and manage employee expectations, awareness, and consent are important steps to getting it right. Nobody wants to be the employee that leaves the CIO holding the liability bag because he realized after the launch that he accepted more risk than he thought by failing to have requested or accepted a comprehensive risk analysis from all the key stakeholders. That should be part of the return on investment analysis prior to service launch.

In addition, a company can take a number of practical steps for proper planning and management of a BYOD program, including:

- Identify all key global stakeholders, including employees from IT, privacy, security, legal, employee communications, training, e-discovery, and human resources

- Ask the launch team to conduct a real return on investment analysis to evaluate the tradeoff of service value vs. cost and privacy risk

- Prioritize global rollouts according to import and ease of offering the service, considering privacy and related laws, enforcement schemes, types of data involved, ease of giving employees notice and obtaining consent, number of employees, operational readiness in each location, and importance of the service to the employees

- Find the right balance when monitoring employee data: failure to monitor can lead to loss of intellectual property, PI loss, excess cost (e.g., bandwidth use), and lawsuits (e.g., employee harassment). Overmonitoring can lead to decreased morale, covert rogue behavior, and lawsuits (e.g., privacy violations)

- Remember proportionality—for example, many data-protection authorities frown on using biometrics or location tracking for employee monitoring when something less will suffice

- Leverage existing corporate policies, such as acceptable use of electronic devices and the corporate network, information security policies, software licensing policies, etc.;

- Don't forget cultural differences – both jurisdictionally and within the company; and

- Ask the launch team to create global program managers for proper ongoing maintenance of the program.

Finally, employee behaviors in the BYOD context can make or break the program. With proper planning and execution, a company can do a number of things to create the right employee behaviors and make the service a better experience for everyone:

- Make BYOD policies and guidelines easy for employees to find and understand

- Create short, understandable employee agreements

- Create and launch employee trainings—you need real employee awareness, not just constructive notice, of how the program works and the expectations the company has on employees to participate in the program

- Technology can help: separate work and personal data, secure the device (e.g., strong passwords) and data (e.g., mobile device management technologies), create trusted access based on context (employee and location)

- Regularly revisit the program specifics—authorized types of devices, technologies, employee behaviors and agreements, laws and regulations, enforcement

By embracing BYOD programs instead of avoiding or ignoring them, companies can focus on the fun and games of a great place to work, and not on the loss of PI.

# Communicating

Once the privacy strategy and operational plan have been completed, a strategic plan document should be published internally so that all stakeholders involved can gain a better understanding of the objectives of the plan. These reviewers likely will have excellent suggestions for improvements before a final plan is adopted.

The benefit is that it makes the stakeholders part of the process and owners of a stake in the outcome. An auxiliary benefit is that the process of receiving stakeholder input also provides a sense of who will be willing participants, who is going to be dragged along (or cajoled into compliance), and where each type of party's interests lie.

It is important, however, to not let the process of gathering feedback derail the process. Be prepared to set limits to the number of review cycles and timing of the assessment phase so things do not get out of hand.

Once the strategic plan document is considered final, the key ideas of the plan should be communicated broadly within the organization and, where appropriate, with outside parties or stakeholders who may have access to the organization's data.

Another step in the process is to identify the parts of the plan that can be made public, and—if practically and strategically important—make a big public relations deal about it. For example, where a business model is built offering a product or service that benefits from having a strong publically articulated privacy policy (i.e., it requires a great deal or unexpected types or uses of personal information), it may be strategically important to broadcast what measures the enterprise has taken. Because data privacy is synonymous with trustworthy management and sharing of personal information, similar tactics of truthfulness and transparency often work for the enterprise as they do in person-to-person communication and relationship building.[13]

# Internal Communications

Concurrent to the policies, procedures, standards, guidelines, and privacy rules being developed, a communications plan should be developed to ensure that all members of the enterprise know that the privacy policies are, which standards and guidelines exist, where to find them, what they are, why they are available, and what their responsibilities are.

Once things are ready, the privacy team should focus on working with the key privacy stakeholders, explaining things and providing training where needed. The availability of this information through such things as internal web sites, newsletters, all-hands meetings, and leadership training will also help people who are new to the enterprise or new to privacy to become educated more quickly.

As much as possible, privacy materials should be written to the specific audiences and avoid too much legalese and jargon (even for lawyers). This will help everyone see the issues in their own areas and recognize that it is also their responsibility and not just the specialized domain of privacy professionals or legal teams.

To this end, it may be helpful to leverage both human resources and communication specialists within an enterprise or organization. Having this information easily accessible and available will also enable those within the company interested in doing so to make helpful, constructive suggestions.

# External Communication

As important as the internal community is, external parties of interest—including customers, partners, suppliers, consultants, media, industry analysts, and regulators—are important targets of the communication plan.

There must be an external communication plan delivering the right messages to these audiences to help build awareness of the enterprise privacy program and its benefits. Because regulators and policymakers look at privacy material published by the enterprise, these externally communicated messages need to be well orchestrated and transparent.

Customers and other impacted parties of interest will review these external privacy communications to ensure that their personally identifiable information and the confidential data related to it are handled in an acceptable way. Reasonable fears of these parties of interest should be anticipated. If people fear that their personal data will be sold, for example, the information transfer and sharing policies need to be communicated as clearly as possible to alleviate such fears.

---

[13]The opposite is true as well. Hiding the type and kind of processing and collection performed, even for the most virtuous of intentions, may cause a rift in respect that may never be repaired. The "trust" that is thus engendered is a trust that this company will always be a jerk. Individual customers and businesses will only remain with jerks until alternatives inevitably appear.

The best outcome for a data subject from an enterprise perspective is one in which the data subject knows which PI is needed, why it is important to engage with this enterprise with this type and amount of data required for the task, and how it is being used and protected. Most important, the data subject should not be surprised by unexpected practices or creeped out by inappropriate or excessive data practices. The more clear, engaging, and complete the communication, the more likely it is an actual asset to the overall program.

# A Word About What Are Usually Important, but Boring Words

It is time for an overhaul of how enterprises design privacy notices. As much as regulators and advocates demand transparency and simplicity, they also have become much more demanding about adding required elements and magic language to data subject–facing privacy notices. As a result, the Privacy Notice has drifted in function and efficacy from a document intended to teach and illuminate the user to an element of enterprise self-insurance. The shift in external requirements has also caused the external Privacy Notice to become a creator of risk rather than a means of engagement (which it *should* be in a privacy-engineered environment).

As privacy engineering practices become ubiquitous, so too can the Privacy Notice become an object of innovation and community creation in context rather than lead undercoating for the enterprise.

As with technology innovation, notice and policy innovation can benefit from a multidisciplinary approach. For example, there are vast resources available outside enterprise legal teams focused exclusively on learning, communication, and persuasion. Large enterprises often have internal communications, public relations, marketing, learning, designers, user interface, branding, human resources, and other similar professionals from whom an intrepid privacy engineering team can benefit.

---

**THE PRIVACY NINJA: PRIVACY NOTICE AS GRAPHIC NOVEL**

McAfee's turning its external Privacy Notice into a graphic novel is one such example of a privacy-engineered notice. The inspiration for this approach came from several divergent requirements to explain a very complex data relationship between security services and data subjects. The Privacy Notice needed to transcend many different international contexts.[14] It is needed to respect and provide a counterbalance to the research that said that no users were ever actually taking the opportunity to read policies. Finally, the comparisons in the technology—and most other vertical marketplaces—were comprised on privacy notices that were heavy, confusing, and not the first impression McAfee hoped to make with its customers.

---

[14]In full disclosure, two of this book's authors, Michelle Dennedy and Jonathan Fox, are employees of McAfee and were responsible for the creation of the Ninja and the graphic novelization of the McAfee Privacy Notice. We and many others who have since contacted us and well as Tom Finneran, our third coauthor, think they happen to be awesome.

Figure 11-2 shows examples of the illustrations used by to communicate privacy information to customers and web site visitors in its graphic novel Privacy Notice.

**Figure 11-2.** *Animated Privacy Notice example from the McAfee Privacy Notice*[15]

The process benefited from collaboration with McAfee's Chief Design Officer who happened to have a PhD in psychology (sometimes you just get lucky and the combination of one professional with creative and communication expertise is powerful). The team also included international data privacy external counsel to control the risk of innovation, information architects and designers, as well as the McAfee Privacy Team.

The McAfee notice benefited from concepts in two excellent books: *Blah Blah Blah*[16] by Dan Roam and *Resonate*[17] by Nancy Duarte. Both are examples of sources from which to draw, or begin drawing, visual representations of complex ideas such as PI and security data flows. Also, the project team benefited from research such as that performed by Carnegie Mellon regarding policies and the survey performed by the trustmark firm Truste regarding the abysmal record of policies engaging users in toto.

Finally, the idea to work up a visual notice was also inspired by School House Rock, a series of animated musical short films that aired in between Saturday morning cartoons in the United States from 1973 to 1985. In that series, American children learned to recite the US Constitution Preamble, cite their three's multiplication tables, and learn a wide range of sometimes complex facts and ideas in 3-minute segments set to music and animation. As of the first printing of this book, the McAfee Ninjas remain silent though illustrative. The future may be more melodious for the Ninjas as data use continues to grow, business models become more complex, and users of security software become more sophisticated (Figure 11-3).

---

[15]mcafee.com/privacy, December 7, 2013
[16]www.danroam.com/blah-blah-blah/
[17]www.duarte.com/book/resonate/

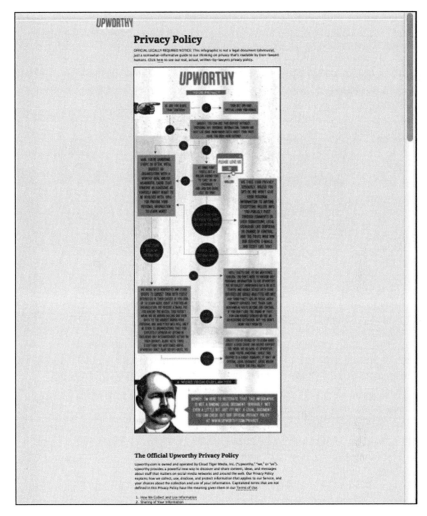

***Figure 11-3.*** *Another great example of a graphic depiction of a privacy policy. This one comes from* Upworthy.com

The basic requirements for privacy policies and a public-facing privacy notice include legal requirements, acknowledgment of evolving standards, and global requirements regarding data processing. The other critical role of the public facing notice is to provide transparency to users of systems and services. In the case of security products and services or other complex data intensive services[18], extensive use of aggregate data processing to predict, protect, and block informational threats on multiple platforms should also be described as clearly as possible.

The need for clarity and simplicity in the Privacy Notice was driven by the requirement to raise understanding and engagement in a business where data—sometimes personal data—is necessary to protect all data (Figure 11-4).

**We use physical safeguards to prevent data loss or misuse**

We use physical security to prevent access to equipment, personnel, or facilities that manage your data.

**We use technological safeguards to keep data secure**

Data is encrypted using sophisticated encryption methods and other technical safeguards. For example, when you make a payment on our website, we use SSL encryption.

*Figure 11-4.* *More Privacy Notice examples from the McAfee Privacy Notice on* mcafee.com[19]

Timothy Pilgrim, the Australian privacy commissioner, stated that we need to innovate for privacy to be more effective and accessible to consumers at an Industry and Government Privacy Conference in Australia in 2013 Celebrating Data Privacy Week. He cited, as one example, McAfee's use of animated Ninja characters to encourage people to read and understand their Privacy Notice.

Even when privacy engineers commit to innovation, when considering the best approaches for communicating to any audience, keep communications concise and use simple language. Playful and fun communications will generally get good results, as long as they are honest, accurate, and respectful. However, iconography and illustration and other techniques are not yet expected and accepted as best practices. Until these are best practices, infographics, images, or graphic novels are best done in *addition* to full text of privacy notices and related documents for those who may want detail in a more traditional format.

It is also absolutely crucial to note that playfulness and humor do not always translate across cultures or demographics. Privacy notice creation must include the requirement of learning for the intended audience of the notice, designing it according to those preferences and biases.

---

[18]Data intensive services may include things like what is currently called the Internet of Things (IoT) or Cloud services. However, even well known traditional services like retail or real estate may require massive amounts of data processing, particularly given how much data is available for analytics and other services.

[19]mcafee.com/privacy, December 7, 2013

# DATA CLASSIFICATION AND RISK ASSESSMENT

By Ed Glover, Client Services Director, Security and Privacy at Resources Global Professionals (RGP)

Too often, senior management who are responsible for the business units view their data needs as unique from other areas of their enterprise. Failure to come to a consensus on common data classification has potential risk implications. Even if they do come to a consensus about the criticality of the data, are their classification standards documented and communicated across the company's business units? Are the metadata used to describe the data consistent across systems? Unfortunately, this is usually a onetime event, and as the nature of the data changes within the business units, management does not reassess the critically of their data to determine if appropriate safeguards are in place or enforce consistent data definitions.

The first step to address risks implications of the data is to ensure that information receives an appropriate level of protection in accordance with the importance to the organization. The company should develop an information classification standard that considers legal requirements, value, criticality, and sensitivity to unauthorized disclosure or modification of the data.

When determining data classification, ISO 27001/2 (ISO/IEC 2013) provides an excellent framework for identifying organization assets and defining appropriate protection responsibilities.

The process of compiling and classifying a list of information assets is an important first step for performing a risk management assessment to identify the level of risk to the information. One needs to understand the criticality of the data in order to assess the risks to the data.

Although there are many ways to classify data, the following list is an example of an information classification standard:

- *Public information:* Any information that, if disclosed, causes no harm or embarrassment to the company. An example of this could be the company's address or main phone number, published annual report, or approved press releases.

- *Internal information:* Any information not approved for general circulation outside the organization, where its disclosure would cause minor embarrassment or operational inconvenience, but more than likely will not result in financial loss or serious damage to credibility or reputation of the company. An example of this could be internal memos, internal project reports, or minutes of meetings.

- *Critical information:* Any information that is considered critical to the organization's ongoing operations and could seriously impede or disrupt them if shared internally or made public. An example of this type of information could be accounting information prior to the approved quarterly and annual announcements, corporate or divisional business plans, customer information of banks, patients' medical records, and similar highly sensitive personal data. Some of these data elements could have privacy implications and should be assessed and evaluated against local or regional laws.

- *Sensitive and confidential information:* Any information that has a serious impact on long-term strategic objectives of the company. This could put the company at risk, if disclosure, and could result in violations of various domestic and international Laws and Regulations. For example: customer databases that include personal information of the employees, etc., pending mergers or acquisitions, investment strategies, intellectual property that could seriously damage the organization if lost or made public. Information classified as sensitive and confidential should have a very restricted distribution/usage labels assigned to it, and must have the appropriate safeguards in place at all times. This information should be identified, assessed for the level of risk, and appropriate safeguards are in place to mitigate the risk to an acceptable level.

Once you understand the importance of data the corporation is responsible for protecting, one should perform a risk assessment to understand the potential threats and vulnerabilities of disclosure of the data. When assessing risk in business terms, there are a number of different methodologies you can use. The following are a few of the many risk assessment frameworks that can be used when assessing risk.

CobiT (© ISACA) Information Criteria[20] consists of seven information criteria in expressing IT Risk in business terms. They are:

Efficiency, Effectiveness, Confidentiality, Integrity, Availability, Compliance, and Reliability

---

[20]Information Systems Audit and Control Association (ISACA) publication "The Risk IT Practitioner Guide."

The four A's (Westerman) is another way to express risk in business terms. This defines IT risk as the potential for an unplanned event involving IT to threaten any of the four interrelated enterprise objectives[21]:

- *Agility:* Process the capability to change

- *Accuracy:* Provide correct, timely, complete, information

- *Access:* Ensure appropriate access to data and systems, so that the right people have access to the information they need and the wrong people do not

- *Availability:* Keep the systems running and the ability to recover in a timely manner

The COSO ERM – Integrated Framework lists the following criteria[22]:

- Strategic criteria consist of high-level goals, aligned with supporting the enterprise mission

- Operations criteria pertain to the effectiveness and efficiency of the enterprise's operations

- Reporting criteria pertain to the reliability of reporting, including both internal and external reporting.

- Compliance criteria pertain to adherence to relevant laws and regulations

These are just a few options to consider when expressing IT risk in business terms. There are many other risk frameworks to use, and it boils down to choosing a framework that best fits what your company is trying to accomplish when performing a risk assessment.

Having a data classification standard and a holistic risk management process in place to assess risk is a huge challenge and, in most instances, is not addressed or incomplete. Most of the time, corporations at one point in time have developed a data classification definition standard and have not revise it since its inception. This alone is a huge issue because as the business grows and evolves, the original definition may no longer pertain to the business and can result in not addressing, through a risk assessment, the potential threats and vulnerabilities to the corporation's data.

---

[21]Westerman (Westerman, G.; R. Hunter, *IT Risk—Turning Business Threats into Competitive Advantage*, Harvard Business School Press, 2007)
[22]COSO (© by the Committee of Sponsoring Organizations of the Treadway Commission) Enterprise Risk Management (ERM)

An example of this is when a company started a professional services organization and provided services to their clients. Their consultants would use laptops (company owned or their own personal laptop) to download client data in order to perform their work. Depending on the nature of the engagement, the data may contain personal information of the employees, network topology maps, credit card information, among others. In most cases, there was information that would be considered private and confidential residing on the personal laptop of the consultant. When performing a risk assessment, it was identified that their consultants were exposing their customers' data to risk of disclosure because they did not understand their clients' data classification and security requirements for data and how to ensure that appropriate security measures were in place depending on the criticality of data.

Furthermore, not every client assessed the criticality of data in the same manner. This proved to be a huge risk issue for the professional services group and the potential impact to their reputation and resulting lawsuits were identified as high or critical. The result of the risk assessment's finding was to encrypt all company-owned laptops to protect client information that is stored on it. Furthermore, a policy was developed to prohibit the use of personal laptops while performing work on behalf of a client. Although this is somewhat restrictive in today's environment, especially with the push for BYOD, it was necessary to ensure that the clients' data was protected and did not expose the company to potential lawsuits if a disclosure were to happen.

There are many stories like this out there. Has your company performed a recent review to determine the criticality of its data, assessed the risk to the company if this data element is disclosed, and implemented the necessary security to reduce the risk to an acceptable level?

# Monitoring and Adapting the Strategy

Ongoing review processes are needed to monitor progress in the area of privacy awareness and readiness so that the program can be adapted as needed. Monitoring can take many forms, but objective metrics must be used so that progress can be measured. For example, one metric might be the number of privacy issues that are uncovered in a privacy impact assessment. This particular metric may arise initially as management teams become more aware of privacy issues and thus spot them in PIAs. However, this knowledge will flow down through the ranks over time and the number of privacy issues discovered in PIAs should then begin to decline.

Other metrics to consider are:

- Number of real and unfounded incidents reported

- Program maturity model level

- Percentage of employees who have completed training

- Size and coverage of the "volunteer" army helping the privacy program

Another way that privacy awareness and readiness can be monitored is through a privacy audit, a thorough annual review of the privacy program and its results done in conjunction with either the internal audit team or a certified third-party auditor versed in privacy. In addition to identifying privacy vulnerabilities and areas for improvement in privacy engineering practices, the audit might also be used to monitor the level of privacy awareness and readiness based on a set of agreed-upon metrics. The audit may be conducted by a third party or by an internal audit group and may include a gap analysis that compares an ideal future scenario against the current environment.

Most organizations will not be able to do all of the privacy awareness and readiness assessment steps outlined in this chapter due to resource or time constraints. They are included in this chapter to provide an overview of what should be considered within the context of your organization's needs.

A summary of the phases and key activities of a privacy awareness and readiness assessment is provided in Table 11-2.

***Table 11-2.*** *Summary of the Phases and Activities in a Privacy Awareness and Readiness Assessment*

| Phase | Key Activities |
| --- | --- |
| Information gathering | • Document existing business processes and data flows.<br>• Document privacy awareness and readiness maturity levels across different organizational functions and across different levels of management.<br>• Assess skills throughout the organization.<br>• Determine how well the organizational structure supports privacy engineering objectives. |
| Analysis and strategy | • Define a privacy awareness and readiness strategy, including goals and objectives with metrics for success.<br>• Communicate the strategy throughout the organization. |
| Operational plan | • Develop a privacy awareness and readiness operational plan with a prioritized list of actions and a timeline for execution.<br>• Define the budget needed to execute the privacy awareness and readiness operational plan. |
| Monitor and adapt | • Ongoing reviews to monitor privacy awareness and readiness can be used to identify additional action items and adapt the program as needed. |

# Conclusion

This chapter presented a foundation for how to begin to assess the work to build an organizational privacy development structure. We will continue to build on the actual organizational structures in the next chapter.

# CHAPTER 12

▨ ▨ ▨

# Organizational Design and Alignment

*My model for business is the Beatles. They were four guys who kept each other's kind of negative tendencies in check. They balanced each other, and the total was greater than the sum of the parts. That's how I see business: Great things in business are never done by one person. They're done by a team of people.*

—Steve Jobs, interview on *60 Minutes*, 2003

This chapter discusses options for the organizational placement and structure of the privacy team in an organization that has embraced privacy engineering. It describes the new and evolving roles necessary to support a successful effort and suggests best practices for aligning key organizational functions with your privacy program and privacy engineering goals. Finally, this chapter explores the key organizational challenges for privacy programs.

Just as privacy engineering requires rethinking responsibilities across the organization, so too it may require redesigning the privacy team and the organization's information governance function. Traditional organizational structures may not be sufficient to support the cross-functional demands of privacy or privacy engineering, especially because these structures have not historically emphasized roles that contain deep privacy expertise.

## Organizational Placement and Structure

The organizational placement and structure of the privacy team can be critical to the success of a privacy engineering program and therefore deserves careful consideration. The optimal location and team structure may vary, depending on factors such as the organization's goals, requirements, and culture.

First, let's look at leveling of the CPO (chief privacy officer—or whomever leads the privacy function); where in the organizational hierarchy should the CPO sit? Titles aside, the CPO should have equal footing with the head of IT and the head of product engineering. This is to facilitate alignment as well as governance (i.e., checks and balances). Also, it is equally important that unless the CPO is also the head of the privacy engineering program, the CPO should be at a higher or equal management level than that of the lead for privacy engineering. This helps avoid competing empires and lessens hindrances to alignment. Ideally, the privacy function would report directly to executive management.

The truth is, however, that many organizations have taken an organic approach and have located privacy groups within the organization that initially recognized the need (e.g., human resources, legal, marketing) and were willing to staff and fund such initiatives. If this is the case in your organization, it's important to reconsider the location of the privacy office: it is more than likely to tilt its charter, its focus, and its goals (official and unofficial). Where in your organization the privacy team is located will also affect how the privacy function is viewed and its reach across programs and divisions of the enterprise.

Any location, even one that is legitimately enterprise wide, will involve tradeoffs. For example, it may often make sense to place the privacy office within product engineering, to make it easier to engineer privacy into products and services. However, in this case, a CPO who resides within the product engineering group may have to work harder to exert influence within business groups that have a very different culture and focus, such as marketing or IT. The converse is true as well: An enterprise-wide privacy function, hosted in human resources will have trouble getting attention from engineering. The fact is that in most organizational cultures, there is no absolutely perfect location. Even if the privacy group is positioned as a legitimate enterprise-wide function reporting to the CEO, it runs the risk as being perceived as "corporate" or outside the business. Thus, the goal should be to position the privacy group where it has the greatest reach and opportunity to be effective across the organization. Fortunately (or perhaps unfortunately), there is no wholly right or wrong answer to this question—just a best one for the given circumstances.

Note that the challenges that come with organizational placement are not impossible to overcome. They just require acknowledgment and factoring into the overall change management plan.

## Horizontal Privacy Team: Pros

Because the implementation of privacy engineering requires a substantial privacy focus within other functional groups, many privacy professionals find that a horizontal or virtual privacy team structure is more effective than a traditional vertically integrated group. A horizontal structure spans traditional organizational boundaries by building a team of people from different functional groups. Horizontal teams typically use a matrix management reporting structure in which team members report directly to their business groups and also to the CPO (Figure 12-1).

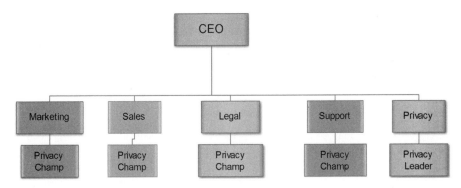

*Figure 12-1.* *An example of an horizontal organization chart*

A horizontal structure or matrix management reporting structure offers several important advantages. Because team members reside within business groups, they may already have existing personal alliances within the business group, and they may have accumulated valuable domain knowledge. Not only can they leverage these relationships and their knowledge for the good of the overall program, but they can also use it to help the CPO build strong alliances with those groups. In addition, they are ideally positioned to develop a deep understanding of the business group's privacy program needs and to accelerate the group's adoption of a privacy program, ensuring that the program and its goals are aligned. In short, horizontal teams can help ensure that different groups work toward the same privacy goals to the benefit of the organization overall. For example, a horizontal privacy team with members in both marketing and engineering can help ensure both functional groups' leverage and apply the same policies and, where it makes sense, the same tools for handling PI.

One caveat is that horizontal organizations can require more effort from the CPO to manage, coordinate, and guide. It may be harder to make progress on privacy initiatives when team members need to deal with other urgent issues that affect their functional groups. The CPO may need to expend more effort to maintain communication among team members, ensure the team shares information, and gain agreement about how to handle problems. The CPO and the privacy team will also have to learn how to speak to each domain in terms it understands.

Additionally, in this scenario the structure must provide incentives for the people performing the roles to collaborate with other people involved in privacy-related tasks. Sometimes these incentives are provided by a matrix management structure in which individuals report both to a manager in their host organization and to a manager in a centralized privacy office. In other cases, collaboration may be incentivized through goals and objectives within the host organizations.

## Horizontal Privacy Teams: Cons

There are some situations in which a horizontal organization may not be adequate. Typically, these are where the risks of a privacy breach are so high that extremely close collaboration among privacy team members is vital to the organization's success. These situations may require a vertically structured privacy team rather than a horizontally structured team. At a company in a regulated industry, such as banking or health care, a breach involving customer or patient data might jeopardize the future of the entire organization. A colocated privacy team, with all members reporting directly to the CPO, may find it easier to continuously share information in ways that help the team identify additional privacy vulnerabilities or new opportunities (Figure 12-2).

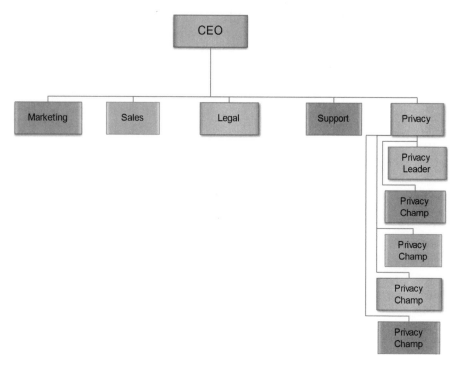

*Figure 12-2.* *An example of a vertical organization chart*

# Common Privacy Engineering Roles

Regardless of the organizational structure, there is a set of privacy roles that typically need to exist in an organization that has embraced privacy and privacy engineering. The following are important roles[1] to consider when defining a privacy organization:

- *Chief privacy officer (CPO):* The CPO carries the responsibility for building a privacy program designed to protect business and personal interests, as well as working with business users and IT teams to identify ways to create value from data.

---

[1]These are *roles*, not necessarily *job titles*.

- *Privacy architect:* The privacy architect is responsible for designing and implementing process, product, system, and service architectures designed to protect personal information.

- *Privacy engineer:* The privacy engineer uses engineering principles and processes to build controls and measures into processes, systems, components, and products that enable the authorized processing of personal information.

- *Privacy analyst:* The privacy analyst assesses whether processes, products, services, and systems (including third-party vendors and service providers) that process personal information meet privacy policy, standards, and guidelines to ensure that personal information is being processed in a fair and legitimate way.

- *Privacy attorney:* The privacy attorney provides legal analysis of laws and regulations and makes recommendations regarding their application. The privacy attorney also performs the same functions for internal policies, guidelines, and standards.

- *Chief information security officer (CISO):* The CISO is in charge of protecting against security risks related to an organization's information assets, systems, and processes.

In large organizations, each role may be performed by a single dedicated individual. In smaller organizations, an individual may perform multiple roles.

# Challenges of Bringing Privacy Engineering to the Forefront

Organizations tend to resist change. Because of this, implementing privacy programs or privacy engineering can be challenging, especially in large organizations. Functional groups across the entire organization, at all levels, must become attuned to privacy requirements and apply consistent principles and policies to its use. Also, they must pay heed and respond to governance models that may not be hierarchal. The following sections outline some of the typical challenges that such privacy initiatives must overcome.

## Expanding Executive Management Support

To be effective, any organization-wide privacy program requires support from senior management. Privacy engineering may require an even higher level of executive engagement and sponsorship because it involves designing privacy into the organization's products, processes, and infrastructure. If you don't already have this level of commitment, you will need to push toward this goal. Strong executive support helps ensure funding and provides the privacy team with the authority to implement privacy engineering across the organization. Executive-level commitment also means you'll have more places to turn for help when the inevitable problems arise.

## Spreading Awareness and Gaining Cultural Acceptance

Privacy engineering programs often initially face the challenge that many people across the organization have little awareness or understanding of the program's purpose and value. There may be confusion about why privacy engineering is necessary, how it differs from existing efforts to keep information secure and confidential, and whether projects need to involve the privacy team or require its approval. The success of a privacy engineering effort will rely on its ability to work within the existing culture, add value to other groups and functions, and ultimately create understanding and recognition of the responsibility for privacy throughout the organization. These changes may take time and require considerable patience.

## Extending Your Reach with Limited Resources

Even with executive sponsorship, privacy programs often operate with limited resources. Privacy engineering places even greater demands on resources because its scope is both broad and deep, spanning multiple functional groups and people at different organizational levels. To maximize its reach and effectiveness, the privacy engineering team may need to creatively evolve new roles within different groups across the organization, as we'll discuss later in this chapter. For the CPO, this creates the challenge of managing a large team of people who are distributed across multiple groups the organization. Keys to success include effective communication, training, and leveraging processes and resources across the extended privacy team.

## Creating Alliances

Due to the need to influence the way personal information is handled across the entire organization, any privacy program is likely to require partnerships with key business groups, especially those that use PI intensively. Privacy engineering makes it even more important to identify important partners and build strategic alliances with them, because it will require the involvement of a broader range of people within each group, including product developers, quality assurance specialists, IT professionals, data stewards, and program managers.

## Expanding the Scope of Data Governance

Implementing privacy engineering requires that business groups actively participate in the protection of personal information. Some organizations may already have existing data governance programs, as discussed in Chapter 3 and in parts of Chapter 6, including data stewards responsible for maintaining data quality, accessibility, and availability. However, these existing data governance programs often do not consider privacy requirements. The challenge for the CPO is therefore to expand the scope of data governance to include privacy. Data stewards should be a crucial part of the privacy engineering team, ensuring that privacy rules are followed throughout the development process in requirements, specifications, use cases, and metadata.

# Remaining Productive Amid Competing Priorities and Demands

The ultimate success of the privacy engineering program depends on continuing to make progress on foundational tasks such as forging alliances, creating program structure, and developing policies. But the privacy team also has to react to day-to-day operational emergencies such as the discovery of new vulnerabilities. With limited resources, it can be challenging to make progress toward long-term goals amid competing demands and priorities. This is particularly the case because privacy roles may be embedded in other groups that have their own pressing business needs.

The use of a privacy component, as defined in Part 2 of this book, can help the privacy engineering team remain productive by reducing the effort required to change privacy rules throughout the enterprise. This will require the privacy team to work with data stewards and data administrators to amend privacy indicators and metadata with the new or changed rules.

## NAVIGATING PRIVACY AND GOVERNANCE IN THE HIGHLY REGULATED FINANCIAL SERVICES INDUSTRY

By Janet F. Chapman, Senior Vice Vice President, Chief Privacy Officer and Manager, Compliance Group, at Union Bank

To many, it seems that there are many "cooks in the kitchen" when it comes to privacy. In the financial services sector, this analogy is not far off the mark. Financial institutions frequently have an alphabet soup of federal and state regulators depending on the size of the institution, the actual component (organizational) parts, and the jurisdiction of the federal regulatory agencies. Depending on the charter, the services, and the customer base, a bank may deal with, among others, the Office of the Comptroller of the Currency (OCC), the Federal Reserve Board (FRB), the Securities and Exchange Commission (SEC), the Federal Deposit Insurance Corporation (FDIC), the Federal Trade Commission (FTC), the Federal Commerce Commission (FCC), and the newest, the Consumer Financial Protection Bureau (CFPB). Don't forget to add a dash of jurisdiction under the Health and Human Services (HHS) and its enforcement agency, the Office of Civil Rights (OCR) if the financial institution handles protected health information (PHI) via operations such as lockbox processing. Mix well with the additional global privacy and data security laws and regulations, and we have ourselves a hearty soup.

At the state level, there are also many laws, banking regulators, attorneys general, and departments of consumer protection. For example, in 2013, at the time of writing, there were over 25 state privacy-related laws—in such areas as social media, identity theft and fraud prevention, credit freeze rights, and data breach amendments.

All these laws and regulatory bodies are focused on the protection and proper handling of consumer personally identifiable information, or the industry term "consumer nonpublic personal information" (NPI).

With all this regulatory jurisdiction and oversight, financial institutions have a regulatory governance model in addition to whatever internal governance framework exists within the institution.

### Financial Regulatory Focus on Governance

The regulatory examiners are increasingly focused on an institution's internal governance processes in the course of their supervisory activities. Among the components they look for are board and senior management oversight; formal meetings with minutes; evidence of a decision-making chain of command; and review of emerging threats, key issues, and relevant risk factors in the organization.

In relation to privacy and data protection, the financial services industry was first called upon to demonstrate a formal governance process with the enactment of the Gramm-Leach-Bliley Act in 1999 and the subsequent publication of Regulations P (for banks) and SP (for brokerage firms) that included governance requirements for the protection of consumer customer data. Because the law covered the entire financial services industry, all the financial services regulators cooperated to develop consistent guidance via the Federal Financial Institutions' Examination Council (FFIEC).

The FFIEC is a formal council of federal agencies that collaborates to develop regulatory guidance and uniform principles, standards, and reporting forms for the federal examination of financial institutions that is consistent across the various financial services jurisdictions. The FFIEC consists of the FRB, the FDIC, the OCC, the CFPB, the SEC, and the National Credit Union Administration (NCUA).

The FFIEC routinely publishes regulatory guidance on various issues and requirements involving governance. The current version of the FFIEC Guidance on Information Security (*IT Examinations Handbook*) has a chapter devoted to governance.

### Governance

"Governance is achieved through the management structure, assignment of responsibilities and authority, establishment of policies, standards and procedures, allocation of resources, monitoring, and accountability. Governance is required to ensure that tasks are completed appropriately, that accountability is maintained, and that risk is managed for the entire enterprise."[2]

The section goes on to address the elements of management structure, responsibilities, and accountability.

---

[2]FFIEC Information Security IT Examination Standards; July, 2006; page 4

- *Management structure:* This regulation requires the active engagement of the Board of Directors and senior business management. Financial services examiners look for demonstrated discussions by board-level risk committees along with annual approval of an annual report on a financial institution's information security program.

- *Responsibility and accountability:* As stated above, the Board of Directors, or an appropriate committee of the board, is responsible for overseeing an institution's information security program and providing formal approval of the annual program. Examiners are looking to executive management to be aware of the components of the program, be advised of emerging threats and risks, and have an understanding of the action plans designed to address identified issues. Executive engagement and support are crucial, and failure at that level could undermine the entire organization's commitment to security.

More recently, in early 2013, the FFIEC published proposed its "Social Media Guidance," with the final version published in December 2013, which requires each financial institution that engages in social media activities to implement a formal risk management program to provide oversight of all associated activities. As noted in the Federal Register, the Guidance states:

"Components of a risk management program should include the following:

- A governance structure with clear roles and responsibilities whereby the board of directors or senior management direct how using social media contributes to the strategic goals of the institution (for example, through increasing brand awareness, product advertising, or researching new customer bases) and establishes controls and ongoing assessment of risk in social media activities."[3]

Essentially, each bank that uses social media as a channel for communicating with customers and the community must now establish an oversight committee of senior management that reviews the bank's social media program in light of overall strategy and how the program complies with all the requirements of the risk management program. The Guidance expects that banks should address an array of risks, including compliance and legal considerations, payments, consumer privacy,

---

[3] www.fdic.gov/news/news/financial/2013/fil13056.html?source=govdelivery&utm_medium=email&utm_source=govdelivery

and reputational and operational concerns. The Guidance also requires the ongoing risk management program to identify, measure, monitor, and control the risks related to social media, including:

- Governance structure

- Policies and procedures for employees

- Due diligence process for third-party service providers

- Employee training

- Monitoring and oversight for all postings to proprietary social media sites

- Audit and compliance reviews

- Periodic reporting to the financial institution's Board of Directors or senior management for purposes of gauging program effectiveness.

- Complaint management

- Incident response

The underlying theme in the Guidance is governance, integration with key risk management controls, and senior management awareness and accountability.

### Governance Applied to Privacy Programs

Recognizing that, in a regulated environment, the focus on governance is here to stay for the foreseeable future, the next concern is applying it to an individual privacy program inside a financial institution.

Financial institutions frequently place privacy functions within legal or compliance departments, appropriate organizations, given the typical privacy office charter, which provides enterprise-wide direction and support on all matters associated with consumer privacy rules and regulations, as well as risk management. Some privacy functions also have responsibility for overseeing compliance with information security laws and regulations and data breach or incident response programs.

The privacy office is typically responsible for guiding a financial institution in the establishment and implementation of controls to manage privacy risk. The privacy office also serves as the clearinghouse for any privacy-related customer concerns or complaints, policy questions, and implementation of new regulations and engages the appropriate parties within the financial institution to participate and support implementation of relevant initiatives and ongoing programs. Because privacy requirements impact every area within the organization that collects, accesses, or uses consumer data, a broad-based governance model is key to increased awareness and acceptance, as well as successful risk management.

An effective method to accomplish this is the creation of an enterprise-wide privacy governing committee or council. Depending on the scope of the privacy program, the CPO should consider including representatives from all affected lines of business: compliance, marketing, legal, information security, operations, fraud, physical security, the online channel, customer service, corporate communications or public relations, records management, human resources, vendor management, and internal audit. A council composed of a variety of business and risk personnel can effectively bring multiple points of view to assessments of privacy requirements, helping all to understand the core purpose behind a requirement and thereby reducing the risk of "unintended consequences." Unintended consequences can be the result of short-term (quick and dirty), overly onerous, or inconsistent implementations of solutions to privacy requirements. An example of this would be adding all "unsubscribe" requests to a "do not e-mail list" and not simply unsubscribing the person. Although the solution may adequately meet one team's goals, it unnecessarily undermines or jeopardizes the goals or longer-term strategy of another.

A governance committee so designed can provide a forum for communication, help build awareness of data privacy practices and policies, and help integrate proper handling, protection, and use and sharing of consumer data into the everyday business activities of the financial institution. In short, the committee can serve as privacy evangelists as well as help the privacy office to leverage its typically small resources.

In addition to the privacy governing committee, integration with the overall risk management committee structure is important to ensure that a formal escalation route up to the Board of Directors can be demonstrated. Typically, financial institutions' governance models are designed to provide executive management and the board with comprehensive reporting of a full array of risks including compliance and operational risks to ensure awareness of material issues and action plans, regulatory developments, and emerging risks or trends. In addition, executive management and the board must be apprised of regulatory examinations, as well as any findings or regulatory concerns.

As privacy professionals, we have a lot of complexity to manage, and this will likely increase. How we coordinate our internal processes and stay abreast of regulatory and industry changes will make all the difference for us and our organizations.

# Best Practices for Organizational Alignment

Some organizational functions are critical to the success of a privacy engineering program, and the CPO and privacy team should therefore invest in building strategic alliances with these functions. The CPO should first seek out those alliances that have the greatest potential, both in terms of meeting the organization's needs and the strength of preexisting personal or business relationships. Alliances should then be prioritized based on their ability to help the CPO achieve his or her business goals. Often, a few key relationships with other information-intensive groups, such as IT, human resources, and sales, can produce the biggest impact. The privacy team should first invest time in these relationships; other, less-critical relationships can be addressed later.

## Aligning with Information Technology and Information Security

Privacy engineering is dependent on IT both for implementing privacy policies (by means of privacy rules, as discussed in Part 2) and for securing data. It is impossible to control access to data stored in IT systems if those systems and their physical environment are not adequately secured. Therefore, it is particularly important that the privacy function is closely aligned with IT and information security. Yet, traditionally, there have often been inconsistencies between privacy policies and the protection provided by IT systems.

Using privacy engineering, privacy and IT teams can work together more closely to reduce the likelihood of such disparities. The CPO and the chief information officer can better align their teams, take advantage of each other's expertise, jointly establish efficient processes, and define IT requirements related to privacy. The result of this cooperation is better protection for the organization as a whole.

## Aligning with Data Governance Functions

Ultimately, an organization's privacy strategy is about data governance—how information is managed and used. Therefore, alignment between the privacy and data governance functions is critical to the success of a privacy engineering effort. Engineers, data analysts, business analysts, and system designers should all work with the CPO and privacy team, following the privacy engineering methodology.

An example of data governance structure, based on a structure that we helped a few of our clients establish, is shown in Figure 12-3. The structure is headed by a steering committee, comprised of senior managers from key domains across the organization, which sets data governance direction and strategy. The CPO should be a member of this committee. The steering committee resolves major issues and authorizes solutions—even if those decisions impact organizational structure or project costs and timelines.

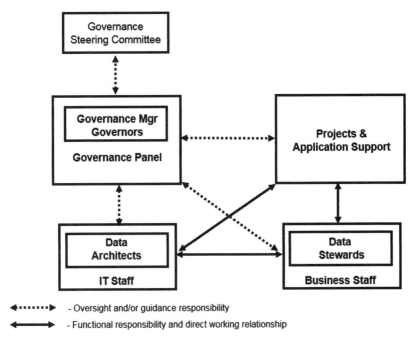

**Figure 12-3.** *Data governance organization*

The next level of the data governance structure consists of data governors and governance managers, who define overarching data governance requirements based on the strategy set by the steering committee. Below this level are the data stewards and data architects responsible for the day-to-day operational data governance activities required for specific projects. They ensure that the way information is used in these projects is aligned with the overall strategy set by the steering committee. The privacy function is represented at each level of this structure, either directly by one of the CPO's delegates or by ensuring that the person performing each role has adequate knowledge of privacy strategy and principles.

The phases required to create this governance structure include:

- *Gain executive sponsorship*: The CPO works with other stakeholders to build understanding among senior executives of the data governance concept and its value. This helps ensure that executives will agree to be part of the data governance steering committee. Executive backing also is helpful when recruiting people at other levels of the governance structure.

- *Define policies*: As the data governance structure is being established, data governance policies are proposed. These policies define governance rules that are used to create standards and guidelines covering areas such as data management and administration, security, emergency fix procedures, privacy issues, common business definitions, and allowable data values and ranges.

- *Select data governors*: Data governors and governance managers are selected or recruited for each major subject area, such as customer, product, employee, vendor, finance, and human resources. The data governors, who include members of the privacy team, are responsible for the development and implementation of the policies, guidelines, and standards for managing the corporation's data assets.

- *Identify data stewards*: Data stewards, together with content managers, represent the business community. They work with dedicated governance managers to administer data based on business rules. Together with the privacy team, data architects, and data analysts, they manage the data entities and attributes that are used in each project. Data stewards and data analysts share project decisions and concerns at regular data stewardship meetings, which are often held in an agile scrum format. The key data management tasks performed by data stewards include:

  - Creating standard definitions for data

  - Establishing the authority to create, read, update, and delete data

  - Ensuring consistent and appropriate usage of data, including privacy rules

  - Providing subject matter expertise to help resolve data issues

# Benefits of Data Governance

Establishing strong data governance delivers a range of benefits to the organization, including:

- Ensuring the effective introduction, implementation, and evolution of architectures within the organization, to guarantee high-quality systems and information that enhance data and privacy protection

- Encouraging reuse of designs, models, information, services, and technology to increase productivity and agility

- Ensuring consistent outcomes and products

- Ensuring that technology investments and capabilities align with business strategy and objectives

- Supporting privacy engineers and data stewards who ensure the quality of information throughout its lifecycle.

# ACT TO CREATE ALIGNMENT AND GOVERNANCE

By Richard Purcell, CEO, Corporate Privacy Group

In *Out of the Crisis*, W. Edwards Deming promoted 14 key principles for transforming businesses into effective and efficient engines of success. His principles have been widely adopted by enterprises intent on building reliable and sustainable processes. Principle 13 encouraged businesses to "institute a vigorous program of education and self-improvement." Principle 14 stated "put everybody in the company to work to accomplish the transformation. Every activity and every job is a part of the process."[4]

Deming was focused on optimizing repetitive processes with an engaged workforce to improve efficiency and quality in manufacturing. Putting those principles into action at companies heavily invested in information management requires new approaches. As businesses focused on their digital futures, we developed an education model that adheres to Deming's principles. We call it ACT: Awareness, Communications, and Training. This approach drives understanding of the context, teaches applied skills, and supports empowered employees.

The ACT education strategy is based on learning theories about how information is absorbed, processed, and retained. It starts with building *awareness*, encouraging individuals to recognize beliefs they value and reflect on how their actions support those values.

This is followed by *communications* that stimulate understanding of how individual actions can accomplish specific goals and objectives. Individuals evaluate how their routine activities contribute to the desired transformation of the company, becoming more engaged and involved in the process of self-improvement.

It is critical to then *train* individuals to apply specific skills to their work product, encouraging them to create novel approaches and innovative solutions to challenges. People then learn how to perform a function reliably to achieve the same outcome consistently, greatly increasing effectiveness and efficiency.

For privacy and security, the ACT model creates a foundation of awareness, or context, about how business success and customer trust rely on proper handling of personal information. Detailed information that is realistic and practical leads to a reduction in adverse outcomes, like data breaches. And training individuals to become proficient at specific procedures increases their efficiency and effectiveness in driving business objectives.

---

[4]W. Edward Deming, *Out of the Crisis*. Cambridge: MIT Press, 2000, p. 24.

The ACT model serves many goals, including regulatory compliance, employee empowerment, process efficiency, and product quality. After more than a decade of employing the ACT model at small and large companies operating locally and globally, each deployment has its own set of stories; here are a few.

### Awareness in Action

In the late 1990s, the employees at a large technology company were deeply occupied in developing Internet-enabled products and services. They built web pages, configured web servers, developed backend databases, and generally rushed to utilize this direct communication channel. About that time, the privacy leader developed and released an online privacy awareness course that highlighted principles for collecting, using, and sharing personal information throughout the company. These principles called for transparency through "Notices," individual respect through "Choices," and information protection through "Safeguards" while transferring and sharing personal information. Within 3 months, over 6,000 people had taken the course, connecting their beliefs about fairness, respect, and dignity with the principles in the course. As a result, the privacy office received hundreds of inquiries for more information and guidance. People got it, and they wanted to do something about it. One program manager called the privacy leader to say how much she had learned from the course and how effectively it had created awareness of the issues involved in information privacy. "The only problem," she said, "is that our developer network program, with 27,000 members, doesn't do any of this stuff."

After a long discussion, they decided the program should go dark while they worked on the solution. Over the next 3 weeks, they worked together to develop appropriate notices to the members and choices allowing members to select whether they wanted their information shared with third parties. They developed appropriate policies and protections to maintain control over the information and protect it from unauthorized disclosure and loss. After testing the revisions, the program manager brought the server back online. Immediately, member feedback demonstrated that, although they didn't like being offline for 3 weeks, they appreciated the fact that their personal information was being treated in a trusted way.

### Communication in Action

A multinational company had great success in building and distributing personal technology products. Customers registered their purchases, downloaded software updates, bought product accessories, and sought support through the company's web site. Staff in marketing, sales, support, information technology, and other areas all directly collected, used, or managed customer information.

As in many companies, each department was managed with relative independence from the others. The privacy office had been working with each department with what could charitably be called limited success. They struggled with the independent and siloed nature of each.

What they needed was a way to inform each group within the context of each group's language, function, and culture while maintaining a centrally consistent vocabulary and policy framework. Using a communications approach, they developed a single online personal information management course for all the groups.

The privacy office led the development of short online courses for each department with a common introduction. Each module addressed issues specific to the subject department using real-world scenarios. The shared introduction focused on common vocabulary and principles underlying each course's lesson. For instance, the sales group's messaging was about providing notice, the marketing group's was about checking choices, and the database management group's was about running suppression lists. Each was appropriate to its audience, and all audiences got consistent messages.

At the end of 3 months, the privacy office noticed a distinct easing in the way different departments worked together on managing privacy issues. They were sharing a common vocabulary, knew their own jobs within their functions, and recognized the skills that others contributed to achieve the program's objectives.

Short, targeted, and consistent messaging began to link the silos together, and employees were able to apply their efforts to solutions rather than problems.

### Training in Action

Don't you just hate it when you have an assignment and no one has told you how to do it? Of course, you try your best to do the task and it might work out. Then again, it might not. All of the awareness and skill development in the world is not going to help when you are given a new task with little or no instruction. It's even worse when several people are all trying in their own way to complete a task and everyone does it differently. The chances that something is going to go horribly wrong for someone are very high.

One multinational consumer goods company discovered how painful this is when the Children's Online Privacy Protection Act (COPPA) was passed in the late 1990s. The act requires that all US-based web sites directed toward children or that know the actual age of children using their sites gain verifiable parental consent before collecting personal information from anyone under 13 years old.

At this company, each product group was responsible for its own web site construction and maintenance. Several marketed children's products like toothpaste, soap, and shampoo, while others marketed products that are not age targeted. Some of the web sites for children's products complied with COPPA, others did not. Although the other product web sites didn't target kids, many of them did collect their users' ages. It was apparent that the COPPA requirements were not part of the web site specifications.

In the end, the company suffered severe reputational damage when the FTC examined all of their web sites and determined that many were out of compliance with COPPA. Following the investigations, negotiations, and fines, the company decided it would be a good idea to train all its webmasters in compliance mechanisms for COPPA and other regulatory requirements.

The privacy office led an effort to develop a single online course that provided detailed instructions about COPPA's requirements and accepted methods of complying. These included age-gating mechanisms, various methods of collecting parental consent, alternatives when consent wasn't available, and even a process to stop collecting age or delete records for those under 13.

In the end, the company was not only able to deploy compliant web sites, but it also provided the compliance training to all its global web operations as a corporate commitment to a single standard for protecting children online.

# Business Benefits of Alignment

Greater alignment with key partners can deliver major benefits to the entire organization. Key benefits include:

- *Greater business value from data, with less risk of misuse*: By improving structure and oversight of data collection and management, alignment between the privacy team and other groups helps the organization acquire greater understanding and control over data. The better your understanding of the data, the more value you can derive from its use. Greater control over data use also means there's less likelihood of data misuse or data fatigue.

- *Increased operational efficiency*: Alignment with other groups can eliminate duplication of effort. Without alignment, privacy and information security teams may ask each business group many of the same questions as they seek to understand how the group plans to use personal information. Alignment between privacy and information security means they can create a single set of questions and share the answers. This reduces the effort for each team. It also means less work for business groups, which now need to explain their requirements only once instead of multiple times.

- *Better business decisions*: Cooperation between privacy and other groups enables a broader view of the multiple perspectives and factors that should be considered in business decisions. For example, decision makers can gain a better understanding of the costs, risks, opportunities, and tradeoffs of different approaches for achieving privacy and security goals.

- *Lower cost of developing and deploying products, processes, systems, and applications*: Greater alignment helps identify all privacy, security, and business requirements early in the development cycle. This reduces overall development and deployment costs, reducing the need for costly changes or retrofits. An associated benefit is the reduced risk of impact to development or deployment schedules due to last-minute discovery of unforeseen privacy concerns. The privacy component can lower the cost of privacy rules change management.

- *Reduced risk of privacy or security breaches*: Alignment between privacy, security, data governance, and other functions drives greater awareness of privacy throughout the organization, with stronger data governance and adherence to privacy policies. A broad understanding of privacy requirements helps ensure, for example, that new internally developed systems and third-party solutions receive timely compliance reviews. The increased privacy awareness makes it easier to identify vulnerabilities, reduce the risk of compromise, and recover more quickly if problems occur.

- *Improved brand image and marketing data*: When an organization demonstrates that it employs consistent and clear privacy practices, its brand image is enhanced and users are more willing to honestly share personal information. This information helps the organization build a more accurate and valuable marketing database.

## Other Benefits

Alignment can also deliver benefits that are less tangible but equally valuable, while helping avoid common mistakes that lead to inefficiencies or reputational damage. Some of these benefits include:

- *A clearer picture of the organization*: An organization typically contains many information owners, spread across different functional groups, each with its own charter and goals. By aligning, these information owners obtain a clearer picture of others' roles, helping to avoid redundancy, overlap, or confusion. Alignment also creates communication channels that help different groups collaborate to solve problems and identify new opportunities to optimize business processes.

- *Better-understood policies*: Better communication and broader involvement in privacy means policies are likely to be better understood across the organization. This helps create greater accountability. There is less chance that different departments will create conflicting or confusing policies, which can be difficult to implement and result in failed or incomplete controls.

- *A more comprehensive risk dashboard*: Alignment provides the organization with a better view of all the risks associated with the use of data by different groups. It helps avoid redundant or overlapping risk management and compliance activities such as internal audits and investigations. Executives obtain a single unified view containing all the information required to make decisions, rather than having to sift through multiple reports.

- *Avoiding dangerous false assumptions*: If privacy and other groups are not aligned, application developers may believe they understand privacy requirements when in fact they do not. Because of this assumption, the developers may not ask for the privacy team's help in assessing potential risks. As a result, they may design a system with privacy risks that could have been avoided.

## Conclusion

It is important to ensure that privacy leadership is well placed within the enterprise. The privacy team must be given serious executive support, strong people resources, robust support of the privacy-oriented roles, and alignment with information technology and with a strongly supported privacy-aware data governance structure. Strong privacy organization management provides business and technological enterprise benefits. The next chapter will discuss the valuation and metrics of our data assets.

**PART 4**

■ ■ ■

# Where Do We Go from Here?

# CHAPTER 13

■ ■ ■

# Value and Metrics for Data Assets

*It is the mark of an educated mind to rest satisfied with the degree of precision which the nature of the subject admits and not to seek exactness where only an approximation is possible*

—Aristotle

*Or, put another way, don't go over thinking things—or over measuring things.*

—Steve Weiss, Editor

No precision is possible to quantify or qualify the value of data, well or poorly designed system efficiencies, or brand value if we fail to begin. Yet, the reality is that enterprises run on well-trod resources such as money, real estate, and property. They also run on brand loyalty, percentage of churn, customer satisfaction, and leverage. The point here is that it is hard to measure the value of intellectual or virtual property such as the right to use, process, or remain a fiduciary for data. This chapter will put forth some ideas and concepts about potential data or data-centric systems. A privacy engineer holding this book will recognize that, here too, is a topic rife with opportunity for quiet incremental improvement and bold innovation.

One of the most elusive, yet impactful, tasks before the privacy engineer is to find measurements for incremental progress in designing and executing data governance standards and utilities and to report those metrics in terms of value. Value may come in many forms:

- Qualitative value as in improved efficacy of data system flows and customer satisfaction

- Quantitative value in terms of:

  - Loss avoidance

  - Incremental gains in information-based products and services or those accelerated by PI

  - A lower percentage of churn

  - Lower perceived "creepiness"

It makes sense here to have a little refresher from a discussion we began in Chapter 2 that covered some of the differences among privacy, confidentiality, and security before addressing value and metrics directly. These differences are particularly interesting, as data privacy tools and models are built, differentiated, and measured for value creation among a thicket of security or general "compliance" goods and services.

Data privacy is, in a very real sense, the most immature of the categories of intellectual property (IP), even though its roots travel far back in time. Traditional notions of IP include patents, trademarks, copyright, trade dress, trade secrets, and the contractual or social concepts of confidentiality. Of course, these notions often offer up models of "ownership" or "control" beyond that comfortably conceived for data privacy and protecting information about humans, but the models are helpful when discussing or determining measurement or quantitative models deployed to arbitrarily value it.

Trademarks (and other IP analogous legal objects) designate the origin of a good or service. For better or worse, a trademark's social utility is to alert end users to the origin or owners, creators, or controllers of goods or services. As part of the exchange for a limited monopoly right to trade goods under an exclusive mark, the owner of the trademark has a bundle of rights and obligations (assets and liabilities) associated with such ownership. For example, under US law,[1] a trademark owner must police his mark to be sure consumers are not fooled into believing imposters' goods are masquerading as his own (the cost of these efforts may be viewed as an expense undertaken for securing or protecting the right to remain the sole source of goods). Similarly, an IP owner must also ensure that goods or services are of a consistent quality (another cost center or liability undertaken both to protect the asset and protect the consumer). On the balanced side of the economic valuation, a trademark owner is entitled to have a limited monopoly as the source of a good or service as a direct market advantage and is also entitled to gain an extra boost and intangible advantage as a greater brand strategy to build emotional or other customer equity.

Data privacy may be considered as the bundle of rights and obligations that arise from the data emanating from or describing a person. Whereas the trademark owner is the origin of the good or service, so too is the human an identifiable individual data subject the origin of personal information. Current laws, regulations, and culture create the obligations for those who wish to remain fiduciaries or processors of data, and those same contextual requirements also create a platform for opportunities for asset management and leverage.

There are a number of imperfect analogies and models to help guide the way to begin the measurement and evaluation of the asset and liability balance for data privacy. None are perfect, but they are a good start in the absence of existing practices. (Remember Aristotle: don't seek exactness when only approximation is possible.)

---

[1] In other countries, laws around IP differ much as they do for data protection as a reflection of local or regional custom and commerce. A trademark owner may, for example, be allowed to own a trademark for a certain period of time without proving commercial use of that mark or have differing rights in his ability to alienate his rights to the mark.

# DO WE TREAT DATA AS ASSETS?

By Rena Mears, Managing Principal of RMCS, LLC

"We treat data as an asset . . ."

A ubiquitous phrase found in hundreds of thousands of online privacy policies[2] that succinctly conveys a sense of shared value and due care on the part of the enterprise to the web site user. Given its widespread use in privacy policies, it may be surprising to note that managing personal information as an asset is still in the very early stages of development within most enterprises. Many of the basic asset management processes such as inventorying, cost analysis, and asset valuation are in a nascent state, and consequently the tools and processes considered standard when managing other enterprise assets may be nonexistent or only minimally applied to personal information (PI) assets. So is it worth the effort and cost to develop these processes? Does adopting a more asset-based approach support or inhibit the effective and efficient management of personally identifiable information in the enterprise?

To answer that question, it is important to consider the definition of an asset, the various uses of PI in the organization, and the impact of valuation on the allocation of enterprise resources and shareholder value. The definition of an asset is deceptively simple:

- A resource controlled by an entity

- As a result of a past event

- From which future economic benefits are expected to flow to the entity[3]

However, when the criteria are applied to PI, the complexity of the management challenge becomes readily apparent. Diverse cultural, regulatory, and marketplace requirements have an enormous impact on defining and managing PI assets. Where, when, and how data is acquired ("past event") can determine what is considered a PI asset, how it can be used, and the level of control that must be exercised to effectively manage the asset throughout its lifecycle.

In response to this complexity, the general tendency has been to treat all PI assets as similar in nature and manage them on a tactical level as a cost-center issue. This approach often results in some or all of the following:

- PI asset management processes focus on risk reduction and cost minimization rather than asset optimization.

---

[2]Internet search results from "treat data as an asset" "privacy policies."
[3]International Accounting Standards Board. (2003). International financial reporting standards (IFRS's): Including international accounting standards (IAS's) and interpretations as at. London: International Accounting Standards Board. Elements of financial statements (IAS 1 article 10)

- Senior management involvement is limited to crisis response (e.g., breach, regulatory, enforcement action) or periodic reporting of risk (e.g., changing law, audit findings) and does not extend to consideration of strategies to maximize return on the PI assets.

- Managing PI assets defaults to the midmanagement layer of the organization and is treated primarily as a legal and compliance issue.

- PI assets are maintained in silos and management may be inconsistent and unaligned with company strategy.

- Enterprise resources (e.g., budget, human capital, technologies) are allocated evenly across all PI assets regardless of the value of individual assets, resulting in misallocation of resources, hidden costs, and unnecessary expense.

- Inventory of PI assets is incomplete or nonexistent, thereby limiting management's ability to evaluate, manage, and optimize the asset.

Changing market conditions are forcing a reexamination of this cost-based approach to managing PI assets. Companies that once considered themselves solely product oriented now see themselves as "information-driven" businesses that rely on data assets, including PI assets, to compete effectively in the marketplace. Innovative technologies and reduced storage costs support the acquisition and mining of vast amounts of data. The rapidly expanding definition and changing role of PI assets in current business models is driving the need for a more nuanced approach to evaluating and managing these assets.

A utility-based approach to asset management examines the "usefulness" or net contribution of individual or subclasses of PI assets to the value chain of an organization. The approach considers the various use cases of PI assets to identify future economic benefits (e.g., revenues, product enhancement), associated costs, and potential risks to determine net contribution values. Assets with similar use cases, characteristics, and values may be grouped into asset profiles that form the basis for asset optimization through strategy development and the application of customized management processes. It is important to note that asset optimization of PI assets is not the same as merely maximizing direct revenue from the use of personal information. There are many use cases for PI assets, and enterprise utility may relate to support activities and contributions through risk or cost reduction (e.g., meeting legal requirements, optimizing talent acquisition). Some advantages that may be expected when adopting a utility-based approach to PI asset management are:

- PI asset management approach focuses more broadly on asset optimization and considers opportunities and risks beyond legal and compliance requirements.

- Senior management involvement extends to the development of PI asset strategies and supports enterprise recognition of the strategic value of PI assets.

- Management of PI is appropriately positioned at all levels in the organization, resulting in more efficient use and effective control of the asset.

- Enterprise resources (e.g., budget, human capital, technologies) are allocated in a more "value-based" manner, thereby focusing expenditures on assets with the highest contribution to the enterprise value chain.

- Basic asset lifecycle processes (e.g., inventorying, cost analysis) are applied to PI assets and may result in identification of new management options (e.g., "build or buy," outsourcing).

- Underperforming assets can be identified and managed appropriately (e.g., retired or deleted, access/use limitation).

Many organizations consider it too costly and very difficult to adopt a utility-based approach to PI asset management. However, the cost of not adopting such an approach may mean that PI assets continue to be treated as "white noise" in the enterprise, widely distributed throughout the organization and relatively homogeneous in nature. That approach ignores the very essence of the definition of an asset and will likely ensure that PI continues to be a source of high risk, hidden cost, and unnecessary expense to the enterprise. Suboptimized assets whose risks and cost outweigh their contributions are more commonly known as liabilities.

# Finding Values for Data

*Some day, on the corporate balance sheet, there will be an entry which reads, "Information"; for in most cases, the information is more valuable than the hardware which processes it.*

—Rear Admiral Grace Murray Hopper

Values for data protection measures have been based on survey and anecdotal evidence relating to reported data breaches. Such breach reporting is typically thrust upon an enterprise by prevailing data breach legislation, best practices relating to credit monitoring or other services, and legal or marketing expenses undertaken in response to the negative perceptions caused by such breaches.[4] Another method for measurement

---

[4]"Ponemon study shows the cost of a data breach continues to increase." www.ponemon.org/news-2/23

may be to analyze prior fines or other regulatory requirements, such as Federal Trade Commission Consent decrees requiring as much as 20 years' oversight by a third-party audit company or other self-reporting mechanism.[5]

These traditional methods for data valuation fall short of the hoped for objective in a few fundamental ways. First, they are retrospective and often based on internal process or insider bad action—often quite difficult for an enterprise to anticipate or prevent. The incident may have arisen from a criminal actor, such as a hacker, or from product vulnerability in an increasingly complex IT ecosystem.[6] Second, the cost of a failure is but one component of risk avoidance—inefficiency, uncurated data mismanagement and waste, and, most important, true data asset prospective value are rarely addressed and even more rarely managed as sources of proactive investment.

Uncurated data is data that is not assigned to, owned by, or governed through specific methodologies or specific responsibilities. In short, this is data that is not being actively processed or organized to add value to either the data subject or the enterprise. For example, special events and business conferences require a great deal of personal data to accept payment, organize meetings, arrange travel, and more. Some of that data remains and grows in value as it is leveraged to build relationships with participants and personalize goods or services while the same data poses a risk only if left neglected or unused for its intended purpose.

Some data loses its relevance and becomes a compliance liability or risk where the data directly related to ended events or meetings for logistics, for example, is no longer needed for any relevant conference-related purpose. Retaining irrelevant portions of collected materials (or information) costs an enterprise money, time, and other resource expenditures. Although hardware storage may seem inexpensive and the myth persists that retention of data past its original purpose may create a "what if" or potential asset value, such is rarely the case. In fact, an enterprise may not have the legal right to process uncurated data if the future purpose of processing is beyond the original purpose.[7]

A mental experiment is helpful here, where a CFO continues to pay to store and move a warehouse filled with notebooks and pencils. These office supplies may be useful for future meetings or for scratch paper if date embossed. Nonetheless, if no one understands where the warehouse is located, if it has doors or a lock, and the nature of the supplies, and if no one has any responsibility for the warehouse's content,

---

[5]There are many examples of FTC Consent decrees and Data Privacy Authority sanctions with a variety of financial or other equitable remedies. In many countries, sanctions are either fines or undertakings to alter activities. In the United States, most federal-level penalties also contain the obligation for an enterprise to pay for annual audits of the enterprise privacy compliance efforts. See Microsoft's consent decree settling allegations with the FTC that the company made false statements regarding its ability to provide privacy or security to its customers. www.ftc.gov/opa/2002/08/microsoft.shtm. See also France's Commission nationale de l'informatique et des libertés (CNIL) sanctions against Google and its specific requirements that it hopes to impose on Google for its processing of French PI. www.cnil.fr/english/news-and-events/news/article/google-failure-to-comply-before-deadline-set-in-the-enforcement-notice/

[6]See "Predicting the unpredictable: Detecting chaos in mathematical equations." www.mit.edu/newsoffice/1998/chaos.html

[7]See OECD Guidelines Purpose Principle, discussed in Chapter 2.

the enterprise must continue to pay for its management, realizing no further value and risking further losses by fire or workplace injury for movers or other unexpected problems. Just as the information ecosphere provides the potential for massive data stores and assets, so too does it create the very real possibility for waste, loss, and unplanned risk.

# KNOWLEDGE GOVERNANCE

By Kenneth P. Mortensen, Chief Governance Officer at CVS Caremark

*What is a system? A system is a network of interdependent components that work together to try to accomplish the aim of the system. A system must have an aim. Without an aim, there is no system. The aim of the system must be clear to everyone in the system. The aim must include plans for the future. The aim is a value judgment.*

—Dr. W. Edwards Deming,
*The New Economics for Industry, Government, Education*

In the age of "big data" and "advanced persistent threats," a privacy professional can no longer focus solely on developing and implementing the processes and procedures to drive information governance, but rather she needs to advance her organization through the optimization of risk while facilitating core management decision making in order to create real value. This is the new world of "knowledge governance."

In the past, an organization looked simply to corral its data into a warehouse so that it could be understood which datasets and which data elements provided operational leverage within the activities or functions of the organization—otherwise known as "data governance." By producing a common or uniform view into the organization's data, data governance allowed, for the first time, an understanding of which data fed the organization's activities or functions. Nevertheless, this was a single dimension view that lacked the ability to understand the utility of the data within those activities and functions. Without a view to the data utility, an organization flies blind to legal and regulatory compliance issues, such as with privacy and information security. Thus just having a common understanding or reference model for the data of an organization does not open up those data for use and disclosure without significant risk regarding privacy and security.

From that gap, the privacy profession promoted the concept of "information governance" that allows for the data to communicate information. In literal etymological terms, information means to give form to something. In business terms, the word focuses on the ability to transmit data by providing form to a message by casting it into a profile or pattern for communication (sharing). This means definitions for information can be grouped roughly into quantitative and qualitative categories.

The qualitative definitions focus on the criteria that add meaning to the message that is communicated. The quantitative definitions focus on measuring the quantity of information units or the strength of its transmission. But this alone did not address the risks inherent with data governance. The governance aspect at the information level comes from the effective and efficient management of information within organizations. Management is the process of getting activities completed efficiently and effectively through the enterprise. The goal (or function) of management is to get the best return on enterprise resources by getting things done efficiently.

There are four basic pillars to any management process: plan, organize, direct, and monitor. An organization must, through data governance programs, *plan* the path for information within any organization as well as address any external collection or disclosure. Next, the organization will need to *organize* not only the data, which gets the organization only as far as data governance, but also the uses and disclosure to discover the utility of the information. From those uses and disclosures, the organization can *direct* protections and safeguards so that the organization can not only use the information thoroughly, but also in a compliant manner. Last, the *monitoring* of the processes and procedures is crucial to ensure that governance works to drive continuous compliance.

At this point, many organizations put down their tools, convinced that they have full use of their information in a methodology that ensures compliance with needed privacy protections and necessary security safeguards.

Unfortunately, these organizations, while able to survive the enforcement environments because they operate in a compliant manner, cannot progress into having full enterprise understandings of what value they can extract from all the information. Legal compliance does not optimize risk to the organization; nor does this coordination of effort address more than one facet of risk. The organization must look to all functionalities of the organization to understand the impact of risks associated with the information resources. To move to the next level and attain "knowledge," the organization must address information and its management strategically. Strategic management of information across the organization addresses not only the need to optimize the risk to the organization, but by establishing all the information as a critical organizational (or, better put, *enterprise*) asset, if not the most critical asset, the organization can introduce effective efficiencies into the decision-making processes for management, enhancing the return on the investment in information. An organization needs wide-ranging processes to capture not only data protection, but also data compliance, which takes in the complexity and diversity of the risk and legal environments. Knowledge is the value form of information, just as information is the communicative form of data. To accomplish this objective, an organization must employ enterprise governance that addresses all aspects of information within the organization with processes and procedures to deconflict and reconcile priorities to ensure governance efficiency.

Once knowledge governance has been achieved, an organization can extract the value of core data and information. The organization's leadership will be guided by this knowledge in advancing the goals and objectives of the organization, or as Dr. Deming noted when addressing similar issues from a quality management aspect:

> *The prevailing style of management must undergo transformation. A system cannot understand itself. The transformation requires a view from outside. The aim . . . is to provide an outside view—a lens—that I call a system of profound knowledge. It provides a map of theory by which to understand the organizations that we work in.*[8]

Knowledge governance for data assets can only be enhanced by further exploring other metric and valuation models. As is true for other sections of **The Privacy Engineering Manifesto**, methodologies and processes have been undertaken to create useful valuations of difficult-to-measure tangible and intangible inputs and outcomes. Data privacy is neither the most unique problem in the world nor the least measurable. Nonetheless, to quote the late American novelist David Foster Wallace, sometimes "the most obvious, ubiquitous, important realities are often the ones that are hardest to see and talk about."[9] Once discovered, the language of value for data privacy may be the key to opening the door to more practical matters.

# Valuation Models

The following potential models should be viewed as a sketch pad of sorts; a group of potential techniques and tactics for assigning values or making concrete the value for data and data-centric systems. As technologies become more deliberately designed for data protection and policies evolve to become both legally more efficient and compatible with requirements setting, so too should valuation models evolve.

## Model 1

Find something to count and count it:

- Data breach, customer churn after direct enterprise activity, or other regionally relevant contextual activity (such as a significant breach or a news-making threat or economic instability that causes data or customer contacts to increase or decrease).

- Leverage the GAPP maturity model and gauge costs to move to a higher maturity model. Balance cost against brand valuation, data reliant programs, or marketing events to the percentage spent to acquire customers.

---

[8]W. Edwards Deming, The New Economics for Industry, Government, Education, Ch. 4 (1994)
[9]"This is Water", Commencement Speech to Kenyon College class of 2005 written by David Foster Wallace.

- Read 10K annual reports or other publicly available, legally binding documents to find data-critical programs such as expansions into new jurisdictions, outsourcing, or cloud shifting business models or determine the geographic mix of customer or employees who provide critical data to the enterprise. Make an educated or sample-based guess regarding the importance of employee or customer data access based on these disclosures.

- Estimate IT spent regarding data-centric systems, and measure the cost of management and governance for technology in terms of full-time employees headcount's, legal, or other professional services or audit requirements (i.e., How much do the systems, processes, and technologies that process personal data cost?).

# Model 2

Track time to deployment or proof of concept in a privacy engineering instance vs. traditional deployment. Start and track improvements in development, speed to deal closure, or other processes to attempt to measure organizational efficiencies.

# Model 3

Work within the grain of cyber insurance. An enterprise will only be covered by cyber insurance where certain conditions are met to prove that the enterprise has taken at least reasonable steps to prevent loss. Create a checklist for coverage for various relevant scenarios based on the current level of cyber coverage or similar coverage within a relevant industry or size of enterprise for incidents such as hacker or other criminal external compromise, advanced persistent threat (APT) exploitation, negligent loss of media device, or physical encroachment. Generate the cost of repair or staffing to attain reasonable coverage in the event of a cyber incident.

# Model 4

Look for qualitative or reputational examples rather than numerical values. For example, there are tools and techniques leveraging other individual's expressed curiosity, socially networked assertions, or trends according to big datasets or other analytics that can show relevance to the enterprise and value to individual customers.

# Model 5

Leverage the known unknowns of brand valuation. Brand value determination is calculated using certain evidential or inferential techniques. Roughly stated, brand is measured as the difference between book value (adding all countable assets such as real estate and improvements, manufacturing assets, and the combination of financial assets relating to currency and investments) and market capitalization value. Where there is a market and that market decides that a company is worth more than tangible assets, that differential is the collection of intangibles, potentials, and connective tissue that ties customers and employees to an enterprise and allows investors to decide an enterprise's potential.

## PRIVACY IN THE ERA OF THE DATA ECONOMY

Chenxi Wang, Ph.D. Vice President of Market Insights at McAfee

We are living in the era of the data economy. The advent of consumer mobility and social media gave rise to a massive amount of readily available data to mine, aggregate, share, and analyze. IDC estimates that by 2020, there will be "40 zettabytes of information in the digital universe".[10] What's more, the composition of data products and applications can lead to brand new business models and previously impossible value propositions : consider Uber (the private, on-demand car service ) in a world without Google maps.

Modern businesses now understand that access to data equals power and competitive advantages , and there is an increasingly large appetite to collect, store, and mind data. It is entirely possible that soon we will see a global market where data products and applications are routinely traded and exchanged. This trend has led to data obesity, heightened risk for data misuse, and an increasing concern for the threat to privacy.

Just like any other market, the data economy is governed by supply-and-demand and a value/pricing framework. Privacy regulations, however, typically seek to govern the supply and demand relationships, while completely ignoring the value framework. We argue that privacy is not attainable unless the value/pricing framework takes privacy impact into consideration. In other words, the value assessment of the data should not be solely based on their potential for creating valuable data products, but also based on their potential exposure to privacy risks.

Consider, for example, the case of a patron entering a bar. To gain admittance, today the patron needs to show her driver license, which discloses his date of birth, weight, height, and home address. Much of this information is beyond what the bar needs to know to permit entrance to the premises.

Consider again the same case when the patron approaches the bar, she is presented with three options: a) minimum disclosure to gain entrance (i.e., prove that she is over 21, the legal drinking age), b) disclose demographic information (i.e., age, gender) for a drink coupon, and c) consent for location tracking and ad serving for a much larger drink coupon.

---

[10]IDC's latest Digital Universe Report, released in December 2012, estimates that the amount of digital data produced will exceed 40 Zettabytes by 2020. This assumes all data is expected to double every two years.

If the patron chooses option A, her picture will be taken and sent to an information cloud for age verification. The answer that comes back from the cloud will be either a "yes (over 21)" or a "no (below 21)" , with no additional information such as date of birth. The picture is then deleted and the patron gains access to the premises.

If the patron chooses option B, the information cloud would disclose, along with age verification, demographic information such as age group, gender, etc. This information will be used in the bar operator's data mining and marketing efforts.

If the patron chooses option C, she would be asked to download an ad-serving app, which serves her relevant ads based on her location and activities.

Of course there could be other levels of information disclosure, but let's look at what just happened in the above scenario:

First, the customer has all the control: she can decide how much information to disclose.

Second, the marketers are not completely ignored here: they can get opt-in information, for a price.

The minimum disclosure is contextual: here the information disclosed is whether the user is above or below 21 years of age, but in other cases minimal disclosure can be about other data that make sense in the specific context of the activity. For example, location for local Yelp services may make sense in context.

There is a trusted intermediary—the info cloud in the example—that brokers the data exchange. The data broker does not have to be a singular party, but it needs to be a public entity trusted by the data owner.

To make this a reality, we need to establish a data value framework and a new model for the data supply chain. The data supply chain should include the designation of authoritative data suppliers, an access authorization model, authentication, data aggregation models, etc. The work done by UMA, for instance, is an example of an user-centric authorization model.[11]

The data value framework is arguably the most interesting, because it denotes how data will be assessed and traded, which are fundamental elements of an economy. One can consider a rudimentary value framework as follows: Pick your favorite data taxonomy, order the categories based on their exposure to privacy risks (if possible), and price them accordingly (the higher the risk, the higher the price tag). Afterwards, for each user-authorized data access, if the data required fall into minimal disclosure, they are supplied free of charge. Outside minimal disclosure, the data are

---

[11]UMA: User Managed Access (UMA) is an industry working group that is developing specifications that will allow an individual to control the authorization of data sharing and service access made between online services on the individual's behalf.

supplied with the attached price. For those data items that the user does not wish to grant third party access, the price tag can be set to infinite.

Clearly there are many options and intricacies to data value assessment beyond this basic framework. For example, how do you handle derived data, those that only exist based on previous data accesses? Similarly, the issue of what is considered minimal disclosure can be debatable.

However, we argue that without such a contextual data value model, either consumer privacy or the increasingly flourishing economy built on data sharing will be undermined. Businesses who truly understand the business impact of data and adopt this privacy-embedded data value framework will see consumers as willing participants in the data economy, where data exchanges are contextually relevant, properly priced, and in a manner that respects their privacy.

So, in many ways, the formula under a brand-based methodology could be that "brand" is the superset where intellectual property (IP) plus personal information (PI) are significant subsets of that market-driven asset. It is also illustrative that countries such as the United Kingdom, France, Australia, and New Zealand allow for intangibles to be included as part of an enterprise's balance sheet.

Brand values have been used to defend against a hostile takeover, as an investor relations tool, and, sometimes, as a performance indicator for the long-term investor. International standards that allow for intangible values may be leveraged and borrowed to assist in documenting PI value for the privacy engineer. For example, the International Accounting Standards Board (IAS 38), UK Accounting Standards (FRS 10 & 11), and US Accounting Standards Board (FASB 141 & 142 under Generally Accepted Accounting Principles) all may be used to determine or infer acquired goodwill. If the analogy from brand value to a subset of PI plus IP value is to be considered, it should be carefully noted and considered that the concept of "impairment"—roughly, the extent to which the stated value does not reach market value for a market-based enterprise—also impacts the PI value.

Here, the process and practice of privacy engineering becomes conceptually very interesting. Part of the controversial nature of valuing intangible assets is where those assets defy measurement. Compliance for data protection measures can be similarly difficult to achieve where enterprise governance professionals are unaware where data reside and how it is actually processed, and they do not have a means with which to measure processing over time. Where privacy engineering practices are followed, data is managed from its earliest analysis, design, and instantiation throughout its lifecycle. In such systems, active management and impairments based on market perception or active risk taking using data assets can be known and tested.[12]

---

[12]For example: www.nysscpa.org/cpajournal/2002/0202/features/202fp.22.htm

# PRIVACY MATTERS BLOG SERIES: QUANTIFYING REPUTATIONAL RISK[13]

By Michelle Finneran Dennedy, published on Jan 06, 2012

There are many kinds of risk: operational, legal, and reputational risk. Most large enterprise IT teams are comfortable and proficient at measuring operational risk. It features in reports as minutes of downtime, incidents of endpoint reimages, number of patches installed, hours of overtime.

Legal risk isn't that hard to handle, either. IT can draw on peers, auditors, and legal staff for expertise.

However, reputational risk seems to be a far more unfriendly concept. I find technical people typically consider reputation a soft science, a squishy topic that can't be measured. As a result, IT can't set goals, gauge progress, or claim success based upon "reputation," and product creators cannot specify requirements for "reputation." Because it can't be managed like other metrics, IT staff and technical business units may ignore or downplay reputational risk's potential impact on the business—and their roles in protecting it.

## IT is Missing a Gigantic Opportunity

I believe you *can* measure—or at least approximate—reputation, applying metrics to the same influences that affect your customers and your C-Suite executives: news headlines and stock prices. If you count the number of published, reputation-buffeting events each month—the headlines in the email news summaries you receive from SC Magazine, for example—you can see what the public is talking about, and that dialog will affect the rise and fall of organizational stock prices. Reputation and market sentiment are huge factors in market valuation, which is something your CMO and CFO are tracking. Although your interest may be in the technical security side of the business, you can take actions to measure, manage, or mitigate reputational risk.

## Building a Reputational Heat Map

Well before the mortgage crisis was discussed in the public and mainstream press, it was anticipated in whispers at investment community conferences and insider blogs. Eventually, and much too late for most people and the economy, it was covered in USA Today and other mainstream papers on the doormats of hotel rooms coast to coast.

---

[13]This blog entry is reprinted in its entirety from McAfee's external web site:
`http://blogs.mcafee.com/business/security-connected/privacy-matters`

Security issues that affect risk appear first in smaller, insider places, too. Then they migrate to the mainstream, to NPR, the Washington Post, Wired, and Vanity Fair. (Look at Stuxnet references on Wikipedia for a great example of this sequence.) With enough mainstream angst, trends start to register on the regulatory radar—with the European Community, the Federal Trade Commission, and others. We experienced this pattern with behavioral marketing. Privacy advocates raised objections in 2005, well before the FTC published its principles for behavioral marketing in December 2007. We are still seeing news and blog coverage on this topic today as companies experiment and push the envelope leveraging new technologies and relationships.

By the time a security topic attracts a reporter in the mainstream press, you had better have a strategy for that problem. You should be able to brief your boss with an assessment of your business's risk, including the risk to your reputation.

This assessment is possible, but you need to be selective. Just as you don't want to read every log entry from your IPS, you don't want to attempt to assess all topics everywhere on the Net. Instead, think about YOUR audience and what they read—or you wish they would read. Look at two tiers of publications: mainstream media and online influencers, including blogs and news feeds. Sign up for emailed daily updates if they are available from the 3–5 most relevant sources. Also, if there is an "insider" conference, you can look at the session titles and monitor news summaries for perspective on what the industry thinks is hot.

Next, think about what risks would affect your business and its reputation. The tech bloggers today might be talking about SQL injection, advertising dollars, identity theft, or phishing. What is newsworthy for your audience? Would a successful hack at a competitor raise questions about your security? Would regulation banning use of cookies affect your service offerings? If yes, use these ideas to set up RSS feeds.

That's your pre-work. You should revisit these decisions at least once a year, or when your business or the markets change significantly.

Now, the ongoing process. Your workflow is to:

Notice topics that relate to your risks.

Count the number of times these topics are mentioned in headlines or news stories. Depending on your work style (and the frequency of the publications you are tracking), you might either jot down mentions as you see them or save these mentions in a file for review monthly.

Create a spreadsheet: rows are the topics, columns are the dates. In each cell, note the number of headlines or significant mentions. If you think it's going to be important, start to capture dates and publications (use links if you can) so you can back up your ideas. (Store this info somewhere else, not in the mention count cell, or you won't be able to convert to a chart.)

Once a month, use the spreadsheet's charting function to generate a "heat map," an assessment of which topics have generated the most energy in the news.

If a relevant topic has generated significant coverage in insider publications, there's a good chance it will reach the mainstream press. If you think this might happen, summarize your findings in a concise note to your boss and your security team. Include an overview of what the issue is, what the coverage has been so far, what the impact would be on your business, and what efforts might be appropriate to mitigate these risks.

Voila.[14] You have quantified reputational risk.

Do this well, and you will be prepared if and when you need to discuss ideas with others. Instead of coming in with only technical data about a problem, you can talk with your colleagues in the context of the risk landscape. You look more strategic and more business-oriented. You are doing more, considering more, and recommending risk management efforts that are proportional to security. This position supports IT's increasing need to do internal selling to non-IT people in order to get the right projects funded.

At a minimum, this exercise will keep your knowledge of the risk landscape current, and you will be more fun at parties. You can talk to non-security people about ideas that they will recognize and explain risks in terms that they can understand. Perhaps you will detect the next "mortgage crisis" level event in time to help a few people avoid its devastation.

# Building the Business Case

Measurements are only science projects until they are leveraged for positive progress. A privacy engineer's innovation can be lost without a market into which to sell the goods and services created with these methodologies or, similarly, it can be lost where internal enterprise measures are not sustained for continued improvement that results in better knowledge governance.

One approach is to treat privacy engineering products, services, and processes as *intrapreneurial* opportunities. An *intrapreneur* is an innovator within an enterprise who takes on the responsibilities for creating and "selling" new techniques or even new privacy business units. To become successful, intrapreneurial teams must connect with executive and operational teams to fit new things into existing environments effectively.

---

[14]Okay, so nothing is that easy, particularly in the world of data privacy and security, but hyperbole is a gimmick and the "voila" was a dead giveaway that I was trying to be dramatic for effect.

For example, when talking to the C-Suite:

- They hate details

- They don't know about detailed data privacy laws

- They hate details

- They have never seen a data valuation model, but they do like cost/benefit analysis where benefits are costed out realistically and the cost side looks real

- They hate details

## PERVASIVE RISK MANAGEMENT APPROACH FOR EFFECTIVE PRIVACY ENGINEERING

By Vidya Phalke, Chief Technology Officer , MetricStream

A comprehensive and sustained risk management program is critical for an enterprise's long-term sustainability and predictability. Risk management needs to be comprehensive across all facets of operational, financial, legal, regulatory, reputational, data security, and intellectual property risks. In addition, it needs to permeate into an organization in a *pervasive* and deep fashion. The basic recipe for this pervasive treatment of governance, risk, and compliance is created by putting together models—both qualitative as well as quantitative—so that decision makers in an enterprise can create a deep understanding of their risks and then use that understanding effectively for planning and managing the short- as well as the long-term objectives at each level of the organization.

Although pervasive risk management is a broader topic, I will use this book's privacy focus to describe a mechanism by which a quantitative model can be orchestrated that will help management of risk that is based on how well privacy risk is understood and managed. This same mechanism can then be extrapolated for other areas of risks to arrive at a pervasive risk management architecture.

Whether it is government agencies or private organizations like banks, insurance companies, or health care providers, the need for incorporating privacy protection and managing privacy risk is not only a regulatory and legal obligation but it also has to be part of the risk management plan. The first step in tackling this risk is to create a comprehensive list of enterprise-wide assets and processes and map them to their privacy risk. This exercise typically is done in conjunction with IT and various functional units. If an enterprise already has a risk or compliance office, then that is usually a good place to start.

Second, a comprehensive assessment across all these assets and processes should be done along the dimension of privacy from a risk as well as a regulatory standpoint. If that has been done already, then that assessment can be leveraged.

The key here is to look for *privacy component* capabilities as described in this book in each of the assets and processes. In addition to looking for those components or their surrogates, a review of past audits, control or compliance testing, industry events or incidents, and other management evidence needs to be taken into account as well. Remember, this assessment needs to be wrapped into overall change management processes and frameworks.

Typically risks due to privacy issues will flow into both legal and regulatory risk as well as reputational risk, and assessment of the likelihood and impact has to be done based on qualitative and quantitative factors followed by evaluation of mitigating controls. As discussed in this book, the assessment need not be extremely precise but can start with an approximation. For example, measuring the privacy controls and usage of privacy components (or lack thereof) can lead to a score ranging from 0 to 5. These scores multiplied by the value of the asset or process they are tied to creates a weighted risk score. The process of assigning value to an asset or process in an enterprise is a well-defined science, so I will not spend time on that here; however, it suffices to state that it is tied to business criticality, footprint, and extent of being proprietary. For example, a database that contains PI that is accessible to an outsourced data analysis company will have a much higher footprint weight as compared to one that is accessible to a fixed known set of data analysts that are internal employees of that company. Once the comprehensive asset and process privacy risk assessments are computed, they need to be multiplied by the organizational weight of that business unit or functional division and then rolled into a score visible to the senior management.

Once this quantitative framework for risk management is put together, the next important aspect is to ensure that it is brought under the umbrella of enterprise change management; this is critical to ensure that as changes happen and new information is discovered, the impact of those changes is captured in the risk management framework. For example, in the above case of a database with PI, if a new application is being brought in that will be integrated within this database and will expose the data to a bigger set of users, then the risk parameters need to be reassessed and appropriate mitigation and controls need to be updated.

Figure 13-1 presents a pictorial summarization of this architecture and flow that should be applied to assets and processes to build a pervasive risk management framework and system.

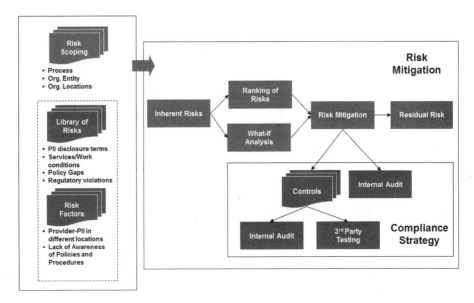

**Figure 13-1.** *Risk management with privacy use case*

# Turning Talk into Action

Allies and other enterprise sponsors can help add to value models and create momentum. Privacy engineers *must* find allies such as the CFO, auditor, CMO, CTO, or any other leader willing to innovate with them and take on a bit of personal credibility risk. New things such as data valuation models can be perceived as unnecessary or not impactful or already managed by audit committees or compliance teams. Innovation in valuation models may require as many facts being marshaled from various measurement techniques as possible before a persuasive technique is selected for the enterprise.

# Conclusion

The word "privacy" creates a marketing challenge. The paradox for creating data value models and systems can begin with this marketing issue. If enterprise stakeholders do not perceive or measure data risks and opportunities, they may well fall into a common trap. They may falsely assume that there is no need for privacy (after all, everyone says so). Another false assumption, if they do understand data about people or data derivatives have value, true stakeholders may feel that "someone else" owns or is accountable for the issue. Both false assumptions also suppose that data value is a thing or a static object as opposed to a flow, as is the case in capital- or currency-based value systems.

297

Finding enterprise allies may mean establishing common definitions, a common lexicography, and value models. It is also true that various enterprise stakeholders may have different relationships to PI's derivative value and, thus, may respond to different valuation models and measurements. In those cases, it is important to have interoperable value models. Although it is an extremely worthwhile effort that will drive ultimate results and systemic change, extracting these common measurement models is not easy.

The privacy engineer's task is to communicate and clarify data values across such stakeholders to drive innovation. Clearly, such value methodologies must provide a coordinated cumulative view to top management. The methodologies and models must also make sense to operational teams gathering data for the models.

Once data assets are properly measured and values understood through innovative techniques and tools—many of which have yet to be invented—data economies based on personal information can thrive and benefit from further investment. The time to start counting and accounting is now.

The final chapter will discuss thoughts and musings about the future and the Privacy Engineer's Manifesto.

# CHAPTER 14

■ ■ ■

# A Vision of the Future: The Privacy Engineer's Manifesto

*There is one thing stronger than all the armies in the world, and that is an idea whose time has come.*

—Victor Hugo

In this final chapter, we propose that this beginning framework for privacy engineering should become amplified like the open mouth of a megaphone (to invoke an oldie-but-goody technology) to enlighten and guide future data privacy and security professionals in a world of increasing pervasive computing. Taken together, the known standards and lessons from past waves of innovation can lead to an explosive and productive information society; but we need to acknowledge the historical certainty that individuals do, in fact, desire a certain degree of freedom to live a life of their own determination without excessive government or corporate interference. These same individuals may wish to communicate, socialize, and receive personalized services. At the same time, individuals should be free from "services that penalize" their users (i.e., those that are encumbered by excessive peeping, overenthusiastic assumptions about preferences, a false sense of safety, undue influence, a filter that causes an information bubble, or other dystopia-like scenarios).

We are creatures of ever-changing context. To meet requirements based on values of ethics, safety, morality, and even fun and laden with every imaginable deconstuctable, predictive, or analytical dataset, we must design forward and fearlessly, with a solid foundation grounded in the experiences of the past. Passive drifting into ever fewer controls and greater obscurity of purpose is not a viable option.

So, this chapter considers two visions of the future: one, where we continue our present technology-centric ways, drifting relentlessly toward chaotic mismanagement of data, or two, where we learn how to thrive in a world with unfettered volumes of data. In this privacy-engineered world, metrics are available to create, manage, and extend information markets that are available to enterprises and individuals alike.

Finally, we propose a privacy engineer's manifesto. A good revolution requires a manifesto, and what we've described in this book documents nothing short of a revolution in how humans look at themselves and think about their world. Innovation in data governance over intellectual property and personally identifiable data (and the gray overlapping spectrum including machine data between), technology enhancements, and societal pressures affects the way we look at privacy. The question remains: Will our views on data privacy drive us forward into greater innovation and markets or shall we, as a global community with differing views on data, retreat into informational and legal stasis, with little or no pragmatic protections for data assets?

Privacy can become a strong platform for relating to customers and users upon which individuals can stand to communicate with governments and commercial enterprises—if we make the conscious decision to create that reality.

# Where the Future Doesn't Need Us

In 1999, Scott McNealy, cofounder and CEO of Sun Microsystems, Inc., infamously harumphed "You have zero privacy anyway. Get over it!" in response to questions about technologies designed to help devices and users communicate to do things like printing documents remotely.[1] Although that technology may seem benign compared with wide-scale open datasets, government intelligence gathering, and wearable computing, the dialogue remains an open one today. Is there an either/or choice to be made between new features, old-time spying, and personal respect and privacy? Has an information-hungry world simply vetoed data protection?

Perhaps data privacy—or any sort of privacy—is simply too hard to protect; perhaps we should accept living in a surveillance state and submit any rights to self-determinism to some higher power that will keep us safe. Perhaps the root of substantive privacy belongs to some Orwellian, Big Brother entity, and our technology, legal, and procedural models should reflect our placid acceptance of an omniscient, "public," and centrally organized and governed IT infrastructure.

It certainly can *appear* that technophilliacs and young people have decided that the future is one where all information is "free" (i.e., neither owned nor managed by them) and that no one should have anything to hide. The truth, however, is likely far different from the myth. The real answer is more complex and a lot more exciting where young people routinely present themselves how and to whom they see fit. Technophiles reject and actively protest overreaching interference and peeping by governments and technology features and settings.

## CALCULATING THE COST OF PRIVACY

By Raj Samani, Vice President, Chief Technical Officer, EMEA, McAfee

Society demands privacy, yet ironically many seem happy to share their deepest secrets to the world for nothing more than a handful of magic beans and the promise of a new feature. It must seem incredibly frustrating for professionals who dedicate their working lives to preserve privacy, when again and again consumers hand over their data like it is absolutely worthless.

---

[1] www.wired.com/politics/law/news/1999/01/17538

I experienced this frustration many times, but none more so than in 2012. A plucky confectioner decided to run a promotion giving away "free" chocolate. The "cost"? Their personal data of course! Perhaps more remarkable were the long lines of willing participants, and in the 10 minutes I stood there, incredulously not one single person read the privacy statement collecting cobwebs just beside the chocolate station.

This experience compelled me to write an article titled "How Much Do You Value Your Personal Data?"[2] in which I made the bold claim that the disparity between the perceived value of personal data and its actual value was at its widest.

How wrong I was! At the time it did not cross my mind that things could be worse than consumers perceiving their privacy as being worth less than a bar of chocolate, but sadly in the past 12 months the perceived value has dropped to zero. Recent retail experiences would suggest that not only is the value at its lowest, but there is no shortage of consumers willing to check out of the personal data economy just before it really takes off.

Most people use corporate loyalty cards, justifying the value they provide in discounts as a fair exchange for their personal and transactional data. Equally, many use social networks with the value they provide seen as a fair exchange. Others may argue, at the very least, there is a value associated with their personal data, be that discounts, or belonging to a social network, amongst others. However, recent experiences would suggest that some organisations are now charging for their loyalty cards, sorry I meant double charging. Not only are consumers expected to pay with their data, but they are also being asked to pay via monetary means. Furthermore, it would appear that 200,000 consumers were already members of one particular scheme!

This is not an isolated example, with more than one retailer actively double charging consumers who seem more than willing to pay twice. What is clearly evident is that while large corporations and privacy professionals clearly understand the value of personal data, the consumer is facing personal data bankruptcy. Sadly, this decline will mean for many that they will fail to realise the financial benefits of this emerging economy.

Twitter @Raj_Samani

---

The collection of thoughts presented in the sidebar may seem better suited in the discussion in Chapter 13 regarding value models. Upon examination, the ideas and attitudes of today's consumers are instructive for the privacy engineer. In the store loyalty example, the consumer pays twice. First, the customer gives away his shopping data to the retailer. Second, he pays to have the card at all. Because the system is neither

---

[2]www.telegraph.co.uk/technology/internet-security/9605078/How-much-do-you-value-your-personal-data.html

customer centric nor does it clearly disclose the ultimate purpose for processing of the customer data, it seems likely that the current system has deployed few, if any, privacy engineering techniques. In this environment, the enterprise risks customer loyalty and trust by continuing to take advantage of its customers rather than providing real and transparent value.

It may be possible for retail brands to be strong enough to withstand charging its customers for giving away their own data. However, once these same consumers are faced with the slimmest margin of choice or price variance, the customer churn for those employing such tactics becomes intolerable. Alternatively, the enterprise may have to flatten its margins, pay a premium to maintain brand stickiness, or employ other costs to compensate.

Instead, a data scheme deploying fair information principles should be a better predictor of success and, thus, a better longer-term investment. The customer would be more engaged, the enterprise at less risk of disclosure of embarrassing practices, and the systems protecting data can be engineered accordingly.

# Even Social Networks (and Their Leaders) Get Cranky When Their Privacy Is Compromised

To continue the interesting scenario of a future where each person is reduced to an object of data mapping and subject to the data observations of others, it is worth exploring how privacy can fit into current social networks.

The earliest days of the now infamous social networking site, Facebook, is a fascinating example of how data privacy can actually act as a business accelerator to start ups.

Facebook's current privacy profile is, perhaps, best known for its founder's rather glib statements about privacy's demise and the many governments worldwide that have investigated and attempted to regulate its privacy settings[3] and advertising models. But the history of Facebook and its implications for innovation is the more interesting story for the purposes of this chapter's discussion.

Social networking, blogging, and other online sharing began before Facebook became the dominant player in that market. In fact, MySpace, an early dominant force, was once the mainstream social sharing platform for music, gossip, meeting friends—and strangers. It has since become more of a music specialty boutique. In its heyday in 2006, the site was lambasted for failing to protect users from predators and peepers. Meanwhile, start up Facebook sold itself as the velvet-roped "in" place for "good" kids with .edu e-mail addresses. Only certain kinds of kids were allowed on the site, and users had to have specific school .edu domains to be allowed on the platform as a "Friend."

The ivy and elite schools that were acceptable circles for Facebook acted as their own type of authentication and limit to the platform—you may call a boy disgusting for gawking at girls in his college dorm, but he'sa well-heeled fancy school kid and, therefore, okay. Privacy of a sort was protected within these elite social and economic circles. Similarly, the ad business that would pay for the "free" use of the site was nowhere near

---

[3]See Canadian PIPEDA Case Summary 2009-008 at
www.priv.gc.ca/cf-dc/2009/2009_008_0716_e.asp

the current sophisticated online behavioral models nor tracking capabilities of the same company, a mere decade later.

The controls for privacy grew more complex and nearly unfathomable to the average user. The social "circles" circumscribed by the social network became ever larger while the original controls and protections for information shared on the Facebook platform have eroded. Accordingly, users and regulators have increasingly grown weary of constant change and eroding policies regarding the monetization of the personal information of social users.

Irony still rules the day in the evolution of social and ad-based businesses. In a recent California conference, the CEOs for Facebook and Yahoo! were asked about revelations regarding US government activities. Facebook's Mark Zuckerberg's response should be very interesting to any privacy engineer. According to the press coverage, "Zuckerberg said the government had done a 'bad job' of balancing people's privacy and its duty to protect. 'Frankly I think the government blew it,' he said."[4]

Several of the CEOs who claim that privacy is an artifact of an earlier era or that it is no longer a necessary social norm have purchased extraordinarily expensive homes that surround their own suburban lodgings. It seems that their own behavior and desire for privacy remain of social and personal value. In these cases, architecture for privacy can indeed be inferred in the most literal sense. The extra homes and real estate are the ultimate in "hardware" protections for privacy.

This chapter concludes—as a capstone to the entire book—with a manifesto that summarizes how seemingly opposing motives of creating corporate profit, maintaining public safety, and respecting individual privacy can live in harmony. The manifesto provides some simple guiding principles and a vision for creating value in the complex world of product development where user needs and corporate motives must find a meeting grounds in mutual respect.

# Let's Remember How We Got Here

Privacy is not a new concept. It has been around since before biblical times in some form or another. However, modern technologies such as databases and the Internet browser have changed some of our ideas about privacy in the sense that they have enabled a cyber world in which one's neighbors are faceless and powerful. Although the intent of an organization may be simply to extract value and intelligence from PI, sharing and using the data are much easier and more ubiquitous than before. It is the speed and reach of today's information age technologies that make the risk of misuse more noteworthy. There is no dispute that preservation and innovation around data protection or privacy are challenging and complex. Only the smart and courageous or, perhaps, adventurous and entrepreneurial, may wish to venture into this arena. No one ever said this was going to be easy.

In the opening chapter, we discussed how the boundaries surrounding an organization's information systems and data have become much more permeable in the past two decades. These advancements have opened up information systems so that people, devices, and systems are now nearly seamlessly connected. Today's users not

---

[4]www.theguardian.com/technology/2013/sep/11/yahoo-ceo-mayer-jail-nsa-surveillance

only have access to a vast amount of information but also typically pay a price for it in terms of sharing their personal information with or without permission or contextual understanding.

The aftermath of this sea change is that vast troves of data are now collected by applications and web sites, creating an opportunity for organizations to mine that data and profit from it. Analysis of this  data enables products and services to be tailored to each user's unique personal preferences, but more often, the "personal" preferences are actually an enterprise's guess at the type of product, service, or information that that enterprise wishes to push. Marketing promotions can also be carefully targeted to very fine-grained audiences or even individuals. Although this may have some limited benefits to users, it often creates a risk that personal information might be used inappropriately or neglected by an enterprise, resulting in the additional risk of loss or theft by malevolent third parties.

Privacy regulations have grown out of the need for consequences for organizations that may be tempted to misuse personal information. What we're striving for in today's information economy is to re-create a sense of mutual respect so users feel they can trust how their information will be used.

# Privacy Is Not a One-Size-Fits-All Formula

There is a broad spectrum of acceptable privacy policies for complying with today's regulations, and many approaches to privacy can fall within the spectrum. The spectrum ranges from a scenario in which user choices about privacy are predominantly controlled by the organization vs. a scenario that represents almost complete freedom of choice for users. There are pros and cons for each approach, and an enterprise's approach will depend on many different factors. Each organization must decide which point on the spectrum best serves the needs of its community.

The organizational control scenario taken to the extreme can amount to a Big Brother approach: In this extreme side of the spectrum, users' decisions about privacy are turned over to the organization and thus users are basically submitting to a higher power that determines the best way to process personal information and ensure its safety. In this scenario, the IT infrastructure and applications are centrally governed and are designed to make "safe" choices for the user on his or her behalf. Users do not have to spend time thinking about privacy options or how much sharing to allow for their personal information. There will be options available to users, but most decisions will have preset defaults that the organization has determined are best for users. Where this scenario is deployed with a high degree of transparency, accountability to the user for error and a healthy respect for the ultimate uses of data, an organizational control method can work for the benefit of both users and the enterprise.[5]

An example of this scenario can be seen with medical records. The Health Insurance Portability and Accountability Act of 1996 (HIPAA) requires that health care providers follow strict procedures to protect patient information. Health care providers were collecting patient data long before HIPAA was enacted. Most were very careful about

---

[5]The new OECD privacy guidelines (2013) tend toward more enterprise data protection responsibility. If the enterprise fails in its responsibility, some legal liability would be expected. www.oecd.org/sti/ieconomy/2013-oecd-privacy-guidelines.pdf

protecting this data even though there was no law specifying how to do so. If health care patients want service, they have no choice about disclosing their personal information to the health care provider. They are thus submitting to a higher power to protect them and must essentially trust the health care provider to keep their data safe.

The biggest benefit to users in this scenario is that it requires very little effort on the part of the users. There is no need to study the privacy options and make choices. In theory, the health care providers can do a better job of understanding what's best for the users, but this requires that they have the users' best interests in mind. The enactment of HIPAA is an attempt to collectively govern the health care providers and make sure that providers do not misuse the information or fail to properly safeguard it. The US government is watching the watchers, so to speak. There are stiff penalties for noncompliance, so health care organizations pay close attention to HIPAA. The enactment of the law is an attempt to enforce proper ethics and moral standards.

At the other end of the spectrum is a scenario in which the user is given great freedom to share personal information and almost total discretion about what he or she would like to share. Social network sites can be an example of such a scenario. Many of the choices in social networks are set by default to enable broad sharing when the user does not specify a preference. The social network enterprise can argue that the entire intent and purpose of the site is to facilitate "open" sharing and, thus, may believe that the default to share settings are understood and even desired by users. For users who want to use greater discretion, such networks may offer options for limiting the sharing of information, but these choices require users to take action to learn how to implement the choice. Users must take the initiative if they want to manage their privacy settings.

The main benefit to users for the social sharing scenario is that users have greater freedom of choice. The massive potential downside to these social sites is that currently an information asymmetry exists where users do not have simple-to-use, clear, or transparent controls that result in reasonable protective outcomes. Additionally, many current social sites have buried analytics and algorithms used to process and make decisions on behalf of users and sell and resell personal information with no participation on behalf of the user in this economic boom. The users become, typically unwittingly, inventory rather than customers, and the actual economic drivers, those buying and selling advertisements, become the Customer who must be Obeyed.

For savvy users who can easily understand the impact of their choices, there are clear benefits to being given the freedom. Less savvy users tend to fail to research their options and typically go along with the default settings without really understanding the implications. Governance is essentially performed at the societal level in this situation. If enough users get upset about a change in privacy policy, they can take a stand together and rise up against the institution to ask for changes in how PI is managed or how privacy options are presented, or they can rely on regulators to step in on their behalf.

Does this situation create risk for the institution? One potential risk is that the early adopters of the technology will drive the future direction and enhancements. This might mean that the system will evolve to meet the needs of its early users but miss emerging market opportunities for users who might prefer a different approach to privacy. Another potential risk is that users could argue that they are governing the PI and thus the data should be considered a joint asset of all users rather than an asset of the institution. Would users then be eligible for a percentage of the profits from the organization's use of the data? And would the user community have rights to the data if the institution dissolved?

Most environments will be somewhere in between these two scenarios. You may decide that it's best to give significant freedom to your users or you may want to closely manage the usage and sharing of data. Perhaps your organization will want to set defaults that limit data sharing unless a user intentionally chooses something different. Woe betide the company that fails to contemplate or plan for the changing character of its users or business model.

As you choose your approach, be mindful of how your users will perceive your approach and how your approach will affect your organization's future vision for itself. Regardless of what your approach is, it will be important to be transparent to users and ensure that there is a fair exchange with users in terms of the value provided by your application or service.

# Innovation and Privacy

The opportunities for innovation around privacy are almost endless and can span the entire product lifecycle from early product design through marketing, distribution, and support. Rather than try to summarize the different ways you could innovate around privacy, we'd like to think about where the future might be headed and what you can do to take action to move in that direction.

First, let's consider what makes a product innovative. Most of the great product and service innovations throughout history were not products that customers were already asking for. They were products—such as the Java programming language and the Apple iPhone—that made new markets, not because they were completely new inventions, but because they took a new approach to meeting a customer need.

The Java programming language, for instance, had many similarities to C and C++ languages. The uniqueness of Java was its ability to make code completely portable across operating systems and platforms. Thus it offered a new benefit while carrying forward the familiar syntax of existing and popular programming languages. Similarly, the iPhone was not the first cell phone, but it was the first one that was really integrated with Internet technologies in a way that made it easy for customers to understand and use these new technologies.

An earlier example of innovative or disruptive development is the combination of recordable media and entertainment. The VCR vs. Betamax war was the technology side of the revolution. The real innovation, however, that upended the entire entertainment industry and paved the way for new technologies like TiVo and other digital video recorders and business combinations like streaming video rentals, was the ability to use recordable media to easily "time shift" or play back entertainment when and where the user desired. All of these products and innovations have a common thread in that they met a need that had not yet been anticipated by the customers themselves. If you want to do more than just satisfy your customers, you have to anticipate their desires and deliver something that is different from that offered in the mainstream market.

So, what does this have to do with privacy? If you agree with the concept that we've reached a point where privacy requirements must be integrated into a product and cannot be just an afterthought, then you realize that how you address the privacy needs of your users must be part of your product development process.

True innovators around privacy will be those that build products that anticipate users' desires. For example, it's feasible to build a privacy tool that makes choices and suggestions for the user by making inferences from the user's past choices. In the field of online radio, Pandora has invested in such an approach and has designed a product that makes music selections for users based on an in-depth analysis of their past choices.

What's interesting about Pandora's approach, which they call the Music Genome Project, is that it has analyzed the musical attributes of hundreds of thousands of songs to create a database that can be used to match listener preferences against other songs the listener is likely to enjoy. Users are served up songs on their radio channel based on their individual tastes in music rather than based on simple categories such as music genre or artist name.[6] Like everything else, there are privacy risk/reward tradeoffs with a Pandora approach.

A similar approach could be taken with privacy. If a broad base of user preferences about privacy were captured, it could be possible to analyze these data and find common characteristics about privacy choices and thus predict a user's preference in a given scenario. This would allow an application to set privacy defaults based on a deep understanding of the user's privacy choices. Alternatively, the application could also present privacy options to users in ways that required only a minimal amount of clicks if the preference were accurately predicted. Each choice made by the user would add further accuracy to future predictions.

This is just one example of how a product might anticipate the privacy needs of its users. There are many other ways to innovate and open new market opportunities. It's nearly impossible to predict what the next big thing will be in the technology revolution, but we can be pretty certain that there *will* be a next big thing. It's our belief that privacy will be an integral part of the next wave in the technology revolution and that innovators who are emphasizing privacy as an integral part of the product lifecycle are on the right track. The sidebar delves into the idea of privacy needs.

## PRIVACY NEEDS TO EVOLVE BETTER DECISION-MAKING MECHANISMS

By Dr. Eric Bonabeau, PhD, Chairman, Icosystem, Inc., and Dean of Computational Sciences, Minerva Schools at KGI

Privacy is that sense of control and safety you have when you know you can share information about yourself selectively and knowingly; when you know, often incorrectly, that your personal information will not fall into the wrong hands—scammers, spammers, nosy employers, overbearing parents, unforgiving peers. It is a fundamental human need, and yet it can be violated in an instant. Privacy has been a topic of social psychology for a long time, but there is an urgent need for a new cognitive framework in an age of permanent connectivity. If decisions affecting privacy were

---

[6]"How Pandora Radio Works," Julie Layton, May 23, 2006. http://computer.howstuffworks.com/internet/basics/pandora.htm.

complex 20 years ago, today the situation is beyond human comprehension because privacy is an emergent property resulting from myriad decisions, conscious or not, combining and interacting in ways that have become impossible to predict. Would E. M. Forster still urge us to "only connect"?

Today, more than ever, with powerful tools at our fingertips, there is a tension between our desire to connect and the fear of indelible digital trails we may one day regret leaving behind. But most often we push away the fear—it can't happen to me, or it won't, or I don't care. And we succumb to the temptation and give away information about ourselves. In fact, the most likely scenario is one where we are not even aware of our loss of privacy and its dangers, where the fear, if it exists at all, is diffuse and unattributable. Therein lies the privacy conundrum: privacy as we experience it today is misunderstood as a barrier between an individual and her desire to connect, or, also incorrectly, as an annoyance she will brush away in one instant, paving the way for a lifetime of unintended consequences. We need ways to make better decisions about privacy. To change this unfortunate state of affairs, there are a few things we can do that will yield a disproportionate return on investment:

*The first is to recognize that privacy is, or should be, to a large extent, a topic of the behavioral sciences.* Our sense of privacy is derived from being part of complex sociotechnical systems in which we have to resort to simple, probably inappropriate, heuristics to deal with all these little decisions that need to be made. They have been reduced to the deceivingly simple choices of opt-in and opt-out, install or cancel, a choice architecture that masks its deep and potentially dark consequences. The menus of privacy options available to you when you set up online accounts range from the binary ("our way or the highway") to the horribly complex ("would you like your friends whose birthdates are prime numbers to see your personal information?"). A different choice architecture (in particular, how defaults are defined) needs to be offered that makes it clear what the privacy options are and, even more importantly, what the consequences of your choice will be. It is one thing to agree to have a social network share your information with select advertisers, but quite another to find out that no one is accountable when the select advertisers have mishandled your data, which can now be exploited by scammers on the other side of the world to steal your identity.

*The second is to create a compelling value framework for individual data, a topic addressed in Chapter 13 of this book.* Beyond the definition and implementation details of this value framework, it is important to realize that the world of privacy is one that currently thrives on information asymmetry: companies that successfully exploit individual data understand the value of it while the individual has at best vague notions about it. Only when individuals understand the value of their personal data, and not just the bad things that can happen to them if it falls into the wrong hands, will they begin to take control of their personal information. As a driver of decisions, the promise of a short-term carrot always works better than the possibility of a stick in the distant future; instead of letting this fact help advertisers promote $1 coupons for hamburgers in exchange for all your family's personal facts and figures, this should be leveraged to offer individuals value they can understand and control.

*The third is to empower individuals to make informed choices about privacy.*
One of the most difficult tasks in this endeavor is to make it simple for the individual: there is no empowerment without ease of use. It is worth noting that making choices and consequences explicit and simpler is not just good for individuals but also for companies having to navigate an increasingly complex legal landscape around privacy: indeed, designing and implementing privacy policies is no less daunting a task in a world where network effects and cascading events produce hard-to-predict consequences.

I am not an expert on privacy but have spent most of the past decade studying choice and decision-making in complex, uncertain situations. Privacy strikes me as a perfect example. Below is an excerpt from a blog post I wrote for the Atlantic a few years back:

There is an intriguing parallel I want to expose in more detail between biological evolution and decision-making: search and evaluation in decision-making are similar to variation and selection in evolutionary theory. Search is all about creating a variety of options and possible answers to a query; evaluation is the process through which some or none of the options are selected. Nature thus provides us with a powerful metaphor for decision-making, and in that context genetic algorithms are decision-support tools. With interactive genetic algorithms, variation is performed by a non-human device while options generated by the device are evaluated by a human being.

In fact, we humans have been using this technique for hundreds of years, it is known under various names such as breeding, animal husbandry or directed evolution. To name one famous example, corn was bred about 9,000 years ago by Mexican farmers. Teosinte, the plant they started with, is so different from modern corn, that it was originally classified in a different genus. Teosinte is barely edible, while corn is today one of the leading sources of calories for humans.

The story of how such a transformation was made possible, by the combination of careful selection by farmers with a genetic structure that enabled dramatic morphological changes, is still being uncovered by ongoing research. Which means that humans have been using a powerful biological engine called variation which they did not understand at all; all they knew was that it worked for producing the requisite amount of variation and they could provide selective pressure.

The philosopher Daniel Dennett uses the phrase "competence without comprehension" to describe the strange value proposition of Darwinian evolution, that "to make a perfect and beautiful machine, it is not requisite to know how to make it" [MacKenzie RB. (Nisbet & Co., London, 1868), cited by Dennett]. Indeed, what McKenzie, a 19th-century critic of Darwin, calls "a strange inversion of reasoning" has been one of the weapons creationists have used.

But directed evolution is a highly successful embodiment of that inversion of reasoning—of competence without comprehension. Corn is the descendant through directed evolution of teosinte. The domestic dog, in its apparently infinite variety, is the product of many generations of breeding from just one common ancestor, the gray wolf. Examples abound.

*In silico* evolution, in the form of genetic algorithms, creates an opportunity for competence without [necessary] comprehension. You may be able to comprehend—either during or after the design process, but *you don't have to.* The machine takes care of the variation process. This is a powerful concept: think about all the situations in which you have to rely on an expert to produce variations for you—an architect, a designer, a brand naming consultant, etc. The expert is the gatekeeper between you and your dreams, and defines the possible on the basis of her own biases.

Your dreams are bounded by the expert. Yet you are an expert on knowing whether you like something or not. You may not understand how the expert comes up with the variations, but you're competent (in fact, you're likely the most competent) when it comes to your own tastes. Competence without comprehension empowers you to innovate far beyond your comprehension. One caveat is obviously that whatever new stuff you produce be safe.[7]

Privacy choices may be considered in a similar fashion. To wit, the average person will never be an expert in the many rules and requirements, some of which are discussed in this book. The average builder of systems or marketer of product or consumer of information similarly may never be an expert in the nearly infinite data points, information artifacts, and choices that may be made with regard to personal data or in the personal data economy.

A privacy component or privacy rules engine, however, may be developed to provide modeling or choice variants that can empower the most competent innovator to innovate far beyond her individual comprehension by providing reasonable and relevant choices that fit the criteria of the rules engine and enterprise objectives or desires. Similarly, the object of data processing (i.e., and the individual person who is described by personal data elements) may be able to choose from variants of privacy settings to optimize her selection to fit culture, taste, and general context without ever becoming an expert in the complexity that lies within.

These are some of the ways forward to address the conundrum of privacy. The objective is to strike a balance between the risks and rewards of personal information sharing, which requires a clear and explicit exposition of the risks and rewards. Contrary to what a certain social network executive stated, privacy is not a binary property rejected by the new social norms; the reality is so much more complex. And so much more fun.

---

[7]www.theatlantic.com/technology/archive/2011/03/how-evolution-helps-us-when-it-comes-to-making-decisions/72883/

# Societal Pressures and Privacy

Social norms are always a part of the process when new technologies are being adopted by society. There are many examples of how technology has ushered in new changes that affect the way our world works. These changes must be accepted and adopted at a cultural level. Therefore, they typically occur in a wave-like fashion rather than as a disruptive event that happens overnight.

If we look at the Internet browser as an example, the initial concept created a disruption in the sense that it suddenly offered a new way to share information. Someone could publish data to a worldwide audience just by posting the data in one place. However, the implications of this have taken years to manifest and become part of our culture. The process has involved many twists and turns, including many unexpected effects on society, such as the current phenomenon that a person previously unknown in the public eye can become a virtual celebrity almost overnight after publishing information that goes viral.

Our society has now learned how to use the technology to make people's lives better. The first Mosaic browser was released to the public in 1993, but the idea of social networking was inconceivable at that time. It evolved after more than a decade of technology innovations[8] that eventually led to mass acceptance of Internet technologies. These technologies have provided a means to connect our global human race and have changed our society: We now can more easily connect to family and friends, get broad perspectives on specialized topics (like privacy), or learn of overseas disasters much more quickly; often we get the best insights from ordinary people who just happened to be at the scene at the time of a major event and chose to share their experience via social networking.

Social norms have no doubt shifted along the way and have affected the way we think about privacy. These social norms are different among different age groups. Some people have gone so far as to suggest that privacy is disappearing as a social norm in the younger generation and that they don't really care about keeping anything private. However, research evidence points to the contrary. There are clear generational differences about what constitutes privacy, but the younger generation still wants a world where they can share freely and yet have their privacy respected for the things that do matter to them.

> *And these children that you spit on, as they try to change their world, are immune to your consultations. They're quite aware of what they're going through.*
>
> —David Bowie, "Changes"

---

[8]Complex and convoluted technologies were a part of this evolution, but the graphical user interface is a prime example of outward simplicity and user centricity that took the Mosaic flash of brilliance to a worldwide revolution.

Recent research by danah boyd and Alice Marwick has shown that even though today's teens routinely use social networking to share information that many adults would consider private, they still care about their privacy on other fronts. The research found that teens want the ability to control their social situations and that it matters to them who is in their physical presence as well as who's watching when they are online or talking with friends. Like most of us, they act differently if they think they are being monitored. So, while they may not be concerned about sharing certain types of information, they do care about having control over their environment and about being able to exercise free will without concern about judgment or other consequences from parents or other authorities.[9]

If we look at history, we can see that our society has not only experienced shifting social norms over time but also has shown an incredible ability to adapt to change. The Industrial Revolution in the 19th century created sweeping changes that affected both social norms and economics. It enabled our society to build an educated workforce and a strong middle class. However, in that process our society had to learn how to balance the human needs of working-class citizens against corporate profit. Laborers formed unions to help make sure that the working class was not being taken advantage of by the elite. Society stood behind the notion that financial security should not be traded for a humane existence.

In today's information age, privacy has surfaced as a similar means by which the elite can in some ways take advantage of the masses. Humanity has a way of making sure that these imbalances don't last forever: We may not yet be able to see how balance will be restored in the area of privacy, but it is our belief that such a balance is virtually inevitable. Those individuals who embrace the need for privacy and bring innovations that help move humanity toward the balance we are seeking will likely find a surprisingly strong embrace by the general public and may be carried by a powerful new wave that ushers in the balance.

It's also important to think about what might happen to those who choose to ignore the call to action. As public awareness of privacy issues has grown, users expect organizations to be considerate of privacy rights. Management teams can no longer get away with big mistakes under the guise of naivety or ignorance: You're expected to be on top of privacy issues. Oversights will be seen as willful acts of betrayal or manifestations of gross incompetence that could quickly turn into bad press in addition to dissatisfied customers.

# It Still Comes Down to Trust and Value

Although we may not know where technology will lead us, we do know that there is a central theme for users when it comes to privacy. At the end of the day, users want to do business with organizations they trust and where there is significant value. Can users trust your organization to safeguard their data? And do they see enough value in your product or service to want to hand over some personal data?

---

[9]"Social Privacy in Networked Publics: Teens' Attitudes, Practices, and Strategies," danah boyd and Alice Marwick, September 2011. www.danah.org/papers/2011/SocialPrivacyPLSC-Draft.pdf

Trust is built by respecting the user's right to privacy and by openly communicating as well as adhering to a coherent privacy policy. The fair use principles discussed in the early part of this book are just common sense. It's a matter of seeing things from the user's perspective and then putting some governance in place to make these principles an integral part of your organization and your product lifecycle.

Trust requires more than just doing the right thing: It's also about communication. If your communication is misleading or vague, it can create mistrust even though you may be technically doing what was said.

Trust can also be broken when we do something slightly different from what was communicated. An action that would fall within the fair-use principles but was not properly communicated to users can open the door for misinterpretation or mistrust.

Building trust also requires repeated behaviors over time. This is especially true if you're making changes to your privacy policy or how it is implemented. If there was reason to mistrust in the past, users may be reluctant to believe that your new approach represents a real change of heart. If you've adopted the privacy engineering principles espoused in this book, your privacy policy will be embedded in your products and services. However, it may take a full product cycle before your users recognize the change. If your organization can be consistent and transparent about treating PI with respect, the long run result will be a trusting user community and a positive public image.

# A New Building Code for Privacy

Privacy is at an inflexion point. It has become a mainstream discipline, and organizations are beginning to take advantage of some of the old-school ways of engineering to build privacy into their products and build out their privacy vision. And yet, privacy engineering is more of an aspiration and a wish than a prolific practice in the face of massive collections of data and a greater ability to analyze, group, and decide based on these data artifacts. Many of the techniques spelled out in Part 2 of this book represent computer science disciplines that have been around for decades. These disciplines are being applied in new ways to leverage tried-and-true design principles while making privacy an integral part of product design.

History has shown that the best innovations are actually built on top of previously successful approaches. We believe that governance and evaluation models can and will evolve toward approaches that are both data centric and person centric. Today's product design reviews are still predominantly focused on protecting corporate interests; protecting privacy (a human right) rarely enters the conversation. To change this requires a new definition of corporate or organizational interests. Corporate interests must include not only building products to address market needs but also protecting users by protecting their data. A balanced approach would have equal focus on how to deliver value to the customer and how to protect the customer's right to privacy.

But how can we fulfill the human desire to be connected online in a way that does not feel like Big Brother is watching while also delivering value to the organization in which we work? It's complex and messy to attempt integrating these two vantage points. However, that doesn't mean we can't break down the complexity and use the techniques and best practices presented in this book to take the first steps toward the goal.

We may think we need a crystal-clear vision of the future of privacy in order to design for privacy, but if we look at nature and organic systems, we can find many examples of things that are created out of orderly chaos. Flocks of birds, schools of fish, and ant colonies are all good examples of organic systems that create a beautiful and elegant result even though the individual participants don't really know the final result toward which they are headed. Organic systems follow simple rules that enable cooperation and steady progress toward a common goal. Each component of an organic system acts with consistency and integrity, and the components interact with one another in close proximity.

Organic systems also have a lifecycle. At some point, old plants die out and their seeds regenerate to form new plants. The human body expels or kills bad bacteria. Similarly, with our information systems, there is a need to either recycle or expel data that have reached the end of their lifecycle and become a potential risk. In the same way that computer viruses or malware can be detected and disabled to prevent damage, data that are no longer useful can be purged from the system to protect personal privacy. Many organizations tend to hoard data while attempting to find ways to derive value from them. If there is no clear use for the data, then they are simply a threat and it's best to properly dispose of them.

If we believe that our customers want to buy from organizations that not only offer valuable products and services but also are respectful of user rights and provide transparency, then we have our design principles. Personal information can be treated as a living entity that must be shared or stored in ways that preserve integrity and enable an elegant outcome. Perhaps there are innovative ways to give users more choice about when their data are saved and for how long. Data retention rules could then be different for different users and yet be implemented automatically with great efficiency.

We can build great products around these lofty goals without knowing how the future of privacy will look a decade from now. Innovation requires taking action from where we are today. Perhaps we can even design systems in which there are frequent interactions between data elements and system or machine components. This can let the system itself determine if there is value in continuing to maintain and store the data. If we've modeled our data well, we will know the places and times in the lifecycle where the data have value. Then we can automate the movement of data through the lifecycle in a way that preserves value and minimizes risk.

Meeting user needs for privacy in new and innovative ways will allow you to be part of a revolution that may help to bring humanity back into balance.

# Getting Started

Now is the time to decide your direction regarding the building blocks that you will create for constructing your privacy foundation. Your building blocks will be based on an overall approach to privacy and will determine how PI is treated within your products or services. The approach must be determined first because it could be difficult to change course after implementing parts of your privacy vision. Think about how difficult it would be for Facebook to change their privacy orientation now that users have become accustomed to the free sharing of information that is promoted in the current environment.

Once your overall approach and orientation are defined, it should be easy to determine what steps to take next because you'll notice areas that are not well aligned with your new approach. You may notice both new opportunities and unchecked risks. To get started, you'll need to take stock of where you are today. By surveying the situation, you can identify areas that need immediate attention and also envision new long-term opportunities. It's not necessary to have a complete long-term plan to begin taking action. The important thing is that action can be taken from where you are today. In many cases, it's possible to identify short-term goals and get the ball rolling in the right direction. A more comprehensive planning process can be concurrent with addressing some of the short-term needs.

The following are examples of some of the actions that may be good starting points once you've surveyed your situation:

- Build consensus among functional organizations regarding how privacy requirements can become part of your overall process for defining product requirements

- Add privacy as a component of your organization's ethics

- Decide to adopt some of the structured approaches for product development that are defined in Part 2 of this book

- Modify your governance processes

- Train your engineers so they know what their options are

- Create organizational incentives for privacy so that privacy gets baked into product design and other parts of the product lifecycle

Whatever course you choose, it's important to be mindful of fair-use principles and the inherent value of data as you move forward on your course to embed privacy principles into all phases of your product lifecycle.

# A Privacy Engineer's Manifesto

We'd like to leave you with a manifesto that provides some guiding principles for you as a privacy engineer. These principles are an attempt to illuminate a belief system in which the seemingly opposing motives of creating corporate profit and respecting individual privacy can live in harmony. Here you may find a meeting grounds that enables both your organization and your customers to profit—each in their own ways.

1. ***Data about people is valuable in and of itself.***

    Data provide commercial value to businesses in addition to their inherent value from a personal perspective. They also provide value as an exchange or a unique identifier to build social connections. A privacy engineer understands this principle as bedrock and strives to find innovative ways to extend the value of data while protecting their inherent value.

2. *A privacy engineer needs more than just technical skills to protect and extend the value of data.*

   The inherent value of data that is attained from or attributable to human beings requires a number of different perspectives and skill sets to be effective. The privacy engineer, as a modern renaissance type discipline, views personal data through legal, creative, and personal lenses.

3. *A privacy engineer draws from artistic creativity and expression to innovate and communicate.*

   Beyond learning from sister disciplines to add to the known world of technology, the privacy engineer seeks to create simplicity, clarity, and beauty to engage and inform users and owners of systems. The tools of engagement can use sound, taste, touch, sight, smell, intuition, or any other artistic medium. Technologies, policies, laws, organization, and metric modalities all have interfaces. Effective interfaces can be engaging, challenging, educational, elegant, emotive, and even beautiful where innovation meets art.

4. *A privacy engineer learns from, but disregards, the failures of the past.*

   While building on past successes as well as the remnants of previous attempts at success, a privacy engineer closely regards and incorporates existing tools, policies, and frameworks as scaffolding to create something wonderful. (Borrowed heavily from Intel founder Bob Noyes.) A privacy engineer strives to map and develop data systems in a scientific fashion in order to create new or improved means of delivering value to all parties who have a vested interest in the data.

5. *We are all privacy engineers.*

   We all possess or are the subject of PI and have a vested interest in protecting it. Some of us have occasion to operate as "professional privacy engineers," but all of us at least operate as "citizen privacy engineers" when we act as stewards of our own PI and the PI of others.

6. *For the privacy engineer, with the mantra to innovate comes the mantra to do no harm.*

   The privacy engineer's goal should be to harness the inherent value of data and innovate to create additional value. But the most basic requirement for the privacy engineer is to do no harm and to plan to eliminate as much secondary or unanticipated harm as possible.

7. *Innovation and complexity need not be the adversary of privacy engineering, although failure of imagination may be.*

What is not thought of cannot be recognized and therefore cannot be managed. Failures of imagination are thus the biggest enemy of the privacy engineer. Failure to imagine a new possibility means that a value creating opportunity or a risk mitigation opportunity has been missed.

8. *The privacy engineer must be able to understand, calculate, mitigate, and accept risk.*

The privacy engineer cannot ignore risk or fall prey to the idea that it can be completely eliminated. By embracing both risk and value, the privacy engineer can strive to find solutions that deliver maximum value at an acceptable risk level to the organization and the individual.

9. *Privacy engineering happens inside and outside of code.*

Coding, building systems, and the business processes that support the product lifecycle are critical. A foundation of privacy principles and operational business processes can support development of products that promote privacy. At the same time, the individual doing the developing may see opportunities for innovation that can only be envisioned by one who is at the proverbial drawing board.

10. *A privacy engineer needs to differentiate between bad ideas and bad implementations.*

A *bad idea* is one that goes against privacy principles or lacks sound judgment about using and protecting PI. A *bad implementation* is when the design goal is sound but the implementation is not due to poor usability, unmitigated risks, or an approach that weakens the bond of trust with users. In the latter scenario, a bad implementation that may harm data privacy may be rearchitected or protected in another layered fashion, whereas, in the former, a bad idea should be acknowledged and quickly ended before damage is done.

# Conclusion

If you've taken the time to read this book, you've already made a commitment to be a change agent in the field of privacy. Our hope is that we've presented some new ideas for you and that you'll use these ideas to help make the world a better place.

We've done our best to lay out some concrete steps that you can adopt today while your future vision continues to evolve over time. Taken to heart, the principles in the manifesto can both shape your future vision and guide your daily activities.

May you achieve success by innovating in ways that align with the trends already shaping our shared world. The future we inhabit together is being shaped by the big and small decisions that each of us make daily.

Go forth and innovate!

*Often when you think you're at the end of something, you're at the beginning of something else.*

—Mister Rogers

# APPENDIX A

■ ■ ■

# Use-Case Metadata

As defined previously in Chapter 5, a "Use Case constitutes a complete course of events initiated by an Actor and it specifies the interaction that takes place between the actor and the system."[1] Actors are people, functional roles, or interfacing systems that interact with the enterprise. One or more use cases are developed for each non-system actor. The following table represents a form that has been used to document use cases and the information that is gathered for each use case. Note that, the bracketed text explains the content expected to be included in the section.

## Example Use-Case Format

| | |
|---|---|
| Use-Case Name | Receive a Reinsurance Request |
| Unique ID | UC000001 |
| **Course of Action** | *[Does the use case represent an "ideal" or "alternative" course of action?* <br><br> • *Ideal: The steps (processes, decisions, deliverables, etc.) taken by the actor(s) within the context of the use case, under ideal circumstances.* <br><br> • *Alternative: The alternative steps (processes, decisions, deliverables, etc.) and the conditions under which the ideal may not be followed.]* |
| **Parent Use Case** | *[The name of a use case from which this use case is derived.]* |
| **Use-Case Description** | *[The description briefly conveys the role and purpose of the use case. A single paragraph will suffice for this description.]* |
| **Primary Actor** | *[The primary role that performs the work associated with the business functionality represented by the use case.]* |

*(continued)*

---

[1] I. Jacobsen, *Software Engineering.* Addison-Wesley, 1992, p. 159.

| | |
|---|---|
| **Support Actor(s)** | *[The roles that assist (support) the work effort associated with the business functionality represented by the use case.]* |
| **Preconditions** | *[A precondition of a use case is the state of the system that must be present prior to a use case being performed.]* |
| **Assumptions** | *[An assumption helps to scope the use case and provide context for its execution.]* |
| **Measures of Success** | *[Tangible metrics and intangible factors (key components of business goals and objectives) that management has determined are success factors for the functionality represented by the use case.]* |
| **Use-Case Location(s)** | *[The location(s) where the use-case functionality takes place.]* |
| **Use-Case Frequency** | *[The frequency (per hour, day, etc.) by which the work effort associated with the use-case functionality is conducted.]* |
| **Main Course** | *[This use case starts when the actor does something. An actor always initiates use cases. The use case describes what the actor does and what the system does in response. It is phrased in the form of a dialogue between the actor and the system.* |
| | *The use case describes what happens inside the system, but not how or why. If information is exchanged, be specific about what is passed back and forth. For example, it is not very illuminating to say that the actor enters customer information. It is better to say the actor enters the customer's name and address. A glossary of terms is often useful to keep the complexity of the use case manageable—you may want to define things like customer information there to keep the use case from drowning in details.* |
| | *Simple alternatives may be presented within the text of the use case. If it only takes a few sentences to describe what happens when there is an alternative, do it directly within the main course section. If the alternative flow is more complex, use a separate section to describe it. For example, an alternative course subsection explains how to describe more complex alternatives.* |

(*continued*)

*A picture is sometimes worth a thousand words, although there is no substitute for clean, clear prose. If it improves clarity, feel free to paste graphic depictions of user interfaces, process flows, or other figures into the use case. If a flow chart is useful to present a complex decision process, by all means use it! Similarly for state-dependent behavior, a state-transition diagram often clarifies the behavior of a system better than pages upon pages of text. Use the right presentation medium for your problem, but be wary of using terminology, notations, or figures that your audience may not understand. Remember that your purpose is to clarify, not obscure.]*

1. **Triggering Event 1**[2]

   a. **Decision 1-1**

      i. **Business Rules 1-1-1: Decision Criteria**

      ii. **Business Rules 1-1-2: Decision Criteria**

      iii. **...**

      iv. **Business Rules 1-1-n: Decision Criteria**

   b. **Decision 1-2**

      i. **Business Rules 1-2-1– Decision Criteria**

      ii. **Business Rules 1-2-2– Decision Criteria**

      iii. **...**

      iv. **Business Rules 1-2-n– Decision Criteria**

   c. **Process 1-1-1**

   d. **Process 1-1-2**

2. **Triggering Event 2**

   a. **Decision 2-1**

      i. **Business Rules 2-2-1– Decision Criteria**

      ii. **Business Rules 2-2– Decision Criteria**

   b. **Decision 2-2**

      i. **Business Rules 2-1– Decision Criteria**

   c. **Process 2-1-1**

   d. **Process 2-1-2**

3. **If X then Alternate 1 else Alternate 2**

4. **Step 4**

*(continued)*

---

[2]See Chapter 5 for the explanation of this content.

| | |
|---|---|
| **Alternate Course 1** | *[More complex alternatives are described in a separate section, referred to in the main course subsection of the flow of events section. Think of the alternative course subsections as an alternative behavior—each alternative flow represents an alternative behavior usually due to exceptions that occur in the main flow. They may be as long as necessary to describe the events associated with the alternative behavior. When an alternative flow ends, the events of the main flow of events are resumed unless otherwise stated.]* |

1. **Step 1**
2. **Step 2**

| | |
|---|---|
| **Alternate Course 2** | *[There may be, and most likely will be, a number of alternative flows in a use case. Keep each alternative flow separate to improve clarity. Using alternative flows improves the readability of the use case, as well as prevents use cases from being decomposed into hierarchies of use cases. Keep in mind that use cases are just textual descriptions, and their main purpose is to document the behavior of a system in a clear, concise, and understandable way.]* |
| **Postconditions** | *[A postcondition of a use case is a list of possible states the system can be in immediately after a use case has finished.]* |
| **Nonfunctional Requirements** | *[These are typically specific to a use case but are not easily or naturally specified in the text of the use case's event flow. Examples of these requirements include legal and regulatory requirements, application standards, and quality attributes of the system to be built including usability, reliability, performance, or supportability requirements. Additionally, other requirements—such as operating systems and environments, compatibility requirements, and design constraints—should be captured in this section.]* |
| **Business Rules** | *[Use cases may contain specific business rules or logic. These are defined as the criteria by which a decision is made within a flow of events. If these rules are complex or lengthy and do not affect the flow of the use case, they should be described here.]* |
| **Issues** | *[During the requirements-gathering and analysis process, issues will crop up. These issues can initially be captured here if they pertain to this use case.]* |

The following "For Each Use Case" table gives an explanation of the information gathered for each use case.

| For Each Use Case | | |
|---|---|---|
| **Type of Information** | **Description of Information** | **When Needed** |
| **Use-Case Name** | The name that will be used by business personnel to represent business functionality encompassing a set of input and output deliverables, actors (roles), processes, decisions, business rules, triggering events, and other information that provides adequate business context to develop automated IT support mechanisms. | Business Requirements Definition |
| **Course of Action** | Does the use case represent an "ideal" or "alternative" course of action? Ideal: The steps (processes, decisions, deliverables, etc.) taken by the actor(s) within the context of the use case, under ideal circumstances. Alternative: The alternative steps (processes, decisions, deliverables, etc.) and the conditions under which the ideal may not be followed. | Business Requirements Definition |
| **Parent-Use Case** | The name of a use case from which this use case is derived. | Business Requirements Definition |
| **Use-Case Description** | An overview of the work that is accomplished within the business scenario scope represented by the use case. For example, an overview of the courses of action taken by the actor(s), within the context of the use case, under ideal circumstances or alternative courses of action and the conditions under which the ideal may not be followed. | Business Requirements Definition |
| **Expected Use-Case Results** | The results (e.g., expected outputs such as products or other deliverables) as expected from the execution of the processes defined within the use case. | Business Requirements Definition |
| **Preconditions** | None | Business Requirements Definition |
| **Assumptions** | None | Business Requirements Definition |

*(continued)*

## For Each Use Case

| Type of Information | Description of Information | When Needed |
|---|---|---|
| **Measures of Success** | Tangible metrics or intangible factors (key components of business goals and objectives) that management has determined are success factors for the functionality represented by the use case. | Business Requirements Definition |
| **Primary Actor** | The primary role that performs the work associated with the business functionality represented by the use case. | Business Requirements Definition |
| **Support Actor(s)** | The roles that assist (support) the work effort associated with the business functionality represented by the use case. | Business Requirements Definition |
| **Use-Case Location(s)** | The location(s) where the use-case functionality takes place. | Business Requirements Definition |
| **Use-Case Frequency** | The frequency (per hour, day, etc.) by which the work effort associated with the use-case functionality is conducted. | Business Requirements Definition |

As shown in the Example Use-Case Format table and as explained in Chapter 5, within both the main course and alternative courses there are a series of events, decisions, and rules that need to be defined. The information types may be data attributes within the Use Case Metadata Model as show in Figure 5-3 and explained in the next "For Each Use Case Course of Action" table.

## For Each Use Case Course of Action

| Type of Information | Description of Information | When Needed |
|---|---|---|
| Use-Case Name | The name that will be used by business personnel to represent a business functionality encompassing a set of input and output deliverables, actors (roles), processes, decisions, business rules, triggering events, and other information that provides adequate business context to develop automated IT support mechanisms.<br><br>*An entry should be established in the general use-case information spreadsheet prior to generating this entry in the use-case course of action spreadsheet.* | Business Requirements Definition |

*(continued)*

## For Each Use Case Course of Action

| Type of Information | Description of Information | When Needed |
|---|---|---|
| Event Name | The name commonly referred to for a business event that triggers the execution of one or more business processes within the use-case scope.<br><br>*This attribute is repeated for each event that can occur within the use-case scope.* | Business Requirements Definition |
| Event Description | A short definition for a business event that triggers the execution of one or more business processes within the business scenario scope defined by the use case.<br><br>*This attribute is repeated for each event that can occur within the use-case scope.* | Business Requirements Definition |
| Event Frequency Mean | The average number of times this business event is expected to occur over a specific time (day, week, etc.) period. For example, guests booked 200 times per day on average.<br><br>*This attribute is repeated for each event that can occur within the use-case scope.* | Business Requirements Definition |
| Maximum Event Frequency | The maximum number of times this business event is expected to occur over a specific time (day, week, etc.) period. For example, guest bookings could reach 1,000 per day during the busiest seasons.<br><br>*This attribute is repeated for each event that can occur within the business scenario scope defined by the use-case scope.* | Business Requirements Definition |
| Spontaneity | Is the business event scheduled, schedulable, or randomly occurring from the perspective of the business-user community?<br><br>*This attribute is repeated for each event that can occur within the use-case scope.* | Business Requirements Definition |

*(continued)*

## For Each Use Case Course of Action

| Type of Information | Description of Information | When Needed |
|---|---|---|
| Scheduling Method | The method for determining the scheduling of the business event. For example, monthly, at the first of the month, daily at 12:00 p.m., etc. | Business Requirements Definition |
| | *This attribute is repeated for each event that can occur within the business scenario scope defined by the use case. In addition, this attribute is optional depending on the type of event spontaneity.* | |
| Event Location(s) | The specific location(s) (e.g., Epcot Welcome Center) or location type(s) (e.g., hotels) where the business event occurs. | Business Requirements Definition |
| | *This attribute is repeated for each event that can occur within the business-scenario scope defined by the use case. In addition, this attribute is optional depending on the type of event spontaneity.* | |
| Decision Name | The name commonly referred to for a business decision that represents the outcome of one or more business rules. A decision is more completely defined within the context of an activity diagram where one or more processes are related to each branch (decision output path) of the decision. | Solution Design |
| | *This attribute is repeated for each decision that can occur within each event and within the use-case scope.* | |
| Decision Description | The short description that defines a business decision that represents the outcome of one or more business rules. | Solution Design |
| | *This attribute is repeated for each decision that can occur within each event and within the use-case scope.* | |
| Business-Rule Description | The name of a business condition or group of conditions that drive a decision to execute one or more business processes. | Solution Design |
| | *This attribute is repeated for each business rule, within each decision that can occur within each event and within the use-case scope.* | |

*(continued)*

## For Each Use Case Course of Action

| Type of Information | Description of Information | When Needed |
|---|---|---|
| Business-Rule Source | The business SME (subject-matter expert) responsible for defining or maintaining the business rule.<br><br>*This attribute is repeated for each business rule, within each decision that can occur within each event and within the use-case scope.* | Solution Design |
| Business-Rule Entity/ Object Name | The descriptive name of a real-world object that contains information used to derive business-rule results and thus determine a business decision.<br><br>*This attribute is repeated for each entity/object name, required by each business rule, within each decision that can occur within each event and within the use-case scope.* | Business Requirements Definition |
| Business-Rule Attribute Name | The name of a discrete, atomic element of information associated with a real-world business object that contains information used to derive business-rule results and thus determine a business decision.<br><br>*This attribute is repeated for each entity/object name, required by each business rule, within each decision that can occur within each event and within the use-case scope.* | Solution Design |

Decision events, as discussed in Chapter 5, trigger system or business processes. In the following "For Each Use-Case Process" table, the class names are decision event actions.

## For Each Use Case Process

| Type of Information | Description of Information | When Needed |
|---|---|---|
| Use-Case Name | The name that will be used by business personnel to represent business functionality encompassing a set of input and output deliverables, actors (roles), processes, decisions, business rules, triggering events, and other information that provides adequate business context to develop automated IT support mechanisms. | Business Requirements Definition |

*(continued)*

| For Each Use Case Process | | |
|---|---|---|
| **Type of Information** | **Description of Information** | **When Needed** |
| Event Name | The name commonly referred to for a business event that triggers the execution of one or more business processes within the scope defined by the use case. | Business Requirements Definition |
| Process Name | The name of a business process representing a real-world business activity or software routine that is triggered by a business event.<br><br>*This attribute is repeated for each process triggered by each event that can occur within the scope defined by the use case.* | Business Requirements Definition |
| Business-Process Description | The short description of a business process representing a real-world business activity or software routine that is triggered by a business event.<br><br>*This attribute is repeated for each process triggered by each event that can occur within the scope defined by the use case.* | Business Requirements Definition |
| Process Frequency Mean | The average number of times this business process is expected to occur over a specific time (day, week, etc.) period. For example, "guest credit check" occurs 300 times per day on average.<br><br>*This attribute is repeated for each process triggered by each event that can occur within the scope defined by the use case.* | Same as above |
| Maximum Process Frequency | The maximum number of times this business process is expected to occur over a specific time (day, week, etc.) period. For example, "guest credit check" could reach 1,000 per day during the busiest seasons.<br><br>*This attribute is repeated for each process triggered by each event that can occur within the scope defined by the use case.* | Same as above |

*(continued)*

| For Each Use Case Process | | |
| --- | --- | --- |
| **Type of Information** | **Description of Information** | **When Needed** |
| Process Location(s) | The specific location(s) (e.g., Epcot Welcome Center) or location type (e.g., hotels) where the business process is executed. | Business Requirements Definition |
| | *This attribute is repeated for each event that can occur within the scope defined by the use case. In addition, this row is optional depending on the type of event spontaneity.* | |
| Required Response | Must an immediate response occur or can a delayed (e.g., batch) response satisfy the requirement? If the response may be delayed, what is the acceptable timeframe? | Business Requirements Definition |
| | *This attribute is repeated for each event that can occur within the scope defined by the use case. In addition, this row is optional depending on the type of event spontaneity.* | |
| Process Entity/Object Name | The descriptive name of a real-world object that contains information used to develop outputs (deliverables) from a business process. | Business Requirements Definition |
| | *This attribute is repeated for each entity/object name, required by each business rule, within each decision that can occur within each event and within the scope defined by the use case.* | |
| Process Attribute Name | The name of a discrete, atomic element of information associated with a real-world business object that contains information used to develop outputs (deliverables) from a business process. | Business Requirements Definition |
| | *This attribute is repeated for each entity/object name, required by each business rule, within each decision that can occur within each event and within the scope defined by the use case.* | |

In Chapters 5 and 6, we introduce data models using UML class models. In the data model examples (Figures 5-4, 6-8, and 6-9, among others in Chapters 7, 8, and 9), we presented class names. The following "For Each Class or Data Entity" table shows the metadata attributes for each class or data entity.

| For Each Class or Data Entity | | |
|---|---|---|
| **Type of Information** | **Description of Information** | **When Needed** |
| Class/Data Entity Name | The descriptive name of a real-world object (person, place, thing, event, concept, or event) and information represented by that object that is of importance to the enterprise. | All Data Entities must be included in the Conceptual Data Model |
| Synonyms | By what other names is this data entity called? | Logical Data Model |
| Data-Entity Description | What is a short description of the data entity from a business perspective? | Conceptual Data Model |
| Responsible Person | Who is responsible for maintaining the quality of the information in this data entity? | Conceptual Data Model |
| Metadata Supplier | Who supplied the information used to populate the data entity metadata? | Conceptual Data Model |
| Instance Example | What would be an example of an instance of this data entity if needed to understand the nature of it? | Conceptual Data Model |
| Supertype Data Entity | If this is a subtype data entity, what is the supertype? | Conceptual Data Model |
| Uniqueness Identifier | What data element(s) uniquely identify the data entity? | Logical Data Model |
| Other Data Elements | What data elements are contained within this data entity, including foreign keys and derivable data elements? | Logical Data Model |
| Average Volume | What is the expected number of instances (records or rows) that this data entity may occur? | Required for Database Design (Logical Data Model) |
| Maximum Volume | What would be the largest number of instances (records or rows) that this data entity may occur? | Required for Database Design (Logical Data Model) |
| Growth Rate | What is the annual rate of increase of the number of instances? | Required for Database Design (Logical Data Model) |
| CRUD Actor(s) | What business role(s) creates, retrieves, updates, and deletes (CRUD) this data entity? | Required for Database Design (Logical Data Model) |

*(continued)*

| For Each Class or Data Entity | | |
|---|---|---|
| **Type of Information** | **Description of Information** | **When Needed** |
| Archiving Rules | How long will information be kept, and how should the history be handled? | Required for Database Design (Logical Data Model) |
| Data-Content Quality Rules | What domain rules and valid value sets should apply? | Required for Database Design (Logical Data Model) |
| Data-Presentation Quality Rules | What data-presentation quality should apply to information-bearing documents and media such as reports or screens presenting the results of queries from data to database? | Required for Database Design (Logical Data Model) |
| Data-Residency Business Rules | How long should data reside in the various levels of storage (e.g., operational data store, data warehouse, or archive)? | Required for Database Design (Logical Data Model) |
| Security Rules | What security rules govern the adding, accessing, and updating of this data entity? | Required for Database Design (Logical Data Model) |
| Data Source | What system or existing database will be used to populate this data entity? | Required for Database Design (Logical Data Model) |
| Refreshment Timing | How often should this data entity be refreshed? | Required for Database Design (Logical Data Model) |
| Availability Requirements | What, if any, special rules govern the availability of these data? | Required for Database Design (Logical Data Model) |

The following "For Each Data Attribute" table shows metadata attributes for each data attribute. (See Figure 6-8 for an example.)

| For Each Data Attribute | | |
|---|---|---|
| **Type of Information** | **Description of Information** | **When Needed** |
| Data-Attribute Name | The name of a discrete, atomic element of information associated with a real-world business object that is of importance to WDW. | All Data Elements must be included in the Logical Data Model |
| Synonyms | By what other names is this data attribute called? | Logical Data Model |

*(continued)*

| For Each Data Attribute | | |
| --- | --- | --- |
| Type of Information | Description of Information | When Needed |
| Data-Attribute Description | What is a short description of the data attribute from a business perspective? | Logical Data Model |
| Metadata Source | Who supplied the information used to populate the data attribute metadata? | Logical Data Model |
| Example | What would be an example of an instance of this data entity if needed to understand the nature of the data attribute? | Logical Data Model |
| Responsible Person | Who is responsible for maintaining the quality information in this data attribute? | Logical Data Model |
| Data Entity (where contained) | What data entity contains this data attribute? | Logical Data Model |
| Data Type | What is the nature of the data attribute? Is it always alphabetic (character), alphanumeric, binary, text, iconic, etc.? | Logical Data Model |
| Maximum Characters | What is the maximum number of characters or digits required for this attribute? | Logical Data Model |
| Decimal Position | What is the maximum number of characters right of a decimal point? | Logical Data Model |
| Required or Optional | Must this data attribute always be entered when the data entity is added? A data attribute should be considered optional unless it is required under all circumstances. | Logical Data Model |
| Percentage of Used | What percentage of the time will an optional data attribute contain data? | Logical Data Model |
| Conditions Used | Under which conditions will an optional data attribute be populated? For instance, the shipment date would be populated only when the shipment is made. | Logical Data Model |
| Edit Rules | What rules determine whether an entry is valid? It may be a formula, range of characters, or a list of valid values. | Logical Data Model |

*(continued)*

| For Each Data Attribute | | |
|---|---|---|
| **Type of Information** | **Description of Information** | **When Needed** |
| Default Value | This is the standard value that should be entered if no information is provided at the stage that an entity occurrence. | Logical Data Model |
| Derived? | Does this data attribute represent a lowest common denominator data value or is it derivable from one or more atomic data attributes? | Logical Data Model |
| Derivation Rules | For derived data attributes, how is this data attribute derived? | Logical Data Model |
| Processing Rules | What business rules govern the adding, updating, and deletion of information in this data attribute? For instance, if the shipment date is entered, the shipment data entity may need to be added and an invoice may need to be generated. | Logical Data Model |
| CRUD Actor(s) | What business role(s) creates, retrieves, updates, and deletes (CRUD) this data attribute? | Required for Database Design (Logical Data Model) |
| Archiving Rules | How long will information be kept, and how should the history be handled? | Required for Database Design (Logical Data Model) |
| Data-Content Quality Rules | What domain rules and valid value sets should apply? | Required for Database Design (Logical Data Model) |
| Data-Presentation Quality Rules | The data-presentation quality that should apply to information bearing documents and media such as reports or screens presenting the results of queries from data to database. | Required for Database Design (Logical Data Model) |
| Data-Residency Business Rules | How long should data reside in the various levels of storage (e.g., operational data store, data warehouse, or archive)? | Required for Database Design (Logical Data Model) |
| Privacy Indicator | Indicates the privacy component that should be invoked. | Required for Database Design (Logical Data Model) |

*(continued)*

## For Each Data Attribute

| Type of Information | Description of Information | When Needed |
| --- | --- | --- |
| Privacy Rules | What privacy rules govern the adding, accessing, or updating of this data attribute? | Required for Database Design (Logical Data Model) |
| Encryption Indicator | Indicates whether an encryption component should be used. | Required for Database Design (Logical Data Model) |
| Encryption Rules | What encryption rules govern? | Required for Database Design (Logical Data Model) |
| Security Rules | What security rules govern the adding, accessing, and updating of this data attribute? | Required for Database Design (Logical Data Model) |
| Data Source | What system or existing database will be used to populate this data attribute? | Required for Database Design (Logical Data Model) |
| Availability Requirements | What, if any, are the special rules governing the availability of these data? | Required for Database Design (Logical Data Model) |
| Refreshment Timing | How often should this data attribute be refreshed? | Required for Database Design (Logical Data Model) |
| Abbreviated Name | What acceptable abbreviation can be used on a screen or report? | Needed for prototyping |

The following "For Each Data Relationship" table shows metadata attributes for each class or data relationship shown in the various data models.

## For Each Data Relationship

| Type of Information | Description of Information | When Needed |
| --- | --- | --- |
| Data Relationship Name | How is the data relationship to be referred to? | All Data Relationships must be included in the Conceptual Data Model |
| Data Entities Related | How do the two data entities relate to each other? | Conceptual Data Model |

*(continued)*

## For Each Data Relationship

| Type of Information | Description of Information | When Needed |
| --- | --- | --- |
| Nature of the Relationship | What is the business purpose of each side of the relationship? For example, "A customer *places* a customer order." | Conceptual Data Model |
| Expected Cardinality | How many times will each side of the relationship occur? For instance, a customer is expected to place 200 customer orders a year, but a given customer order may be placed by one and only one customer. | Conceptual Data Model |
| Maximum Cardinality | What is the maximum number of times each side of the relationship may occur? For instance, a customer may place 1,200 customer orders during the busiest year. | Logical Data Model |
| Insert Referential Integrity Rule | What is the impact on the related data entity when a new instance of the data entity is added? For instance, a customer order may not be added unless the customer who placed the order exists in the system. A new customer may be added even though there are no customer orders to be added. The referential integrity rules will use both business terminology and data modeling terminology. | Logical Data Model |
| Delete Referential Integrity Rule | What is the impact on the related data entity when a new instance of the data entity is deleted? For instance, a customer order may be deleted independent of the customer who placed the order. A customer may not be deleted if there are still outstanding customer orders in the system. If a customer order is deleted, all order line items are also deleted. The referential integrity rules will use both business terminology and data-modeling terminology. | Logical Data Model |
| Relationship Constraint Rule | Is there any business rule that impacts or constrains the relationship? | Logical Data Model |

■ ■ ■

# Meet the Contributors

Martin Abrams
Executive Director and Chief Strategist for the
Information Accountability Foundation

Martin Abrams, Executive Director and Chief Strategist
for the Information Accountability Foundation, has
35 years of experience as an information and consumer
policy innovator. Multi-stakeholder collaboration
has been a key for Abrams in developing practical
solutions to dilemmas in information policy. His
most recent work has been on big data governance
and privacy compliance driven by demonstrable data
stewardship. For the past five years he has led the
Global Accountability Project, which has refined the accountability principle that is part
of various data protection laws and guidance documents. Abrams was the co-founder
and President of the Centre for Information Policy Leadership at Hunton & Williams LLP,
which he led for 13 years.

Dr. Annie I. Antón
Professor in and Chair of the School of Interactive
Computing at the Georgia Institute of Technology

Dr. Annie I. Antón is a Professor in and Chair of
the School of Interactive Computing at the Georgia
Institute of Technology in Atlanta. She has served the
national defense and intelligence communities in
a number of roles since being selected for the
IDA/DARPA Defense Science Study Group in
2005–2006. Antón is a three-time graduate of the
College of Computing at the Georgia Institute of
Technology, receiving a Ph.D. in 1997 with a minor
in Management & Public Policy, an M.S. in 1992, and
a B.S. in 1990 with a minor in Technical and Business
Communication.

John Berard
Founder, Credible Context

John Berard is a visible and vocal privacy advocate. He has spent the last 15 years at the intersection of data protection and privacy and marketing communications. A founding member of the board of TRUSTe and twice a member of the board of the International Association of Privacy Professionals, Berard understands the call for transparency, access, and restraint. Working for companies in data-driven industries like health care, financial services, and telecommunications, he is a communications professional who sees data protection and privacy, when paired with security and product performance, as the raw material of trust. And it is trust that grants companies permission to market. As an advisor to start-ups seeking to take the right first steps with regard to privacy and larger companies hoping to maximize the value of the data in their custody, Berard's goal is to help guide business and consumers to common ground.

Eric Bonabeau
PhD, Chairman, Icosystem, Inc., and Dean of Computational Sciences, Minerva Schools at KGI

Eric Bonabeau is one of the world's leading experts in complex systems and distributed adaptive problem solving and is known worldwide for his ability to apply the concepts of complexity science to real-world problems. His work focuses on the limits of human decision-making in a complex, decentralized, and unpredictable world. Read more about these topics on Icosystem's blog. Prior to founding Icosystem, Eric was involved in research and development for US and European telecommunications and software companies. He has written three books, including the perennial scientific bestseller, *Swarm Intelligence*, which provided the inspiration for another bestseller, Michael Crichton's *Prey*. He has published more than 140 scientific articles in international journals and conference proceedings and is a regular contributor to the *Harvard Business Review* and the *MIT Sloan Management Review*. He has a Ph.D. in Theoretical Physics from Paris-Sud University in France, and is an alumnus of France's Ecole Polytechnique and Ecole Nationale Supérieure des Télécommunications.

Ann Cavoukian, Ph.D.
Information and Privacy Commissioner, Ontario, Canada

Dr. Ann Cavoukian is recognized as one of the world's leading privacy experts. Her *Privacy by Design* framework seeks to proactively embed privacy into the design specifications of information technologies and business practices, thereby achieving the strongest protection possible. In October 2010, regulators at the conference of International Data Protection and Privacy Commissioners in Jerusalem unanimously passed a Resolution recognizing *Privacy by Design* as an essential component of fundamental privacy protection. This was followed by the U.S. Federal Trade Commission's inclusion of *Privacy by Design* as one of three recommended practices for protecting online privacy – a major validation of its significance. In November 2011, Dr. Cavoukian was ranked as one of the top 25 Women of Influence, recognizing her contribution to the Canadian and global economy. In October 2013, she was named one of the Top 100 City Innovators Worldwide by UBM Future Cities for her passionate advocacy of *Privacy by Design*. She is now tackling Big Data, for which she says, "Big Privacy" is the answer.

Janet F. Chapman
Senior Vice Vice President, Chief Privacy Officer and Manager, Compliance Group, at Union Bank

Janet F. Chapman currently serves as Senior Vice President, Chief Privacy Officer and Manager, Compliance Group, at Union Bank in San Francisco. She currently serves as Chair of the Privacy Working Committee of the Financial Services Roundtable (FSR) and, as a member of FSR BITS Regulatory Steering Committee, and is a founding member of the advisory board of the Ponemon Institute's Responsible Information Management Council. She is a Certified Information Privacy Professional (CIPP) and is a frequent speaker on privacy issues.

Ms. Chapman is the former Chief Privacy Officer (CPO) for The Charles Schwab Corporation. During her tenure as CPO, Schwab ranked in the top 10 in the Ponemon Institute-Trust-e survey of the Top Most Trusted Companies for Privacy from 2006–2008.

R. Traver Clifford

R. Traver Clifford is a senior at North Central High School in Indianapolis, Indiana. He is an Eagle Scout, a member of the Cross Country team, and an intern at Developer Town, a technology business that works with start-ups and existing companies. He plans to earn an undergraduate degree in computer science and a masters in business administration.

Jay Cline
President of privacy consulting firm MPC

Jay Cline is a former chief privacy officer, IT management consultant, and international trade-law expert in the U.S. government. Cline also has held leadership positions in the IAPP, is the privacy columnist for *Computerworld*, and was the winner of the Barbara Wellbery Memorial Award for his proposal for an international Safe Harbor agreement. Cline's Privacy Maturity Model won the HP-IAPP Privacy Innovation Award. Cline founded the Twin Cities Privacy Network and Minnesota Privacy Consultants in 2006, and the Bay Area Privacy Network in 2013.

Peggy Eisenhauer
Founder of Privacy & Information Management Services—Margaret P. Eisenhauer, P.C.

Peggy Eisenhauer is the founder of Privacy & Information Management Services—Margaret P. Eisenhauer, P.C., an Atlanta, Georgia based law firm. She is recognized by *Chambers Global: Guide to Leading Business Lawyers* in the area of privacy and data security. She earned a J.D. with honors from the University of Georgia and a Masters of Science in Information & Computer Science from the Georgia Institute of Technology. She is a member of the IAPP, a Certified Information Privacy Professional (CIPP/US), Chair Emeritus of the CIPP Advisory Board, a Fellow of the Ponemon Institute, a member of the Nymity Advisory Council, the BNA Privacy Law Advisory Board, and the 501st Legion. She is the author of the case book, *A Global Survey of Privacy & Security Enforcement Actions with Recommendations for Reducing Risk* (IAPP, May 2008).

Francoise Gilbert
Founder and Managing Director of the IT Law Group and author and editor of *Global Privacy and Security Laws*

Francoise Gilbert, founder and managing director of the IT Law Group, is an internationally recognized thought leader and expert in information privacy and security law. She regularly advises public companies and other businesses on a variety of information privacy, security, cloud computing, and big data matters. She is the primary author and editor of the reference two-volume treatise *Global Privacy and Security Law* (www.globalprivacybook.com) (3,000 pages, 2-volume, Aspen Publishers / Wolters Kluwer Law and Business), an in-depth analysis of the data protection laws of 66 countries. Named Best Lawyers' "2014 San Francisco Lawyer of the Year for Information Technology Law," Francoise was selected as one of the "2013 Northern California's Top Attorneys." She has received consistent accolades from *Chambers USA, Chambers Global, the Best Lawyers in America, Ethisphere Who's Who in E-Commerce,* and *Computerworld* for her work in the information privacy and security field.

Ed Glover
Client Services Director, Security and Privacy at Resources Global Professionals (RGP)

Ed Glover has over 30 years of experience in the information technology field as a senior executive driving, vision, and strategy. Currently, Ed is working at Resources Global Professionals (RGP) as a client services director in the Northern California Region focusing on GRC, Security, and Privacy. Prior to RGP, Ed was a member of the executive IT team, reporting to the EVP CIO of Sun Microsystems. While his responsibilities covered the IT Compliance and Risk Management organization, he provided leadership and direction for SunIT's Vision and Strategic initiatives. Prior to Ed's time in SunIT, Ed was responsible for defining, developing, implementing, and managing Sun's worldwide security and custom engineering consulting practice. Before joining Sun, Ed was a Senior Manager at Price Waterhouse responsible for providing security, IT Risk, and Compliance to a wide variety of clients. Ed is a graduate of The University of California–Berkeley and obtained an Executive MBA from St. Mary's College.

Dawn N. Jutla, PhD
Board Director, OASIS, and Professor, Sobey School
of Business, Saint Mary's University, Halifax,
Nova Scotia, Canada

Dawn Jutla is a Professor of Business and Computer
Science and founder of the Master of Technology
Entrepreneurship and Innovation Program in the
Sobey School of Business at Saint Mary's University,
Halifax, Nova Scotia. An industry consultant in
emerging information technologies, big data
management, strategy, privacy, and governance,
she currently sits on the Board of Directors for the
Organization for the Advancement of Structured
Information Standards (OASIS) and the Saint Mary's
Board of Governors. In 2012, she convened the OASIS
Privacy by Design for Software Engineers Technical Committee to co-lead the creation of
a standard that would help software engineers more easily embed privacy mechanisms
for users into their software. Her honours include the 2009 World Technology Award for
IT Software, given to researchers in academia and industry in science and technology
for innovative work of the greatest likely long-term significance, and the Jutla SimplyCast
Scholarship, donated by a former student and technology entrepreneur.

Leslie K. Lambert
Chief Security and Strategy Officer for
GuruCul Solutions

Leslie K. Lambert is the Chief Security and Strategy
Officer for GuruCul Solutions and is responsible for
company and product strategy, executive relations,
strategic partnerships, as well as chairing the GuruCul
Executive Advisory Council. Most recently, Lambert
was the CISO for Juniper Networks, with responsibility
for information security, IT risk and compliance,
including the development and deployment of
policies, standards, and procedures. She oversaw
Juniper's security practice of incident management,
intrusion detection, the prevention/protection against
spam and malware attacks, security awareness,
threat vulnerability assessments and mitigation, and partnered with Juniper Legal in
the protection of intellectual property. With more than 30 years' experience, Lambert's
deep IT knowledge base extends across architecture, business infrastructure, operations,
security, and technical infrastructure. Prior to Juniper, Lambert was an IT executive at
Sun Microsystems for 18 years, and served as Sun's CISO. She received *CSO Magazine*'s
2010 Compass Award for security leadership and was named one of Computerworld's
Premier 100 IT Leaders in 2009.

Barb Lawler
Chief Privacy Officer at Intuit

Barbara Lawler is the first Chief Privacy Officer at Intuit, makers of, TurboTax®, QuickBooks®, and other online financial services, and is responsible for creating and driving data stewardship, privacy and data use strategy, policy and implementation, and regulatory analysis to deliver the best experiences to customers and employees. Intuit tied for first as the "Most Trusted Company for Privacy in America" in 2007, and finished in the top 10 every year since 2006. Before Intuit, Ms. Lawler spent over 20 years in privacy, data management, and marketing at Hewlett Packard, and was their first Chief Privacy Officer. While there, she led a global team whose work culminated in HP's selection as the inaugural "Most Trusted Company for Privacy" in 2004. She is a member of the International Association of Privacy Professionals (IAPP) and is a previous member of its Board of Directors. She has testified about privacy and accountability before the U.S. Congress House and Senate.

Virginia Lee
Senior Attorney, Privacy and Security Legal,
Intel Corporation

Ginny Lee has worked in the high-tech industry for over twenty years. At Intel Corporation, she is responsible for providing legal guidance on privacy and security matters, especially as they relate to "Privacy by Design." Prior to Intel, Ginny was the Director of Platform and Product Privacy at Yahoo! where she was responsible for the policy direction of Yahoo!'s varied products and platforms. Ginny also ran a boutique law practice focused on privacy and intellectual property law. She has worked on policy, regulatory, and compliance issues for the Network Advertising Initiative. In addition to her legal experience, Ginny has held positions in engineering and product management and technical support. Ginny holds a BA in Applied Mathematics from the University of Maine, a MBA from the University of New Hampshire, and a JD from the University Of Maine School Of Law. Ginny is also a Certified Information Privacy Professional (CIPP) and Manager (CIPM).

Tyson Macaulay
Vice President, Global Telecommunications Strategy at McAfee

Tyson Macaulay is the Vice President - Global Telecommunications Strategy for McAfee. In this role, Mr. Macaulay drives security solutions development supporting the Telecommunications Service Provider vertical, representing McAfee capabilities integrated with those of its parent, Intel Corporation. Mr. Macaulay is accountable for the definition of value-added solutions, business models, and thought -leadership specifically for the global telecommunications industry. Mr. Macaulay has an impressive pedigree of achievements in the Telecom space, most recently at Bell Canada as the Security Liaison Officer for the past 8 years. A well-respected speaker and researcher since 1993, he regularly lectures at the university level, and has many books, periodical publications, and patent applications to his name. Mr. Macaulay also supports the development of engineering and security standards through the Professional Engineers of Ontario, the International Standards Organization (ISO), the Internet Engineering Task Force (IETF), and the newly formed oneM2M.

Rena Mears
Managing Principal of RMCS, LLC

Rena Mears is the Managing Principal of RMCS, LLC providing privacy and data protection consulting services to enterprises managing and protecting customer and employee data in complex regulatory environments. Prior to her recent retirement, Rena was a partner in Deloitte's Audit & Enterprise Risk Services, where she founded and led the national and global Privacy & Data Protection services. She has more than twenty-five years of experience supporting clients in the areas of privacy, enterprise risk and controls, data protection, and information security.

Kenneth P. Mortensen
Chief Governance Officer at CVS Caremark

Kenneth P. Mortensen is VP, Assistant General Counsel & Chief Governance Officer at CVS Caremark, where he has enterprise responsibility for knowledge governance to empower application of information as an enterprise asset to optimize risk and facilitate innovation while protecting individual privacy. Ken serves on the Board of Directors for the International Association of Privacy Professionals. He is also on the boards of the National Health ISAC and Health Information Trust Alliance (HITRUST). Before CVS Caremark, Ken was Boston Scientific's first ever CPO with responsibility for global privacy. Before that, Ken served in the Administration of President George W. Bush as Associate Deputy Attorney General for Privacy and Civil Liberties for the Department of Justice, acting as primary counsel and policy advisor to the Attorney General and Deputy Attorney General on privacy and civil liberties, including revisions to the Attorney General Guidelines for Domestic FBI Operations, updates to EO 12333, and the FISA Amendments Act.

David Mortman
Chief Security Architect, Dell Enstratius and Contributing Analyst, Securosis

David Mortman is the Chief Security Architect for Dell Enstratius and a Contributing Analyst at Securosis and has been doing Information Security for well over 15 years. Prior to Dell, he was the Director of Security and Operations at C3. Previously, David was the CISO at Siebel Systems and the Manager of Global Security at Network Associates. David speaks regularly at Blackhat, Defcon, RSA, and other conferences. Additionally, he blogs at emergentchaos.com, newschoolsecurity.com, and securosis.com. David sits on a variety of advisory boards, including Qualys, Lookout, and Virtuosi. David holds a B.S. in Chemistry from the University of Chicago.

Vidya Phalke
Chief Technology Officer at MetricStream

As the CTO of MetricStream, Dr. Vidya Phalke is responsible for MetricStream's global product architecture and technology strategy. He has been the technology visionary behind MetricStream's GRC platform that has transformed Risk Intelligence and GRC Programs across a broad range of industries. He also leads MetricStream's innovation hub -- —MetricStream Labs -- —which is responsible for several leading- edge innovations including Big Data Analytics, GRC Cloud, and Social Media GRC. Dr. Phalke has held various senior product management and engineering positions in Narus and Network Programs, - building Enterprise Grade Business and Operations Support Systems. Before joining the software industry, Dr. Phalke was an Academic at Rutgers University where he won several SBIR grants on cutting- edge research on Very Large Databases and Network Optimization. Besides a Ph.D. in Computer Science from Rutgers University, Dr. Phalke holds a management degree from MIT Sloan. He is a graduate of IIT, Delhi, India.

Jules Polonetsky
Executive Director, Future of Privacy Forum

Jules serves as Executive Director and Co-chair of the Future of Privacy Forum, a Washington, D.C.--based think tank that seeks to advance responsible data practices. Founded five years ago, FPF is supported by more than 80 leading companies, as well as an advisory board of comprised of the country's leading academics and advocates. FPF's current projects focus on online data use, smart grid, mobile data, big data, apps, location, and social media. Jules previous roles have included serving as Consumer Affairs Commissioner for New York City., Jules currently chairs the privacy advisory board of Gigya, and serves on the Advisory Boards of the Cookie Clearinghouse, Frankly, and the Center for Copyright Information. He has served on the boards of a number of privacy and consumer protection organizations including TRUSTe, the International Association of Privacy Professionals, and the Network Advertising Initiative. From 2011-2012, Jules served on the Department of Homeland Security Data Privacy and Integrity Advisory Committee.

Richard Purcell
CEO, Corporate Privacy Group

Richard Purcell is a privacy pioneer and supports information management programs through planning, developing, and implementing protocols designed to respect and protect personal information. Corporate Privacy Group also offers award-winning Web-based education and training courseware for security and privacy awareness, knowledge, and skills development. As Microsoft's original privacy officer, Richard designed, developed, implemented, and oversaw one of the world's largest and most advanced privacy programs spanning Internet properties, software products, end-user support, and information systems. Richard served as Chairman of the Data Privacy and Integrity Advisory Committee to the Department of Homeland Security and as Executive Director of the non-profit research agency, the Privacy Projects. He served on the Online Access & Security Advisory Committee of the Federal Trade Commission and as Chairman of TRUSTe, the pioneering online privacy certification agency. He sits on several corporate advisory boards and regularly addresses issues of information privacy and data protection domestically and globally.

James Ransome, PhD, CISSP, CISM
Senior Director, Product Security at McAfee

Dr. James Ransome, CISSP, CISM, is the Senior Director of Product Security and responsible for all aspects of McAfee's Product Security Program, a corporate-wide initiative that supports the delivery of secure software products to customers. His career is marked by leadership positions in the private and public industries, having served in three chief information security officer (CISO) and four chief security officer (CSO) roles. Prior to the corporate world, Ransome had 23 years of government service in various roles supporting the Unites States intelligence community, federal law enforcement, and the Department of Defense. He holds a Ph.D. specializing in Information Security from a NSA/DHS Center of Academic Excellence in Information Assurance Education program. Ransome is a member of Upsilon Pi Epsilon, the International Honor Society for the Computing and Information Disciplines. He recently authored his 10th information security book *Core Software Security: Security at the Source.*

Stewart Room
Partner, Field Fisher Waterhouse LLP

Stewart Room is a dual qualified solicitor and barrister, with 20 years' experience as a litigator and advocate. Stewart is rated as one of the UK's leading data protection lawyers, with considerable expertise and reputation in data protection and data security matters. He is a leading lawyer on contentious aspects of privacy and data protection law, informational security, and the operational implications of the law within complex technologies, networks, and communications systems. Stewart also specializes in data security breaches and the theft or loss of personal data, and leads on major international compliance projects. Stewart heads the Telecommunication sector group for Field Fisher Waterhouse LLP. and has authored three leading text books on data protection law, including "*Butterworth's Data Security Law and Practice*", the pre-eminent work in this field.

Raj Samani
Vice President, Chief Technical Officer, EMEA, McAfee

Raj is currently working as the VP, Chief Technical Officer for McAfee EMEA, having previously worked as the Chief Information Security Officer for a large public sector organization in the UK. He volunteers as the Cloud Security Alliance Chief Innovation Officer, and Special Advisor for the European CyberCrime Centre, and is on the advisory councils for Infosecurity Europe, and *Infosecurity Magazine.* In addition, Raj was previously the VP for Communications in the ISSA UK Chapter, having presided over the award for Chapter communications program of the year for 2008, and 2009, and was inducted into the Infosecurity Europe Hall of Fame in 2012.

Richard Schaefer
Director Technical Alliances, Good Technology

Richard Schaefer is the Director Technical Alliances at Good Technology. He is responsible for all aspects of ISV integration with Good's secure mobility platform including security compliance. His longtime career focus is market adoption of evolutionary technologies primarily via partner eco-systems. His roles have spanned engineering, marketing, and business development in the application of nascent computing platforms and processes to a broad range of industries. His achievements have earned him awards and executive recognition at Sun Microsystems and Good. He has edited and contributed to books on the Solaris operating system, multi-threading, and Java. Michelle frequently introduces him as the one who taught her about garbage collection.

Denise Schoeneich, CIPM, CIPP/IT, CISA, PMP
IT Risk, Compliance, and Audit Professional at Resources Global Professionals (RGP)

As an IT professional Denise Schoeneich has experience in project and program management, and information technology risk, compliance, and audit. Denise She currently is a consultant with Resources Global Professionals (RGP). As a subject matter expert, Denise has managed compliance projects and conducted risk assessments and audits in information security, IT governance, system development lifecycle (SDLC), Payment Card Industry Standards (PCI), and business continuity/disaster recovery for a variety of industry sectors, including financial services, health care, hospitality, retail, and software. She is a Certified Information Privacy Professional/IT (CIPP/IT), Certified Information Privacy Manager (CIPM), Certified Information Systems Audit (CISA), and Certified Project Manager Professional (PMP) and holds an MBA in Management Information Systems from Wayne State University and a BBA from Eastern Michigan University.

Peter Swire
Nancy J. & Lawrence P. Huang Professor of Law and Ethics, Georgia Institute of Technology, Georgia Tech

Peter Swire is the Nancy J. & Lawrence P. Huang Professor at the Georgia Institute of Technology, in the Scheller College of Business, with courtesy appointments in the College of Computing and the School of Public Policy. He is a Senior Fellow with the Future of Privacy Forum and the Center for American Progress, and Policy Fellow with the Center for Democracy and Technology. In the fall of 2013, Swire served as a member of President Obama's Review Group on Intelligence and Communications Technology. Previously, he co-chaired the Do Not Track standards process of the World Wide Web Consortium. In 2009--2010 Professor Swire was Special Assistant to the President for Economic Policy, serving in the National Economic Council under Lawrence Summers. From 1999 to early 2001, Professor Swire served as the Clinton Administration's Chief Counselor for Privacy, in the U.S. Office of Management and Budget, the only person to date to have government-wide responsibility for privacy issues. Many of his writings appear at www.peterswire.net.

Eduardo Ustaran
Data Protection Lawyer and author of *The Future of Privacy*

Eduardo advises some of the world's leading companies on the adoption of global privacy strategies and is closely involved in the development of the new EU data protection framework. He has been named by *Revolution* magazine as one of the 40 most influential people in the growth of the digital sector in the UK and is ranked as a leading privacy and internet lawyer by prestigious international directories. Eduardo is a member of the Board of Directors of the IAPP and the editor of *Data Protection Law & Policy*. Eduardo is the author of *The Future of Privacy* (DataGuidance, 2013), executive editor of *European Privacy: Law and Practice for Data Protection Professionals* (IAPP, 2011), and co-author of *E-Privacy and Online Data Protection* (Tottel Publishing, 2007) and of the Law Society's *Data Protection Handbook* (2004). Eduardo regularly lectures at the University of Cambridge on data protection law as part of its Masters of Bioscience Enterprise.

Chenxi Wang, Ph.D.
Vice President of Market Insight at McAfee

Dr. Wang is VP of Market Insight at McAfee, responsible for market research and intelligence worldwide for McAfee. Prior to McAfee, Chenxi was a highly respected industry analyst, with the roles of Vice President and Principal Analyst at Forrester Research. During her tenure at Forrester, Chenxi led a number of high- profile research areas, including mobile security, cloud, and application security. She was also the lead on Forrester's global privacy heat map project. Prior to Forrester, Chenxi was Associate Professor of Computer Engineering at Carnegie Mellon University. At CMU, Chenxi led a number of large research projects funded by the National Science Foundation and the Department of Defense. She was one of the founding faculty members of CMU's CyLab. Chenxi holds a Ph.D. in Computer Science from the University of Virginia. Her Ph.D. thesis work received ACM's Samuel Alexander Award. She is a contributing author to the book "*Beautiful Security*."

Dr. Dr Mark Watts
Head of Information Technology Law, Bristows

Mark Watts is an IT specialist with over 18 years' experience. He advises many of the world's best- known companies on the legal issues arising out of IT issues such as system development, outsourcing, social networking, cloud computing, mobile apps, and online trading. Mark also has a doctorate in semiconductor physics from Oxford University. He has particular expertise in data protection and for many years was Global Privacy Counsel at IBM. Mark's busy practice involves assisting multinationals on global compliance projects, such as those based on Binding Corporate Rules, advising technology companies on product development to ensure compliance with applicable law, and advising companies on how to respond to data protection enforcement actions, including Monetary Penalty Notices issued by the UK's Information Commissioner.

Joel Weise
Director of Security and Compliance, Hootsuite

Joel Weise has worked in the field of information security for over 30 years. He is the Director of Security and Compliance at Hootsuite in Vancouver, British Columbia. Joel is a founding member of the Information Systems Security Association and an ISSA Distinguished Fellow, the chairman of the *ISSA Journal*'s Editorial Advisory Board, and a member of and Subject Matter Expert for the American Bar Association Science and Technology working committee.

Ruby Zefo
Chief Privacy and Security Counsel Counsel,
Intel Corporation

Ruby Zefo, CIPP/US, CIPM, is Intel Corporation's Chief Privacy & Security Counsel. Zefo manages Intel's global privacy and security legal group, whose charter is to provide legal counseling that enables Intel's business to appropriately manage risks and opportunities related to privacy, data security, and cyber security. In addition, Zefo manages the teams responsible for legal support of Intel's IT department and Intel's global trademark practice. Zefo began her law career at Fenwick & West LLP, specializing in intellectual property and general commercial litigation. She later joined Sun Microsystems, Inc., specializing in licensing, marketing, and trademark law. She joined Intel in 2003. Zefo has a B.S. in Business Administration from the University of California– at Berkeley, and a J.D. from Stanford Law School. She is a frequent speaker on legal practice excellence and leadership topics.

# Index